The Short Fiction of
AMBROSE BIERCE

II

The Short Fiction of
AMBROSE BIERCE

A Comprehensive Edition

Edited by
S. T. Joshi
Lawrence I. Berkove
David E. Schultz

II

The University of Tennessee Press / Knoxville

The Short Fiction of
AMBROSE BIERCE

A Comprehensive Edition

Edited by
S. T. Joshi
Lawrence I. Berkove
David E. Schultz

The University of Tennessee Press / Knoxville

Copyright © 2006 by The University of Tennessee Press / Knoxville.
All Rights Reserved. Manufactured in the United States of America.
First Edition.

This book is printed on acid-free paper.

LIBRARY OF CONGRESS CATALOGING-IN-PUBLICATION DATA

Bierce, Ambrose, 1842–1914?
[Short stories]
The short fiction of Ambrose Bierce : a comprehensive edition / edited by S.T. Joshi,
Lawrence I. Berkove, and David E. Schultz.— 1st ed.
    p. cm.
Includes bibliographical references and index.
ISBN 1-57233-475-4 (set : acid-free paper) — ISBN 1-57233-537-8 (v. 2 : acid-free paper)
I. Joshi, S. T., 1958– II. Berkove, Lawrence I. III. Schultz, David E., 1952– IV. Title.
PS1097.A1 2006
813'.4—dc22

2006001036

CONTENTS
VOLUME 1

Part 1. 1868–1876

Part 2. 1878–1886

VOLUME 2
Part 3. 1887–1893

VOLUME 3
Part 4. 1895–1904

Part 5. 1905–1910

Ambrose Bierce after the Civil War, in his early career as a writer. University of Virginia Library, Manuscript Division.

PART 3

1887–1893

INTRODUCTION

Most of the best stories that Bierce wrote date from this, the prime stage of his career. In 1887, he was personally solicited by the young William Randolph Hearst to become a feature writer for his newly acquired newspaper, the *San Francisco Examiner*. Hearst set out to hire the best journalistic talent he could find on the West Coast, and Bierce was one of the first people he wanted on his staff. Because Bierce already had a twenty-year reputation from various San Francisco newspapers and magazines for being a brilliant, albeit controversial, journalist, he was in a good position to bargain. Although the specific details of his contract are not presently known, they can be inferred from the practical results. Bierce was, first of all, very well paid by Hearst, enough to make him relatively comfortable. His main work consisted of writing occasional editorials and contributing his famous feature column, "Prattle," to the editorial page once or twice a week, especially Sundays. "Prattle" was a miscellany of comments on personalities and events in the news, and Bierce apparently worked out an understanding with Hearst that his columns were not to be subject to editorial dictation or revision in either form or content. It appears, also, that the contract might have been for "Prattle" and editorial work only and that he would be paid extra for any fiction he contributed to the paper, and that he was free to submit stories to other periodicals and publishers. As Bierce notes in his fascinating memoir of Hearst, "A Thumb-Nail Sketch" (*SS* 201–5), Hearst kept his part of the bargain fairly well, and the files show that in 1887, shortly after Bierce started to work for the *Examiner*, he began either to substitute stories for "Prattle" on the editorial page or to supplement "Prattle" with stories in the Sunday feature section. The stories met with instant success, and by 1891 there were enough of them for Bierce to select sixteen (adding three more from other sources) for his first American book, *Tales of Soldiers and Civilians*. Bierce's fame largely rests on the stories in this book.

Knowledge of the periodical backgrounds of these and other stories of this period is important because it supplies us with information and insights that would otherwise be unavailable. From their respective dates of publication, for instance, it is apparent that Bierce wrote them in an extended surge of creativity. Perhaps *Examiner* employment freed him from the heavy workloads and financial insecurity of his previous jobs, and perhaps the memories and thoughts that his mind had been turning over since his war years finally ripened; in any case, it is obvious that in his first six or seven years on the newspaper he not only produced stories with extraordinary rapidity while also writing "Prattle" and editorials, but also advanced his artistry to its acme. As the *Examiner* prospered and grew larger, increased its coverage of news stories and feature articles, and began a Sunday supplement that included fiction and nonfiction from other local and national American authors, as well as such internationally famous writers as Robert Louis Stevenson, Rudyard Kipling, Guy de Maupassant, and even Lev Tolstoy, Bierce unavoidably read his own newspaper and found material that stimulated him and became the germs of new stories. Evidence of this stimulation regularly occurs in his "Prattle" columns, which of course fed on current events, and which sometimes afford us autobiographical glimpses of his earlier life. As a consequence, "Prattle" is the largest and most valuable trove of biographical information about Bierce, but the rest of the *Examiner* is also a valuable source of insights on what spurred his creativity.

Nineteenth-century newspapers were far more different from today's periodicals than a superficial glance would indicate. In addition to the conventional fare of local, national, and foreign news, and sports and business coverage, the newspapers carried out an educational function by being compendia of entertaining and instructive feature articles; humor; discussions of history, archeology, science, and comparative religion; and literature, ranging from poetry and short stories to serialized novels. Newspapers also regularly ran articles on topics that today seem far-fetched or gruesome but were of current interest at the time: people buried alive, animals eating corpses, and supernatural occurrences. Bierce wrote in all these categories, but especially the supernatural. Undoubtedly, a main reason was that these topics were popular and sold well. Additionally, in the category of the supernatural, it is fair to say that he was himself interested in supernatural phenomena. He did not believe in ghosts and demons and not only ridiculed such beliefs during his entire career but also wrote ghost stories that are excellent examples of verisimilitude replete with "convincing" details that he cheerfully manufactured as needed. The prominence, therefore, of supernatural narratives in this section should not be read as indicating a sincere belief on his part. On the other hand, he did keep an open albeit skeptical mind on certain paranormal experiences—for example, hypnosis, dreams, and visions, phenomena which he regarded as beyond our present but perhaps not eventual ability to explain. All his writings in these categories, however, have their counterparts in the standard journalistic fare of his day.

Bierce also contributed fiction to other periodicals in the San Francisco area. Chief among these was the *Wave*, edited by Hugh Hume, one of Bierce's friends. It published some important stories of his, and its editorial columns gave him personal as well as critical support. The *Oakland Tribune* also published some of his work. Undoubtedly, Bierce also read these other periodicals to which he contributed, and in their pages he would have encountered additional ideas and information of use to him, and the works of other authors of his time.

Like many other authors of his era, Bierce was an autodidact, and the education he gave himself was by no means restricted to periodicals and popular literature. His "Prattle" columns are an extraordinary record of the growth of his mind and art. While a list of the books he read has yet to be compiled, it is possible to see that philosophy, ethics, the familiar classics of literature, and religion constituted important elements. Like many other authors of those years, Bierce seasoned his writing with quotations from Shakespeare and more recent English and American authors. Despite his overt scorn of religion, Bierce knew the Bible and was able to cite not only its famous lines but also unusual passages in ways that suggest that he had given them thought. In short, he was not a talented but narrowly read iconoclast. He gained an impressive and broad education over the years, and as he read and studied, he meditated over the lessons he learned from books as well as experience. He therefore entered into his mature phase.

The stories of this, his best period reflect a mind that was searching and probing with painful honesty conventions of thought and morality and was approaching the conviction that all conventions and all systems of thought were ultimately limited, and that human beings were sentient victims of an indifferent universe. This was not a unique position in the late nineteenth century, but Bierce did not begin with that conclusion and work deductively to particular cases, but rather the reverse, from the particular to the general. He had years earlier encountered classical Stoicism and found in the teachings of Epictetus and Marcus Aurelius some comfort in their assurance that through reason human beings might inure themselves to tragedy. What was now becoming apparent to him, however, was that even Stoicism failed in the final analysis because it overestimated the mind and underestimated the heart. The mind might be protected from tragedy but not the heart, and the heart to him was the essence of humanity. Many of the most poignant stories of this period depict situations that lead to this conclusion and carry within them some hint of self-directed irony, some rueful recognition that the search for meaning was coming up with blanks because there were no answers and no way of escaping all the tragedies that were concomitant with life. Reason and philosophy could reduce but not eliminate the pain of living, and neither could supply what was for Bierce life's greatest good, happiness.

Tales such as "A Son of the Gods," "Chickamauga," "The Affair at Coulter's Notch," and "A Horseman in the Sky" allegorize with rapidly accelerating power the limitations of reason and philosophy, and "Haïta the Shepherd" dramatizes the fleeting nature of happiness. All are pertinent as exempla to the lives of readers, but all have elements of tragedy in them. Bierce could be and was sharply critical of human beings who acted foolishly and meanly—that is what "An Occurrence at Owl Creek Bridge" incomparably illustrates—but he had only compassion for good people whose humanly best was not good enough, and especially those whose virtues or innocence made their tragedies more severe. Bierce was passionately involved in these stories. Carey McWilliams astutely observed that Bierce had a horror of pain and suffering. It took Bierce almost a quarter of a century of recalling searing memories and meditating on the brutal chaos of life to be able to advance as far as those stories did on the grim enigmas that tormented him. What pained him is what he projected into his stories, and often the irony with which he wrote was only a means of getting distance from emotions that would otherwise still be too strong for him. Responsive readers have always been able to sense something absolutely authentic about them; those situations, those terrible choices occur in real life.

Bierce's personal life during this, the artistic peak of his career, was not at all calm. In the winter of 1888–89 he discovered that another man had written his wife, Mollie, ardent letters. She had done nothing wrong except not to terminate the correspondence immediately, yet this relatively trivial indiscretion had a drastic consequence. Their marriage had not been smooth for years, and this discovery was too much for his proud nature; he separated permanently from her. Several months later, his talented seventeen-year-old son, Day, whom Bierce once characterized as "another Chatterton," died in a tragic shootout with a friend who eloped with his fiancée. Bierce was hit very hard by these twin blows, especially the latter, but except for a brief response to a mean-spirited enemy who gloated in print over his tragedy, he made no explicit mention of his feelings in his work. Critics who have treated this silence as evidence of Bierce's heartlessness have fundamentally misinterpreted their man. Bierce was very strict about keeping his personal life out of his professional work. In this respect, he resembled Mark Twain, who wrote some of the funniest stories and essays of his career for the *Galaxy* between 1868 and 1871, yet confessed in his last contribution that he had driven himself to write them despite dire illness in the family and a death in his house. Again, probably like Twain in another way, Bierce's professional work must have been an escape for him from his tragedies. Finally, given that Bierce had specifically selected Stoic philosophy because it taught him to expect, and how to endure, pain and loss, his personal tragedies, though they shook him, probably only confirmed the Stoic view of life. The stories that he wrote at this time, therefore, were all the more pointed and intense because they sublimated his griefs.

No doubt Bierce would have been a less complicated author to study if only he had confined himself to the overtly serious stories and not alternated them with simultaneously composed tales of outrageous black humor such as the "Parenticide Club" set and others like it; supernatural stories about uncanny disappearances, haunted houses, and dead bodies, which we know he did not believe; and Gulliverian narratives about the strange customs of the inhabitants of imaginary countries. But apart from the biographical background of his stories, Bierce wrote for a living, and if he could earn extra money by publishing more, it is understandable that he wrote more, even though not everything was up to his highest standards. On the other hand, the "Parenticide Club" and related stories are powerful and very skillfully written satires whose subtle ironies have eluded even most Bierce scholars; and the satires and supernatural stories carry on, in their own way, Bierce's fascination with the human susceptibility, often enhanced by rationalism, to credulousness and folly. His lesser works are lesser only by his own standards; in comparison with similar work by other authors, they are quite well done. In retrospect, this mature period must be respected for its production not only of Bierce's best stories but also stories that the world now regards as classic.

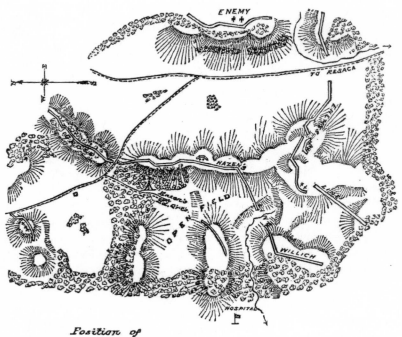

Position of
HAZEN'S BRIGADE
AT RESACA.

A. G. Bierce
Lt & Actg. Top. Engineer

Scale—Yds.

Traced in Adjutant General's Office.
From Original Records.

KILLED AT RESACA

The best soldier of our staff was Lieutenant Herman Brayle, one of the two aides-de-camp. I don't remember where the general picked him up; from some Ohio regiment, I think; none of us had previously known him, and it would have been strange if we had, for no two of us came from the same State, nor even from adjoining States. The general seemed to think that a position on his staff was a distinction that should be so judiciously conferred as not to beget any sectional jealousies and imperil the integrity of that part of the country which was still an integer. He would not even choose officers from his own command, but by some jugglery at department headquarters obtained them from other brigades. Under such circumstances, a man's services had to be very distinguished indeed to be heard of by his family and the friends of his youth; and "the speaking trump of fame"[1] was a trifle hoarse from loquacity, anyhow.

Lieutenant Brayle was more than six feet in height and of splendid proportions, with the light hair and gray-blue eyes which men so gifted usually find associated with a high order of courage. As he was commonly in full uniform, especially in action, when most officers are content to be less flamboyantly attired, he was a very striking and conspicuous figure. As to the rest, he had a gentleman's manners, a scholar's head and a lion's heart. His age was about thirty.

We all soon came to like Brayle as much as we admired him, and it was with sincere concern that in the engagement at Stone's River[2]—our first action after he joined us—we observed that he had one most objectionable and unsoldierly quality: he was vain of his courage. During all the vicissitudes and mutations of that hideous encounter, whether our troops were fighting in the open cotton fields, in the cedar thickets or behind the railway embankment, he did not once take cover, except when sternly commanded to do so by the general, who usually had other things to think of than the lives of his staff officers—or those of his men, for that matter.

In every later engagement while Brayle was with us it was the same way. He would sit his horse like an equestrian statue, in a storm of bullets and grape, in the most exposed places—wherever, in fact, duty, requiring him to go, permitted him to remain—when, without trouble and with distinct advantage to his reputation for common sense, he might have been in such security as is permissible on a battlefield in the brief intervals of personal inaction.

On foot, from necessity or in deference to his dismounted commander or associates, his conduct was the same. He would stand like a rock in the open when officers and men alike had taken to cover; while men older in service and years, higher in rank and of unquestionable intrepidity, were loyally preserving behind the crest of a hill lives infinitely precious to their country, this fellow would stand, equally idle, on the ridge, facing in the direction of the sharpest rifle.

When battles are going on in open ground it frequently occurs that the opposing lines, confronting each other within a stone's throw for hours, hug the earth as closely as if they loved it. The line officers in their proper places flatten themselves no less, and the field officers, their horses all killed or sent to the rear, crouch beneath the infernal canopy of hissing lead and screaming iron without a thought of personal dignity.

In such circumstances the life of a staff officer of a brigade is distinctly "not a happy one," mainly because of its precarious tenure and the unnerving alternations of emotion to which he is exposed. From a position of that comparative security from which a civilian would ascribe his escape to a "miracle," he may be dispatched with an order to some commander of a prone regiment in the front line—a person for the moment inconspicuous and not always easy to find without a deal of search among men somewhat preoccupied, and in a din in which question and answer alike must be imparted in the sign language. It is customary in such cases to duck the head and scuttle away on a keen run, an object of lively interest to some thousands of admiring marksmen. In returning—well, it is not customary to return.

Brayle's practice was different. He would consign his horse to the care of an orderly,—he loved his horse,—and walk quietly over on his perilous errand with never a stoop of the back, his splendid figure, accentuated by his uniform, holding the eye with a strange fascination. We watched him with suspended breath, our hearts in our mouths. On one occasion of this kind, indeed, one of our number, an impetuous stammerer, was so possessed by his emotion that he shouted at me:

"I'll b-b-bet you t-two d-d-dollars they d-drop him b-b-before he g-gets to that d-d-ditch!"

I did not accept the brutal wager; I thought they would.

Let me do justice to a brave man's memory; in all these needless exposures of life there was no visible bravado nor subsequent narration. In the few instances when some of us had ventured to remonstrate, Brayle had smiled pleasantly and made some light reply, which, however, had not encouraged a further pursuit of the subject. Once he said:

KILLED AT RESACA

"Captain, if ever I come to grief by forgetting your advice, I hope my last moments will be cheered by the sound of your beloved voice breathing into my ear the blessed words, 'I told you so.'"

We laughed at the captain—just why we could probably not have explained—and that afternoon when he was shot to rags from an ambuscade Brayle remained by the body for some time, adjusting the limbs with needless care—there in the middle of a road swept by gusts of grape and canister! It is easy to condemn this kind of thing, and not very difficult to refrain from imitation, but it is impossible not to respect, and Brayle was liked none the less for the weakness which had so heroic an expression. We wished he were not a fool, but he went on that way to the end, sometimes hard hit, but always returning to duty about as good as new.

Of course, it came at last; he who ignores the law of probabilities challenges an adversary that is seldom beaten. It was at Resaca, in Georgia, during the movement that resulted in the taking of Atlanta. In front of our brigade the enemy's line of earth-works ran through open fields along a slight crest. At each end of this open ground we were close up to him in the woods, but the clear ground we could not hope to occupy until night, when darkness would enable us to burrow like moles and throw up earth. At this point our line was a quarter-mile away in the edge of a wood. Roughly, we formed a semicircle, the enemy's fortified line being the chord of the arc.

"Lieutenant, go tell Colonel Ward to work up as close as he can get cover, and not to waste much ammunition in unnecessary firing. You may leave your horse."

When the general gave this direction we were in the fringe of the forest, near the right extremity of the arc. Colonel Ward was at the left. The suggestion to leave the horse obviously enough meant that Brayle was to take the longer line, through the woods and among the men. Indeed, the suggestion was needless; to go by the short route meant absolutely certain failure to deliver the message. Before anybody could interpose, Brayle had cantered lightly into the field and the enemy's works were in crackling conflagration.

"Stop that damned fool!" shouted the general.

A private of the escort, with more ambition than brains, spurred forward to obey, and within ten yards left himself and his horse dead on the field of honor.[3]

Brayle was beyond recall, galloping easily along, parallel to the enemy and less than two hundred yards distant. He was a picture to see! His hat had been blown or shot from his head, and his long, blond hair rose and fell with the motion of his horse. He sat erect in the saddle, holding the reins lightly in his left hand, his right hanging carelessly at his side. An occasional glimpse of his handsome profile as he turned his head one way or the other proved that the interest which he took in what was going on was natural and without affectation.

The picture was intensely dramatic, but in no degree theatrical. Successive scores of rifles spat at him viciously as he came within range, and our own line in the edge

KILLED AT RESACA

of the timber broke out in visible and audible defense. No longer regardful of themselves or their orders, our fellows sprang to their feet, and swarming into the open sent broad sheets of bullets against the blazing crest of the offending works, which poured an answering fire into their unprotected groups with deadly effect. The artillery on both sides joined the battle, punctuating the rattle and roar with deep, earth-shaking explosions and tearing the air with storms of screaming grape, which from the enemy's side splintered the trees and spattered them with blood, and from ours defiled the smoke of his arms with banks and clouds of dust from his parapet.

My attention had been for a moment drawn to the general combat, but now, glancing down the unobscured avenue between these two thunderclouds, I saw Brayle, the cause of the carnage. Invisible now from either side, and equally doomed by friend and foe, he stood in the shot-swept space, motionless, his face toward the enemy. At some little distance lay his horse. I instantly saw what had stopped him.

As topographical engineer I had, early in the day, made a hasty examination of the ground, and now remembered that at that point was a deep and sinuous gully, crossing half the field from the enemy's line, its general course at right angles to it. From where we now were it was invisible, and Brayle had evidently not known about it. Clearly, it was impassable. Its salient angles would have afforded him absolute security if he had chosen to be satisfied with the miracle already wrought in his favor and leapt into it. He could not go forward, he would not turn back; he stood awaiting death. It did not keep him long waiting.

By some mysterious coincidence, almost instantaneously as he fell, the firing ceased, a few desultory shots at long intervals serving rather to accentuate than break the silence. It was as if both sides had suddenly repented of their profitless crime. Four stretcher-bearers of ours, following a sergeant with a white flag, soon afterward moved unmolested into the field, and made straight for Brayle's body. Several Confederate officers and men came out to meet them, and with uncovered heads assisted them to take up their sacred burden. As it was borne toward us we heard beyond the hostile works fifes and a muffled drum—a dirge. A generous enemy honored the fallen brave.

Amongst the dead man's effects was a soiled Russia-leather pocketbook. In the distribution of mementoes of our friend, which the general, as administrator, decreed, this fell to me.

A year after the close of the war, on my way to California, I opened and idly inspected it. Out of an overlooked compartment fell a letter without envelope or address. It was in a woman's handwriting, and began with words of endearment, but no name.

It had the following date line: "San Francisco, Cal., July 9, 1862." The signature was "Darling," in marks of quotation. Incidentally, in the body of the text, the writer's full name was given—Marian Mendenhall.

KILLED AT RESACA

The letter showed evidence of cultivation and good breeding, but it was an ordinary love letter, if a love letter can be ordinary. There was not much in it, but there was something. It was this:

"Mr. Winters, whom I shall always hate for it, has been telling that at some battle in Virginia, where he got his hurt, you were seen crouching behind a tree. I think he wants to injure you in my regard, which he knows the story would do if I believed it. I could bear to hear of my soldier lover's death, but not of his cowardice."

These were the words which on that sunny afternoon, in a distant region, had slain a hundred men. Is woman weak?

One evening I called on Miss Mendenhall to return the letter to her. I intended, also, to tell her what she had done—but not that she did it. I found her in a handsome dwelling on Rincon Hill.[4] She was beautiful, well bred—in a word, charming.

"You knew Lieutenant Herman Brayle," I said, rather abruptly. "You know, doubtless, that he fell in battle. Among his effects was found this letter from you. My errand here is to place it in your hands."

She mechanically took the letter, glanced through it with deepening color, and then, looking at me with a smile, said:

"It is very good of you, though I am sure it was hardly worth while." She started suddenly and changed color. "This stain," she said, "is it—surely it is not—"

"Madam," I said, "pardon me, but that is the blood of the truest and bravest heart that ever beat."

She hastily flung the letter on the blazing coals. "Uh! I cannot bear the sight of blood!" she said. "How did he die?"

I had involuntarily risen to rescue that scrap of paper, sacred even to me, and now stood partly behind her. As she asked the question she turned her face about and slightly upward. The light of the burning letter was reflected in her eyes and touched her cheek with a tinge of crimson like the stain upon its page. I had never seen anything so beautiful as this detestable creature.

"He was bitten by a snake," I replied.

E (5 June 1887): 11 (with subtitle: "An Incident of the Civil War"); *TSC* 93–104; *IML* 88–100; *CW* 2.93–104.

NOTES

AB was recruited by young William Randolph Hearst in 1887 to write for his newly acquired *E*, the first of what was to become his nationwide chain of newspapers. AB was expected to contribute a signed column of opinion to the editorial page once a week, but he soon began occasionally contributing stories as well as the column. "Killed at Resaca" is the first story to appear in *E*. With "George Thurston" (1883), AB entered his mature period, and by 1887 the stories are beginning to come fast, most of them having at their core troubling issues that had been germinating in him since the Civil War.

KILLED AT RESACA

AB mentions Resaca in the autobiographical essay "The Crime at Pickett's Mill" (*SS* 37–44). As topographical engineer under Gen. William B. Hazen, he produced a map of the battlefield (subsequently published in Hazen's *A Narrative of Military Service* [Boston: Ticknor & Co., 1885], facing p. 251). The Union forces moved through Dalton, Georgia, on 7 May, Resaca on 14–15 May, Adairsville on 17 May, and Kingston and Cassville on 18 May 1864. Beyond relating to "A Son of the Gods" in showing how a display of what appears to be heroic self-sacrifice can have the opposite of its intended effect, this story is a searching study in its own right of the delicate balance between bravery and cowardice. In addition, it is one of the period's few literary works that challenged the prevailing tendency to put women on a pedestal. AB has often been charged with misogyny, but in this story his refusal to subscribe to the mores that condescended to women is an acknowledgment of their power, and a bold step forward for realism. The story is discussed more fully in *PA* 66–68.

1. Byron, *English Bards and Scotch Reviewers* (1809), l. 400: "To fill the speaking trump of future fame."

2. The battle of Stone's (or Stone) River, in Tennessee, occurred on 31 December 1862–2 January 1863, and was one of the bloodiest battles of the Civil War (total casualties for both sides numbered nearly 25,000). It resulted in a victory for the Federal army, led by Gen. William S. Rosecrans, commanding the Army of the Cumberland. The Confederate general, Braxton Bragg (commanding the Army of Tennessee), was ultimately forced to retreat to Tullahoma, Tennessee. For AB's discussion of the battle see *SS* 26–27.

3. Cf. George Lunt (1803–85), "Requiem: Dedicated to the Memory of the Slain in Battle" (1862): "Upon his shield, / Upon his shield returning, / Borne from the field of honor / Where he fell" (ll. 8–11). AB's frequent use of the phrase "field of honor" is nearly always mocking.

4. Rincon Hill is a sand ridge located south of Market Street in San Francisco. Although once filled with large Victorian mansions built by wealthy residents, the neighborhood was gradually abandoned by the well-to-do because of the increasing prevalence of factories and shanties in the area. The Old Mint, where AB worked, is located near this region. Cf. the discussion of the locale in "Beyond the Wall" (p. 1029).

KILLED AT RESACA

THE MAN OUT OF THE NOSE

At the intersection of two certain streets in that part of San Francisco known by the rather loosely applied name of North Beach,[1] is a vacant lot, which is rather more nearly level than is usually the case with lots, vacant or otherwise, in that region. Immediately at the back of it, to the south, however, the ground slopes steeply upward, the acclivity broken by three terraces cut into the soft rock. It is a place for goats and poor persons, several families of each class having occupied it jointly and amicably "from the foundation of the city."[2] One of the humble habitations of the lowest terrace is noticeable for its rude resemblance to the human face, or rather to such a simulacrum of it as a boy might cut out of a hollowed pumpkin, meaning no offense to his race. The eyes are two circular windows, the nose is a door, the mouth an aperture caused by removal of a board below. There are no doorsteps. As a face, this house is too large; as a dwelling, too small. The blank, unmeaning stare of its lidless and browless eyes is uncanny.

Sometimes a man steps out of the nose, turns, passes the place where the right ear should be and making his way through the throng of children and goats obstructing the narrow walk between his neighbors' doors and the edge of the terrace gains the street by descending a flight of rickety stairs. Here he pauses to consult his watch and the stranger who happens to pass wonders why such a man as that can care what is the hour. Longer observations would show that the time of day is an important element in the man's movements, for it is at precisely two o'clock in the afternoon that he comes forth 365 times in every year.

Having satisfied himself that he has made no mistake in the hour he replaces the watch and walks rapidly southward up the street two squares, turns to the right and as he approaches the next corner fixes his eyes on an upper window in a three-story building across the way. This is a somewhat dingy structure, originally of red brick and now gray. It shows the touch of age and dust. Built for a dwelling, it is now a factory. I do not know what is made there; the things that are commonly made in a factory, I suppose. I only know that at two o'clock in the afternoon of every day but Sunday it is full of activity and clatter; pulsations of some great engine shake it and there are recurrent screams of wood tormented by the saw. At the window on which the man fixes an intensely expectant gaze nothing ever appears; the glass, in truth, has such a coating of dust that it has long ceased to be transparent. The man looks at it without stopping; he merely keeps turning his head more and more backward as he leaves the building behind. Passing along to the next corner, he turns to the left, goes round the block and comes back till he reaches the point diagonally across the street from the factory—a point on his former course, which he then retraces, looking frequently backward over his right shoulder at the window while it is in sight. For many years he has not been known to vary his route nor to introduce a single innovation into his action. In a quarter of an hour he is again at the mouth of his dwelling, and a woman, who has for some time been standing in the nose, assists him to enter. He is seen no more until two o'clock the next day.

The woman is his wife. She supports herself and him by washing for the poor people among whom they live, at rates which destroy Chinese and domestic competition.[3]

This man is about fifty-seven years of age, though he looks greatly older. His hair is dead white. He wears no beard, and is always newly shaven. His hands are clean, his nails well kept. In the matter of dress he is distinctly superior to his position, as indicated by his surroundings and the business of his wife. He is, indeed, very neatly, if not quite fashionably, clad. His silk hat has a date no earlier than the year before the last, and his boots, scrupulously polished, are innocent of patches. I am told that the suit which he wears during his daily excursions of fifteen minutes is not the one that he wears at home. Like everything else that he has, this is provided and kept in repair by his wife, and is renewed as frequently as her scanty means permit.

Thirty years ago John Hardshaw and his wife lived on Rincon Hill in one of the finest residences of that once aristocratic quarter. He had once been a physician, but having inherited a considerable estate from his father concerned himself no more about the ailments of his fellow-creatures and found as much work as he cared for in managing his own affairs. Both he and his wife were highly cultivated persons, and their house was frequented by a small set of such men and women as persons of their tastes would think worth knowing. So far as these knew, Mr. and Mrs. Hardshaw lived happily together; certainly the wife was devoted to her handsome and accomplished husband and exceedingly proud of him.

Among their acquaintances were the Barwells—man, wife and two young children—of Sacramento. Mr. Barwell was a civil and mining engineer, whose duties took him much from home and frequently to San Francisco. On these occasions his wife commonly accompanied him and passed much of her time at the house of her friend,

THE MAN OUT OF THE NOSE

Mrs. Hardshaw, always with her two children, of whom Mrs. Hardshaw, childless herself, grew fond. Unluckily, her husband grew equally fond of their mother—a good deal fonder. Still more unluckily, that attractive lady was less wise than weak.

At about three o'clock one autumn morning Officer No. 13 of the Sacramento police saw a man stealthily leaving the rear entrance of a gentleman's residence and promptly arrested him. The man—who wore a slouch hat and shaggy overcoat—offered the policeman one hundred, then five hundred, then one thousand dollars to be released. As he had less than the first mentioned sum on his person the officer treated his proposal with virtuous contempt. Before reaching the station the prisoner agreed to give him a check for ten thousand dollars and remain ironed in the willows along the river bank until it should be paid. As this only provoked new derision he would say no more, merely giving an obviously fictitious name. When he was searched at the station nothing of value was found on him but a miniature portrait of Mrs. Barwell—the lady of the house at which he was caught. The case was set with costly diamonds; and something in the quality of the man's linen sent a pang of unavailing regret through the severely incorruptible bosom of Officer No. 13. There was nothing about the prisoner's clothing nor person to identify him and he was booked for burglary under the name that he had given, the honorable name of John K. Smith. The K. was an inspiration upon which, doubtless, he greatly prided himself.

In the mean time the mysterious disappearance of John Hardshaw was agitating the gossips of Rincon Hill in San Francisco, and was even mentioned in one of the newspapers. It did not occur to the lady whom that journal considerately described as his "widow," to look for him in the city prison at Sacramento—a town which he was not known ever to have visited. As John K. Smith he was arraigned and, waiving examination, committed for trial.

About two weeks before the trial, Mrs. Hardshaw, accidentally learning that her husband was held in Sacramento under an assumed name on a charge of burglary, hastened to that city without daring to mention the matter to any one and presented herself at the prison, asking for an interview with her husband, John K. Smith. Haggard and ill with anxiety, wearing a plain traveling wrap which covered her from neck to foot, and in which she had passed the night on the steamboat, too anxious to sleep, she hardly showed for what she was, but her manner pleaded for her more strongly than anything that she chose to say in evidence of her right to admittance. She was permitted to see him alone.

What occurred during that distressing interview has never transpired; but later events prove that Hardshaw had found means to subdue her will to his own. She left the prison, a broken-hearted woman, refusing to answer a single question, and returning to her desolate home renewed, in a half-hearted way, her inquiries for her missing husband. A week later she was herself missing: she had "gone back to the States"—nobody knew any more than that.

THE MAN OUT OF THE NOSE

On his trial the prisoner pleaded guilty—"by advice of his counsel," so his counsel said. Nevertheless, the judge, in whose mind several unusual circumstances had created a doubt, insisted on the district attorney placing Officer No. 13 on the stand, and the deposition of Mrs. Barwell, who was too ill to attend, was read to the jury. It was very brief: she knew nothing of the matter except that the likeness of herself was her property, and had, she thought, been left on the parlor table when she had retired on the night of the arrest. She had intended it as a present to her husband, then and still absent in Europe on business for a mining company.

This witness's manner when making the deposition at her residence was afterward described by the district attorney as most extraordinary. Twice she had refused to testify, and once, when the deposition lacked nothing but her signature, she had caught it from the clerk's hands and torn it in pieces. She had called her children to the bedside and embraced them with streaming eyes, then suddenly sending them from the room, she verified her statement by oath and signature, and fainted—"slick away," said the district attorney. It was at that time that her physician, arriving upon the scene, took in the situation at a glance and grasping the representative of the law by the collar chucked him into the street and kicked his assistant after him. The insulted majesty of the law was not vindicated; the victim of the indignity did not even mention anything of all this in court. He was ambitious to win his case, and the circumstances of the taking of that deposition were not such as would give it weight if related; and after all, the man on trial had committed an offense against the law's majesty only less heinous than that of the irascible physician.

By suggestion of the judge the jury rendered a verdict of guilty; there was nothing else to do, and the prisoner was sentenced to the penitentiary for three years. His counsel, who had objected to nothing and had made no plea for lenity—had, in fact, hardly said a word—wrung his client's hand and left the room. It was obvious to the whole bar that he had been engaged only to prevent the court from appointing counsel who might possibly insist on making a defense.

John Hardshaw served out his term at San Quentin, and when discharged was met at the prison gates by his wife, who had returned from "the States" to receive him. It is thought that they went straight to Europe; anyhow, a general power-of-attorney to a lawyer still living among us—from whom I have many of the facts of this simple history—was executed in Paris. This lawyer in a short time sold everything that Hardshaw owned in California, and for years nothing was heard of the unfortunate couple; though many to whose ears had come vague and inaccurate intimations of their strange story, and who had known them, recalled their personality with tenderness and their misfortunes with compassion.

Some years later they returned, both broken in fortune and spirits and he in health. The purpose of their return I have not been able to ascertain. For some time they lived, under the name of Johnson, in a respectable enough quarter south of Market street, pretty well out, and were never seen away from the vicinity of their dwelling. They

THE MAN OUT OF THE NOSE

must have had a little money left, for it is not known that the man had any occupation, the state of his health probably not permitting. The woman's devotion to her invalid husband was a matter of remark among their neighbors; she seemed never absent from his side and always supporting and cheering him. They would sit for hours on one of the benches in a little public park, she reading to him, his hand in hers, her light touch occasionally visiting his pale brow, her still beautiful eyes frequently lifted from the book to look into his as she made some comment on the text, or closed the volume to beguile his mood with talk of—what? Nobody ever overheard a conversation between these two. The reader who has had the patience to follow their history to this point may possibly find a pleasure in conjecture: there was probably something to be avoided. The bearing of the man was one of profound dejection; indeed, the unsympathetic youth of the neighborhood, with that keen sense for visible characteristics which ever distinguishes the young male of our species, sometimes mentioned him among themselves by the name of Spoony Glum.

It occurred one day that John Hardshaw was possessed by the spirit of unrest. God knows what led him whither he went, but he crossed Market street and held his way northward over the hills, and downward into the region known as North Beach. Turning aimlessly to the left he followed his toes along an unfamiliar street until he was opposite what for that period was a rather grand dwelling, and for this is a rather shabby factory. Casting his eyes casually upward he saw at an open window what it had been better that he had not seen—the face and figure of Elvira Barwell. Their eyes met. With a sharp exclamation, like the cry of a startled bird, the lady sprang to her feet and thrust her body half out of the window, clutching the casing on each side. Arrested by the cry, the people in the street below looked up. Hardshaw stood motionless, speechless, his eyes two flames. "Take care!" shouted some one in the crowd, as the woman strained further and further forward, defying the silent, implacable law of gravitation, as once she had defied that other law which God thundered from Sinai. The suddenness of her movements had tumbled a torrent of dark hair down her shoulders, and now it was blown about her cheeks, almost concealing her face. A moment so, and then—! A fearful cry rang through the street, as, losing her balance, she pitched headlong from the window, a confused and whirling mass of skirts, limbs, hair and white face, and struck the pavement with a horrible sound and a force of impact that was felt a hundred feet away. For a moment all eyes refused their office and turned from the sickening spectacle on the sidewalk. Drawn again to that horror, they saw it strangely augmented. A man, hatless, seated flat upon the paving stones, held the broken, bleeding body against his breast, kissing the mangled cheeks and streaming mouth through tangles of wet hair, his own features indistinguishably crimson with the blood that half-strangled him and ran in rills from his soaken beard.

The reporter's task is nearly finished. The Barwells had that very morning returned from a two years' absence in Peru. A week later the widower, now doubly desolate, since there could be no missing the significance of Hardshaw's horrible

THE MAN OUT OF THE NOSE

demonstration, had sailed for I know not what distant port; he has never come back to stay. Hardshaw—as Johnson no longer—passed a year in the Stockton asylum for the insane,[4] where also, through the influence of pitying friends, his wife was admitted to care for him. When he was discharged, not cured but harmless, they returned to the city; it would seem ever to have had some dreadful fascination for them. For a time they lived near the Mission Dolores,[5] in poverty only less abject than that which is their present lot; but it was too far away from the objective point of the man's daily pilgrimage. They could not afford car fare. So that poor devil of an angel from Heaven—wife to this convict and lunatic—obtained, at a fair enough rental, the blank-faced shanty on the lower terrace of Goat Hill.[6] Thence to the structure that was a dwelling and is a factory the distance is not so great; it is, in fact, an agreeable walk, judging from the man's eager and cheerful look as he takes it. The return journey appears to be a trifle wearisome.

E (10 July 1887): 10 (unsigned; as "John Hardshaw: The Story of a Man Who May Be Seen Coming out of the Nose"); CSTB 61–72; **CW 2.233–46.**

NOTES

Next to "The Haunted Valley," this is AB's longest story in the conventional local color genre. It is sentimental, but the sentiment is restrained by the pose that the narrator is acting as a reporter.

1. For North Beach, see "A Providential Intimation," p. 293 note 3.
2. The standard English translation of the Latin phrase *ab urbe condita* (literally, "from the city [i.e., Rome] having been founded"). Livy's history of Rome bears this title, since it commences from the traditional date of Rome's founding (753 B.C.E.).
3. Inasmuch as the Chinese had the reputation of being the cheapest laborers available, it is clear that Mrs. Hardshaw, in underselling them, was earning severely substandard wages.
4. The Insane Asylum of California was established in Stockton in 1853 by an act of the state legislature; the facility opened on 1 July 1853. It is now the Stockton State Hospital.
5. The Mission San Francisco de Assis (or Mission Dolores), on Dolores between Sixteenth and Seventeenth streets (south of Market), is the oldest religious edifice in San Francisco. It was founded in 1776 by Father Junipero Serra.
6. Goat Hill is apparently a reference to Billy Goat Hill, in the Noe Valley district south of Market Street. It is about eight blocks south of the Mission Dolores.

A BOTTOMLESS GRAVE

My name is John Brenwalter. My father, a drunkard, had a patent for an invention for making coffee-berries out of clay; but he was an honest man and would not himself engage in the manufacture. He was, therefore, only moderately wealthy, his royalties from his really valuable invention bringing him hardly enough to pay his expenses of litigation with rogues guilty of infringement. So I lacked many advantages enjoyed by the children of unscrupulous and dishonorable parents, and had it not been for a noble and devoted mother, who neglected all my brothers and sisters and personally supervised my education, should have grown up in ignorance and been compelled to teach school. To be the favorite child of a good woman is better than gold.

When I was nineteen years of age my father had the misfortune to die. He had always had perfect health, and his death, which occurred at the dinner table without a moment's warning, surprised no one more than himself. He had that very morning been notified that a patent had been granted him for a device to burst open safes by hydraulic pressure, without noise. The Commissioner of Patents had pronounced it the most ingenious, effective and generally meritorious invention that had ever been submitted to him, and my father had naturally looked forward to an old age of prosperity and honor. His sudden death was, therefore, a deep disappointment to him; but my mother, whose piety and resignation to the will of Heaven were conspicuous virtues of her character, was apparently less affected. At the close of the meal, when my poor father's body had been removed from the floor, she called us all into an adjoining room and addressed us as follows:

"My children, the uncommon occurrence that you have just witnessed is one of the most disagreeable incidents in a good man's life, and one in which I take little pleasure, I assure you. I beg you to believe that I had no hand in bringing it about. Of course," she added, after a pause, during which her eyes were cast down in deep thought, "of course it is better that he is dead."

She uttered this with so evident a sense of its obviousness as a self-evident truth that none of us had the courage to brave her surprise by asking an explanation. My mother's air of surprise when any of us went wrong in any way was very terrible to us. One day, when in a fit of peevish temper, I had taken the liberty to cut off the baby's ear, her simple words, "John, you surprise me!" appeared to me so sharp a reproof that after a sleepless night I went to her in tears, and throwing myself at her feet, exclaimed: "Mother, forgive me for surprising you." So now we all—including the one-eared baby—felt that it would keep matters smoother to accept without question the statement that it was better, somehow, for our dear father to be dead. My mother continued:

"I must tell you, my children, that in a case of sudden and mysterious death the law requires the Coroner to come and cut the body into pieces and submit them to a number of men who, having inspected them, pronounce the person dead. For this the Coroner gets a large sum of money. I wish to avoid that painful formality in this instance; it is one which never had the approval of—of the remains. John"—here my mother turned her angel face to me—"you are an educated lad, and very discreet. You have now an opportunity to show your gratitude for all the sacrifices that your education has entailed upon the rest of us. John, go and remove the Coroner."

Inexpressibly delighted by this proof of my mother's confidence, and by the chance to distinguish myself by an act that squared with my natural disposition, I knelt before her, carried her hand to my lips and bathed it with tears of sensibility. Before five o'clock that afternoon I had removed the Coroner.

I was immediately arrested and thrown into jail, where I passed a most uncomfortable night, being unable to sleep because of the profanity of my fellow-prisoners, two clergymen, whose theological training had given them a fertility of impious ideas and a command of blasphemous language altogether unparalleled. But along toward morning the jailer, who, sleeping in an adjoining room, had been equally disturbed, entered the cell and with a fearful oath warned the reverend gentlemen that if he heard any more swearing their sacred calling would not prevent him from turning them into the street. After that they moderated their objectionable conversation, substituting an accordion,[1] and I slept the peaceful and refreshing sleep of youth and innocence.

The next morning I was taken before the Superior Judge, sitting as a committing magistrate, and put upon my preliminary examination. I pleaded not guilty, adding that the man whom I had murdered was a notorious Democrat. (My good mother was a Republican, and from early childhood I had been carefully instructed by her in the principles of honest government and the necessity of suppressing factional opposition.) The Judge, elected by a Republican ballot-box with a sliding bottom, was visibly impressed by the cogency of my plea and offered me a cigarette.

"May it please your Honor," began the District Attorney, "I do not deem it necessary to submit any evidence in this case. Under the law of the land you sit here as a committing magistrate. It is therefore your duty to commit. Testimony and argument alike would imply a doubt that your Honor means to perform your sworn duty. That is my case."

My counsel, a brother of the deceased Coroner, rose and said: "May it please the Court, my learned friend on the other side has so well and eloquently stated the law governing in this case that it only remains for me to inquire to what extent it has been already complied with. It is true, your Honor is a committing magistrate, and as such it is your duty to commit—what? That is a matter which the law has wisely and justly left to your own discretion, and wisely you have discharged already every obligation that the law imposes. Since I have known your Honor you have done nothing but commit. You have committed embracery,[2] theft, arson, perjury, adultery, murder— every crime in the calendar and every excess known to the sensual and depraved, including my learned friend, the District Attorney. You have done your whole duty as a committing magistrate, and as there is no evidence against this worthy young man, my client, I move that he be discharged."

An impressive silence ensued. The Judge arose, put on the black cap and in a voice trembling with emotion sentenced me to life and liberty. Then turning to my counsel he said, coldly but significantly:

"I will see you later."

The next morning the lawyer who had so conscientiously defended me against a charge of murdering his own brother—with whom he had a quarrel about some land—had disappeared and his fate is to this day unknown.

In the meantime my poor father's body had been secretly buried at midnight in the backyard of his late residence, with his late boots on and the contents of his late stomach unanalyzed. "He was opposed to display," said my dear mother, as she finished tamping down the earth above him and assisted the children to litter the place with straw; "his instincts were all domestic and he loved a quiet life."

My mother's application for letters of administration stated that she had good reason to believe that the deceased was dead, for he had not come home to his meals for several days; but the Judge of the Crowbait Court—as she ever afterward contemptuously called it—decided that the proof of death was insufficient, and put the estate into the hands of the Public Administrator, who was his son-in-law. It was found that the liabilities were exactly balanced by the assets; there was left only the patent for the device for bursting open safes without noise, by hydraulic pressure and this had passed into the ownership of the Probate Judge and the Public Administraitor—as my dear mother preferred to spell it. Thus, within a few brief months a worthy and respectable family was reduced from prosperity to crime; necessity compelled us to go to work.

In the selection of occupations we were governed by a variety of considerations, such as personal fitness, inclination and so forth. My mother opened a select private school for instruction in the art of changing the spots upon leopard-skin rugs; my eldest brother, George Henry, who had a turn for music, became a bugler in a neighboring asylum for deaf mutes; my sister, Mary Maria, took orders for Professor Pumpernickel's Essence of Latchkeys for flavoring mineral springs, and I set up as an adjuster and gilder of cross-beams for gibbets. The other children, too young for labor, continued to steal small articles exposed in front of shops, as they had been taught.

In our intervals of leisure we decoyed travelers into our house and buried the bodies in a cellar.

In one part of this cellar we kept wines, liquors and provisions. From the rapidity of their disappearance we acquired the superstitious belief that the spirits of the persons buried there came at dead of night and held a festival. It was at least certain that frequently of a morning we would discover fragments of pickled meats, canned goods and such débris, littering the place, although it had been securely locked and barred against human intrusion. It was proposed to remove the provisions and store them elsewhere, but our dear mother, always generous and hospitable, said it was better to endure the loss than risk exposure: if the ghosts were denied this trifling gratification they might set on foot an investigation, which would overthrow our scheme of the division of labor, by diverting the energies of the whole family into the single industry pursued by me—we might all decorate the crossbeams of gibbets. We accepted her decision with filial submission, due to our reverence for her worldly wisdom and the purity of her character.

One night while we were all in the cellar—none dared to enter it alone—engaged in bestowing upon the Mayor of an adjoining town the solemn offices of Christian burial, my mother and the younger children, holding a candle each, while George Henry and I labored with a spade and pick, my sister Mary Maria uttered a shriek and covered her eyes with her hands. We were all dreadfully startled and the Mayor's obsequies were instantly suspended, while with pale faces and in trembling tones we begged her to say what had alarmed her. The younger children were so agitated that they held their candles unsteadily, and the waving shadows of our figures danced with uncouth and grotesque movements on the walls and flung themselves into the most uncanny attitudes. The face of the dead man, now gleaming ghastly in the light, and now extinguished by some floating shadow, appeared at each emergence to have taken on a new and more forbidding expression, a maligner menace. Frightened even more than ourselves by the girl's scream, rats raced in multitudes about the place, squeaking shrilly, or starred the black opacity of some distant corner with steadfast eyes, mere points of green light, matching the faint phosphorescence of decay that filled the half-dug grave and seemed the visible manifestation of that faint odor of mortality which tainted the unwholesome air. The children now sobbed and clung about the limbs of their elders, dropping their candles, and we were near being left in total darkness, except for that sinister light, which slowly welled upward from the disturbed earth and overflowed the edges of the grave like a fountain.

Meanwhile my sister, crouching in the earth that had been thrown out of the excavation, had removed her hands from her face and was staring with expanded eyes into an obscure space between two wine-casks.

A BOTTOMLESS GRAVE

"There it is!—there it is!" she shrieked, pointing; "God in Heaven! can't you see it?"

And there indeed it was!—a human figure, dimly discernible in the gloom—a figure that wavered from side to side as if about to fall, clutching at the wine-casks for support, had stepped unsteadily forward and for one moment stood revealed in the light of our remaining candles; then it surged heavily and fell prone upon the earth. In that moment we had all recognized the figure, the face and bearing of our father— dead these ten months and buried by our own hands!—our father indubitably risen and ghastly drunk!

On the incidents of our precipitate flight from that horrible place—on the extinction of all human sentiment in that tumultuous, mad scramble up the damp and mouldy stairs—slipping, falling, pulling one another down and clambering over one another's back—the lights extinguished, babes trampled beneath the feet of their strong brothers and hurled backward to death by a mother's arm!—on all this I do not care to dwell. My mother, my eldest brother and sister and I escaped; the others remained below, to perish of their wounds, or of their terror—some, perhaps, by flame. For within an hour we four, hastily gathering together what money and jewels we had and what clothing we could carry, fired the dwelling and fled by its light into the hills. We did not even pause to collect the insurance, and my dear mother said on her death-bed, years afterward in a distant land, that this was the only sin of omission that lay upon her conscience. Her confessor, a holy man, assured her that under the circumstances Heaven would pardon the neglect.

About ten years after our removal from the scenes of my childhood I, then a prosperous forger, returned in disguise to the spot with a view to obtaining, if possible, some treasure belonging to us, which had been buried in the cellar. I may say that I was unsuccessful: the discovery of many human bones in the ruins had set the authorities digging for more. They had found the treasure and had kept it for their honesty. The house had not been rebuilt; the whole suburb was, in fact, a desolation. So many unearthly sights and sounds had been reported thereabout that nobody would live there. As there was none to question nor molest, I resolved to gratify my filial piety by gazing once more upon the face of my beloved father, if indeed our eyes had deceived us and he was still in his grave. I remembered, too, that he had always worn an enormous diamond ring, and never having seen it nor heard of it since his death, I had reason to think he might have been buried in it. Procuring a spade, I soon located the grave in what had been the backyard and began digging. When I had got down about four feet the whole bottom fell out of the grave and I was precipitated into a large drain, falling through a long hole in its crumbling arch. There was no body, nor any vestige of one.

Unable to get out of the excavation, I crept through the drain, and having with some difficulty removed a mass of charred rubbish and blackened masonry that choked it, emerged into what had been that fateful cellar.

All was clear. My father, whatever had caused him to be "taken bad" at his meal (and I think my sainted mother could have thrown some light upon that matter) had

A BOTTOMLESS GRAVE

indubitably been buried alive.[3] The grave having been accidentally dug above the forgotten drain, and down almost to the crown of its arch, and no coffin having been used, his struggles on reviving had broken the rotten masonry and he had fallen through, escaping finally into the cellar. Feeling that he was not welcome in his own house, yet having no other, he had lived in subterranean seclusion, a witness to our thrift and a pensioner on our providence. It was he who had eaten our food; it was he who had drunk our wine—he was no better than a thief! In a moment of intoxication, and feeling, no doubt, that need of companionship which is the one sympathetic link between a drunken man and his race, he had left his place of concealment at a strangely inopportune time, entailing the most deplorable consequences upon those nearest and dearest to him—a blunder that had almost the dignity of crime.[4]

E (26 Feb. 1888): 9 (with subheads: "How a Good Mother Reared Noble Sons and Daughters; 'Brenwalter Returns'; The Short and Simple Annals of a Worthy But Most Unfortunate Family"); *CW* 8.9–22.

NOTES

This is another AB social satire in the vein of the "Parenticide Club" series. The well-spoken narrator is unreliable. He is sanctimonious, as fastidious about formalities as he is indifferent to substance, and given to employing euphemisms to describe the immoral acts that he, with refined amorality, considers only as logical means to his materialistic ends. The narrator, moreover, is in tune with his family and the hypocritical society in which they dwell. Any sin or crime may be overlooked or even pardoned as long as superficial appearances are kept up and honest directness avoided.

1. Cf. *DD*: "ACCORDION, *n*. An instrument in harmony with the sentiments of an assassin."
2. That is, the attempt to influence a jury or court by bribes, threats, or other unlawful means.
3. The nineteenth century had a fascinated horror of premature burial. Newspapers printed with some frequency incidents or rumors of them with sensational luridness. AB follows Poe in using the motif in his stories, but typically mocks the excessive public fear of it.
4. The obvious sarcasm of the subheads that are appended in *E* to the title is paralleled in the last line of *E*. In place of the last clause ("a blunder . . . crime") is a final sentence with this ironic moral: "Let the lesson of his error sink deeply into the human heart." AB probably eliminated both it and the subheads as being too heavy-handed.

ONE OF THE MISSING

Jerome Searing, a private soldier of General Sherman's army, then confronting the enemy at and about Kennesaw Mountain, Georgia,[1] turned his back upon a small group of officers with whom he had been talking in low tones, stepped across a light line of earthworks and disappeared in a forest. None of the men in line behind the works had said a word to him, nor had he so much as nodded to them in passing, but all who saw understood that this brave man had been intrusted with some perilous duty. Jerome Searing, though a private, did not serve in the ranks; he was detailed for service at division headquarters, being borne upon the rolls as an orderly. "Orderly" is a word covering a multitude of duties. An orderly may be a messenger, a clerk, an officer's servant—anything. He may perform services for which no provision is made in orders and army regulations. Their nature may depend upon his aptitude, upon favor, upon accident. Private Searing, an incomparable marksman, young, hardy, intelligent and insensible to fear, was a scout. The general commanding his division was not content to obey orders blindly without knowing what was in his front, even when his command was not on detached service, but formed a fraction of the line of the army; nor was he satisfied to receive his knowledge of his *vis-à-vis* through the customary channels; he wanted to know more than he was apprised of by the corps commander and the collisions of pickets and skirmishers. Hence Jerome Searing, with his extraordinary daring, his woodcraft, his sharp eyes and truthful tongue. On this occasion his instructions were simple: to get as near the enemy's lines as possible and learn all that he could.

In a few moments he had arrived at the picket-line, the men on duty there lying in groups of two and four behind little banks of earth scooped out of the slight depression in which they lay, their rifles protruding from the green boughs with which they had masked their small defenses. The forest extended without a break toward the front, so solemn and silent that only by an effort of the imagination could it be conceived as populous with armed men, alert and vigilant—a forest formidable with possibilities of battle. Pausing a moment in one of these rifle-pits to apprise the men of his intention Searing crept stealthily forward on his hands and knees and was soon lost to view in a dense thicket of underbrush.

"That is the last of him," said one of the men; "I wish I had his rifle; those fellows will hurt some of us with it."

Searing crept on, taking advantage of every accident of ground and growth to give himself better cover. His eyes penetrated everywhere, his ears took note of every sound. He stilled his breathing, and at the cracking of a twig beneath his knee stopped his progress and hugged the earth. It was slow work, but not tedious; the danger made it exciting, but by no physical signs was the excitement manifest. His pulse was as regular, his nerves were as steady as if he were trying to trap a sparrow.

"It seems a long time," he thought, "but I cannot have come very far; I am still alive."

He smiled at his own method of estimating distance, and crept forward. A moment later he suddenly flattened himself upon the earth and lay motionless, minute after minute. Through a narrow opening in the bushes he had caught sight of a small mound of yellow clay—one of the enemy's rifle-pits. After some little time he cautiously raised his head, inch by inch, then his body upon his hands, spread out on each side of him, all the while intently regarding the hillock of clay. In another moment he was upon his feet, rifle in hand, striding rapidly forward with little attempt at concealment. He had rightly interpreted the signs, whatever they were; the enemy was gone.

To assure himself beyond a doubt before going back to report upon so important a matter, Searing pushed forward across the line of abandoned pits, running from cover to cover in the more open forest, his eyes vigilant to discover possible stragglers. He came to the edge of a plantation—one of those forlorn, deserted homesteads of the last years of the war, upgrown with brambles, ugly with broken fences and desolate with vacant buildings having blank apertures in place of doors and windows. After a keen reconnoissance from the safe seclusion of a clump of young pines Searing ran lightly across a field and through an orchard to a small structure which stood apart from the other farm buildings, on a slight elevation. This he thought would enable him to overlook a large scope of country in the direction that he supposed the enemy to have taken in withdrawing. This building, which had originally consisted of a single room elevated upon four posts about ten feet high, was now little more than a roof; the floor had fallen away, the joists and planks loosely piled on the ground below or resting on end at various angles, not wholly torn from their fastenings above. The supporting posts were themselves no longer vertical. It looked as if the whole edifice would go down at the touch of a finger.

ONE OF THE MISSING

Concealing himself in the débris of joists and flooring Searing looked across the open ground between his point of view and a spur of Kennesaw Mountain, a half-mile away. A road leading up and across this spur was crowded with troops—the rear-guard of the retiring enemy, their gun-barrels gleaming in the morning sunlight.

Searing had now learned all that he could hope to know. It was his duty to return to his own command with all possible speed and report his discovery. But the gray column of Confederates toiling up the mountain road was singularly tempting. His rifle—an ordinary "Springfield," but fitted with a globe sight and hair-trigger—would easily send its ounce and a quarter of lead hissing into their midst. That would probably not affect the duration and result of the war, but it is the business of a soldier to kill. It is also his habit if he is a good soldier. Searing cocked his rifle and "set" the trigger.

But it was decreed from the beginning of time that Private Searing was not to murder anybody that bright summer morning, nor was the Confederate retreat to be announced by him. For countless ages events had been so matching themselves together in that wondrous mosaic to some parts of which, dimly discernible, we give the name of history, that the acts which he had in will would have marred the harmony of the pattern. Some twenty-five years previously the Power charged with the execution of the work according to the design had provided against that mischance by causing the birth of a certain male child in a little village at the foot of the Carpathian Mountains,[2] had carefully reared it, supervised its education, directed its desires into a military channel and in due time made it an officer of artillery. By the concurrence of an infinite number of favoring influences and their preponderance over an infinite number of opposing ones, this officer of artillery had been made to commit a breach of discipline and flee from his native country to avoid punishment. He had been directed to New Orleans (instead of New York), where a recruiting officer awaited him on the wharf. He was enlisted and promoted, and things were so ordered that he now commanded a Confederate battery some two miles along the line from where Jerome Searing, the Federal scout, stood cocking his rifle. Nothing had been neglected—at every step in the progress of both these men's lives, and in the lives of their contemporaries and ancestors, and in the lives of the contemporaries of their ancestors, the right thing had been done to bring about the desired result. Had anything in all this vast concatenation been overlooked Private Searing might have fired on the retreating Confederates that morning, and would perhaps have missed. As it fell out, a Confederate captain of artillery, having nothing better to do while awaiting his turn to pull out and be off, amused himself by sighting a field-piece obliquely to his right at what he mistook for some Federal officers on the crest of a hill, and discharged it. The shot flew high of its mark.

As Jerome Searing drew back the hammer of his rifle and with his eyes upon the distant Confederates considered where he could plant his shot with the best hope of making a widow or an orphan or a childless mother,—perhaps all three, for Private

ONE OF THE MISSING

Searing, although he had repeatedly refused promotion, was not without a certain kind of ambition,—he heard a rushing sound in the air, like that made by the wings of a great bird swooping down upon its prey. More quickly than he could apprehend the gradation, it increased to a hoarse and horrible roar, as the missile that made it sprang at him out of the sky, striking with a deafening impact one of the posts supporting the confusion of timbers above him, smashing it into matchwood, and bringing down the crazy edifice with a loud clatter, in clouds of blinding dust!

When Jerome Searing recovered consciousness he did not at once understand what had occurred. It was, indeed, some time before he opened his eyes. For a while he believed that he had died and been buried, and he tried to recall some portions of the burial service. He thought that his wife was kneeling upon his grave, adding her weight to that of the earth upon his breast. The two of them, widow and earth, had crushed his coffin. Unless the children should persuade her to go home he would not much longer be able to breathe. He felt a sense of wrong. "I cannot speak to her," he thought; "the dead have no voice; and if I open my eyes I shall get them full of earth."

He opened his eyes. A great expanse of blue sky, rising from a fringe of the tops of trees. In the foreground, shutting out some of the trees, a high, dun mound, angular in outline and crossed by an intricate, patternless system of straight lines; the whole an immeasurable distance away—a distance so inconceivably great that it fatigued him, and he closed his eyes. The moment that he did so he was conscious of an insufferable light. A sound was in his ears like the low, rhythmic thunder of a distant sea breaking in successive waves upon the beach, and out of this noise, seeming a part of it, or possibly coming from beyond it, and intermingled with its ceaseless undertone, came the articulate words: "Jerome Searing, you are caught like a rat in a trap—in a trap, trap, trap."

Suddenly there fell a great silence, a black darkness, an infinite tranquility, and Jerome Searing, perfectly conscious of his rathood, and well assured of the trap that he was in, remembering all and nowise alarmed, again opened his eyes to reconnoitre, to note the strength of his enemy, to plan his defense.

He was caught in a reclining posture, his back firmly supported by a solid beam. Another lay across his breast, but he had been able to shrink a little away from it so that it no longer oppressed him, though it was immovable. A brace joining it at an angle had wedged him against a pile of boards on his left, fastening the arm on that side. His legs, slightly parted and straight along the ground, were covered upward to the knees with a mass of débris which towered above his narrow horizon. His head was as rigidly fixed as in a vise; he could move his eyes, his chin—no more. Only his right arm was partly free. "You must help us get out of this," he said to it. But he could not get it from under the heavy timber athwart his chest, nor move it outward more than six inches at the elbow.

ONE OF THE MISSING

Searing was not seriously injured, nor did he suffer pain. A smart rap on the head from a flying fragment of the splintered post, incurred simultaneously with the frightfully sudden shock to the nervous system, had momentarily dazed him. His term of unconsciousness, including the period of recovery, during which he had had the strange fancies, had probably not exceeded a few seconds, for the dust of the wreck had not wholly cleared away as he began an intelligent survey of the situation.

With his partly free right hand he now tried to get hold of the beam that lay across, but not quite against, his breast. In no way could he do so. He was unable to depress the shoulder so as to push the elbow beyond that edge of the timber which was nearest his knees; failing in that, he could not raise the forearm and hand to grasp the beam. The brace that made an angle with it downward and backward prevented him from doing anything in that direction, and between it and his body the space was not half so wide as the length of his forearm. Obviously he could not get his hand under the beam nor over it; the hand could not, in fact, touch it at all. Having demonstrated his inability, he desisted, and began to think whether he could reach any of the débris piled upon his legs.

In surveying the mass with a view to determining that point, his attention was arrested by what seemed to be a ring of shining metal immediately in front of his eyes. It appeared to him at first to surround some perfectly black substance, and it was somewhat more than a half-inch in diameter. It suddenly occurred to his mind that the blackness was simply shadow and that the ring was in fact the muzzle of his rifle protruding from the pile of débris. He was not long in satisfying himself that this was so—if it was a satisfaction. By closing either eye he could look a little way along the barrel—to the point where it was hidden by the rubbish that held it. He could see the one side, with the corresponding eye, at apparently the same angle as the other side with the other eye. Looking with the right eye, the weapon seemed to be directed at a point to the left of his head, and *vice versa*. He was unable to see the upper surface of the barrel, but could see the under surface of the stock at a slight angle. The piece was, in fact, aimed at the exact center of his forehead.

In the perception of this circumstance, in the recollection of that just previously to the mischance of which this uncomfortable situation was the result he had cocked the rifle and set the trigger so that a touch would discharge it, Private Searing was affected with a feeling of uneasiness. But that was as far as possible from fear; he was a brave man, somewhat familiar with the aspect of rifles from that point of view, and of cannon too. And now he recalled, with something like amusement, an incident of his experience at the storming of Missionary Ridge,[3] where, walking up to one of the enemy's embrasures from which he had seen a heavy gun throw charge after charge of grape among the assailants he had thought for a moment that the piece had been withdrawn; he could see nothing in the opening but a brazen circle. What that was he had understood just in time to step aside as it pitched another peck of iron down that

ONE OF THE MISSING

swarming slope. To face firearms is one of the commonest incidents in a soldier's life—firearms, too, with malevolent eyes blazing behind them. That is what a soldier is for. Still, Private Searing did not altogether relish the situation, and turned away his eyes.

After groping, aimless, with his right hand for a time he made an ineffectual attempt to release his left. Then he tried to disengage his head, the fixity of which was the more annoying from his ignorance of what held it. Next he tried to free his feet, but while exerting the powerful muscles of his legs for that purpose it occurred to him that a disturbance of the rubbish which held them might discharge the rifle; how it could have endured what had already befallen it he could not understand, although memory assisted him with several instances in point. One in particular he recalled, in which in a moment of mental abstraction he had clubbed his rifle and beaten out another gentleman's brains, observing afterward that the weapon which he had been diligently swinging by the muzzle was loaded, capped and at full cock—knowledge of which circumstance would doubtless have cheered his antagonist to longer endurance. He had always smiled in recalling that blunder of his "green and salad days"[4] as a soldier, but now he did not smile. He turned his eyes again to the muzzle of the rifle and for a moment fancied that it had moved; it seemed somewhat nearer.

Again he looked away. The tops of the distant trees beyond the bounds of the plantation interested him; he had not before observed how light and feathery they were, nor how darkly blue the sky was, even among their branches, where they somewhat paled it with their green; above him it appeared almost black. "It will be uncomfortably hot here," he thought, "as the day advances. I wonder which way I am looking."

Judging by such shadows as he could see, he decided that his face was due north; he would at least not have the sun in his eyes, and north—well, that was toward his wife and children.

"Bah!" he exclaimed aloud, "what have they to do with it?"

He closed his eyes. "As I can't get out I may as well go to sleep. The rebels are gone and some of our fellows are sure to stray out here foraging. They'll find me."

But he did not sleep. Gradually he became sensible of a pain in his forehead—a dull ache, hardly perceptible at first, but growing more and more uncomfortable. He opened his eyes and it was gone—closed them and it returned. "The devil!" he said, irrelevantly, and stared again at the sky. He heard the singing of birds, the strange metallic note of the meadow lark, suggesting the clash of vibrant blades. He fell into pleasant memories of his childhood, played again with his brother and sister, raced across the fields, shouting to alarm the sedentary larks, entered the somber forest beyond and with timid steps followed the faint path to Ghost Rock, standing at last with audible heart-throbs before the Dead Man's Cave and seeking to penetrate its awful mystery. For the first time he observed that the opening of the haunted cavern was encircled by a ring of metal. Then all else vanished and left him gazing into the barrel of his rifle as before. But whereas before it had seemed nearer, it now seemed an inconceivable distance away, and all the more sinister for that. He cried out and, startled by something in his own voice—the note of fear—lied to himself in denial: "If I don't sing out I may stay here till I die."

He now made no further attempt to evade the menacing stare of the gun barrel. If he turned away his eyes an instant it was to look for assistance (although he could not see the ground on either side the ruin), and he permitted them to return, obedient to the imperative fascination. If he closed them it was from weariness, and instantly the poignant pain in his forehead—the prophecy and menace of the bullet—forced him to reopen them.

The tension of nerve and brain was too severe; nature came to his relief with intervals of unconsciousness. Reviving from one of these he became sensible of a sharp, smarting pain in his right hand, and when he worked his fingers together, or rubbed his palm with them, he could feel that they were wet and slippery. He could not see the hand, but he knew the sensation; it was running blood. In his delirium he had beaten it against the jagged fragments of the wreck, had clutched it full of splinters. He resolved that he would meet his fate more manly. He was a plain, common soldier, had no religion and not much philosophy; he could not die like a hero, with great and wise last words, even if there had been some one to hear them, but he could die "game," and he would. But if he could only know when to expect the shot!

Some rats which had probably inhabited the shed came sneaking and scampering about. One of them mounted the pile of débris that held the rifle; another followed and another. Searing regarded them at first with indifference, then with friendly interest; then, as the thought flashed into his bewildered mind that they might touch the trigger of his rifle, he cursed them and ordered them to go away. "It is no business of yours," he cried.

The creatures went away; they would return later, attack his face, gnaw away his nose, cut his throat—he knew that, but he hoped by that time to be dead.

Nothing could now unfix his gaze from the little ring of metal with its black interior. The pain in his forehead was fierce and incessant. He felt it gradually penetrating the brain more and more deeply, until at last its progress was arrested by the wood at the back of his head. It grew momentarily more insufferable: he began wantonly beating his lacerated hand against the splinters again to counteract that horrible ache. It seemed to throb with a slow, regular recurrence, each pulsation sharper than the preceding, and sometimes he cried out, thinking he felt the fatal bullet. No thoughts of home, of wife and children, of country, of glory. The whole record of memory was effaced. The world had passed away—not a vestige remained. Here in this confusion of timbers and boards is the sole universe. Here is immortality in time—each pain an everlasting life. The throbs tick off eternities.[5]

Jerome Searing, the man of courage, the formidable enemy, the strong, resolute warrior, was as pale as a ghost. His jaw was fallen; his eyes protruded; he trembled in

ONE OF THE MISSING

every fiber; a cold sweat bathed his entire body; he screamed with fear. He was not insane—he was terrified.

In groping about with his torn and bleeding hand he seized at last a strip of board, and, pulling, felt it give way. It lay parallel with his body, and by bending his elbow as much as the contracted space would permit, he could draw it a few inches at a time. Finally it was altogether loosened from the wreckage covering his legs; he could lift it clear of the ground its whole length. A great hope came into his mind: perhaps he could work it upward, that is to say backward, far enough to lift the end and push aside the rifle; or, if that were too tightly wedged, so place the strip of board as to deflect the bullet. With this object he passed it backward inch by inch, hardly daring to breathe lest that act somehow defeat his intent, and more than ever unable to remove his eyes from the rifle, which might perhaps now hasten to improve its waning opportunity. Something at least had been gained: in the occupation of his mind in this attempt at self-defense he was less sensible of the pain in his head and had ceased to wince. But he was still dreadfully frightened and his teeth rattled like castanets.

The strip of board ceased to move to the suasion of his hand. He tugged at it with all his strength, changed the direction of its length all he could, but it had met some extended obstruction behind him and the end in front was still too far away to clear the pile of débris and reach the muzzle of the gun. It extended, indeed, nearly as far as the trigger guard, which, uncovered by the rubbish, he could imperfectly see with his right eye. He tried to break the strip with his hand, but had no leverage. In his defeat, all his terror returned, augmented tenfold. The black aperture of the rifle appeared to threaten a sharper and more imminent death in punishment of his rebellion. The track of the bullet through his head ached with an intenser anguish. He began to tremble again.

Suddenly he became composed. His tremor subsided. He clenched his teeth and drew down his eyebrows. He had not exhausted his means of defense; a new design had shaped itself in his mind—another plan of battle. Raising the front end of the strip of board, he carefully pushed it forward through the wreckage at the side of the rifle until it pressed against the trigger guard. Then he moved the end slowly outward until he could feel that it had cleared it, then, closing his eyes, thrust it against the trigger with all his strength! There was no explosion; the rifle had been discharged as it dropped from his hand when the building fell. But it did its work.

Lieutenant Adrian Searing, in command of the picket-guard on that part of the line through which his brother Jerome had passed on his mission, sat with attentive ears in his breastwork behind the line. Not the faintest sound escaped him; the cry of a bird, the barking of a squirrel, the noise of the wind among the pines—all were anxiously noted by his overstrained sense. Suddenly, directly in front of his line, he heard a faint, confused rumble, like the clatter of a falling building translated by distance.

ONE OF THE MISSING

The lieutenant mechanically looked at his watch. Six o'clock and eighteen minutes. At the same moment an officer approached him on foot from the rear and saluted.

"Lieutenant," said the officer, "the colonel directs you to move forward your line and feel the enemy if you find him. If not, continue the advance until directed to halt. There is reason to think that the enemy has retreated."

The lieutenant nodded and said nothing; the other officer retired. In a moment the men, apprised of their duty by the non-commissioned officers in low tones, had deployed from their rifle-pits and were moving forward in skirmishing order, with set teeth and beating hearts.

This line of skirmishers sweeps across the plantation toward the mountain. They pass on both sides of the wrecked building, observing nothing. At a short distance in their rear their commander comes. He casts his eyes curiously upon the ruin and sees a dead body half buried in boards and timbers. It is so covered with dust that its clothing is Confederate gray. Its face is yellowish white; the cheeks are fallen in, the temples sunken, too, with sharp ridges about them, making the forehead forbiddingly narrow; the upper lip, slightly lifted, shows the white teeth, rigidly clenched. The hair is heavy with moisture, the face as wet as the dewy grass all about. From his point of view the officer does not observe the rifle; the man was apparently killed by the fall of the building.

"Dead a week," said the officer curtly, moving on and absently pulling out his watch as if to verify his estimate of time. Six o'clock and forty minutes.

E (11 Mar. 1888): 10; *TSC* 69–91; *IML* 63–87; **CW** 2.71–92. Reprinted in *Current Literature* 1, no. 1 (July 1888): 54–57.

NOTES

The chief feature of this tale is the penetrating psychological analysis it brings to bear on the Biercian theme of the narrow separation of bravery from cowardice. "Insensible to fear" at the beginning of the story, in a matter of minutes the protagonist Jerome Searing is literally terrified to death. The story is also one of the few in the Bierce canon which flirt with the idea of destiny. Nowhere in the canon, however, and certainly not in this story is much done with the idea. More well developed is the theme of justice, as Searing's cold-blooded ambition to impartially kill Confederates and inflict collateral pain on their civilian survivors first characterizes him as a rat, and ends in his own impartial victimization by a seemingly random but predestined shell. Frank Norris parodied this story in "Ambrosia Beer," one of six sketches that comprise his "Perverted Tales," published in the Christmas 1897 issue of *Wa*. (For more discussion see Lawrence I. Berkove's article "The Romantic Realism of Bierce and Norris," *Frank Norris Studies* 15 [Spring 1993]: 13–17.)

1. The battle of Kennesaw Mountain, about twenty miles northwest of Atlanta in Georgia, occurred on 27 June 1864. Although the Confederate forces, led by Gen. Joseph E. Johnston, defeated the Federals, led by William Tecumseh Sherman, the victory was short-lived, as Sherman nevertheless proceeded on his march to Atlanta. AB received a serious head wound in the battle (see *SS* 51–52).

2. The Carpathian Mountains are located in eastern Europe, on the borderline between Poland and Czechoslovakia.
3. The battle of Missionary Ridge, in central Tennessee, occurred on 24–25 November 1863, between Federal forces led by Gen. Ulysses S. Grant and Confederate forces led by Gen. Braxton Bragg. Heavy losses were sustained on both sides, but the battle is considered a Federal victory. Poor coordination by Grant's army, however, prevented the Federals from destroying Bragg's forces. For AB's memories of the battle see *SS* 27–29.
4. Cf. Shakespeare, *Antony and Cleopatra,* 1.5.73–74: "My salad days, / When I was green in judgment."
5. This brief mention of the subjective character of time adumbrates the famous and fuller treatment of it in "An Occurrence at Owl Creek Bridge" (p. 725) and incidentally shows that the subject was on AB's mind.

ONE OF THE MISSING

FOR THE AHKOOND

In the year 4591 I accepted from his gracious Majesty the Ahkoond of Citrusia[1] a commission to explore the unknown region lying to the eastward of the Ultimate Hills,
the range which that learned archæologist, Simeon Tucker, affirms to be identical
with the "Rocky Mountains" of the ancients. For this proof of his Majesty's favor I was
indebted, doubtless, to a certain distinction that I had been fortunate enough to
acquire by explorations in the heart of Darkest Europe. His Majesty kindly offered to
raise and equip a large expeditionary force to accompany me, and I was given the
widest discretion in the matter of outfit; I could draw upon the royal treasury for any
sum that I might require, and upon the royal university for all the scientific apparatus and assistance necessary to my purpose. Declining these encumbrances, I took my
electric rifle and a portable waterproof case containing a few simple instruments and
writing materials and set out. Among the instruments was, of course, an aerial
isochronophone which I set by the one in the Ahkoond's private dining-room at the
palace. His Majesty invariably dined alone at 18 o'clock, and sat at table six hours: it
was my intention to send him all my reports at the hour of 23, just as dessert would
be served, and he would be in a proper frame of mind to appreciate my discoveries
and my services to the crown.

At 9 o'clock on the 13th of Meijh I left Sanf Rachisco and after a tedious journey
of nearly fifty minutes arrived at Bolosson, the eastern terminus of the magnetic tube,
on the summit of the Ultimate Hills. According to Tucker this was anciently a station
on the Central Peaceful Railway,[2] and was called "German," in honor of an illustrious
dancing master. Prof. Nupper, however, says it was the ancient Nevraska, the capital
of Kikago, and geographers generally have accepted that view.

Finding nothing at Bolosson to interest me except a fine view of the volcano Car-
lema, then in active eruption, I shouldered my electric rifle and with my case of

instruments strapped upon my back plunged at once into the wilderness, down the eastern slope. As I descended the character of the vegetation altered. The pines of the higher altitudes gave place to oaks, these to ash, beech and maple. To these succeeded the tamarack and such trees as affect a moist and marshy habitat; and finally, when for four months I had been steadily descending, I found myself in a primeval flora consisting mainly of giant ferns, some of them as much as twenty *surindas* in diameter. They grew upon the margins of vast stagnant lakes which I was compelled to navigate by means of rude rafts made from their trunks lashed together with vines.

In the fauna of the region that I had traversed I had noted changes corresponding to those in the flora. On the upper slope there was nothing but the mountain sheep, but I passed successively through the habitats of the bear, the deer and the horse. This last mentioned creature, which our naturalists have believed long extinct[3] and which Dorbley declares our ancestors domesticated, I found in vast numbers on high table lands covered with grass upon which it feeds. The animal answers the current description of the horse very nearly, but all that I saw were destitute of the horns, and none had the characteristic forked tail. This member, on the contrary, is a tassel of straight wiry hair, reaching nearly to the ground—a surprising sight. Lower still I came upon the mastodon, the lion, the tiger, hippopotamus and alligator, all differing very little from those infesting Central Europe, as described in my "Travels in the Forgotten Continent."

In the lake region where I now found myself, the waters abounded with ichthyosauri, and along the margins the iguanodon dragged his obscene bulk in indolent immunity. Great flocks of pterodactyls, their bodies as large as those of oxen and their necks enormously long, clamored and fought in the air, the broad membranes of their wings making a singular musical humming, unlike anything that I had ever heard. Between them and the ichthyosauri there was incessant battle, and I was constantly reminded of the ancient poet's splendid and original comparison of man to

> dragons of the prime
> That tare each other in their slime.[4]

When brought down with my electric rifle and properly roasted, the pterodactyl proved very good eating, particularly the pads of the toes.

In urging my raft along the shore line of one of the stagnant lagoons one day I was surprised to find a broad rock jutting out from the shore, its upper surface some ten *coprets* above the water. Disembarking, I ascended it, and on examination recognized it as the remnant of an immense mountain which at one time must have been 5,000 *coprets* in height and doubtless the dominating peak of a long range. From the striations all over it I discovered that it had been worn away to its present trivial size by glacial action. Opening my case of instruments, I took out my petrochronologue and applied it to the worn and scratched surface of the rock. The indicator at once pointed to K 59 xpc 1/2! At this astonishing result I was nearly overcome by excitement: the

FOR THE AHKOOND

last erosions of the ice-masses upon this vestige of a stupendous mountain range which they had worn away, had been made as recently as the year 1945! Hastily applying my nymograph, I found that the name of this particular mountain at the time when it began to be enveloped in the mass of ice moving down upon it from the north, was "Pike's Peak."⁵ Other observations with other instruments showed that at that time the country circumjacent to it had been inhabited by a partly civilized race of people known as Galoots,⁶ the name of their capital city being Denver.

That evening at the hour of 23 I set up my aerial isochronophone* and reported to his gracious Majesty the Ahkoond as follows:

"*Sire:* I have the honor to report that I have made a startling discovery. The primeval region into which I have penetrated, as I informed you yesterday—the ichthyosaurus belt—was peopled by tribes considerably advanced in some of the arts almost within historic times: in 1920. They were exterminated by a glacial period not exceeding one hundred and twenty-five years in duration. Your Majesty can conceive the magnitude and violence of the natural forces which overwhelmed their country with moving sheets of ice not less than 5,000 *coprets* in thickness, grinding down every eminence, destroying (of course) all animal and vegetable life and leaving the region a fathomless bog of detritus. Out of this vast sea of mud Nature has had to evolve another creation, beginning *de novo,* with her lowest forms. It has long been known, your Majesty, that the region east of the Ultimate Hills, between them and the Wintry Sea, was once the seat of an ancient civilization, some scraps and shreds of whose history, arts and literature have been wafted to us across the gulf of time; but it was reserved for your gracious Majesty, through me, your humble and unworthy instrument, to ascertain the astonishing fact that these were a pre-glacial people—that between them and us stands, as it were, a wall of impenetrable ice. That all local records of this unfortunate race have perished your Majesty needs not to be told: we can supplement our present imperfect knowledge of them by instrumental observation only."

To this message I received the following extraordinary reply:

"All right—another bottle of—ice goes: push on—this cheese is too—spare no effort to—hand me those nuts—learn all you can—damn you!"

His most gracious Majesty was being served with dessert, and served badly.

I now resolved to go directly north toward the source of the ice-flow and investigate its cause, but examining my barometer found that I was more than 8,000 *coprets*

*This satire was published in the San Francisco *Examiner* many years before the invention of wireless telegraphy; so I retain my own name for the instrument.—A. B.⁷

FOR THE AHKOOND

below the sea-level; the moving ice had not only ground down the face of the country, planing off the eminences and filling the depressions, but its enormous weight had caused the earth's crust to sag, and with the lessening of the weight from evaporation it had not recovered.

I had no desire to continue in this depression, as I should in going north, for I should find nothing but lakes, marshes and ferneries, infested with the same primitive and monstrous forms of life. So I continued my course eastward and soon had the satisfaction to find myself meeting the sluggish current of such streams as I encountered in my way. By vigorous use of the new double-distance telepode, which enables the wearer to step eighty *surindas* instead of forty, as with the instrument in popular use, I was soon again at a considerable elevation above the sea-level and nearly 200 *prastams* from "Pike's Peak." A little farther along the water courses began to flow to the eastward. The flora and fauna had again altered in character, and now began to grow sparse; the soil was thin and arid, and in a week I found myself in a region absolutely destitute of organic life and without a vestige of soil. All was barren rock. The surface for hundreds of *prastams,* as I continued my advance, was nearly level, with a slight dip to the eastward. The rock was singularly striated, the scratches arranged concentrically and in helicoidal curves. This circumstance puzzled me and I resolved to take some more instrumental observations, bitterly regretting my improvidence in not availing myself of the Ahkoond's permission to bring with me such apparatus and assistants as would have given me knowledge vastly more copious and accurate than I could acquire with my simple pocket appliances.

I need not here go into the details of my observations with such instruments as I had, nor into the calculations of which these observations were the basic data. Suffice it that after two months' labor I reported the results to his Majesty in Sanf Rachisco in the words following:

"*Sire:* It is my high privilege to apprise you of my arrival on the western slope of a mighty depression running through the center of the continent north and south, formerly known as the Mississippi Valley. It was once the seat of a thriving and prosperous population known as the Pukes,[8] but is now a vast expanse of bare rock, from which every particle of soil and everything movable, including people, animals and vegetation, have been lifted by terrific cyclones and scattered afar, falling in other lands and at sea in the form of what was called meteoric dust! I find that these terrible phenomena began to occur about the year 1860, and lasted, with increasing frequency and power, through a century, culminating about the middle of that glacial period which saw the extinction of the Galoots and their neighboring tribes. There was, of course, a close connection between the two malefic phenomena, both, doubtless, being due to the same cause, which I have been unable to trace. A cyclone, I venture to remind your gracious Majesty, is a mighty whirlwind, accompanied by the most startling meteorological phenomena, such as electrical disturbances, floods of falling water, darkness and so forth. It moves with great speed, sucking up everything and reducing it to powder. In many days' journey I have not found a square *copret* of the country that did not suffer a visitation. If any human being escaped he must speedily have perished from starvation. For some twenty centuries the Pukes have been an extinct race, and their country a desolation in which no living thing can dwell, unless, like me, it is supplied with Dr. Blobob's Condensed Life-pills."

The Ahkoond replied that he was pleased to feel the most poignant grief for the fate of the unfortunate Pukes, and if I should by chance find the ancient king of the country I was to do my best to revive him with the patent resuscitator and present him the assurances of his Majesty's distinguished consideration; but as the politoscope showed that the nation had been a republic I gave myself no trouble in the matter.

My next report was made six months later and was in substance this:

"*Sire:* I address your Majesty from a point 430 *coprets* vertically above the site of the famous ancient city of Buffalo, once the capital of a powerful nation called the Smugwumps.[9] I can approach no nearer because of the hardness of the snow, which is very firmly packed. For hundreds of *prastams* in every direction, and for thousands to the north and west, the land is covered with this substance, which, as your Majesty is doubtless aware, is extremely cold to the touch, but by application of sufficient heat can be turned into water. It falls from the heavens, and is believed by the learned among your Majesty's subjects to have a sidereal origin.

"The Smugwumps were a hardy and intelligent race, but they entertained the vain delusion that they could subdue Nature. Their year was divided into two seasons—summer and winter, the former warm, the latter cold. About the beginning of the nineteenth century according to my archæthermograph, the summers began to grow shorter and hotter, the winters longer and colder. At every point in their country, and every day in the year, when they had not the hottest weather ever known in that place, they had the coldest. When they were not dying by hundreds from sunstroke they were dying by thousands from frost. But these heroic and devoted people struggled on, believing that they were becoming acclimated faster than the climate was becoming insupportable. Those called away on business were even afflicted with nostalgia, and with a fatal infatuation returned to grill or freeze, according to the season of their arrival. Finally there was no summer at all, though the last flash of heat slew several millions and set most of their cities afire, and winter reigned eternal.[10]

"The Smugwumps were now keenly sensible of the perils environing them, and, abandoning their homes, endeavored to reach their kindred, the Californians, on the western side of the continent in what is now your Majesty's ever-blessed realm. But it was too late: the snow growing deeper and deeper day by day, besieged them in their towns and dwellings, and they were unable to escape. The last one of them perished about the year 1943, and may God have mercy on his fool soul!"

To this dispatch the Ahkoond replied that it was the royal opinion that the Smugwumps were served very well right.

Some weeks later I reported thus:

"*Sire:* The country which your Majesty's munificence is enabling your devoted servant to explore extends southward and southwestward from Smugwumpia many hundreds of *prastams,* its eastern and southern borders being the Wintry Sea and the Fiery Gulf, respectively. The population in ancient times was composed of Whites and Blacks in about equal numbers and of about equal moral worth—at least that is the record on the dial of my ethnograph when set for the twentieth century and given a southern exposure. The Whites were called Crackers and the Blacks known as Coons.

"I find here none of the barrenness and desolation characterizing the land of the ancient Pukes, and the climate is not so rigorous and thrilling as that of the country of the late Smugwumps. It is, indeed, rather agreeable in point of temperature, and the soil being fertile exceedingly, the whole land is covered with a dense and rank vegetation. I have yet to find a square *smig* of it that is open ground, or one that is not the lair of some savage beast, the haunt of some venomous reptile, or the roost of some offensive bird. Crackers and Coons alike are long extinct, and these are their successors.

"Nothing could be more forbidding and unwholesome than these interminable jungles, with their horrible wealth of organic life in its most objectionable forms. By repeated observations with the necrohistoriograph I find that the inhabitants of this country, who had always been more or less dead, were wholly extirpated contemporaneously with the disastrous events which swept away the Galoots, the Pukes and the Smugwumps. The agency of their effacement was an endemic disorder known as yellow fever. The ravages of this frightful disease were of frequent recurrence, every point of the country being a center of infection; but in some seasons it was worse than in others. Once in every half century at first, and afterward every year* it broke out somewhere and swept over wide areas with such fatal effect that there were not enough of the living to plunder the dead; but at the first frost it would subside. During the ensuing two or three months of immunity the stupid survivors returned to the infected homes from which they had fled and were ready for the next outbreak. Emigration would have saved them all, but although the Californians (over whose happy and prosperous descendants your Majesty has the goodness to reign) invited them again and again to their beautiful land, where

---

*At one time it was foolishly believed that the disease had been eradicated by slapping the mosquitoes which were thought to produce it; but a few years later it broke out with greater violence than ever before, although the mosquitoes had left the country.

FOR THE AHKOOND

sickness and death were hardly known, they would not go, and by the year 1946 the last one of them, may it please your gracious Majesty, was dead and damned."

Having spoken this into the transmitter of the aerial isochronophone at the usual hour of 23 o'clock I applied the receiver to my ear, confidently expecting the customary commendation. Imagine my astonishment and dismay when my master's well-remembered voice was heard in utterance of the most awful imprecations on me and my work, followed by appalling threats against my life!

The Ahkoond had changed his dinner-time to five hours later and I had been speaking into the ears of an empty stomach!

E (18 Mar. 1888): 13 (as by "A. B."); *CW* **1.199–214**.

NOTES

In contrast to the popular belief in constant progress, AB contemplated both early and late in his career the decline for both internal and external reasons not only of the American republic but also of civilization, and of the rise in some distant future of another civilization which would have to speculate, sometimes wildly, about our civilization from very few archaeological remnants. Noteworthy in this humorous satire is AB's acceptance of Darwinian and geological explanations of physical changes in the earth and its life forms. He was in advance of his time in these matters.

Title: The title "Ahkoond" became popular when in 1878 American poet George Thomas Lanigan (1845–86) wrote a comic poem, "A Threnody" (1878), on the "Akhoond of Swat"—i.e., Abdul Ghafur (1794–1877), the Akhund (or Akhond) of Swat, a region in northwestern India.

1. An allusion to California (*E* actually reads "California" here, and reads "Citrusia" later in the text where the present text reads "California"). See "Prattle," *E* (30 Apr. 1893): 6: "When I am Minister of the Fine Arts to his Majesty the Ahkoond of Citrusia every picture made will be submitted to the untutored eye of a South Sea islander freshly imported. If he sees in it a resemblance to any thing on the earth, in the heavens above the earth, or in waters beneath the earth, it will be destroyed and its maker put to death."

2. A play on the Central Pacific Railroad. AB is making a pun on the root meaning of the word "pacific" (peaceful).

3. For AB's later whimsical ruminations on the future extinction of the horse, see "The Future of the Horse and the Horse of the Future" (*NYA,* 17 Feb. 1903; *E,* 5 Apr. 1903); reprinted as "The Passing of the Horse" (*CW* 9.147–50).

4. Tennyson, *In Memoriam: A. H. H.* (1850), stanza 56, ll. 22–23.

5. Pike's Peak (14,109 ft.) is in central Colorado, about sixty miles south of Denver.

6. "Galoot" was a slang term of humorous contempt used largely in the western states in reference to a man, frequently suggesting awkwardness or weakness.

7. But AB's original name for the instrument (in *E*) was "telephonagraphine," and his use of "isochronophone" dates only to *CW.*

8. "Puke" was originally a nickname for a native of Missouri, and later a slang term for a disgusting person.

9. A play on "mugwump." The term was coined in the 1830s from an Algonquin word, *mugquomp,* meaning "great man, chief, captain, leader." In U.S. slang it came to be used derisively for a man who thought too highly of himself. In 1884 it was a term of abuse directed against Republicans who refused to support their presidential candidate, James G. Blaine. In 1888 AB declared himself a mugwump (see *SS* 219). AB uses the word "smug-wump" on occasion in letters, once in reference to Andrew Carnegie (AB to John H. E. Partington, 7 October 1892 [MS., BL]) and twice in apparent reference to Easterners (AB to S. O. Howes, 5 Apr. 1906 [MS., HL]; AB to George Sterling, 5 Apr. 1906 [MS., NP]). AB's meaning in these instances is unclear, nor is it clear whether he actually coined this term or whether it was a slang term in general use. See also "The Extinction of the Smugwumps."

10. AB, after he moved to Washington, D.C., in late 1899, complained of the extreme heat of the eastern summers; see "The Domestic Heat Escape," *NYA* (5 June 1903): 16.

HADES IN TROUBLE

An Authentic Description of Ancient Pandemonium.

Satan's Bad Mistake.

How Dissension First Crept Into the Happy Home of the Devil.

"Did you ring, your Highness?"

"Put on some coals and stir up the fire; it's getting cold enough to freeze."

"Yes, your Satanic Majesty."

"Anything going on outside?"

"Nothing to speak of, your Highness."

"What are all the devils doing?"

"Very little, your Excellency. They gape and yawn and stretch themselves and look rather blue. Some are aimlessly playing at skittles, others are sorrowfully dawdling over mumbly-peg, divers couples maunder feebly over progressive euchre, while liquor solaces, in a measure, a few sad and forlorn spirits—"

"Stop! Stop! Stop! In pity's sake, stop! Time," burst out Moloch,[1] rousing from the luxurious couch on which he lay extended, "make an end. Existence is tedious enough without listening to a catalogue of the woes of others. Are there no contests, no broils to arouse the slumbering senses?"

"None, your Excellency."

Satan gaped and stretched himself. "Time," he said, slowly, "this has gone far enough. A little monotony goes a great way, even here. You must make a change, or you'll lose your place. You understand, Time, change all this or you'll lose your place."

"Yes, your Satanic Majesty."

"Or we'll have you up, Time," put in Moloch, "and see if we cannot find some diversion in your antics. Not that we'll kill you, Time," he added, with a smile, as the old servitor looked at him askance. "You furnish a great deal more entertainment than any of your predecessors, but if you hope to retain your place change this wearying round of monotony."

Time bowed humbly. "An't please your lordship, there's a wandering minstrel without—"

"Was that the strange noise we heard a short while since?" interrupted Satan, idly swinging his leg against the couch.

"Yes, your Satanic Majesty."

"Well?"

"An't please your Majesty, he's a poor, lone, wandering devil, and he came to the gates turning the crank of what he calls an organ, and he asked for hospitality and I took him in, as your Majesty has ordered that none shall be turned from your gates."

"Quite right! But why ain't he playing? Can he offer us any amusement?"

"Please, your Highness, he's touching up the deviled-ham and chicken. He says he's been wandering about chaos for I don't know how long, and to see him at the deviled-ham and wine you'd think he'd been lost in chaos twice as long. I cannot recommend his instrument for harmony, but the chances are he may be able to narrate something interesting about his travels. He must have seen much and learned more of that great unknown. Assuredly he has learned the good qualities of deviled-ham and wine." And old Time nodded sagely as he pictured the stranger making devastating inroads on his prime edibles and drinkables.

"Have him brought in," proposed Belial.[2] "He may serve to while away a few moments. Anything—anything to mix with this dullness."

"Show the fellow in, Time," ordered Satan, "and let him bring his organ."

Time backed to the heavy curtains and disappeared.

The next moment he reappeared, followed by a devil, whose noble form and lofty bearing only seemed magnified by his coarse and well-worn habiliments.

Satan, Moloch, Mammon[3] and Belial did not even glance up as the stranger entered the gorgeous apartment and deposited his instrument on the floor, but seeking new positions on their couches, they wearily waited for him to attempt their amusement.

Time whispered this in his ear and withdrew.

"Potentates and Princes," he began, "thy servant has been wandering these many seasons in chaos—chaos, that wilderness of hubbub and despair. To beguile the tedium of my unhappy way, I cast about for some instrument to interrupt the din by occasionally whispering in my ear some note of harmony. This mel—music—box was the result." He tapped it fondly and went on hesitatingly. "It—it may not be much, I confess, but considering the place, the means and the expanse I was striving to enliven,

HADES IN TROUBLE

it was doing a—er something. I will first offer a melody very familiar to your Majesties."

Thereupon he seized the crank, and giving it a few vigorous turns, he warmed himself and the instrument, and what might be mistaken for "Give the Devil his Due" began to wail forth.[4]

But hardly had the first strains of the frightful discord broke the air of that quiet apartment than Moloch jumped to his feet with a roar. "Time! Time!" he shouted, banging on the gong, "seize the wretched wanderer and kick him into chaos again!"

The stranger drew himself up proudly, folded his arms composedly and calmly regarded the storming Moloch. "Kick?" was all he vouchsafed, very quietly.

Moloch started toward him, but as his blazing eyes fell upon that noble brow and regal bearing, he paused, gazed and stammered, "Wha—what! Beelzebub,[5] as I'm a sinner!"

"What!" shouted the recumbent majesties, "Beelzebub!" and leaping to their feet they rushed toward the minstrel and fervently wrung his hands.

"Welcome, welcome home, our long lost brother. Time, bring in the wine!"

"Steady, steady, brethren," cried Beelzebub, embracing them heartily and rapidly.

"Where have you been? What have you been doing?" demanded Satan as they reseated themselves on the couches. "Ah, you were right, quite right, as you always are, in embarking on adventures to avoid the inactivity of this place, for I swear nothing can surpass it. We have scarcely moved since you left; we've simply lain stagnant. You'll conceive what it has been in that time when I tell you that that bit of rage just shown by Moloch is all that has stirred him since you left. Nothing can be drearier than our existence. But how has it been with you? Bless my eyes! I feel quite animated, even with the sight of you."

Beelzebub smiled, bowed and quaffed a beaker of wine.

"Bad as this place may seem to you, believe me, there is a worse place—chaos. I've been wandering, swimming, wading, sliding, creeping, floating, climbing, walking, flying, sinking and rolling over, under, around and through its bogs, sands, marshes, rocks, pits and cliffs, tossed in a universal hubbub.[6] Had I not been animated with the labor of trying to escape that dreadful place I shudder to think what might have become of me. Behold your instrument," and he pointed to the hand organ, "consider that I turned it and to it for cheer, and you will form some idea of my dolorous wanderings."

"You must have met with misfortune indeed," confessed Satan. "Stupid as this place has been we couldn't stand *that*. But didn't you find anything novel, see anything interesting, or hear of anything marvelous? You're not the one to do all that plodding without some profit."

"Ah!" said the traveler, his face lighting at the compliment and the remembrance, "that did I."

The audience gazed at him with renewed attention.

HADES IN TROUBLE

"Do you remember," he asked, "that fable, legend, tradition, rumor, tale, prophecy or what you will, of a new race of beings? I know people are always inventing new devils, but this is an old, old story."

"Ha!" exclaimed Satan, "you don't mean that story of the devil with a tail and cloven feet, and long pointed ears, incased in flaming red cloth at $2 a yard and always appearing and disappearing in red fire, popping up from below at unexpected moments and—"

"Hold on," protested Beelzebub, laughing, "you are ornamenting him with all the fantastic attributes that have ever been conceived. But imagine him plain and unadorned and you mention the one I mean. I've seen him!"

"Seen him! Never! It cannot be!"

"I have, though!"

"Then he's a fact?"

"Yes, he sits under a fig tree on a spherical lump of clay down there on the borders of chaos and he's well worth seeing."

"Then it's really so," exclaimed Satan recovering from his surprise. "Has he cloven feet and does he wear a flaming red dress at $2 a yard, and how does he wiggle his tail?"

"Has he got a spear on the end of it, like the stories say?" put in Moloch. "I've seen pictures of him with a spear on the end of it."

"About all you've heard is nonsense," explained Beelzebub, smiling. "Whoever invented the tales about him drew immensely on their imagination, and those who have repeated them have lengthened and adorned the tails. No; the most you have heard is pure fabrication with a fiber of truth to hold the yarn."

"Describe him then; what is he like?" demanded Satan.

"As near like us in form as you can imagine."

"How many are there?" asked Moloch.

"Two, when I left; a man and a woman. Adam and Eve."

"Woman!" echoed Belial, rubbing his hands. "So she—was she—why, the deuce, couldn't you bring her away with you anyway?'"

"I thought of doing a good many things as I contemplated them strolling about. You'll give me credit for knowing a little, won't you?" and he looked at the group interrogatively.

"Oh, a great deal, a great deal!" they hastened to protest.

"Well, then," he continued, "I thought it best to leave them where they are. I studied the species rather carefully, and between us, they have senses lying dormant in their natures that I don't think it would be prudent to awaken, least of all cultivate."

"Yes," urged the eager Belial, "but consider they might serve to liven up this peaceful, slow-going place."

Beelzebub shook his head slowly and said: "You think this place devoid of interest, slow, somniferous; believe me, with all its dullness it is far preferable to the world outside. Rouse yourselves, infuse life into your slothful bodies! Brethren, I have explored chaos and the places adjacent, and I've returned to take up my quarters here, contented. Sheol[7] is good enough for me."

"Yes, yes," protested Belial, rather impatiently, "it's all well enough to talk like that when you have been wandering about, visiting worlds and interviewing strange people, but consider we've been rusting here in the mean while. Now, if we only had that new man and woman to amuse us, life might be bearable. I feel a particular desire to go after that woman."

"And I the man," declared Satan.

"Take my advice and leave them alone," urged Beelzebub. "This is a quiet uneventful place, I know, but mark my words, if you bring those creatures here and let their instincts develop the place will grow too hot to hold us."

"But only one woman!" protested Belial. "Surely one woman can't turn the place topsy turvy."

Beelzebub shrugged his shoulders, seeing the futility of further opposition. "I see you have made up your minds," he said, "and it's useless resisting, but I warn you that the result will be disastrous. As your brother I will stand by you in the consequences, but I affirm firmly and emphatically that I will not stir to bring them here. The fact is I've had enough of them already."

"We'll venture it alone then," replied Satan, rising and stretching himself.

And seizing the hand organ he flung it over his shoulder and disappeared through the curtains.

While the worthies were dubiously speculating on the favorable outcome of this venture, Mammon bethought of calling to their assistance a new art of prognosticating as practiced by inventive Time. The old servitor was accordingly summoned.

"Time," explained Beelzebub, "Mammon tells us that in addition to your many merits you are an excellent medium, a seer, a revealer of the future. Use your arts and tell us what will be the result of Satan's exploit."

The old man bowed, shivered and shook, and rolled his eyes, but before they could ascertain what ailed him he began to speak: "I see a queer place and a queer creature, with long, wavy hair, decorated with plumes. It must be—yes, it is—a woman. She is rubbing red ochre stripes on her arms. Now she sits down and begins to braid her hair. She braids, she rubs a little ochre off one arm, she changes a few feathers in her hair, and steadfastly contemplates a tree opposite. She gazes, fondly, hungrily. It must be the tree she is looking at; no, it is the fruit. I cannot tell from this distance whether it is an apple, or a peach, or—"

"No matter," put in Belial, impatiently.

"Ha! a snake appears. It cogitates. Wonderful! It speaks. The woman looks inspired. She starts to leave. The snake places a detaining coil about her waist and whispers something. The woman blushes and answers bashfully—"

"Time, no levity," put in Beelzebub, sharply.

HADES IN TROUBLE

"They converse quite amiably," went on the rapt medium, not heeding. "Aha! the snake impales the fruit of the tree on the tip of his tail and politely presents it to the blushing woman. She smells it, hesitatingly. The serpent squeezes her, smiles and says something. The woman takes a nip. The snake chuckles and digs her in the ribs with his tail. Ha! it was so sudden the woman bit her tongue. She bolts the fruit. The serpent tries to apologize and attempts to chuck her under the chin. She resents his advancing tail. She grabs a stick and makes a cut at him. The serpent vanishes in the brush and—bless me! it's—"

"What!"

"Satan![8] He seems rather crestfallen. He thinks deeply and sadly. He shakes his head and sighs. I see him go out the garden gates and carefully close them after him. He takes out a card and writes on it, 'Satan, Sheol,' and puts it in his pocket. He picks up a stick and takes the road marked 'Chaos.'"

"What does that mean?" demanded Belial.

"Methinks the card is to insure his identity should he be lost; the address signifies he is returning home."

"Without the man and woman!" exclaimed Belial.

"So it seems."

"Impossible! Time, you're a fraud. You don't know anything about the future unless it is told you. Go out and polish up your glass and con the cards till you can give us a better test than that."

Old Time withdrew, while the potentates, influenced in spite of themselves by his revelations, fell to their old occupation of disconsolately tossing on the couches while they impatiently awaited the return of the crestfallen Satan.

*   *   *   *   *   *   *

Beelzebub, Moloch, Mammon and Belial lay extended upon luxuriant couches in the great chamber of Pandemonium, impatiently awaiting the return of Satan, who had been absent a long time on his extraordinary mission of bringing Adam and Eve to Sheol.

"But why should he remain silent so long, Beelzebub? Surely he must have succeeded by this time," and Belial shook his head rather hopelessly.

"How long has he been gone?" asked Mammon, after a pause.

Beelzebub concentrated his noble brow in thought.

"An't please your lordships," came from Time, as he protruded his head between the curtains.

"Time," interrupted Beelzebub, "how long is it since our worthy brother departed for the earth?"

"Please your lordships, I have trimmed my beard to the ninth number and—"

"So long!" exclaimed Belial. "Then certainly something wrong has happened."

HADES IN TROUBLE

"An't please your Majesties, there is one without, a peculiar sort of devil, who says he bears a message from his Satanic Majesty."

"From Satan! Show him in instantly." And the four worthies sprang from their couches, impatient to greet the courier.

In another moment the curtains parted and their eyes fell upon a comely youth, bearing all the outward semblance of themselves; yet at a second glance he seemed unlike, wanting both the power of physique and loftiness of look that distinguished the people of peaceful Pandemonium from the inhabitants of Earth e'er that unfortunate connection was brought about that destroyed the peace of one and the simplicity of the other.

"From whence come you?" demanded Beelzebub, closely scrutinizing the messenger.

"From the Earth and my—Satan."

"And thy message!"

"Is here," and he touched a scroll in his girdle, "for him who is Beelzebub."

"I am he," replied his interrogator.

The youth extended his scroll and Beelzebub untwisting the thong, proceeded to unroll and read, while his brothers gathered closer with the liveliest interest.

Beelzebub and Brothers All—greeting: This to thee in mine jeopardy. Rouse thee, my brothers, in the morning. Don thy warlike gear; take on the ingenuity to plan great deeds; fling our standards to the breeze, and with martial blasts awake the peaceful. Beelzebub, brighten thou thy wisdom; wake, wake, my Moloch, stir thy spleen and prepare to vent thy rage; Mammon, sharpen thy greed and whet thy avarice; furbish thou thy most insinuating graces, Belial, for I thy fellow, thy brother always, am in deep distress, and call unto thee for aid.

As was thou knowest. Through Chaos I took my devious way, nor did the confusion deter me aught. The organ of discords lies buried in the deepest pit thereof, and there wound up adds discord to the horrid din. Unto the Earth I come. I seek the man and find the woman of whom Beelzebub spake. Like him I blush and grow confused, oh, brothers, and like him, now knowing, I much disprove their transfer to our peaceful home and destroying that which late I knew not how to appreciate and enjoy. My eyes are opened and I see and testify unto you and bear witness that Beelzebub, our brother, was right in opposing the introduction of this couple to peaceful Pandemonium. Yea, and moreover, he was warranted in the exercise of force to prevent what I now perceive is a consequence most dire. But we, who knew not, knew not what we did. The ignorant may overcome the wise for a moment, but folly betrays him e'er the struggle is done.

But how is it with me, oh, my brothers? In truth, I am in much perplexity and extremity, and with contrite voice call upon you to come forth and rescue me from this man and woman. Woman! Belial, simple one, thou knowest not for what thou cravest. If thou art as steadfast in thy delusion, come, for the peace of thy brother come and take her away. For the man I will say nothing. Suffice it that he has initiated me into ways and practices that I fear will work much disturbance and more grief if introduced into our happy home.

Beelzebub, when late thou passed this way there were but two; now there are many, and do not you, my brothers, make the greatest haste to my assistance, there will be

HADES IN TROUBLE

many more. The evils grow apace. Delay not, I beseech you for my own safety and for the security of yourselves. For since my eyes have gathered new light I can easily conceive that these creatures, big with their swelling boldness and rampant in their newly awakened senses, may make a descent upon our happy home and bring you all here to pander to their insatiable greed for amusement.

This will be handed you by my eldest—brethren, I blush myself—whom after much diligence and craft I have succeeded in dispatching on this mission that his life at least may be taken away from this wicked place. Take him in, educate and foster him that he may in time forget the place of his birth and know only the peace of our happy home.

From this infer as you can how I am situate; describe it in detail. I cannot, nor have I the courage to let you learn even a part. Question not my offspring, I beseech you. And further I pray that nought of what I have here set down may be hinted to those poor devils sighing around you with the dolefulness of their position. Come to me quickly, my brothers, once behold my plight and you shall pity, forgive and help me.

Of these words take especial note, and in your preparations hold them constantly before you: the woman and man of whom Beelzebub learned—oh, so little—and their daughters and sons are something far out of the ordinary. Be not exalted in your own valor, nor deem my rescue a trifling matter; for surely, and I speak after much experience and forethought, you will be called upon to exercise your greatest and most subtle powers.

Again, and of the utmost importance: Should I be not discernible on your approach, do not hearken with trusting ears to the words of her who will call herself Eve, or mayhap my mother-in-law, or mayhap my aunt, or mayhap anything that a ready wit may conceive, for her craft passeth our simple understanding. When she speaks, no matter how or why or where, brethren, be on your guard, your stoutest guard.

But come you as indifferent travelers or, better, mongers of new things, and on the crest of opportunity I will be borne to your arms. Till the moment is ripe I will communicate with you privily. It is best, as you will see.

Again I tell you that my relief can be compassed only by the exercise of the greatest wisdom and perseverance.

Come to thy lorn brother in his misfortune and come in thy greatest power, lest we all be undone.

Thy forlorn, penitent and wistful,

SATAN.

Believe not, I beseech you, the wicked stories you may hear concerning me. These people tarnish everything with which they have to do, nor will the reputations of the best escape their vilifications. Believe me, my dear brethren, contrition and tribulation have very much chastened and refined the one whom you esteemed so highly as

S.

Beelzebub heaved a heavy sigh. "As I thought," he murmured, and slowly rolled the scroll, pondering deeply.

Moloch, Mammon and Belial stood lost in wonder while the stranger curiously contemplated them. It was his voice that finally broke the silence.

"He told me to say that he couldn't portray the faintest semblance of his wretched position and feelings in any writing. Then he said to me, kind of white and gulpy like,

'Nick,' said he, 'just do your greatest, my boy, to get them to come to my help; they'll fix you up soft for my sake.' 'Twixt you and me I think the old man was coming uncommonly soft himself. He always does when he talks about his old home. Ah, I see you keep the cheerful here—good custom. If you don't mind I'll try a little bracer. That chaos is about the rockiest section I ever traversed."

"Oh, do you drink?" said Beelzebub. "Certainly, help yourself. Time, attend to the wants of the young man." But the young man was already liberally attending to his own wants.

"He seems to be at home," whispered Belial, as they covertly glanced at the expert traveler.

"Fine stock you keep," he volunteered, after sampling all there was in sight. "Seem to be rather downily fixed here, too. I think I'll like the place after I get acquainted. I'm to stay, I suppose, you know?"

"So Satan says; his word is law here."

"The deuce it is!" replied the youth, grinning. They'd like to hear that on earth. How Eve would smile! I must drop the folks a line and tell them. They'll enjoy the joke. Who's the ancient individual?"

"Time, who looks after our pleasures."

"Chief Keeper of Pleasures, eh? Egad! I must cultivate his acquaintance, sure. Must know a great deal about 'em from his looks. Good Time! Who're the others?"

"Moloch, famed for his strength—"

"He *is* a trifle muscular; more so than my uncle Cain, I should say. I'd like to see them in a little scrap. I suppose you have some lovely set-tos here occasionally? I saw some fine material as I came through the place."

"No," admitted Beelzebub, becoming somewhat puzzled. "The fact is we have very few amusements here. Pandemonium, as you must have observed, is very quiet. Doubtless you will be able to teach us many new games and tell us much of interest. You have—"

"Games! interest! Well, I should say so! I can tell you more tales while a lamb's bleating than you can rake together in all that infernal chaos. You got the king-pin when you got me. I can give the others on earth all the points of the game and then double discount them. Why! didn't you ever hear tell of me, Nick? But who's the one here who gathers the glittering spoils and rakes the tumbling futures?"

"Mammon, there, evinces great foresight in calculating chances and prophesying the future."

"He does, eh! Well, Mr. Mammon, I'd just like to try the stuff that's in you, the first chance we get. Pleased to know you, anyhow. But who's the other fellow? I like his looks and style," and Nick good-naturedly extended his hand.

"Belial, who is grace and affability. He has the art of ingratiating himself with all."

"I knew you were a flower. You and I will get on famously together, I'll be bound. And now, if it ain't forcing the custom of the place too much, and just to give our

HADES IN TROUBLE

friendship a good send-off, suppose we—er—well, I don't know what you call it in this royal abode—but, drink, you know?"

"Call Time!" spoke up Belial, cheerily, who felt he had found his soul's companion. "Time, replenish the beakers!"

"Call Time, is it?" laughed the young man, betraying strong signs of his introduction to the cordials of Sheol. "Ay, call Time, with a will," and he flung himself on the most luxurious couch. "Call Time, and I'll tell you fellows the latest and rummiest yarns on Earth; they'll make your hair curl, I'll stake a stack. You're rather high here, but you ought to see us at home. Can you make a cobbler yet?"

The potentates looked at one another inquiringly and dumbly shook their heads.

"No! Well, of course you can mix a cocktail?"

Again the dumb look of pitiful ignorance.

"What! Not mix a cocktail! Well, this place does need shaking up. You've got lots to learn yet. Fine things, both of 'em. I'll rattle the cups for you on the next round and turn you out some titillations."

He seized the beaker and swallowed the contents in great gulps; as he set it down on the little stand and patronizingly regarded the Princes slowly draining their beverages, he muttered to himself: "Never heard of a cocktail! Suffering Satan, what kind of a place is this you have sent me to?"

"You fellows are really fixed down here, but I don't suppose you know it," he went on, volubly, as his nervous eye glanced admiringly over the luxurious furnishings of the apartment. "So Satan rules this roost!" and he smiled. "I don't wonder he looks so glum now. I suppose you know things have changed a good bit with him?"

Beelzebub nodded gravely, and touched the scroll. "So this letter would seem to imply."

The other laughed boisterously. "Oh, that's nothing, nothing at all! I can tell you more in three breaths than that could if it was trebled. And smash me, but I'll do it! Of course, Satan won't like it; he's my dad, I know, but then, I couldn't help it. You seem to be pretty good fellows if you are his brothers. Once more to our fortune," and he seized the refilled beaker.

"Pretty heady stuff," he remarked, as he set it down. "Stays with one, eh? Like Aggie, she—"

"She!" exclaimed Belial, starting. "A woman?"

"Woman! Well, I should say so! The flower of the lot; red hair, gray eyes and such a figure! Oh, shake me! I'm going to bring her here first chance I get. My eye! but she'll liven up this old slow-going place for you."

"Entrancing is she?" queried Belial, thoroughly aroused.

"Entrancing? She's a stunner! A regular out and outer! I wanted to bring her with me. But, whew! the dander that dad got into when I mentioned it. Mad! I never dreamed he had so much fire in him. I thought the peaceful old curmudgeon was really going to try and lick me right where I stood. 'Take that woman to Pandemonium,' he

HADES IN TROUBLE

screamed, 'and I'll—I'll'—and I'm blest if he wasn't so mad he really couldn't speak. I believe the honest old fellow really swore. If he ever lost his temper like that 'fore I was born, I don't wonder he's got such a bad reputation."

"Is his reputation so bad, then?" inquired Beelzebub.

"Beastly!" replied the eldest son of his father. "To tell the truth, though, I never saw him do anything out of the way. But you see, he seems to have begun somehow with a bad name and it sticks to him. I've heard lots of folks ask how such an innocent, harmless old gent could be such a great villain. Then he's a poor sort of devil all by himself, and humanity kind of looks down on him as being a little out of his regular way. Fact is, they wouldn't tolerate him if he hadn't married into the family long ago, and got a little respectable foothold to hang to. He's my dad, I know," the speaker added, with a hiccough, "but that don't seem to help him much."

"But surely," said Beelzebub, "these people must respect his great attributes, his noble character, his lordly standing."

Nick smiled benignantly. "Go try 't yourself," he said; "'f you think any devil's goin' t' hog our earth an' beat us you're much mistaken. Here, Time, gimme some wine. Good ole boy. Who's your father?"

"But this story you were about telling us," suggested Belial, mildly, "about the—"

"Oh, you want late scan'ls. I've got 'em all. Heard that one about Zel'y? Course you haven't. I forgot. But I'll tell you a better one 'bout Eve—'s 'bout Satan, too."

"What, our brother!" exclaimed Belial.

"Same feller. When he first come to earth, met Eve. Say, when d'ye eat in this place, anyway?"

"But what happened when he met Eve?" persisted Belial, earnestly.

"Oh, that's ole story. Tell you bimeby. I'm sleepy. Chaos too much f'r me; tired; call me s-u-p-p-'r," and the wearied traveler rolled over in a sound sleep.

The tears started to Belial's eyes as he muttered, "I'll find out what happened when Satan met Eve if I have to go to the earth."

The potentates gazed upon the slumbering figure with troubled and anxious faces.

"Well," finally remarked Moloch, breaking the silence, "if this is Satan's eldest, what must his youngest be?"

"I wonder if this is the fruit of his great mission?" hazarded Mammon.

"Of course not!" replied Belial. "He was to bring two—a man and a woman. There's no woman yet."

"It seems he has changed his plans," Beelzebub suggested.

"Not to this extent," protested Beelzebub [*sic*]. "I never dreamed he had changed them to this extent."[9]

"Well, it seems he has," went on Belial, eagerly, "and naught remains for us but to act as his letter prays. We must go to his assistance."

"We must go to his assistance," they all assented.

"And see these strange people."

HADES IN TROUBLE

"And punish them for ill-treating him."

"And bring our Satan home."

"And act a guard about Sheol to prevent their ingress."

And leaving the wearied Nick buried in slumber they went and summoned their hosts, and carefully following the injunctions of the letter, they sped toward the earth to the rescue of the much-persecuted Satan.

A careful and diligent historian, whose reputation for veracity is unimpeachable, has shown in a work in which the brilliancy of argument has only been surpassed by the felicity of expression that the mission of this gallant host was far, very far, from being a success.

E (25 Mar. 1888): 12 (as by "B.").

NOTES

This story, which was rediscovered in 1993 by Lawrence I. Berkove, is here included for the first time in a collection of AB's stories. Pessimistic even for AB, beyond its parody of Milton's *Paradise Lost*, it suggests that the human race may have been created to further punish Satan and the fallen angels by turning their Pandemonium in the underworld of Hades into Hell.

1. The Canaanite god to whom infants (specifically, the firstborn) were sacrificed as burnt offerings; represented by Milton as one of the fallen angels (see, e.g., Milton, *Paradise Lost*, 1.392, 417).

2. A word of obscure origin, used frequently in the Old Testament as a symbol for chaos and evil (see, e.g., Deut. 13:13) and once in the New Testament as a synonym for Satan (2 Cor. 6:15). Milton cites Belial as one of the fallen angels (*Paradise Lost*, 1.490, 502).

3. A word used by Jesus to denote wealth or property (see, e.g., Matt. 6:24, Luke 16:9, 11, 13); personified in medieval times as the devil of covetousness.

4. "Give the Devil His Due" was a British song dating to the 1770s.

5. A name given to "the prince of devils" in the New Testament (see Matt. 12:24) and as a synonym for Satan (Matt. 12:27). The Hebrew word means "lord of the flies." Milton uses the term to refer to the devil second in power to Satan (*Paradise Lost*, 1.81, 271).

6. See *Paradise Lost*, 2.940–50.

7. A Hebrew word of uncertain meaning, signifying the abode of the dead. Initially, the conception did not include the notion of punishment, merely an absence of communication with God (see, e.g., Isa. 38:18); moreover, all souls went to Sheol (as with the Greek Hades), not only those of sinners.

8. The identification of the serpent in Gen. 3:1f. with Satan first occurred in the Wisdom of Solomon (2:23f.), an Alexandrian work dating to the first or second century B.C.E.; it influenced the Book of Revelation, where a similar identification is made (see Rev. 12:9–15).

9. In this line Beelzebub objects to a suggestion he himself made in the previous line. This is an error made either by AB or the typographer. In any case, AB did not catch it in the proofreading.

THE FALL OF THE REPUBLIC

An Article from a "Court Journal" of the
Thirty-First Century

Although many of the causes which finally, in combination, brought about the downfall of the great American republic were in operation from the very beginning of its
political life—being inherent in the system—it was not until the year 1950 that the
collapse of the vast fabric was complete. In that year the defeat of the last republican
army near Smithville, in the lava beds of Northern California, extinguished the last
fires of insurrection against the monarchical revival, and thenceforth armed opposition was confined to desultory and insignificant guerrilla warfare, whose object was
pillage and whose method murder. In that year, too, Field Marshal Sir Henry Burnell,
whose astonishing military genius had subdued all the republican forces west of the
Sierra Nevada, turned his victorious arms against his royal master, Leonard "the
Chicken-Hearted," tore him from the throne of California, suppressed his Legislature, and with it the last remnant of legislative government on the American continent and established himself in absolute power as Emperor of the Occident. His
dynasty, it is needless to say, endured without a break in its continuity almost to our
own times, when, in the year 2781, John XI was compelled to abdicate and the scepter
passed to the hand of our present gracious sovereign, William of Pescadero.[1] For ten
years before the usurpation of Henry I peace had prevailed in all the country east of
the Sierra Nevada to the Atlantic, and the reign of "the Three Kings" was undisputed.
The turbulent period between 1895 and 1940, with its incalculable waste of blood and
treasure, its dreadful conflicts of armies and more dreadful massacres of the people,
its kaleidoscopic changes of government and incessant effacement of boundaries, its
succession of political assassinations, popular insurrections pitilessly subdued—all the
horrors incident to the extirpation of a system rooted in the hearts and traditions of a
mighty race—had so exhausted and dispirited the surviving protagonists of the

republican regime that they made no further head against the inevitable, and were, indeed, glad enough to accept life on any terms, justifying their submission, and at the same time condemning their former obstinacy by quoting the words of the great poet:

> For forms of government let fools contest—
> What e'er is best administered is best.[2]

When at the battle of Smithville the last spark of what had been absurdly known as "civil and religious liberty" was quenched in blood and the Pacific Coast brought under the light and beneficent yoke of Absolute Monarchy, the three kingdoms east of the Sierra Nevada had for a whole decade enjoyed in peace and with increasing satisfaction the advantage of those natural and now universal institutions which their valiant but shortsighted and misguided forefathers had madly flung away. The name of George Washington had already begun to sink into the infamy which now covers it, and that of the illustrious sovereign against whom he raised his impious hand and traitor sword shone with a brightening splendor.

But the purpose of this treatise is not historical, but philosophic; not to recount events familiar to all students of history, but to trace the genesis and development of a few of the causes which produced them. The historians have left nothing undone to give a true account of these events. In Mancher's "Decline and Fall of the American Republics," in Lenwith's "History of Popular Government," in Bardeal's "Monarchical Renascence" and in Staley's immortal work, "The Rise, Progress and Extinction of the United States," the facts are set forth with such copiousness and particularity as to have exhausted all attainable stores of information, and it remains for investigators of this later time only to expound the causes and point the moral.

It may seem needless at this time to point out the inherent defects of a system of government which the logic of events has swept like political rubbish from the face of the earth, but we must not forget that ages before the inception of the American republics and of that of France[3] and Ireland this form of government had been discredited by emphatic failures among the most enlightened and powerful nations of antiquity: the Greeks, the Romans and long before them (as we now know) the Egyptians and the Chinese. To the lesson of these failures the founders of the eighteenth and nineteenth century republics were blind and deaf. Have we then reason to believe that our posterity will be wiser because instructed by a greater number of examples? And is the number of examples which they will have in memory really greater? Already the instances of China, Egypt, Greece and Rome are almost lost in the mists of antiquity; they are known, except by infrequent report, only to the archæologist, and but dimly and uncertainly to him. The brief and imperfect record of yesterdays which we call History is like that traveling vine of India, which, taking new root as it advances, decays at one end while it grows at the other, and so is constantly perishing and finally lost in all the spaces which it has over-passed.

THE FALL OF THE REPUBLIC

Our republican ancestors, with an ignorance of the meaning of words which now seems hardly credible, called theirs a "government of the people, for the people, by the people"—which was to say, that in so far as this catching phrase described it, it was no government at all. Government means control; it means limitation of the will of the governed by some power superior to himself. But if the will of A is limited only by the will of A it is unlimited. We still speak of self-control, but it means now, as it always meant, just nothing at all; for where the will to be controlled and the controlling will are one there can be no limitation: whatever is done is done as much by the will that we figure to ourselves as restrained as by the will that we figure to ourselves as restraining it. Yet our republican ancestors tickled their own ears with this senseless phrase during the whole brief period of their national existence, and all the political literature of the time is full of it, used with ludicrous gravity and doubtless with telling effect upon the popular intelligence. But how, it may be asked, could they go on even so long as they did with no government, properly so called? From the records that have come down to us it does not appear that they went on very well. They were preyed upon by all sorts of political adventurers, whose power in most instances was limited only by the contemporaneous power of other political adventurers equally unscrupulous and mischievous. A full half of the taxes wrung from them were stolen. Their public lands, millions of square miles, were parceled out among banded conspirators. Their roads and the streets of their cities were nearly impassable. Their public buildings, conceived in abominable taste and representing enormous sums of money which never were used in their construction, began to tumble about the ears of the workmen before they were completed. The most delicate and important functions of government were intrusted to men with neither knowledge, heart nor experience, who by their corruption imperiled the public interest and by their blundering disgraced the national name. In short, all the train of evils inseparable from government of any kind beset this unhappy people with tenfold power, together with hundreds of worse ones peculiar to their own faulty and unnatural system. It was thought that their institutions would give them peace, yet in the first three-quarters of a century of their existence they fought three important wars: one of revenge, one of aggression and one—the bloodiest and most wasteful known up to that time—among themselves. And before the full century had passed they had the humiliation to see all their seaport cities destroyed by the Emperor of China in a quarrel which they had themselves provoked, the enormous sums of money taken indirectly from the pockets of the people by a monstrous process known as "Protection to American Industries" having been suffered to lie idle in the treasury instead of being intelligently applied to the defense of their harbors.

In illustration of the means by which their public men climbed to power, and as one of the causes of the final collapse, the learned Professor Dunkle relates this almost incredible instance. At the close of their great civil war—brought about by lack of foresight, political animosity and sheer incapacity on the part of their "public servants," as their tyrants loved to call themselves—there were nearly two millions of mostly young men who had borne arms on the victorious side. These men had been true patriots: they had enlisted from a simple sense of duty, with no desire for, nor thought of, other reward than the nominal pay of the private soldier or the considerable salary of the officer. At the conclusion of hostilities the survivors returned to their homes, happy and proud to have saved their country, as they believed, and wholly content to have escaped with their lives. They were praised and honored by all, even the vanquished. Their service and sufferings constituted them a distinct class, and unhappily, with the best of intentions, they broadened the line which marked them off from their fellow-citizens by forming an association so organized that it was capable, through its officers, of direction as one man. The members all had "votes"; that is, each one was permitted, under the vicious system of republican government, to help select the country's rulers. Here were present all the conditions of political mischief and the demagogues of the time were swift to avail themselves of the opportunity. By the basest sycophancy and the most shameless appeals to the sordid side of the soldiers' nature, these scheming men soon obtained control of the whole organization and used it to elevate themselves to power. When in power they had to retain their places against the efforts of others equally ambitious and equally unscrupulous by distributing the people's money to those who had advanced them. At first the money was given—rightly enough, according to the practice of nations— to those whose wounds in battle had made them wholly or partly unable to support themselves. Afterward, to those who had been wounded at all. Later, to all who were said to have contracted diseases in the service which had become chronic, and still later, to all who for any reason were unable or indisposed to work. Dazzled and corrupted by these successive concessions, the old soldiers, who had been patriots, became perjurers and plunderers; and at last, throwing off all pretense to decency, those whom shame had not compelled to withdraw from the organization demanded as a right that they and all their relatives be supported in comfort and even luxury by the rest of the people; and their demand was granted. In the mean time their numbers, instead of decreasing by death, had doubled and trebled by fraud; and thirty years after the close of the war, during the Presidency of General Ingalls,[4] the annual pension charge, computed in our money, amounted to the prodigious sum of 9,500,000,000 drusoes! Soon afterward the people rose against the Grand Army—as the members called themselves—and being more accustomed to the use of arms, though greatly outnumbered, put them all to death.

I have mentioned "a monstrous practice known as 'Protection to American Industries.'" Modern research has not ascertained precisely what it was: it is known rather from its effects than in its true character, but from what we can learn of it to-day from the fragmentary records that have come down to us, I am disposed to number it among those malefic agencies concerned in the destruction of the American republics,

THE FALL OF THE REPUBLIC

particularly the United States, although it appears not to have been peculiar to "popular government." Some of the contemporary monarchies of Europe were afflicted with it, but by the Divine favor which ever guards a throne its disastrous effects were averted. "Protection" consisted in a number of extraordinary expedients, the purposes of which, and their relations to one another, cannot with certainty be determined in the present state of our knowledge. Barclay, Debrethin, Henley, Villemassant and Schleibach agree that one feature of it was the support, by general taxation, of a few favored citizens in public palaces, where they passed their time in song and dance and all kinds of revelry. They were not, however, altogether idle, being required, out of the sums bestowed upon them, to employ a certain number of men each in erecting great piles of stone and pulling them down again, digging holes in the ground and then filling them up, pouring water into casks and then drawing it off, and so forth. These unhappy laborers were subject to the most cruel oppressions, but the knowledge that their wages came from the pockets of those whom their work nowise benefited was so gratifying to them that nothing could induce them to leave the service of their heartless employers to engage in lighter and more useful labor.

Another characteristic of "Protection" was the maintenance at the principal seaports of "custom-houses," which were strong fortifications, armed with heavy guns, for the purpose of destroying or driving away the trading ships of foreign nations. It was this that caused the United States to be known abroad as the "Hermit Republic," a name of which its infatuated citizens were strangely proud, although they had themselves sent armed ships to open the ports of Japan and other Oriental countries to their own commerce. In their own case, if a foreign ship came empty and succeeded in evading the fire of the "custom-house," as sometimes occurred, she was permitted to take away a cargo. It is obvious that such a system was distinctly mischievous, but it must be confessed our uncertainty regarding the whole matter of "Protection" does not justify us in assigning it a definitive place among the causes of national decay. That in some way it produced an enormous revenue is certain, and that the method was dishonest is no less so; for this revenue—known as a "surplus"—was so abhorred while it lay in the treasury that all were agreed upon the expediency of getting it out again, one great political party existing for apparently no other purpose than the patriotic one of taking it themselves, with all the evils which its possession would entail.

The fundamental fallacy of republican or popular government is now seen to be the extraordinary delusion that two or more follies make one wisdom—the greater the number of added idiocies, the higher the resulting intelligence. It is easy now to trace the origin of this error. When three men engage in any undertaking in which they have an equal interest and in the direction of which they have equal power, it necessarily results that any action approved by two of them, with or without the assent of the third, will be taken. This is called—or was called when it was an accepted principle in political and other affairs—"the rule of the majority." Evidently, under the mischievous conditions supposed it is the only practicable plan of getting anything done. A and B rule and overrule C, not because they ought, but because they can; not because they are wiser, but because they are stronger. In order to avoid a conflict in which he is sure to be worsted, C submits as soon as the vote is taken. C is as likely to be right as A and B; nay, that eminent ancient philosopher, Professor Richard A. Proctor (or Proroctor as the learned now spell the name), has clearly shown by the law of probabilities that any one of the three, all being of the same intelligence, is far likelier to be right than the other two; but submits because he must.

It is thus that the "rule of the majority" as a political system is established. It is in essence nothing but the discredited and discreditable principle that "might makes right"; but early in the life of a republic this essential character of government by majority is lost sight of. The habit of submitting all questions of policy to the arbitrament of counting noses and assenting without question to the result invests the ordeal with a seeming sanctity, and what was at first obeyed as the mandate of power comes to be revered as the oracle of wisdom. Hence originated that ancient blasphemy, adopted and held in high favor in every republic: *Vox populi vox Dei.* The innumerable instances—such as the famous ones of Galileo and Keeley—in which one man has been right and all the rest of the race wrong, are overlooked, or their significance missed and "public opinion" is followed as a divine and infallible guide through every bog into which it blindly stumbles and over every precipice in its fortuitous path. Clearly, there will sooner or later be encountered a bog that will smother, or a precipice that will crush. Thoroughly to apprehend the absurdity of the ancient faith in the wisdom of majorities let the loyal reader try to fancy our gracious Sovereign by any possibility wrong, or his unanimous Ministry by any possibility right!

During the latter half of the nineteenth century there arose in the United States a political element opposed to all government, which frankly declared its object to be Anarchy. This astonishing heresy was not of indigenous growth: its seeds were imported from Europe by the emigration or banishment thence of criminals congenitally incapable of understanding and appreciating the blessings of monarchical institutions, and whose method of protest was murder. The governments against which they conspired in their native lands were too strong in authority and too enlightened in policy for them to succeed in their wicked attempts. Hundreds of them were put to death, thousands imprisoned and sent into exile. But in America, whither those who escaped fled for safety, they found conditions entirely favorable to the prosecution of their designs.

A revered fetish of the Americans was "freedom of speech": it was foolishly believed that if bad men were permitted to proclaim their evil wishes they would go no further in the direction of executing them—that if they might say what they would like to do they would not try to do it. The close relation between speech and action was not understood. Because the Americans themselves had long been accustomed, in their own political debates and discussions, to the use of unmeaning declamation and threats which they had no intention of executing, they reasoned that others were like them, and attributed to the menaces of these desperate and earnest outcasts no greater importance than to their own. They thought also that the foreign Anarchists, having exchanged the tyranny of kings for the tyranny of majorities, would be content with their new and better lot and become in time good and law-abiding citizens. Had their lot been really better this could never have happened; from secretly warring for generations against the particular forms of authority in their native lands they had inherited a bitter antagonism against all authority, even the most beneficent. In their new home they were worse than in their old. In the sunshine of opportunity the rank and sickly growth of their perverted natures became hardy, vigorous, bore fruit. They surrounded themselves with proselytes from the ranks of the idle, the vicious, the unsuccessful. They stimulated and organized discontent. Every one of them became a center of contagion. To those as yet unprepared to accept Anarchy was offered the milder dogma of Socialism, and to those even weaker in the faith something vaguely called Reform. Each was initiated into that degree to which the induration of his conscience and the character of his discontent made him eligible, and in which he could be most useful; the body of the people still cheating themselves with a false sense of security begotten of the belief that they were somehow exempt from the operation of all agencies inimical to their national welfare and integrity. Human nature, they thought, was different in the West from what it was in the East: in the New World the old causes would not have the old effects: a republic had some inherent vitality of its own, entirely independent of any action intended to keep it alive. They felt that words and phrases had some talismanic power, and charmed themselves asleep by repeating "liberty," "all men equal before the law," "dictates of conscience," "free speech" and all manner of such shibboleth to exorcise the evil spirits of the night. And when they could no longer close their eyes to the dangers environing them—when they saw at last that what they had mistaken for the magic power of their form of government and its assured security was really its radical weakness and subjective peril—they found their laws inadequate to repression of the enemy, the enemy too strong to permit the enactment of adequate laws. The belief that a malcontent armed with freedom of speech, a newspaper, a vote and a rifle is less dangerous than a malcontent with a still tongue in his head, empty hands and under police surveillance was abandoned, but all too late. From its fatuous dream the nation was awakened by the noise of arms, the shrieks of women and the glare of burning cities.

Beginning with the slaughter at St. Louis on the night of Christmas in the year 1897, when no fewer than twenty-two thousand citizens were slain in their beds and half of the city destroyed, massacre followed massacre with frightful rapidity. New York fell in the month following, many thousands of its inhabitants escaping fire and sword only to be driven into the bay and drowned, "the roaring of the water in their ears," says Bardeal, "augmented by the hoarse clamor of their red-handed pursuers whose blood-thirst was unsated by the sea." A week later Washington was destroyed, with all its public buildings and archives; the President and his Ministry were slain, the

Parliament was dispersed and an unknown number of officials and private citizens perished. Of all the principal cities, Chicago and San Francisco alone escaped. The people of the former were all Anarchists and the latter was valorously and successfully defended by the Chinese.

In turning from this branch of our inquiry to consider the causes of the failure and bloody disruption of the great American republic other than those inherent in the form of government, it may not be altogether unprofitable to glance briefly at what seems to a superficial view the inconsistent phenomenon of great material prosperity. It is not to be denied that this unfortunate people was singularly prosperous, in so far as national wealth is a measure and proof of prosperity. It was the richest nation among nations. But at how great a sacrifice of better things was its wealth obtained! By the neglect of all education except that crude elementary sort which fit men for the coarse delights of business and affairs, but confers no capacity of rational enjoyment; by exalting the worth of wealth and making it the test and touchstone of merit; by ignoring art, scorning literature and despising science, except as these might contribute to the glutting of the purse; by setting up and maintaining an artificial standard of morals which condoned all offenses against the property and peace of every one but the condoner; by pitilessly crushing out of their natures every sentiment and aspiration unconnected with accumulation of property, these civilized savages and commercial robbers attained their sordid end. Before they had rounded the first half-century of their existence as a nation they had sunk so low in the scale of true morality that it was considered nothing discreditable to take the hand and even visit the house of a man who had grown rich by means notoriously corrupt and dishonorable; and Harley declares that even the editors and writers of newspapers, after fiercely assailing such men in their journals, would be seen "hobnobbing" with them in public places. (The nature of the social ceremony named the "hobnob" is not now understood, but it is known that it was a mark of amity and favor.) When men or nations devote all the powers of their minds and bodies to the heaping up of wealth, wealth is heaped up. But what avails it? It may not be amiss to quote here the words of one of the greatest of the ancient Americans whose works—fragmentary, alas—have come down to us.

> Wealth has accumulated itself into masses; and poverty, also in accumulation enough, lies impassably separated from it; opposed, uncommunicating, like forces in positive and negative poles. The gods of this lower world sit aloft on glittering thrones, less happy than Epicurus's gods, but as indolent, as impotent; while the boundless living chaos of ignorance and hunger welters, terrific in its dark fury, under their feet. How much among us might be likened to a whited sepulcher: outwardly all pomp and strength, but inwardly full of horror and despair and dead men's bones! Iron highways, with their wains fire-winged, are uniting all the ends of the land; quays and moles, with their innumerable stately fleets, tame the ocean into one pliant bearer of burdens; labor's thousand arms, of sinew and of metal, all-conquering everywhere, from the tops of the mount down to the depths of the mine and the caverns of the sea, ply unweariedly for the service of man; yet man remains unserved. He has subdued this planet, his habitation and

inheritance, yet reaps no profit from the victory. Sad to look upon: in the highest stage of civilization nine-tenths of mankind have to struggle in the lowest battle of savage or even animal man—the battle against famine. Countries are rich, prosperous in all manner of increase, beyond example; but the men of these countries are poor, needier than ever of all sustenance, outward and inward; of belief, of knowledge, of money, of food.

To this somber picture of American "prosperity" in the Nineteenth century nothing of worth can be added by the most inspired artist. Let us simply inscribe upon the gloomy canvas the memorable words of our greatest and wisest living poet:

> Ill fares the land, to hastening ills a prey,
> Where wealth accumulates and men decay.[5]

In the space allotted to me in the royal journal by his most gracious Majesty I have room to consider but a single one of the many additional causes that effected the downfall of republican government in the United States. This was the strange and unnatural antagonism known in that far time as the "contest between Capital and Labor." It was the direct result and legitimate sequence of the abolition of that beneficent and advantageous system of slavery (now happily restored) but it was as needless as inhuman and disastrous. Even in that day it was by many seen to be so, but their deprecation was unheeded and their admonition scorned. Some of the philosophers of the period, rummaging amongst the dubious and misunderstood facts of commercial and industrial history, had discovered what they were pleased to term "the law of supply and demand"; and this they expounded with so ingenious sophistry and so copious a wealth of illustration and example that what is at best but a faulty and imperfectly applicable principle, limited and cut into by all manner of other considerations, came to be accepted as the sole explanation and basis of material prosperity and an infallible rule for the proper conduct of affairs. In obedience to its mandate, as they understood it—interpreting it in its narrowest and straitest sense—employers and employees alike regulated by its iron authority all their dealings with one another, throwing off the immemorial relations of mutual dependence and mutual esteem as tending to interfere with the beneficent operation of the new Law. The employer came to believe conscientiously that it was not only profitable and expedient, but under all circumstances his duty to obtain his labor for as little money as possible, even as he sold its product for as much. Considerations of humanity were not banished from his heart, but most sternly excluded from his business. Many of these misguided men would give large sums to various charities; would found universities, hospitals, libraries; would even stop on their way to relieve beggars in the street; but for their own work-people they had no care. Strahan relates in his "Memoirs" that a wealthy manufacturer once said to one of his mill-hands who had asked for an increase of his wages because unable to support his family on the pay that he was receiving: "Your family is nothing to me. I cannot afford to mix benevolence with my business." Yet this man, the author adds, had just given a thousand gold pieces to a "seaman's home."

He could afford to care for other men's employees, but not his own. He could not see that the act which he performed as truly, and to the same degree, cut down his margin of profit in his business as the act which he refused to perform would have done, and had not the advantage of securing him better service from a grateful workman.

On their part, the laborers were no better. Their relations to their employers being "purely commercial," as it was called, they put no heart into their work, seeking ever to do as little as possible for their money, precisely as their employers sought to pay as little as possible for the work they got. The interests of the two classes being thus antagonized, they grew to distrust and hate one another, and each accession of ill feeling produced acts which tended to broaden the breach more and more. There was neither cheerful service on the one side, nor ungrudging payment on the other.

The laborers at last thought they had discovered a plan of power which would give them control of the situation: they began to combine in vast leagues, agreeing that the grievance of one should be the grievance of all. Originally organized for self-protection, and for a while partly successful, these leagues became in the course of time great tyrannies, so reasonless in their demands and so unscrupulous in their methods of enforcing them that the laws were unable to deal with them, and frequently the military forces of the several States were ordered out for the protection of life and property; but in every case the soldiers either fraternized with the leagues, ran away or were easily defeated. The "strikers," as these cruel and mindless mobs were called, had always the hypocritical sympathy and encouragement of the press and the politician, for both feared their power and courted their favor. The judges, dependent for their offices not only on their votes, but on the approval of the press and the politicians, boldly set aside the laws against conspiracy, and strained to the utmost tension those against riot, arson and murder. To such a pass did all this come that in the year 1891 an inn-keeper's denial of a half-holiday to an under cook resulted in the peremptory closing of half the factories in the country, the stoppage of all the railroad travel and the movement of all freight by land and water and a general paralysis of all the industries in the land. Many thousands of families, including those of the "strikers" and their friends, suffered from famine; armed conflicts occurred in every State; hundreds were slain and incalculable amounts of property wrecked and destroyed.

In the mean time capital had not been idle. As it had at first taught labor the law of supply and demand and the mischievous advantages of the "purely commercial relation," so now it learned from labor the malevolent lesson of protective and aggressive leagues. "Strikes" were met by "lockouts," the "boycott" begot the "blacklist," force was repelled by force. The assistance denied by the police and the military was secured by armies of hirelings armed with the most deadly weapons known at the time. In a country where money was all-powerful the power of money was used without stint and without scruple. The judges were bribed to do their duty, juries to convict, newspapers to support and legislators to betray their constituents and pass the most oppressive laws. By these corrupt means, and with the natural advantage of

THE FALL OF THE REPUBLIC

greater skill in affairs and larger experience in concerted action (gained in corporations, syndicates and that form of piracy known as "trusts") the capitalists soon restored their ancient reign and the state of the laborer was worse than it ever had been before. Strahan says that in his time two millions of unoffending workmen in the various industries were once discharged without warning and promptly arrested as vagrants and deprived of their ears because a sulking canal-boatman had kicked his captain's dog into the water. And the dog was a retriever.

Even without these monstrous measures, except for the lawless wrecking of property, capital must eventually have triumphed, and in point of fact commonly did. Cheered and consoled by the knowledge that the whole country suffered with him, the man whose workmen had struck or been locked out could with tranquility forego his profits; but however sustained by spiritual satisfaction the workmen could not forego their dinners. Their leagues, moreover, were at a peculiar and remediless disadvantage in this: the more nearly they succeeded in making their membership universal and their strikes general and ruinous, the stronger was the temptation to treason in and defection from their own ranks. When capital, most imperiled, most needed trusty labor the trade of being a non-union man was most lucrative, and became at last one of the "overcrowded professions." The labor leagues had made the fatal mistake of allowing too little for human cupidity.

The leagues were finally broken up, the laborer, reduced to the condition of a serf, became an Anarchist and his subsequent deeds in that character, briefly glanced at elsewhere in this treatise, are recorded in blood upon his page of the awful annals of that "fierce democracy"[6] of which he was ever the central figure and for long the controlling power.

In reviewing the history of those turbulent times one cannot help thinking how different it all might have been if the "law of supply and demand" and the "purely commercial relation" had remained undiscovered, or had perished unexpounded with their discoverer when he was hanged; if in ancient America, as under the benign sway of our most gracious and ever-blessed sovereign, the employer had studied, not how little he could get his labor for, but how much he could afford to give for it, and if the employee, instead of calculating how badly he could do his work and keep his place, had considered how well he could do it and keep his health.

In concluding this hasty and imperfect sketch I cannot forbear to relate an episode of the bloody and unnatural contest between labor and capital, which I find recorded in the almost forgotten work of Antrolius, who was an eye-witness to the incident. At a time when the passions of both parties were most inflamed and scenes of violence most frequent, it was somehow noised about in Washington that at a certain hour of a certain day some one—none knew who—would stand upon the steps of the Capitol and speak to the people, expounding a plan for the reconciliation of all conflicting interests and the pacification of the quarrel. At the specified hour, there being a general strike and lock-out in the city, thousands of idlers had assembled to hear—glowering capitalists attended by hireling body-guards with repeating rifles, sullen laborers with dynamite bombs concealed beneath their coats. All eyes were directed to the appointed spot, where suddenly appeared (none could say whence—it seemed as if he had been standing there all the time, such were his immobility and composure) a tall, pale man clad in a long robe, bare-headed, his hair falling lightly upon his shoulders, his eyes full of compassion, and with such majesty of face and mien that all were awed to silence ere he spoke. Slightly raising his right hand from the elbow, the index finger extended upward, he said in a voice ineffably sweet and serious: "As ye would that others should do unto you, do ye even so unto them." These words he repeated in the same solemn and thrilling tones three times; then, as the expectant multitude waited breathless for him to begin his discourse, stepped quietly down among them into their very midst, every one afterward averring that he passed within a pace of where himself stood. For an instant the crowd was speechless with surprise and disappointment, then broke into wild, fierce cries of "Lynch him! Lynch him!" and struggling into looser order started in mad pursuit. But each man ran a different way and the stranger was seen again by none of them.

E (25 Mar. 1888): 12. Revised as "Ashes of the Beacon."

NOTES

AB was no monarchist, but his criticism of democracy in this satire is not far from his real political opinions, which were fairly consistent over time. He felt that democracy was leveling downward to mobocracy, a crowd-pandering form of government, and that the people were being manipulated by demagogues, plutocrats, and bureaucrats to the end that they were no longer true to the character and ideals of the Founding Fathers. Repeatedly during his career he warned in satires like this and in "Prattle" essays against the idealization of an imperfect system and against the hubris implicit in the belief that "the voice of the people is the voice of God."

1. Pescadero is a small town near the coast of northern California, about twenty miles west of San Jose.
2. Pope, *An Essay on Man* (1733–34), Epistle 3, ll. 303–4.
3. France permanently became a republic in 1870 with the establishment of the Third Republic.
4. A reference to the Republican politician John James Ingalls (1833–1900), U.S. senator from Kansas (1873–91) and a vigorous supporter of the Grand Army of the Republic.
5. The first line is from Oliver Goldsmith's *The Deserted Village* (1770), l. 51; the second is by AB.
6. Milton, *Paradise Regain'd* (1671), 4.269.

THE KINGDOM OF TORTIRRA

SOME ACCOUNT OF THE PEOPLE OF A RECENTLY DISCOVERED COUNTRY

By the arrival of the schooner *Jabez Jones,* Capt. Taylor, we are put in possession of further knowledge concerning the recently discovered Tortirra Islands, some account of which appeared in this journal last October.[1] The information then obtained from the trading vessel *Ecuador,* which, driven from her course, had touched at one of the smaller islands of the group, was imperfect and fragmentary, the vessel having been compelled by the natives to go to sea again within twenty-four hours after dropping anchor in their port. They discerned her true character of merchantman, despite the clever ruse by which her master and crew endeavored to give her the appearance of a pirate, and sent her to the right about in short order.

Our present advices are less meager, being derived from one James Donelson, who lived on Tanga, the largest of the group, for more than three years, the first European, and, excepting the crew of the *Ecuador,* the only one who is known to have seen these islands. Donelson was an able seaman on board the British barque *Arethusa,* which on the 5th of November, 1884, was wrecked on an uninhabited island some three hundred miles to the northeast of Tanga. As the island upon which the vessel went ashore afforded neither food nor water, the seven survivors, including the Captain, left it in an open boat with such provisions as they had been able to save, choosing a course almost at random in the faint hope of finding a more hospitable land. After incredible sufferings, Donelson, now the sole survivor, unconscious in the bottom of his boat, drifted ashore on Tanga, and was restored to strength and health by the natives. He remained among them until November last, when finding the situation intolerable he embarked in a small boat which he had secretly provisioned, and set sail, trusting to the remote chance of being picked up by some ship, if spared by the winds and waves. In case of failure and the exhaustion of his food and water, he resolved to die by his own hand. By good fortune the *Jabez Jones,* hence from Teluga, which, like the *Ecuador,* had been blown many leagues out of her course, found and rescued him and brought him to this port.

To an EXAMINER reporter, who visited Mr. Donelson on Wednesday last, that gentleman appeared somewhat reluctant to say much concerning the hitherto almost unknown people among whom he had lived so long. He even refused to say what had been the character of his treatment by them; but from the desperate chances of escape which he took it may safely enough be considered to have been not altogether friendly. "I must decline to answer all your questions," said Mr. Donelson. "While on board the Jones I began, at the suggestion of her Captain, a narrative of my adventures and an account of the extraordinary people among whom I was thrown—of whom and of whose no less extraordinary country the world will be first fully apprised by my book. Naturally I do not with to publish in advance any particulars which would add interest to the volume. I appreciate the enterprise of the EXAMINER in trying to obtain them, all the same," he added with a smile. Mr. Donelson, by the way, is an educated and singularly intelligent man—a very able seaman indeed. How he came to ship as a sailor before the mast he declines to say.

At a later interview he said: "On reflection, and influenced, I confess, by the handsome offer that your paper has made me, I am disposed to surrender to you such parts of my manuscript as I think can best be spared from my book. I must tell you frankly that my choice has been determined by considerations purely selfish: I offer to you that part of my narrative which I conceive to be the least credible—that which deals with certain monstrous and astounding follies of that strange people. Their ceremony of marriage by decapitation; their custom of facing to the rear when riding on horseback; their reversal of the law of hereditary succession to the throne—the father succeeding the son; their practice of walking on their hands in all ceremonial processions; their selection of the blind for military command; their pig-worship—these and many other interesting particulars of their religious, political, intellectual and social life I reserve; but if you think that without risking its reputation for veracity the EXAMINER can publish the extraordinary statements contained in the manuscripts which I now hand you, they are at your service. I am convinced that they would seriously impair the reader's faith in the general credibility of my book."

Assuring Mr. Donelson that the EXAMINER would publish them for what they are worth, the reporter accepted the manuscripts, and they are here printed without material alteration.

SOUTH PACIFIC POLITICS.

The politics of Tortirra are no less remarkable than the laws. Something has been already said of the political system—a limited monarchy, with a commonly vacant throne (the sovereign's functions *in interregno* being performed by a designated Minister), a supreme and many subordinate legislatures and an executive head of each island. The system is good enough, but in its practical working the prodigious folly and dark ignorance of the people deprive it of all beneficent effectiveness and make it an instrument of evil. To most of the multitude of offices men are chosen for a brief incumbency by what is called a popular election; that is to say, on certain stated days every adult male not legally disqualified is supposed to designate for any certain office the "man of his choice," and actually believes himself exercising the largest liberty of preference. But by the previous action of a few men whose political existence is un-known to the Constitution, whose meetings are secret and whose methods wicked, his choice is limited to one of two or three men. It is so arranged that he must vote for the man of another man's choice or his vote is wasted. Yet he is no less zealous and enthu-siastic in assertion of this worthless right than if he were really recording an intelligent preference. So great is the earnestness of these voters that they sometimes engage in the most acrimonious disputes, and even in bloody fights, very few important elections taking place without men justifying with their hearts' blood to the worth of candi-dates, about whom they know nothing except what they have been told by interested persons, and to whom they are not only themselves unknown but objects of profound indifference.

In Tortirran politics the population is always divided into two, and sometimes three or four, "parties," each having a "policy" and each conscientiously believing the policy of the other or others erroneous and destructive. In so far as these various and varying policies can be seen to have any relation whatever to practical affairs they can be seen also to be the result of purely selfish considerations. The self-deluded people flatter themselves that their elections are contests of principles, whereas they are only struggles of interests. They are very fond of the word *slagthrit,* "principles"; and when they believe themselves acting from some high moral motive they are capable of almost any monstrous injustice or stupid folly. This insane devotion to principle is craftily fostered by their political leaders, who invent captivating phrases intended to confirm them in it; and these deluding aphorisms are diligently repeated until all the people have them in memory, with no knowledge of the fallacies which they conceal. One of these phrases is, "Principles, not men." In the last analysis this is seen to mean that it is better to be governed by scoundrels professing one set of principles than by good men professing another. That a scoundrel will govern badly, regardless of the principles which he is supposed somehow to "represent," is a truth which, however obvious to our own enlightened intelligences, has never penetrated the dark under-standings of the Tortirrans. It is chiefly through the dominance of the heresy fostered by this popular phrase that the political leaders are able to place base men in office to serve their own nefarious ends. Sometimes they push their power to so bold an extreme, by nomination of a man so notoriously unfit, that an important group of his own party refuse to support him.[2] Upon these conscientious dissenters the great body of the party, taking the cue from the discomfited leaders, heaps the vilest and most opprobrious abuse and fastens some abominable nickname to serve in place of argument. To the civilized observer this is inexpressibly shocking, and he can but wonder that Heaven permits this abominable race to exist.

To show how thoroughly, to the mind of the typical Tortirran, loyalty to party is identical with loyalty to country, and with the service of reason, I may relate that at a public dining-table I once heard a political conversation among five natives, each of whom, with a single exception, boasted that he had never voted anything but the "straight ticket" of his party. If these men had been told that in ignoring such small reason as God had given them for their guidance, and submitting with sheeplike docility to the direction of a long succession of scheming men whom they did not even know by name, they had, within the limits of their narrow capacity, done the worst possible disservice to their country, they would not have known what was meant, or knowing, they would have resented it. The resentment of the ignorant is not a thing to be courted, nor could it be expected that I, a foreigner, should rebuke a savage in his own land, and I was silent, as became me; but I could not help thinking how appropriate to each of these men would be "the Fool's Prayer" of one of our minor poets:

> Earth bears no balsam for mistakes:
> Men crown the knave and scourge the tool
> That did his will; but thou, O Lord,
> Be merciful to me, a fool.[3]

The fifth native of this group of statesmen—he who had not always "voted the straight ticket of his party"—was too young to vote, but I suppose he lived in the comforting hope of always voting it when qualified by age and a ripe judgment.

A "LIVE ISSUE."

I have called the political contests of Tortirra struggles of interests. In nothing is this more clear (to the looker-on at the game) than in the endless disputes concerning restrictions on commerce. It must be understood that lying many leagues to the southeast of Tortirra are other groups of islands, also wholly unknown to people of our race. They are known by the general name of Gropilla-Stron, a term signifying "the Land of the Day-dawn," though it is impossible to ascertain why. They are inhabited by a powerful and hardy race, many of whom I have met in the capital of Tanga, and whom I shall elsewhere describe in this volume. The *Stronagu,* as they are called, are bold navigators and traders, their *proas* making long and hazardous voyages in all the adjacent seas to exchange commodities with other tribes. For many years they were welcomed in Tortirra with great hospitality and their goods eagerly purchased. They took back with them all manner of Tortirran products, and nobody thought of questioning the mutual advantages of the exchange. But early in the present century a powerful Tortirran demagogue named Pragam-Zut began to persuade the people that commerce was piracy—that true prosperity consisted in consumption of domestic products and abstention from foreign. This extraordinary heresy soon gathered such head that Pragam-Zut was appointed Regent and invested with almost dictatorial powers. He at once distributed nearly the whole army among the seaport cities, and whenever a Stronagu trading *proa* attempted to land, the soldiery, assisted by the populace, rushed down to the beach with a terrible din of gongs and an insupportable discharge of ill-smelling hand grenades—the only offensive weapon known to Tortirran warfare—drove the laden vessels to sea, or if they persisted in landing, destroyed them and smothered their crews in mud. The Tortirrans themselves not being a sea-going people, all communication between them and the rest of their little world soon ceased. But with it ceased the prosperity of Tortirra. Deprived of a market for their surplus products and compelled to forego the comforts and luxuries which they had obtained from abroad, the people began to murmur at the effect of their own folly. A reaction set in, a powerful opposition to Pragam-Zut and his policy was organized, and he was driven from power. But the noxious tree which he had planted in the fair garden of his country's prosperity had struck root too deeply to be altogether eradicated. It threw up secret shoots everywhere, and no sooner was one cut down than from the roots underrunning the whole domain of political thought others sprang up with a vigorous and baleful growth. While the dictum that trade is piracy no longer commanded universal acceptance, a majority of the populace still held a modified form of it, and that "importation is theft" is to-day a cardinal political "principle" of a vast body of Tortirra's people. The chief expounders and protagonists of this doctrine are all directly or indirectly engaged in making or growing such articles as were formerly got by exchange with the Stronagu traders. The articles are generally inferior in quality, and consumers, not having the benefit of foreign competition, are compelled to pay extortionate prices for them, thus maintaining the unscrupulous producers in needless industries and a pernicious existence. But these active and intelligent rogues are too powerful to be driven out. They persuade their followers, among whom are many ignorant consumers, that this remnant survival of the old Pragam-Zut policy is all that keeps the nation from being desolated by smallpox; and some go so far as to argue that every instance of a broken leg is clearly traceable to the importation of foreign goods.

It is impossible in these limits to give a full history of the strange delusion whose origin we have described. It has undergone many modifications and changes, as it is the nature of error to do, but the present situation is about this. The trading *proas* of the Stronagu are permitted to enter certain ports, but when one arrives she must anchor at a little distance from shore. Here she is boarded by an officer of the Government, who ascertains her tonnage, the number of souls on board and the amount and character of the merchandise she brings. From these data—the last being the

THE KINGDOM OF TORTIRRA

main factor in the problem—the officer computes her unworthiness and adjudges a suitable penalty. The next day a scow manned by a certain number of soldiers pushes out and anchors within easy throw of her, and there is a frightful beating of gongs. When this has reached its lawful limit as to time it is hushed and the soldiers throw a stated number of stink-pots on board, which, exploding as they strike, stifle the captain and crew with an intolerable odor of decayed eggs. In the case of a large *proa* having a cargo of such commodities as the Tortirrans particularly need this bombardment is continued for hours. At its conclusion the vessel is permitted to land and discharge her cargo without further molestation. Under these hard conditions importers find it impossible to do much business, the exorbitant wages demanded by seamen consuming most of the profit. No restrictions are now placed on the export trade, and vessels arriving empty are subjected to no penalties; but the Stronagu having only a limited sale for their surplus products cannot afford to pay such prices for those of Tortirra as would recoup them for the expense of the unprofitable outward voyage.

It will be obvious to the reader that in all this no question of "principle" is involved. A well-informed Tortirran's mental attitude with regard to the matter may be calculated with unfailing accuracy from a knowledge of his business interests. If he produces anything which his countrymen want, and which in the absence of all restriction they could get more cheaply from the Stronagu than they can from him, he is in politics a *Gakphew,* or "Stinkpotter"; if not, he is what that party derisively calls a *Shokerbom,* which signifies "Righteous Man"—for there is nothing which the Gakphews hold in so holy detestation as righteousness.

THE TORTIRRAN COURTS.

Nominally, Tortirra is an hereditary monarchy, as previously explained; practically it is a democracy, for under the peculiar law of succession there is seldom an occupant of the throne, and all public affairs are conducted by a Supreme Legislature sitting at Felduchia, the capital of Tanga, to which body each island of the archipelago, twenty-nine in number, elects representatives in proportion to its population, the total membership being 317. Each island has a Subordinate Council for the management of local affairs and a Head Chief charged with execution of the laws. There is also a Great Court at Felduchia, whose function it is to interpret the general laws of the Kingdom, passed by the Supreme Council, and a Minor Great Court at the capital of each island, with corresponding duties and powers. These powers are very loosely and vaguely defined, and are the subject of endless controversy everywhere, and nowhere more than in the courts themselves—such is the multiplicity of laws and so many are the contradictory decisions upon them, every decision constituting what is called a *lantrag,* or, as we might say, "precedent." The peculiarity of a *lantrag,* or previous decision, is that it is, or it is not, binding, at the will of the court or judge making a later one on a similar point. If he wishes to decide in the same way he quotes the previous decision with all the gravity that he would give to an exposition of the law itself; if not, he either ignores it altogether, shows that it is not applicable to the case under consideration (which, as the circumstances are never exactly the same, he can always do), or substitutes a contradictory *lantrag* and fortifies himself with that. There is a precedent for any decision that a judge may wish to make, but sometimes he is too indolent to search it out and cite it. Frequently, when the letter and intent of the law under which an action is brought are plainly hostile to the decision which it pleases him to render, the judge finds it easier to look up an older law, with which it is compatible, and which the later one, he says, does not repeal, and to base his decision on that; and there is a law for everything, just as there is a precedent. Failing to find, or not caring to look for, either precedent or statute to sustain him, he can readily show that any other decision than the one he has in will would be *tokoli impelly,* that is to say, contrary to public morals—and this, too, is considered a legitimate consideration, though on another occasion he may say, with public assent and approval, that it is his duty, not to make the law conform to justice, but to expound and enforce it as he finds it. In short, such is the confusion of the law and the public conscience that the courts of Tortirra do whatever they please, subject only to overruling by higher courts in the exercise of *their* pleasure; for so great is the number of minor and major tribunals that a case originating in the lowest is never really settled until it has gone through all the intermediate ones and been passed upon by the highest, to which it might just as well have been admitted in the first place. The evils of this astonishing system could not be even baldly catalogued in this whole volume. They are infinite in number and prodigious in magnitude. To the trained intelligence of the American observer it is incomprehensible how any, even the most barbarous, nation can endure them.

An important function of the Great Court and the Minor Great Court is passing upon the validity of all laws enacted by the Supreme Council and the Subordinate Councils, respectively. The nation as a whole, as well as each separate island, has a fundamental law called the *Trogodal,* or, as we should say, the constitution; and no law whatever that may be passed by the Council is final and determinate until the appropriate court has declared that it conforms to the *Trogodal.* Nevertheless—incredible fatuity—every law is put in force the moment it is perfected and before it is submitted to the court. Indeed, not one in a thousand ever is submitted at all, their submission depending upon the possibility of some individual objecting to their action upon his personal interests. It not infrequently occurs that some law which has for years been rigorously enforced, even by fines and imprisonment, and to which the whole commercial and social life of the nation has adjusted itself with all its vast property interests, is brought before the tribunal having final jurisdiction in the matter and coolly declared no law at all. The pernicious effect may be more easily imagined than related, but those who, by loyal obedience to it all those years, have been injured in property, those who are ruined by its erasure and those who may have suffered the severest penalties for its violation are alike without redress. It seems not to have occurred to these reasonless savages to require the court to inspect the law and determine its validity before it is put in force. It is, indeed, the traditional practice of these strange tribunals when a case is forced upon them to decide not as many points of law as they can, but as few as they must; and this dishonest inaction is not only tolerated, but commended as the highest wisdom. The consequence is that only those who make a profession of the law and live by it, and find their account in having it as little understood by others as is possible, can know what acts are in force and what are not. These higher courts, too, have arrogated to themselves the power of declaring unconstitutional even parts of the constitutions themselves, frequently annulling the most important provisions of the very instrument creating them!

A popular folly in Tortirra is the selection of representatives in the councils from among that class of men who live by the law, whose sole income is derived from its uncertainties and perplexities. Obviously, it is to the interest of these men to make laws which shall be uncertain and perplexing—to confuse and darken legislation as much as they can. Yet in nearly all the councils these men are the most influential and active element, and it is not uncommon to find them in a numerical majority. It is evident that the only check upon their mischievousness lies in the certainty of their disagreement as to the particular kind of confusion which they may think it expedient to create. Some will wish to accomplish their common object by one kind of verbal ambiguity, some by another; some by laws clearly enough (to them) unconstitutional, others by contradictory statutes, or statutes virtually repealing wholesome ones already existing. A clear, simple and just code would deprive them of all their means of livelihood and compel them to seek some honest employment.

So great are the uncertainties of the law in Tortirra that an eminent judge once confessed to the writer that it was his conscientious belief that if all cases were decided by the impartial arbitrament of the *do-tusis* (a process similar to our "throw of the dice") substantial justice would be done far more frequently than under the present system; and there is reason to believe that in many instances cases at law are so decided—but only at the close of tedious and costly trials which have impoverished the litigants and correspondingly enriched the lawyers.

Of the interminable train of shames and brutalities entailed by this reasonless and pernicious tomfoolery, I shall mention here but a single one—the sentencing and punishment of an accused person in the midst of the proceedings against him, and while his guilt is not finally and definitively established. It frequently occurs that a man convicted of crime in one of the lower courts is at once hurried off to prison while he has still the right of appeal to a higher tribunal and while that appeal is pending. In fact, the appeal never operates as a stay of punishment. After months and sometimes years of punishment his case is reached in the appellate court, his appeal found valid and a new trial granted, resulting in his acquittal. He has been imprisoned for a crime which he is eventually declared not to have committed. But he has no redress; he is simply set free, to bear through all his after life the stain of dishonor and nourish an ineffectual resentment. Imagine the storm of popular indignation that would be evoked in America by an instance of so foul injustice!

In the great public square of Itsami, the capital of Otamwee,[4] stands a golden statue of Estari-Kumpro, a famous judge of the Civil Court.* This great man was celebrated throughout the archipelago for the wisdom and justice of his decisions and the virtues of his private life. So great was the veneration in which he was held, so profound the awe that his presence inspired, that none of the advocates in his court ever ventured to address him except in formal pleas: all motions, objections and so forth were addressed to the Clerk and by him disposed of without dissent: the silence of the judge, who never was heard to utter a word in court, was understood as sanctioning the acts of his subordinate. For thirty years, promptly at sunrise, the great hall of justice was thrown open, disclosing the Judge seated on a lofty dais beneath a black canopy, partly in shadow, and quite inaccessible. Promptly at sunset all proceedings for the day terminated, every one left the hall and the portal closed. The decisions of this august and learned jurist were always read aloud by the Clerk and a copy, in the judge's handwriting, furnished to the counsel on each side. They were brief, clear and remarkable not only for their unimpeachable justice, but for their conformity to the fundamental principles of law. Not one of them was ever set aside, and during the last fifteen years of his service no litigant ever took an appeal, although none ever ventured before that infallible tribunal unless conscientiously persuaded that his cause was just. One day it happened during the progress of an important trial that a sharp shock of earthquake occurred, throwing the whole assembly into confusion. When order had been restored a cry of horror and dismay burst from the multitude—the judge's head lay flattened upon the floor, a dozen feet below the Bench, and from the neck of the rapidly collapsing body, which had pitched forward upon his desk, poured a thick stream of sawdust! For thirty years that great and good man had been represented by a stuffed manikin. For thirty years he had not entered his own court, nor heard a word of evidence or argument. At the moment of the accident to his simulacrum he was writing his decision of the case on trial, in his bedroom at home, and was killed by a falling chandelier. It was afterward learned that his Clerk, twenty-five years dead, had all the time been personated by his twin brother, who was an idiot from birth.

---

*Klikat um Delu Ovwi. In revising Mr. Donelson's manuscript it was thought inexpedient and needless to retain many of the native terms for which he gives also the English equivalent. From merely literary considerations a few have been permitted to stand.

THE KINGDOM OF TORTIRRA

E (**22 Apr. 1888**): **12.** Incorporated into "The Land Beyond the Blow."

NOTES

The influence of *Gulliver's Travels* is obvious in this political satire. Tortirra is an offset but transparent stand-in for the United States, as seen by a disinterested and rational observer. AB incisively—and perhaps painfully—exposes the inefficiencies and follies of political, economic, and judicial practices of the Tortirran (i.e., American) systems. Like Swift, AB is more concerned to point out problems than to suggest their remedies. His satire is therefore primarily aimed at those who either are unaware of the systems' failings or have grown complacent about them.

1. No such account by AB has been located in *E* for October 1887.
2. AB alludes to the so-called mugwumps in the presidential campaign of 1884 (see "For the Ahkoond," note 9).
3. Edward Rowland Sill (1841–87), "The Fool's Prayer" (1879), ll. 36–39.
4. Evidently a play on Ottumwa, Iowa, a city founded in 1843. AB apparently found the name amusingly bizarre-sounding.

BODIES OF THE DEAD [I]

SOME ACCOUNTS OF THEIR SEEMING CAPRICES.

DO WE KNOW IT ALL?

When the Breath is Out of a Man is He Therefore Dead and as Nothing?

On the morning of the 14th day of August, 1872, Charles J. Reid, a young man of 25 years, living in Xenia, O.,[1] fell while walking across the dining room in his father's house. The family consisted of his father, mother, two sisters and a cousin, a boy of 15. All were present at the breakfast table, when Charles entered the room, but instead of taking his accustomed seat near the door by which he had entered, passed it and went obliquely toward one of the windows—with what purpose no one knows. He had passed the table but a few steps when he fell heavily to the floor and never again breathed. The body was carried into a bedroom and, after vain efforts at resuscitation by the stricken family, left lying on the bed with composed limbs and covered face. In the mean time the boy had been hastily dispatched for a physician, who arrived some twenty minutes after the death. He afterward remembered as an uncommon circumstance that when he arrived the weeping relations—father, mother and two sisters—were all in the room out of which the bedroom door opened, and that the door was closed. There was no other to the bedroom. This door was at once opened by the father of the deceased, and as the physician passed through it he observed the rigid outlines of the body under the sheet that had been thrown over it; and the profile was plainly discernible under the face-cloth, clear-cut and sharp, as profiles of the dead seem always to be. He approached and lifted the cloth. There was nothing there. He pulled away the sheet. Nothing.

The family had followed him into the room. At this astonishing discovery—if so it may be called—they looked at one another, at the physician, at the bed, in speechless amazement, forgetting to weep. A moment later the three ladies required the physician's care; all had fainted and fallen to the floor. The father's condition was but little better; he stood in a stupor, muttering inarticulately and staring like an idiot.

Having restored the ladies to consciousness the physician went to the window— the only one the room had, opening upon a garden. It was locked on the inside with the usual fastening attached to the bottom bar of the upper sash and engaging with the lower.

No inquest was held—there was nothing to hold it on; but the physician and many others who were curious as to this remarkable occurrence made the most searching investigation into all the circumstances, but without result. Charles J. Reid was dead and "gone," and that is all that is known to this day. It should be stated that previously to Dr. Jarvis' arrival the body had been divested of its outer clothing and these lay on the floor at the foot of the bed where they had been cast. Dr. Jarvis, a most respectable man, was still practicing his profession in Xenia as late as 1885, but the Reids had removed to Fort Wayne, Indiana.

One evening in the summer of 1843 William Hayner Gordon, of Philadelphia, lay in his bed reading Goldsmith's "Traveller," by the light of a wax candle. It was about 11 o'clock. The room was in the third story of the house and had two windows looking out upon Chestnut street; there was no balcony, nothing below the windows but other windows in a smooth brick wall.

Becoming drowsy, Mr. Gordon laid away his book, extinguished his candle and composed himself to sleep. A moment later (as he afterward averred) he remembered that he had neglected to place his watch within reach, and rose in the dark to get it from the pocket of his waistcoat, which he had hung on the back of a chair on the opposite side of the room, near one of the windows. In crossing, his foot came in contact with some heavy object and he was thrown to the floor. Rising, he struck a match and lighted his candle. In the center of the room lay the dead body of a man.

Gordon was no coward, as he afterward proved by his gallant death upon the enemy's parapet at Chapultepec,[2] but this strange apparition of a human corpse where but a moment before, as he believed, there had been nothing, was too much for his nerves, and he cried aloud. Henri Granier, who occupied an adjoining room, but had not retired, came instantly to Mr. Gordon's door and attempted to enter. The door being bolted and Gordon too terrified to open it, Granier burst it in.

Gordon was taken into custody and an inquest held, but what has been related was all that could be ascertained. The most diligent efforts on the part of the police and the press failed to identify the dead. Physicians testifying at the inquest agreed that death had occurred but a few hours before the discovery, but none was able to divine the cause; all the organs of the body were in an apparently healthy condition; there were traces of neither violence nor poison.

Eight or ten months later Gordon received a letter from Charles Ritcher in Bombay, relating the death in that city of Charles Farquharson, whom both Gordon and Richter had known when all were boys. Enclosed in the letter was a daguerreotype of the deceased, found among his effects. So nearly as the living can look like the dead it was an exact likeness of the mysterious body found in Mr. Gordon's bedroom, and it was with a strange feeling that Gordon observed that the death, making allowance for the difference of time, was said to have occurred on that very night. He wrote for further particulars, with especial reference to what disposition had been made of Farquharson's body. "You know he turned Parsee,"[3] wrote Ritcher in reply; "so his naked remains were exposed on the grating of the Tower of Silence, as those of all good Parsees are. I saw the buzzards fighting for them and gorging themselves helpless on his fragments." On some pretense Gordon and his friends obtained authority to open the dead man's grave. The coffin was there and had evidently not been disturbed. They unscrewed the lid. The shroud was there, a trifle mouldy. There was no body nor any vestige of one.

The night of December 31, 1863, was an exceedingly cold one in the vicinity of Murfreesboro, Tenn. The first day's battle at Stone river[4] had been fought, resulting in disaster to the Federal army, which had been driven from its original ground at every point except its extreme left. The weary troops at this point lay behind a railway embankment which had served them during the last hours of the fight as a breastwork to repel repeated charges of the enemy. Behind the line the ground was open and rocky. Great bowlders lay about everywhere, and among them lay many of the Federal dead, where they had been carried out of the way. Before the embankment the dead of both armies lay greatly thicker, but they were not molested. It was not a very dark night, being clear. Among the dead in the bowlders lay one whom nobody seemed to know— a Federal Sergeant, shot directly in the center of the forehead. One of our surgeons, from idle curiosity, or possibly with a view to the amusement of a group of officers during a lull in the engagement (we needed something to divert our minds) had dropped his probe clean through the head. The body lay on its back, its chin in the air, and with straightened limbs, as rigid as steel; frost on its white face and in its beard and hair. Some Christian soul had covered it with a blanket, but when the night became pretty sharp a companion of the writer removed this, and we lay beneath it ourselves. With the exception of our pickets, which had been posted well in front of the embankment, every man lay silent. Conversation was forbidden; to have made a fire, or even struck a match to light a pipe, would have been a grave offense. Stamping horses, moaning wounded—everything that made a noise had been sent to the rear: the silence was absolute. Those whom the chill prevented from sleeping nevertheless reclined as they shivered, or sat with their heads on their arms, suffering but making no sign. Every one had lost friends and all expected death on the morrow. These matters are mentioned to show the improbability of any one going about during those solemn hours to commit a ghastly practical joke.

When the dawn broke, the sky was still clear. "We shall have a warm day," the writer's companion whispered as we rose in the gray light; "let's give back the poor devil his blanket."

The Sergeant's body lay in the same place, two yards away. But not in the same attitude. It was upon its right side. The knees were drawn up nearly to the breast, both hands thrust to the wrist between the buttons of the jacket, the collar of which was turned up, concealing the ears. The shoulders were elevated, the head was retracted, the chin rested on the collar-bone. The posture was that of one suffering from intense cold. But for what had been previously observed—but for the ghastly evidence of the bullet-hole—one might have thought the man had frozen to death.

About ten miles to the southeast of Whitesburg, Kentucky,[5] in a little "cove" of the Cumberland mountains lived for many years an old woman named Sarah (or Mary) Magone. Her house, built of logs and containing but two rooms, was a mile and a half distant from any other, in the wildest part of the "cove," entirely surrounded by forest except on one side, where a little field, or "patch," of about a half-acre served her for a vegetable garden. How she subsisted nobody exactly knew; she was reputed to be a miser with a concealed hoard; she certainly paid for what few articles she procured on her rare visits to the village store. Many of her ignorant neighbors believed her to be a witch, or thought, at least, that she possessed some kind of supernatural powers. In November, 1881, she died and, fortunately enough, the body was found while yet warm by a passing hunter, who locked the door of the cabin and conveyed the news to the nearest settlement. Several of the residents of the vicinity at once went to the cabin to prepare her for her burial; while others were to follow the next day with the coffin and whatever else was needful. Among those who first went was the Rev. Elias Atney, a Baptist minister of Whitesburg, who happened to be in the neighborhood visiting a relation. He was to conduct the funeral services on the following day. Mr. Atney is, or was, well known in Whitesburg and all that country as a good and pious man of good birth and education. He was closely related to the Marshalls and several other families of distinction. It is from him that the particulars here related were learned; and the account is confirmed by the affidavits of John Hershaw, William C. Wrightman and Catharine Doub, residents of the vicinity and eye-witnesses.

The body of "Granny" Magone had been "laid out" on a wide plank supported by two chairs at the end of the principal room, opposite the fireplace, and the persons mentioned were acting as "watchers," according to the local custom. A bright fire on the hearth lighted one end of the room brilliantly, the other dimly. The watchers sat about the fire, talking in subdued tones, when a sudden noise in the direction of the corpse caused them all to turn and look. In a little unglazed aperture which served for a window and was directly above the remains, at a hight of some four or five feet, they saw, with natural alarm, two glowing eyes staring fixedly into the room; and before they could do more than rise, uttering exclamations of terror, a large black cat leaped upon the body and fastened its teeth in the cloth covering the face. Instantly the right hand of the dead was violently raised from the side, seized the cat and hurled it against the wall, whence it fell to the floor, and then dashed wildly through another window into the outer darkness and was seen no more. Inconceivably terrified, the watchers stood for some moments speechless; but finally, with returning courage, approached the body. The face-cloth lay upon the floor; the cheek was terribly lacerated; the right arm hung stiffly over the side of the plank. There was not a sign of life. With trembling hands they chafed the forehead, the witheréd cheeks and neck. They carried the body to the heat of the fire and worked upon it for hours, all in vain. But the funeral was postponed until the fourth day brought unmistakable evidence of dissolution, and poor Granny was buried.

"Ah, but your eyes deceived you," said he to whom the reverend gentleman related the occurrence; "the arm was disturbed by the struggles of the cat, which, taking sudden fright, leaped blindly against the wall."

"No," he answered, "the clenched right hand, with its long nails, was full of black fur."

E (22 Apr. 1888): 9 (as by "A. G. B."). Reprinted in "Bodies of the Dead," *CSTB* 293–95 (as "That of Granny Magone"), 298–300 (as "The Mystery of Charles Farquharson"), 301–2 (as "Dead and 'Gone'"), 303–5 (as "A Cold Night"). "Dead and 'Gone,'" reprinted in *Short Stories* 1, no. 1 (June–July 1890): 59.

NOTES

Nineteenth-century newspapers not infrequently ran sensational stories of odd or uncanny incidents, some of them perhaps verifiable, some of them embellished, and others just rumors or inventions. It is difficult to distinguish the more incredible straight newspaper items from fiction, and it is impossible now to ascertain the sources, if any, of the accounts in these two pieces published with the same title on successive Sundays. As AB was fond of composing tales about the supernatural, he was capable of having made up or altered all or any of these narratives.

1. Xenia is the seat of Greene County in southwestern Ohio.
2. Chapultepec is a hill outside Mexico City, upon which a castle built in the eighteenth century resides. U.S. forces captured the castle on 13 September 1847, signaling the end of the Mexican War.
3. The Parsees are the followers of Zoroaster in India; they still maintain a substantial presence in Bombay, where they settled in 1640. They do not bury their dead, but expose the corpses on the rooftops of towers to scavenging birds. Once a year the Parsees hold a festival in honor of Farvardin, the god who presides over the souls of the dead. The people congregate at the "towers of silence" on hilltops, and priests pray for the deceased souls.

Cf. AB's early series of fables, "The Fables of Zambri, the Parsee" (*F,* 13 July 1872–8 Mar. 1873; repr. *CES* and *CF*).

4. See "Killed at Resaca," p. 507 note 2.

5. Whitesburg is the seat of Letcher County in southeastern Kentucky. AB may have passed through this region during his Civil War service in Virginia and West Virginia.

BODIES OF THE DEAD [II]

ADDITIONAL INSTANCES OF PHYSICAL ACTIVITY AFTER DEATH.

REFLEX ACTION, QUOTH'A

The Dead Child's Ball—A Turner—How Dr. Spier Subdued a Corpse.

In my article under the same heading as this, in last Sunday's EXAMINER, I related, "for what they were worth," two instances, one of the mysterious disappearance, and one the equally mysterious apparition, of a human dead body. Both were from my rather voluminous memoranda on such matters, and it seems almost needless to say that I not only do not vouch for the truth of them, but do not myself believe them. All I did was to present such evidences as had accompanied them into my reading.

That the bodies of the dead, even a long time after the moment of death, do perform actions which have all the appearance of volition, the other and more authentic occurrences related in the same article sufficiently show, without the concurrent testimony of physicians as to instances familiar to every student of medical literature. Physicians, it is true, assure us that in these movements the element of volition does not enter; and they have given to this muscular movement the name of "reflex action"; and this, apparently, we are expected to accept as a perfectly lucid explanation of a phenomenon which without the name would be obscure. Enlightened by the term "reflex action," it must be a discontented and exacting curiosity that would not rest and be thankful. My present purpose is neither inquisitive nor controversial: I wish only to present in a simple, straightforth way a few more instances from my notebook. Science, I suppose, is able to take care of itself.

On the 2d day of May, 1873, the little daughter of James Craven, a linen-draper of Bath, England,[1] died of membranous croup, and was buried in a cemetery a mile or two from the town—the same cemetery, by the way, which contains the ashes of "tower-building Beckford," the author of *Vathek*.[2] When the child's body was put into the casket the hands were crossed upon the breast and tied with a white ribbon. Just before the lid was screwed down a little brother of the deceased came forward with her doll and asked permission to place it in the casket; and this was done, the doll lying upon the breast and left arm of the body. Some weeks after the burial Craven sold out his business and removed with his family to Bristol. The body of the child was exhumed for conveyance to that city, and for some reason the casket was opened in the presence of the father and three or four others. The ribbon confining the hands was found broken, the right hand was clasping the doll, which lay diagonally, pressed against the throat. Excepting a slight displacement of the left hand and forearm, caused by the strain upon the ribbon, no other movement had been made—not even a turning of the head. The face showed nothing but the peaceful tranquillity of death.

John Hoskin, living on Mission street, in this city, had a beautiful wife, to whom he was devotedly attached. In the spring of 1871 Mrs. Hoskin went East to visit her relations in Springfield, Illinois, where a week after her arrival she suddenly died of some disease of the heart; at least the physician said so. Mr. Hoskin was at once apprised of his loss, by telegraph, and requested that the body be sent to San Francisco. On arrival here the metallic case containing the remains was opened. The body was lying on the right side, the right hand under the cheek, the other on the breast. The posture was the perfectly natural one of a sleeping child, and in a letter to the deceased lady's father, Mr. Martin L. Whitney of Springfield, Mr. Hoskin expressed a grateful sense of the thoughtfulness that had so composed the remains as to soften the suggestion of death. To his surprise he learned from the father that nothing of the kind had been done: the body had been put in the casket in the customary way, lying on the back, with the arms extended along the sides. In the mean time the casket had been deposited in the receiving-vault at Laurel Hill cemetery,[3] pending the completion of a tomb. Greatly disquieted by this revelation, Mr. Hoskin did not at once reflect that the easy and natural posture and placid expression precluded the idea of suspended animation, subsequent revival and eventual death by suffocation. He insisted that his wife had been murdered by medical incompetency and heedless haste. Under the influence of this feeling he wrote to Mr. Whitney again, expressing in passionate terms his horror and renewed grief. Some days afterward, someone having suggested that the casket had been opened *en route,* probably in the hope of plunder, and pointing out the impossibility of the change having occurred in the straitened space of the confining metal, it was resolved to reopen the casket to ascertain if this latter consideration were decisive. Removal of the lid disclosed a new horror: the body now lay upon its *left* side. The position was cramped, and to a living person would have been uncomfortable. The face wore an expression of pain. Some costly rings on the fingers were still undisturbed. Overcome by his emotions, to which was now added a sharp, if mistaken, remorse, Mr. Hoskin lost his reason, dying years afterward in the asylum at Stockton.[4]

A physician having been summoned to assist in clearing up the mystery, viewed the body of the deceased lady, pronounced life obviously extinct and ordered the casket closed for the third and last time. "Obviously extinct," indeed: the corpse had, in fact, been embalmed at Springfield.

At Hawley's Bar, a mining camp near Virginia City, Montana,[5] a gambler named Henry Graham, but commonly known as "Gray Hank," met a miner named Dreyfuss one day, with whom he had had a dispute the previous night about a pack of cards, and asked him into a barroom to have a drink. The unfortunate miner, taking this as an overture of peace, gladly accepted. They stood at the counter, and while Dreyfuss was in the act of drinking Graham shot him dead. This was in 1865. Within an hour after the murder Graham was in the hands of the vigilantes, and that evening at sunset, after a fair, if informal, trial, he was hanged to the limb of a tree which grew upon a little eminence within sight of the whole camp. The original intention had been to "string him up," as is customary in such affairs; and with a view to that operation the long rope had been thrown over the limb, while a dozen pairs of hands were ready to hoist away. For some reason this plan was abandoned, the rope was given a single turn about the limb at a suitable distance from the noose, the free end made fast to a bush and the victim compelled to stand on the back of a horse, which at the cut of a whip sprang from under him, leaving him swinging. When steadied, his feet were about eighteen inches from the earth.

The body remained suspended for exactly half an hour, the greater part of the crowd remaining about it: then the "Judge" ordered it taken down. The rope was untied from the bush and two men stood by to lower away. The moment the feet came squarely upon the ground the men engaged in lowering, thinking doubtless that those standing about the body had hold of it to support it, let go the rope. The body at once ran quickly forward toward the main part of the crowd, the rope paying out as it went. The head rolled from side to side, the eyes and tongue protruding, the face ghastly purple, the lips covered with bloody froth. With cries of horror the crowd ran hither and thither, stumbling, falling over one another, cursing. In and out among them—over the fallen, coming into collision with others, the horrible dead man "pranced," his feet lifted so high at each step that his knees struck his breast, his tongue swinging like that of a panting dog, the foam flying in flakes from his swollen lips. The deepening twilight added its terror to this uncanny scene and brave men fled from the spot, not daring to look behind.

Straight into this confusion from the outskirts of the crowd walked with rapid steps the tall figure of a man whom all who saw instantly recognized as a master spirit. This was Dr. Arnold Spier, who with two other physicians had pronounced the man dead and had been retiring to the camp. He moved as directly toward the dead man as the now somewhat less rapid and erratic movements of the latter would permit and seized him in his arms. Encouraged by this a score of men sprang shouting to the free end of the rope, which had not been drawn entirely over the limb, and laid hold of it, intending to make a finish of their work. They ran with it toward the bush to which it had been fastened, but there was no resistance: the physician had cut it from the dead murderer's neck. In a moment the body was lying on its back, with composed limbs and face upturned to the kindling stars, in the motionless rigidity of death. The hanging had been done well enough: the neck had been broken by the drop. Dr. Spier knew that a corpse which, placed upon its feet, would walk and run, would lie still when placed upon its back. The dead are creatures of habit.

E (29 Apr. 1888): 9 (as by "A. G. B."). Reprinted in "Bodies of the Dead," *CSTB* 296–97 (as "A Light Sleeper"), 306–8 (as "A Creature of Habit").

NOTES

1. AB visited Bath on several occasions during his English stay of 1872–75. See "The Early History of Bath" (p. 158).
2. William Beckford (1760–1844) was the author of the mock *Arabian Nights* tale, *The History of the Caliph Vathek* (1786). Beckford, the wealthiest man in England in his day, was known as the Caliph (and also the Fool) of Fonthill, his exotically appointed six-thousand-acre estate in Wilshire. One architectural feature of the so-called Fonthill Abbey, a great neo-Gothic house designed by James Wyatt, was Lansdown Tower, or "Beckford's Tower," as it is known today.
3. See "'The Bubble Reputation,'" p. 452 note 2.
4. See "The Man out of the Nose," p. 518 note 4.
5. This Virginia City is a town in Madison County in southwestern Montana; another, more famous one is in Nevada. AB was in Virginia City, Montana, in 1866–67 during his exploration of the Indian Territory with Gen. William B. Hazen (see *SS* 80).

SONS OF THE FAIR STAR

AN INVOLUNTARY FLIGHT TO ANOTHER AND A BITTER WORLD.

GOLAMPIAN TRAITS.

A COUNTRY WHOSE PEOPLE EXPERIENCE THE DISASTERS OF CONSISTENCY.

"You are a liar!"

These are the last words that I remember to have spoken on that occasion. When consciousness returned the sun was high in the heavens, yet the light was dim and had that indefinable ghastly quality that is observed during a partial eclipse. The sun itself appeared singularly small, as if it were at an immensely greater distance than usual. Rising with some difficulty to my feet I looked about me. I was in an open space among some trees growing on the slope of a mountain range whose summit on the one hand was obscured by a mist of a strange pinkish hue and on the other rose into peaks glittering with snow. Skirting the base at a distance of two or three miles flowed a wide river, and beyond it a nearly level plain stretched away to the horizon dotted with villages and farm-houses and apparently in a high state of cultivation. All was unfamiliar in its every aspect. The trees were unlike any that I had ever seen or even imagined, the trunks being mostly square and the foliage consisting of long filaments resembling hair, in many instances long enough to reach the earth. It was of various colors, and I could not perceive that there was any prevailing one like green in the vegetation to which I was accustomed. So far as I could see there was no grass, weeds nor flowers—

the earth was covered with a kind of lichen, uniformly blue. Instead of rocks, great masses of various metals protruded here and there, and above me on the mountain were high cliffs of what seemed to be brass veined with bronze. No animals were visible, but a few birds of as uncommon appearance as their surroundings glided through the air or perched upon the rocks. I say glided, for their motion was not true flight, their wings being mere membranes extended parallel to their sides and having no movement independent of the body. The bird was, so to say, suspended between them and moved forward by quick strokes of a pair of enormously large webbed feet, precisely as a duck propels itself in water. All these things excited in me no surprise nor even curiosity; they were merely unfamiliar. That which most interested me was what appeared to be a bridge several miles away, up the river, and toward this I directed my steps, hoping to cross over from the barren and desolate hills to the populous plain.

For a full history of my life and adventures in Doosno-Zwair,[1] and a detailed description of the country, its people, their manners and customs, I must ask the reader to await the publication of my book now in the press, entitled "A Black Eye"; in this article I can give only a few of such particulars as seem instructive by contrast with our own civilization.

The inhabitants of Doosno-Zwair call themselves Golampis, a word signifying Sons of the Fair Star. Physically they closely resemble ourselves, being in all respects the equals of the highest Caucasian type. Their hair, however, has a broader scheme of color, hair of any hue known to us, and even of some hues imperceptible to my eyes but brilliant to theirs, being too common to excite remark. A Golampian assemblage with uncovered heads resembles, indeed, a garden of flowers, vivid and deep in color, but no two alike. They wear no clothing of any kind, excepting as protection from the weather, resembling in this the ancient Greeks and the modern Japanese; nor was I ever able to make them comprehend that clothing could be worn for those reasons for which it is chiefly worn among ourselves. They are simply destitute of those feelings of delicacy and refinement which distinguish us from the lower animals and which, in the opinion of our foremost and most pious thinkers, is an evidence of our close alliance to the Power that made us.

Among this people certain ideas, which are current among ourselves as mere barren faiths expressed in purposeless platitudes, receive a practical application in the affairs of life. For example, they hold, with the best, wisest and most experienced of our own race, that wealth does not bring happiness and is a misfortune and an evil. None but the most ignorant and depraved, therefore, take the trouble to acquire or preserve it. A rich Golampi is naturally regarded with contempt and suspicion, is shunned by the good and respectable and subjected to police surveillance. Accustomed to a world where the rich man is profoundly and justly respected for his goodness and wisdom (manifested in part by his own deprecatory protests against the wealth of which, nevertheless, he is apparently unable to rid himself), I was at first greatly pained to observe the contumelious manner of the Golampis toward this class of men, carried in some instances to the length of personal violence; a popular amusement being the pelting them with coins. These the victims would carefully gather from the ground and carry away with them, thus increasing their hoard and rendering themselves all the more liable to popular indignities. When the cultivated and intelligent Golampi finds himself growing too wealthy, he proceeds to get rid of his surplus riches by some one of many easy expedients. One of these I have just described; another is to give his excess to those of his own class who have not sufficient to live upon in comfort; for poverty too is regarded as an evil, chiefly because it entails leisure, which is considered the greatest misfortune of all. "Idleness," says one of their famous authors, "is the child of poverty and the parent of discontent"; and another great writer says: "No one is without employment; the indolent man works for the enemy of his soul." It is interesting to compare this aphorism with our own popular but disregarded proverb: "The devil finds some mischief still for idle hands to do."[2]

In conformity to these ideas, the Golampis—all but the ignorant and vicious rich—look upon labor as the highest good, and the man who is so unfortunate as not to have sufficient money to purchase employment in some useful industry will rather engage in a useless one than not labor at all. It is not unusual to see hundreds of men carrying water from a river and pouring it into a natural ravine or artificial channel, through which it runs back into the stream. Frequently a man is seen conveying stones—or the masses of metal which there correspond to stones—from one pile to another. When all have been heaped in a single place he will convey them back again, or to a new place, and so proceed until darkness puts an end to the work. This kind of labor, however, does not confer the satisfaction derived from the consciousness of being useful, and is never performed by any person having the means to hire another to employ him in some beneficial industry. The wages usually paid to employers are from three to six *balukan* a day. This statement may seem incredible, but I solemnly assure the reader that I have known a bad workman or a feeble woman to pay as high as eight; and there have been instances of men whose incomes had outgrown their desires, paying even more.

Labor being a luxury which only those in easy circumstances can afford, the poor are only the more eager for it, not only because it is denied them, but because it is a sign of respectability. Many of them, therefore, indulge in it on credit and soon find themselves deprived of what little property they had, to satisfy their hardfisted employers. A poor woman once complained to me that her husband spent every *rylat* that he could get in the purchase of the most expensive kinds of employment, while she and the children were compelled to content themselves with such cheap and coarse activity as dragging an old wagon round and round in a small field which a kind-hearted neighbor permitted them to use for the purpose. I afterward saw this improvident husband and unnatural father. He had just squandered all the money he had been able to beg or borrow in purchasing seven tickets, which entitled the holder to that many days' employment pitching hay into a barn. A week later I met him again. He was broken in health, his limbs trembled, his walk was an uncertain shuffle. Clearly he was suffering from excessive exertion. As I paused by the wayside to speak to him a wagon loaded with hay was passing. He fixed his eyes upon it with a hungry, wolfish look, clutched his pitchfork and leaned eagerly forward, watching the vanishing wagon with breathless attention and heedless of my salutation. That night he was arrested, streaming with perspiration, in the unlawful act of unloading that hay and putting it in its owner's barn. He was tried, convicted and sentenced to six months' detention in the House of Indolence.

The whole country in which I found myself (the name Doosno-Zwair seems to have an enormously wide application, far beyond the scope of my observation) is infested by a class of criminal vagrants known as *strambaltis,* or, as we should say, "tramps." These persons prowl about among the farms and villages begging for work in the name of charity. Sometimes they travel in groups, as many as a dozen together, and then the farmers dare not refuse them, and before he can notify the constabulary they will have performed a great deal of the most useful labor that they can find to do and escaped without paying a *rylat.* One trustworthy agriculturist assured me that his losses in one year from these depredations amounted to no less a sum than 700 *balukan.* On nearly all the larger and more isolated farms a strong force of guards is maintained during the greater part of the year to prevent these outrages, but they are frequently overpowered, and sometimes prove unfaithful to their trust by themselves performing labor secretly by night.

The Golampi priesthood has always denounced overwork as a deadly sin, and declared useless and apparently harmless work, such as carrying water from the river and letting it flow in again, a distinct violation of the Divine law, in which, however, I could never find any reference to it: but there has recently arisen a sect which holds that all labor being pleasurable, each kind in its degree is immoral and wicked. This sect, which embraces many of the most holy and learned men, is rapidly spreading and becoming a power in the State. It has, of course, no churches, for these cannot be built without labor, and its members commonly dwell in caves and live upon such roots and berries as can be easily gathered, of which the country produces a great abundance, though all are exceedingly unpalatable. These *Gropoppsu* (as the members of this communion call themselves) pass most of their waking hours sitting in the sunshine with folded hands, contemplating their navels; by the practice of which austerity they hope to obtain, as reward, an eternity of hard labor after death.

The Golampians are an essentially pious and religious race. There are few, indeed, who do not profess one or more religions. They are nearly all, in a certain sense, polytheists: they worship a supreme and beneficent deity by one name or another, but all believe in the existence of a subordinate and malevolent one, whom also, while solemnly execrating him in public rites, they hold at heart in such reverence that needlessly to mention his name or that of his dwelling is considered a sin of hardly inferior rank to blasphemy. I am persuaded that this singular tenderness toward a being whom their theology represents as an abominable monster, the origin of all evil and the foe to souls, is a survival of an ancient propitiatory adoration. Doubtless this wicked deity was once so feared that his placation was one of the serious concerns of life. He is probably as greatly feared now as at any former time, but he is apparently less hated, and is by some honestly admired.

It is interesting to observe the important place held in Golampian affairs by religious persecution. The Government is a pure theocracy, all the Ministers of State and the principal functionaries in every department of control belonging to the priesthood of the dominant church. It is popularly believed in Doosno-Zwair that persecution, even to the extent of death, is in the long run beneficial to the cause enduring it. This belief has, indeed, been crystallized into a popular proverb, not capable of accurate translation into our tongue, but to the effect that martyrs fertilize religion by pouring out their blood about its roots. Acting upon this belief with their characteristically logical and conscientious directness, the sacerdotal rulers of the country mercilessly afflict the sect to which themselves belong. They arrest its leading members on false charges, throw them into loathsome and unwholesome dungeons, subject them to the cruelest tortures and frequently put them to death. The provinces in which the State religion is especially strong are occasionally raided and pillaged by Government soldiery, enlisted for the purpose among the dissenting sects, and are sometimes actually devastated with fire and sword. The result is not altogether confirmatory of the popular belief and does not fulfill the pious hope of the governing powers, who are cruel to be kind. The vitalizing efficacy of persecution is not to be doubted, but the persecuted of too feeble faith frequently thwart its beneficent intent and happy operation by acts of apostasy.

Having in mind the horrible torments which a Golampian General had inflicted upon the population of a certain town I once ventured to protest to him that so dreadful a sum of suffering, seeing that it did not accomplish its purpose, was needless and unwise.

"Needless and unwise it may be," said he, "and I am disposed to admit that the result which I expected from it has not followed; but why do you speak of the *sum* of suffering? I tortured those people in but a single, simple way—by skinning their legs."

"Ah, that is very true," said I, "but you skinned the legs of one thousand."

"And what of that?" he asked. "Can one thousand, or ten thousand, or any number of people suffer more agony than one? A man may have his leg broken, then his nails pulled out, then be seared with a hot iron. Here is suffering added to suffering, and the effect is really cumulative. In the true mathematical sense it is a *sum* of suffering. A single person can experience it. But consider, my dear sir. How can you add one man's agony to that of another? They are not addable quantities. Each is an individual pain, unaffected by the other. The limit of anguish which ingenuity can inflict is that utmost pang which one man has the capacity to endure."

SONS OF THE FAIR STAR

I was convinced but not silenced.

The Golampis believe, singularly enough, that truth possesses some inherent vitality and power that gives it an assured prevalence over falsehood; that a good name cannot be permanently defiled and irreparably ruined by detraction, but, like a star, shines all the brighter for the shadow through which it is seen; that justice cannot be stayed by injustice; that vice is powerless against virtue. I could quote from their great writers hundreds of utterances affirmative of these propositions. One of their poets, for example, has some striking lines, of which the following is a literal but unmetrical translation:

> Truth when flattened out will become again vertical;
> She owns God's everlasting years;
> But a hurt mistake twists in discomfort,
> And its adorers see it breathe its last.

Another, whom their critics esteem the greatest poet who ever lived, writes:

> A man who is in the right has three arms,
> But he whose conscience is rotten with wrong
> Is stripped and confined in a metal cell.

Imbued with these beliefs the Golampis think it hardly worth while to be truthful, to abstain from slander, to do justice and to avoid vicious actions. "The practice," they say, "of deceit, calumniation, oppression and immorality cannot have any sensible and lasting injurious effect, and it is most agreeable to the mind and heart. Why should there be personal self-denial without commensurate general advantage?"

In consequence of these false views, affirmed by those whom they regard as great and wise, the people of Doosno-Zwair are, so far as I have observed them, the most conscienceless liars, cheats, thieves, rakes and all-round, many-sided rascals that God ever made! In attentive contemplation of their incomparable unworth I one day fell asleep. When I awoke I found myself lying in a narrow bed, one of a long row of similar ones. A man in the dress of a hospital attendant was in the act of adjusting a raw beefsteak upon one of my eyes.

"Where am I?" I feebly asked.

"In the hospital of the City Prison," he replied, moving away.

"See here," I said, tapping with my forefinger the beefsteak that lay athwart my eye, "if you leave me some other d—— Golampi will steal this viand off and eat it."

"What is a Golampi?" he inquired with composure.

E (**10 June 1888): 11.** Incorporated into "The Land Beyond the Blow."

NOTES

AB placed a high value on close reasoning but he realized, as this witty narrative demonstrates, that logic could serve any system of thought or values, even those which stand on their heads propositions which our culture considers normal. If work is good, for example, why should not people pay to do it? And if truth inevitably triumphs over falsehood, then cannot deceit and slander be safely indulged in without fear of their being victorious? AB's purpose was to expose the potential dangers of believing in simplistic slogans and proverbs and to show how reasonable-sounding arguments could be devised and twisted to support ludicrous ideas.

1. AB had first coined this name (as Doo-sno-swair) in a fable in "The Fables of Zambri, the Parsee" (1872–73; see *CF*, no. 74). He then used it in several fables in *Fantastic Fables* (1899); see, e.g., *CF*, no. 166 (this fable was first published in *E*, 15 Apr. 1893).

2. "In Works of Labour or of Skill I would be busy too; For Satan finds some mischief for idle Hands to do." Isaac Watts, *Divine Songs for Children* (1715).

SONS OF THE FAIR STAR

HITHER FROM HADES

Do "Millions of Spiritual Creatures Walk the Earth"?

THE NIGHT-FOLK ABROAD

Three Old-Fashioned Ghost Stories from the Note-Book of a Collector.

In the month of July, 1871, near Galesburg, Ill., a farmer named John Harold Wilson was returning home from the harvest-field. He had been unable to procure enough assistance to harvest his grain as fast as it ripened, so he had worked as long as he could see in the evening, and as he made his way to his dwelling it was almost dark. As he was passing through an avenue of trees, the foliage obscuring such faint light as still lingered in the west, he met another man.

"Good evening," said Mr. Wilson, civilly. He supposed the man to be some neighbor, but rural etiquette demanded the salutation, in any case. The person addressed said nothing, but stopped in the middle of the lane, as if to hold a conversation. Mr. Wilson stopped also. They stood thus, not two paces apart, for some moments. Mr. Wilson endeavoring to recognize his *vis-à-vis* in the gloom. Suddenly the figure of the latter was illuminated from head to foot by an intense red light, and at the same moment Wilson heard the words, "Help! Help!" They did not seem to come from the person before him, but faintly, from a great distance, and he recognized the voice as that of his son Joseph, living in Galesburg, whom also he now saw in the person confronting him. At the moment of recognition the cries ceased and the figure disappeared in darkness.

Inexpressibly astonished and alarmed, Mr. Wilson proceeded to his dwelling, where the first person that he saw was his son, sitting comfortably at supper with his mother. He had been in the house for two hours. On being told the adventure he protested that it was an illusion, caused by overwork; and his father finally took that view of it himself.

Five years later the ship *Sparrowhawk,* from New York to Buenos Ayres, was burned at sea, and the younger Wilson lost his life. The disaster occurred on the afternoon of the same day of the year as that on which the father had seen the vision, and as the ship's last overloaded boat pulled away from the blazing wreck in the early evening the survivors whom it contained saw Joseph Wilson standing on the deck in the glare of flames, and heard but could not heed his cries for help.

An old man named Daniel Baker, living near Lebanon, Missouri, was suspected by his neighbors of having murdered a peddler who had obtained permission to pass the night at his house. This was in 1853, when the peddler's vocation in the Western States was more common than it is now, and was attended with considerable danger. The peddler with his pack traversed the country by all manner of lonely roads, and was compelled to rely upon the country people for hospitality, which brought him into relation with queer characters, some of whom were not altogether scrupulous in their methods of making a living, murder being an acceptable means to that end. It occasionally occurred that a peddler with diminished pack and swollen purse would be traced to the lonely dwelling of some rough character and never could be traced beyond. This was so in the case of "old man Baker," as he was always called. (Such names are given in the Western "settlements" only to people who are not esteemed; where possible, to the general disrepute of social unworth is affixed the special reproach of age.) A peddler came to his house and none went away—that is all that anybody knew.

Seven years later the Rev. Mr. Cummings, a Baptist minister well known in that part of the country, was driving by Baker's farm one night. It was not very dark: there was a bit of moon somewhere above the light veil of mist that hung above the earth. Mr. Cummings, who was at all times a cheerful person, was whistling a tune, which he would occasionally interrupt to speak a word of friendly encouragement to his horse. As he came to a little bridge across a dry ravine he saw the figure of a man standing upon it, clearly outlined against the gray background of a misty forest. The man had something strapped on his back and carried a heavy stick—obviously an itinerant peddler. His attitude had in it a suggestion of abstraction, like that of a sleepwalker. Mr. Cummings reined in his horse when he arrived in front of him, gave him a pleasant salutation and invited him to a seat in the buggy—"if you are going my way," he added. The man raised his head, looked him full in the face, but neither

HITHER FROM HADES

answered nor made any further movement. The minister, with good-natured persistence, repeated his invitation. At this the man threw his right hand forward from his side and pointed to his feet as he stood on the extreme edge of the bridge. Mr. Cummings looked past him, over into the ravine, saw nothing unusual and withdrew his eyes to address the man again. He had disappeared. The horse, which all this time had been uncommonly restive, gave at the same moment a snort of terror and started to run away. Before he had regained control of the animal the minister was at the crest of a hill a hundred yards along. He looked back and saw the figure again, at the same place and in the same attitude as when he had first observed it. Then for the first time he was conscious of a sense of the supernatural and drove home as rapidly as his willing horse would go.

On arriving at home he related his adventure to his family, and early the next morning, accompanied by two neighbors, John White Corwell and Abner Raiser, returned to the spot. They found the body of old man Baker hanging by the neck from one of the beams of the bridge, immediately beneath the spot where the apparition had stood. A thick coating of dust, slightly dampened by the mist, covered the planks; there was not a footprint anywhere to be seen.

In taking down the body the men disturbed the loose, friable earth of the slope below it, disclosing human bones already nearly uncovered by the action of water and frost. They were identified as those of the lost peddler. At the double inquest the Coroner's jury found that Daniel Baker died by his own hand while suffering from temporary insanity, and that Samuel Morritz was murdered by some person or persons to the jury unknown.

Henry Saylor, who was killed last month in Covington, Kentucky,[1] in a quarrel with Antonio Finch, was a reporter on the Cincinnati *Commercial.*[2] In the year 1859 a vacant dwelling in Vine street, in Cincinnati, became the center of a local excitement because of the strange sights and sounds said to be observed in it nightly. According to the testimony of many reputable residents of the vicinity these were inconsistent with any other hypothesis than that the house was haunted. Figures with something singularly unfamiliar about them were seen by crowds on the sidewalk to pass in and out. No one could say just where they appeared upon the open lawn on their way to the front door by which they entered, nor at exactly what point they vanished as they came out; or, rather, while each spectator was positive enough about these matters, no two agreed. They were all similarly at variance in the descriptions of the figures themselves. Some of the bolder of the curious throng ventured on several evenings to stand upon the doorsteps to intercept the ghostly visitors or get a nearer look at them. These courageous men, it was said, were unable to force the door by their united strength, and invariably were hurled from the steps by some invisible agency and severely injured; the door immediately afterward opening, apparently of its own motion, to admit or free some ghostly guest. The dwelling was known as the Roscoe house, a family of that name having lived there for some years, and then, one by one, disappeared, the last to leave being an old woman. Stories of foul play and successive murders had always been rife but never authenticated.

One day during the prevalence of the excitement Saylor presented himself at the office of the *Commercial* for orders. He was handed a note from the city editor which read as follows: "Go and pass the night alone in the haunted house in Vine street and make two columns if anything occurs worth while." Saylor obeyed his superior; he could not afford to lose his position on the paper.

Apprising the police of his intention he effected an entrance through a rear window before dark, walked through the deserted rooms, bare of furniture, dusty and desolate, and with feelings which it is perhaps needless to describe seated himself at last in the parlor on an old sofa which he had dragged in from another room, and watched the deepening of the gloom as night came on. Before it was altogether dark the curious crowd had collected in the street, silent, as a rule, and expectant, with here and there a scoffer uttering his incredulity and courage with scornful remarks or ribald cries. None knew of the anxious watcher inside. He feared to make a light: the uncurtained windows would have betrayed his presence, subjecting him to insult, possibly to injury. Moreover, he was too conscientious to do anything to enfeeble his impressions and unwilling to alter any of the customary conditions under which the manifestations were said to occur.

It was now quite dark, but the lights from the street faintly illuminated a part of the room that he was in. He had set open every door in the whole interior, above and below, but all the outer ones were locked and bolted. Sudden exclamations from the crowd caused him to spring to a window and look out. He saw the figure of a man moving rapidly across the lawn toward the building—saw it ascend the steps; then a projection of the wall concealed it. There was a noise as of the opening and closing of the hall door; he heard quick heavy footsteps along the passage—heard them ascend the stairs—heard them on the uncarpeted floor of the chamber immediately overhead. Saylor drew his pistol and groped his way up the stairs, entered the chamber, dimly lighted from the street. There was no one there. He heard footsteps in an adjoining room and entered that. It was black-dark and silent. He struck his foot against some object on the floor, knelt by it and passed his hand over it. It was a human head—that of a woman. Lifting it by the hair, this iron-nerved man returned to the half-lighted room below, carried it to near the window and attentively examined it. While so engaged he was half conscious of the rapid opening and closing of the outer door, of footfalls sounding all about him. He raised his eyes from the ghastly object of his attention and saw himself the center of a crowd of men and women dimly seen; the room was thronged with them. He thought the people had broken in. "Ladies and gentlemen," he said, coolly, "you see me under suspicious circumstances, but——." His voice was drowned in peals of laughter—such laughter as is heard in

HITHER FROM HADES

asylums for the insane. The people about him pointed at the object in his hand and their merriment increased as he dropped it and it went rolling among their feet. They danced about it with gestures grotesque and attitudes obscene and indescribable. They struck it with their feet, urging it about the room from wall to wall: pushed and overthrew one another in their struggles to kick it; cursed and serenaded and sang snatches of ribald songs as the battered head bounded about the room as if in terror and trying to escape. At last it shot out of the door into the hall, followed by them all with tumultuous haste. That moment the door closed with a sharp concussion. Mr. Saylor was alone, in dead silence. Carefully replacing his pistol, which all the time he had held in his hand, he went to the windows and looked out. The street was deserted and silent; the lamps were extinguished; the roofs and chimneys of the houses were sharply outlined against the dawn-light in the east. He left the house, the door yielding easily to his hand, and walked to the *Commercial* office. The city editor was still in his office—asleep. Saylor waked him and said, quietly: "I passed the night in the haunted house."

The editor stared blankly as if not wholly awake. "Good God!" he cried, "are you Saylor?"

"Yes—why not?"

The editor made no answer; the reporter's face was seamed with lines like those of age; his hair and beard were snow-white.

"They say that things were uncommonly quiet out there," the editor said, trifling with a paper-weight upon which he kept his eyes, "did anything occur?"

"Nothing whatever."

E (24 June 1888): 11 (as by "A. B."). Reprinted (in part) in *Current Literature* 2, no. 6 (June 1889): 512; 3, no. 1 (July 1889): 60 (as "'An Assignment'"). Reprinted as "A Fruitless Assignment" (*CSTB* 280–84; *CW* 3.377–82) and "Present at a Hanging" (*CW* 3.327–30).

NOTES

More supernatural narratives that pit incredulity against the plausibility supplied by verisimilitude.

1. For Covington, Kentucky, see "Jupiter Doke, Brigadier-General," p. 437 note 4.
2. The *Cincinnati Commercial* was published from 1843 to 1883, when it became the *Cincinnati Gazette* (1883–96), then the *Commercial Tribune* (1896–1930).

A SON OF THE GODS

A STUDY IN THE PRESENT TENSE

A breezy day and a sunny landscape. An open country to right and left and forward; behind, a wood. In the edge of this wood, facing the open but not venturing into it, long lines of troops, halted. The wood is alive with them, and full of confused noises—the occasional rattle of wheels as a battery of artillery goes into position to cover the advance; the hum and murmur of the soldiers talking; a sound of innumerable feet in the dry leaves that strew the interspaces among the trees; hoarse commands of officers. Detached groups of horsemen are well in front—not altogether exposed—many of them intently regarding the crest of a hill a mile away in the direction of the interrupted advance. For this powerful army, moving in battle order through a forest, has met with a formidable obstacle—the open country. The crest of that gentle hill a mile away has a sinister look; it says, Beware! Along it runs a stone wall extending to left and right a great distance. Behind the wall is a hedge; behind the hedge are seen the tops of trees in rather straggling order. Among the trees— what? It is necessary to know.

Yesterday, and for many days and nights previously, we were fighting somewhere; always there was cannonading, with occasional keen rattlings of musketry, mingled with cheers, our own or the enemy's, we seldom knew, attesting some temporary advantage. This morning at daybreak the enemy was gone. We have moved forward across his earthworks, across which we have so often vainly attempted to move before, through the débris of his abandoned camps, among the graves of his fallen, into the woods beyond.

How curiously we had regarded everything! how odd it all had seemed! Nothing had appeared quite familiar; the most commonplace objects—an old saddle, a splintered wheel, a forgotten canteen—everything had related something of the mysterious personality of those strange men who had been killing us. The soldier never becomes wholly familiar with the conception of his foes as men like himself; he cannot divest himself of the feeling that they are another order of beings, differently conditioned, in an environment not altogether of the earth. The smallest vestiges of them rivet his attention and engage his interest. He thinks of them as inaccessible; and, catching an unexpected glimpse of them, they appear farther away, and therefore larger, than they really are—like objects in a fog. He is somewhat in awe of them.

From the edge of the wood leading up the acclivity are the tracks of horses and wheels—the wheels of cannon. The yellow grass is beaten down by the feet of infantry. Clearly they have passed this way in thousands; they have not withdrawn by the country roads. This is significant—it is the difference between retiring and retreating.

That group of horsemen is our commander, his staff and escort. He is facing the distant crest, holding his field-glass against his eyes with both hands, his elbows needlessly elevated. It is a fashion; it seems to dignify the act; we are all addicted to it. Suddenly he lowers the glass and says a few words to those about him. Two or three aides detach themselves from the group and canter away into the woods, along the lines in each direction. We did not hear his words, but we know them: "Tell General X. to send forward the skirmish line." Those of us who have been out of place resume our positions; the men resting at ease straighten themselves and the ranks are re-formed without a command. Some of us staff officers dismount and look at our saddle girths; those already on the ground remount.

Galloping rapidly along in the edge of the open ground comes a young officer on a snow-white horse. His saddle blanket is scarlet. What a fool! No one who has ever been in action but remembers how naturally every rifle turns toward the man on a white horse; no one but has observed how a bit of red enrages the bull of battle. That such colors are fashionable in military life must be accepted as the most astonishing of all the phenomena of human vanity. They would seem to have been devised to increase the death-rate.

This young officer is in full uniform, as if on parade. He is all agleam with bullion—a blue-and-gold edition of the Poetry of War. A wave of derisive laughter runs abreast of him all along the line. But how handsome he is!—with what careless grace he sits his horse!

He reins up within a respectful distance of the corps commander and salutes. The old soldier nods familiarly; he evidently knows him. A brief colloquy between them is going on; the young man seems to be preferring some request which the elder one is indisposed to grant. Let us ride a little nearer. Ah! too late—it is ended. The young officer salutes again, wheels his horse and rides straight toward the crest of the hill!

A thin line of skirmishers, the men deployed at six paces or so apart, now pushes from the wood into the open. The commander speaks to his bugler, who claps his instrument to his lips. *Tra-la-la! Tra-la-la!* The skirmishers halt in their tracks.

A SON OF THE GODS

Meantime the young horseman has advanced a hundred yards. He is riding at a walk, straight up the long slope, with never a turn of the head. How glorious! Gods! what would we not give to be in his place—with his soul! He does not draw his saber; his right hand hangs easily at his side. The breeze catches the plume in his hat and flutters it smartly. The sunshine rests upon his shoulder-straps, lovingly, like a visible benediction. Straight on he rides. Ten thousand pairs of eyes are fixed upon him with an intensity that he can hardly fail to feel; ten thousand hearts keep quick time to the inaudible hoof-beats of his snowy steed. He is not alone—he draws all souls after him. But we remember that we laughed! On and on, straight for the hedge-lined wall, he rides. Not a look backward. O, if he would but turn—if he could but see the love, the adoration, the atonement!

Not a word is spoken; the populous depths of the forest still murmur with their unseen and unseeing swarm, but all along the fringe is silence. The burly commander is an equestrian statue of himself. The mounted staff officers, their field glasses up, are motionless all. The line of battle in the edge of the wood stands at a new kind of "attention," each man in the attitude in which he was caught by the consciousness of what is going on. All these hardened and impenitent man-killers, to whom death in its awfulest forms is a fact familiar to their every-day observation; who sleep on hills trembling with the thunder of great guns, dine in the midst of streaming missiles, and play at cards among the dead faces of their dearest friends—all are watching with sus- pended breath and beating hearts the outcome of an act involving the life of one man. Such is the magnetism of courage and devotion.

If now you should turn your head you would see a simultaneous movement among the spectators—a start, as if they had received an electric shock—and looking forward again to the now distant horseman you would see that he has in that instant altered his direction and is riding at an angle to his former course. The spectators sup- pose the sudden deflection to be caused by a shot, perhaps a wound; but take this field- glass and you will observe that he is riding toward a break in the wall and hedge. He means, if not killed, to ride through and overlook the country beyond.

You are not to forget the nature of this man's act; it is not permitted to you to think of it as an instance of bravado, nor, on the other hand, a needless sacrifice of self. If the enemy has not retreated he is in force on that ridge. The investigator will encounter nothing less than a line-of-battle; there is no need of pickets, videttes, skirmishers, to give warning of our approach; our attacking lines will be visible, conspicuous, exposed to an artillery fire that will shave the ground the moment they break from cover, and for half the distance to a sheet of rifle bullets in which nothing can live. In short, if the enemy is there, it would be madness to attack him in front; he must be manœuvred out by the immemorial plan of threatening his line of communication, as necessary to his existence as to the diver at the bottom of the sea his air tube. But how ascertain if the enemy is there? There is but one way,—somebody must go and see. The natural and customary thing is to send forward a line of skirmishers. But in this case they will

A SON OF THE GODS

answer in the affirmative with all their lives; the enemy, crouching in double ranks behind the stone wall and in cover of the hedge, will wait until it is possible to count each assailant's teeth. At the first volley a half of the questioning line will fall, the other half before it can accomplish the predestined retreat. What a price to pay for gratified curiosity! At what a dear rate an army must sometimes purchase knowledge! "Let me pay all," says this gallant man—this military Christ!

There is no hope except the hope against hope that the crest is clear. True, he might prefer capture to death. So long as he advances, the line will not fire—why should it? He can safely ride into the hostile ranks and become a prisoner of war. But this would defeat his object. It would not answer our question; it is necessary either that he return unharmed or be shot to death before our eyes. Only so shall we know how to act. If captured—why, that might have been done by a half-dozen stragglers.

Now begins an extraordinary contest of intellect between a man and an army. Our horseman, now within a quarter of a mile of the crest, suddenly wheels to the left and gallops in a direction parallel to it. He has caught sight of his antagonist; he knows all. Some slight advantage of ground has enabled him to overlook a part of the line. If he were here he could tell us in words. But that is now hopeless; he must make the best use of the few minutes of life remaining to him, by compelling the enemy himself to tell us as much and as plainly as possible—which, naturally, that discreet power is reluctant to do. Not a rifleman in those crouching ranks, not a cannoneer at those masked and shotted guns, but knows the needs of the situation, the imperative duty of forbearance. Besides, there has been time enough to forbid them all to fire. True, a single rifle-shot might drop him and be no great disclosure. But firing is infectious—and see how rapidly he moves, with never a pause except as he whirls his horse about to take a new direction, never directly backward toward us, never directly forward toward his executioners. All this is visible through the glass; it seems occurring within pistol-shot; we see all but the enemy, whose presence, whose thoughts, whose motives we infer. To the unaided eye there is nothing but a black figure on a white horse, tracing slow zigzags against the slope of a distant hill—so slowly they seem almost to creep.

Now—the glass again—he has tired of his failure, or sees his error, or has gone mad; he is dashing directly forward at the wall, as if to take it at a leap, hedge and all! One moment only and he wheels right about and is speeding like the wind straight down the slope—toward his friends, toward his death! Instantly the wall is topped with a fierce roll of smoke for a distance of hundreds of yards to right and left. This is instantly dissipated by the wind, and before the rattle of the rifle reaches us he is down. No, he recovers his seat; he has but pulled his horse upon its haunches. They are up and away! A tremendous cheer bursts from our ranks, relieving the insupportable tension of our feelings. And the horse and its rider? Yes, they are up and away. Away, indeed—they are making directly to our left, parallel to the now steadily blazing and smoking wall. The rattle of the musketry is continuous, and every bullet's target is that courageous heart.

Suddenly a great bank of white smoke pushes upward from behind the wall. Another and another—a dozen roll up before the thunder of the explosions and the humming of the missiles reach our ears and the missiles themselves come bounding through clouds of dust into our covert, knocking over here and there a man and causing a temporary distraction, a passing thought of self.

The dust drifts away. Incredible!—that enchanted horse and rider have passed a ravine and are climbing another slope to unveil another conspiracy of silence, to thwart the will of another armed host. Another moment and that crest too is in eruption. The horse rears and strikes the air with its fore-feet. They are down at last. But look again—the man has detached himself from the dead animal. He stands erect, motionless, holding his saber in his right hand straight above his head. His face is toward us. Now he lowers his hand to a level with his face and moves it outward, the blade of the saber describing a downward curve. It is a sign to us, to the world, to posterity. It is a hero's salute to death and history.

Again the spell is broken; our men attempt to cheer; they are choking with emotion; they utter hoarse, discordant cries; they clutch their weapons and press tumultuously forward into the open. The skirmishers, without orders, against orders, are going forward at a keen run, like hounds unleashed. Our cannon speak and the enemy's now open in full chorus; to right and left as far as we can see, the distant crest, seeming now so near, erects its towers of cloud and the great shot pitch roaring down among our moving passes. Flag after flag of ours emerges from the wood, line after line sweeps forth, catching the sunlight on its burnished arms. The rear battalions alone are in obedience; they preserve their proper distance from the insurgent front.

The commander has not moved. He now removes his field-glass from his eyes and glances to the right and left. He sees the human current flowing on either side of him and his huddled escort, like tide waves parted by a rock. Not a sign of feeling in his face; he is thinking. Again he directs his eyes forward; they slowly traverse that malign and awful crest. He addresses a calm word to his bugler. *Tra-la-la! Tra-la-la!* The injunction has an imperiousness which enforces it. It is repeated by all the bugles of all the subordinate commanders; the sharp metallic notes assert themselves above the hum of the advance and penetrate the sound of the cannon. To halt is to withdraw. The colors move slowly back; the lines face about and sullenly follow, bearing their wounded; the skirmishers return, gathering up the dead.

Ah, those many, many needless dead! That great soul whose beautiful body is lying over yonder, so conspicuous against the sere hillside—could it not have been spared the bitter consciousness of a vain devotion? Would one exception have marred too much the pitiless perfection of the divine, eternal plan?

A SON OF THE GODS

E (29 July 1888): 9 (with subtitle: "A Study in the Historical Present Tense"); *TSC* 55–67; *IML* 49–62; **CW** **2.58–70**. Reprinted in *Anti-Philistine*, no. 3 (15 Aug. 1897): 159–68.

NOTE

One of AB's most well-known stories, it may have its genesis in some true events. In "Prattle" he once recalled an incident in his own life when he "recklessly" exposed himself on horseback in order to draw Confederate fire from a hill Union troops were approaching (*W*, no. 363 [14 July 1883]: 5 [repr. *SS* 62]). Anticlimactically, however, there were no shots; the hill had already been taken. A similar incident is recounted of Union Gen. James A. Garfield, who successfully prevented the destruction of the Army of the Cumberland by galloping up a hill to warn almost-encircled Union troops while being shot at by Confederate riflemen. The account, "Between the Bullets," appeared in the *San Francisco Call* ([26 May 1895]: 24), seven years after "A Son of the Gods" was published. AB obviously made no use of this later piece, but it corroborates the likelihood of some historical basis for the story. For a fuller analysis of the story and the significance of its use of the historical present tense, see *PA* 101–5.

BEHIND THE VEIL

WORK FOR THE SOCIETY OF PSYCHICAL RESEARCH.

ARE THE DEAD DEAD?

Two Studies in the Inexplicable—The Dead Physician—A Lost Night.

Some months ago I published in this paper an account of the sudden death of a young man in Xenia, Ohio,[1] and gave such particulars of the strange and apparently unaccountable disappearance of the body as had been recorded in my notebook, it having been my custom for many years to make memoranda of such matters, as they occurred in my reading or observation. I have not at this moment access to either the issue of the EXAMINER containing the account or the memoranda from which it was written, and my memory has not preserved such details as names and dates. Briefly, the story was this:

A young man suddenly fell dead in the dining-room of his father's house, in the presence of the whole family. The body was disrobed and laid upon a bed in a room which opened out of the dining-room, and had no other door and but one window. On arrival of a physician, hastily summoned, he was shown into the bedroom, where he distinctly saw the profile and outline of the body sharply defined under the face-cloth and sheet with which it had been covered; but on removal of these it was not there, nor was it ever discovered. The window remained locked on the inside, the flower-bed outside was undisturbed, the dining-room had not been for a moment vacant; in short, none of the circumstances of the disappearance was consistent with the hypothesis of fraud.

Apropos of this matter I have received the following communication:

BOSTON (Mass.), July 30, 1888.

A. G. B.—DEAR SIR: My attention has been drawn to an account of the remarkable disappearance of the corpse of a young man in Xenia, Ohio. We shall be grateful if you will kindly tell me what foundation in fact the story possesses.

I mail you herewith circulars of our society, including Blank G. We shall be exceedingly obliged for any assistance which you can give us in obtaining answers to the questions set forth in Blank G, even if only a few answers can be obtained. It will be advisable to add after each name and address the numbers of the particular questions which have been answered in the affirmative. Any further information in my power I shall be glad to supply. Yours sincerely, RICHARD HODGSON.

In the absence of my notes I am unable to comply with Mr. Hodgson's request; if in my published account I did not state the source of my information with as great particularity as I am confident I did all the essentials that it embodied, it was an oversight which I promise myself the pleasure of rectifying later, for the benefit of the Society of Psychical Research.[2] In the mean time the data that I have at hand enable me to supply the society with a few facts which it may perhaps deem worthy of its attention.

Something has recently been said in the newspapers about an agreement once made between the late Stephen Pearl Andrews and the late Courtland Palmer, to the effect that the one dying first should communicate to the other a certain message from the spirit land. This kind of undertaking is not, I think, uncommon; certainly I have myself been a party to it more than once without, as yet, having received, in the character of lamented survivor, any spiritual advantage from it.[3] But is it always so?

In the summer of 1881 I met a man named James H. Conway, a resident of Franklin, Tenn.[4] He was visiting San Francisco for his health, deluded man, and brought me a note of introduction from Mr. Lawrence Barting, whom I had known as a Captain in the Federal army during the civil war, and who had settled in Franklin, and in time became, I had reason to think, somewhat prominent as a physician. Barting had always seemed to me an honorable and truthful man, and the warm friendship which he expressed in his note for Mr. Conway was to me sufficient evidence that the latter was in every way worthy of my confidence and esteem. At dinner one day he told me that it had been solemnly agreed between him and Barting that the one who died first should, if possible, communicate with the other from beyond the grave, in some unmistakable way—just how they had (wisely, it seemed to me) left to be decided by the deceased, according to the opportunities that his altered environment might afford.

BEHIND THE VEIL

A few weeks after the conversation in which Mr. Conway spoke of this agreement, I met him one day, walking slowly down Montgomery street, apparently, from his abstracted air, in deep thought. He greeted me coldly with merely a movement of the head and passed on, leaving me standing on the walk, with half-proffered hand, surprised and naturally somewhat pained. The next day I met him again in the office of the Palace Hotel,[5] and, seeing him about to repeat the disagreeable performance of the day before, I intercepted him in a doorway with a friendly good morning, and bluntly requested an explanation of his altered manner. He hesitated a moment; then, looking me frankly in the eyes, said:

"I do not think, sir, that I have any longer a claim to your friendship, since Mr. Barting appears to have withdrawn his own from me—for what reason, I protest I do not know. If he has not already informed you, he probably will do so."

These were nearly his words—I do not profess to report conversations *verbatim;* whoever does attempts to deceive.

"But," I replied, "I have not heard from Mr. Barting."

"Heard from him!" he repeated, with apparent surprise. "Why, he is here. I met him yesterday ten minutes before meeting you. I gave you exactly the same greeting that he had given me. I met him again not a quarter of an hour ago, and the manner was precisely the same: he merely bowed and passed on. I shall not soon forget your civility to me. You know where I live. Good morning, or—as it may please you—farewell."

All this seemed to me singularly gentlemanly and delicate behavior on the part of Mr. Conway.

As dramatic situations and literary effects are foreign to my purpose I will explain at once that Mr. Barting was dead. He had died in Nashville four days before this conversation. Calling on Mr. Conway, I apprised him of our friend's death, showing him the letters announcing it. He was visibly affected in a way that forbade me to entertain a doubt of his sincerity.

"It seems incredible," he said, after a period of reflection. "I suppose I must have mistaken another man for Barting, and that man's cold greeting was merely a stranger's civil acknowledgment of my own. I remember, indeed, that he lacked Barting's mustache."

"Doubtless it was another man," I assented; and the subject was never afterward mentioned between us. But I had in my pocket a photograph of Barting, which had been inclosed in the letter from his widow. It had been taken a week before his death, and was without a mustache.

A week or two later Mr. Conway left San Francisco for Santa Barbara, where he died the following year—at the Arlington Hotel, I think.

It will be observed that the value of this incident to "psychical research" is altogether dependent on the good faith and credibility of the late Mr. Conway—if he was not the subject of a strange hallucination. Even if he was, the fact would itself possess a certain psychical interest within the scope, I suppose, of the society's research. As to his good faith and credibility I can only say that I have myself no greater, nor other, reason to question them than I have now imparted to the reader.

For many years there lived near the town of Gallipolis, Ohio,[6] an old man named Herman Deluse. Very little was known of his history, for he would neither speak of it himself nor suffer others to. It was a common belief among his neighbors that he had been a pirate—if upon any better evidence than his collection of boarding pikes, cutlasses and ancient flint-lock pistols, I do not know. He lived entirely alone, in a small house of four rooms falling rapidly into decay and never repaired further than was required by the imperative mandates of the weather. It was situated on a slight elevation in the midst of a large, stony field overgrown with brambles and cultivated in patches, and that in the most primitive way. It was his only visible property, but could hardly have yielded him a living, simple and few as were his wants. He seemed always to have ready money and paid cash for all his purchases at the village stores round about, seldom buying more than two or three items at the same place until after the lapse of a considerable period. He got no commendation, however, for this equitable distribution of his patronage; people were disposed to regard it as an ineffectual attempt to conceal his possession of so much money. That he had great hoards of ill-gotten gold buried somewhere about his tumble-down dwelling was not reasonably to be doubted by any honest soul conversant with the facts of local traditions and gifted with a sense of the fitness of things.

On the 9th of November, 1867, the old man died; at least his dead body was discovered on the 10th, and physicians testified that death had occurred about twenty-four hours previously—just how, they were unable to say; for the post-mortem examination showed every organ to be absolutely healthy, with no indication anywhere of disorder or violence. According to them the death must have taken place about noon-day, yet the body was found in bed. The verdict of the Coroner's jury was that he "came to his death by a visitation of God." The body was buried and the Public Administrator took charge of the estate. A vigorous search failed to disclose anything more than was already known about the deceased, and much patient excavation here and there about the premises by thoughtful and thrifty neighbors went unrewarded. The Administrator locked up the house against the time when the property, real and personal, should be sold by law with a view to defraying, partly, the expenses of the sale.

The night of November 20th was boisterous. A furious gale stormed across the country, scourging it with desolating drifts of stinging sleet. Great trees were torn from the earth and hurled across the roads. So wild a night had never been known in all that region, but toward morning the storm had blown itself out of breath, and the day dawned bright and clear. At about 10 o'clock that morning the Rev. Henry Galbraith, a well-known and highly esteemed Baptist minister, arrived on foot at his house, a mile and half from the Deluse place—which, by the way, had already acquired the reputation of being "haunted." Mr. Galbraith had been for a month in Cincinnati. He had come up the river in a steamboat, and landing at Gallipolis the previous evening, had immediately obtained a horse and buggy and set out for home. The violence of the storm had delayed him over night, and in the morning the fallen trees had compelled him to abandon his conveyance and continue his journey afoot.

"But where did you pass the night?" inquired his wife, after he had briefly related his adventure.

"With old Deluse at the 'Isle of Pines,'"[7] was the laughing reply; "and a glum enough time I had of it. He made no objection to my remaining, but not a word could I get out of him."

(The Isle of Pines, in the West Indies, was formerly a famous rendezvous of pirates.)

Fortunately for the interests of truth, there was present at this conversation Mr. Robert Mosely Maren, a lawyer and *littérateur* of Columbus, the same who wrote the delightful "Mellowcraft Papers." Noting, but apparently not sharing, the astonishment caused by Mr. Galbraith's answer, this cool-headed cynic checked by a gesture the exclamations that would naturally have followed, and tranquilly inquired: "How came you to go in there?"

This is Mr. Maren's version of Mr. Galbraith's reply:

"I saw a light moving about in the house, and being nearly blinded by the sleet and frozen besides, I drove in at the gate and put up my horse in the old rail stable where he is now. I then rapped at the door, and getting no invitation, went in without one. The room was dark; but, having matches, I found a candle and lit it. I tried to enter the adjoining room; but the door was fast, and although I heard the old man's heavy footsteps in there, he made no response to my calls. There was no fire on the hearth, so I made one, and laying [*sic*][8] down before it with my overcoat under my head, prepared myself for sleep. Pretty soon the door which I had tried silently opened, and the old man came in, carrying a candle. I spoke to him pleasantly, apologizing for my intrusion; but he took no notice of me. He seemed to be searching for something, though his eyes were unmoved in their sockets. I wonder if he ever walks in his sleep. He took a circuit part way round the room, and then went out the same way he came in. Twice more before I slept he came back in the room, acting precisely the same way, and departing as at first. In the intervals I heard him tramping all over the house, his footsteps distinctly audible in the pauses of the storm. When I woke in the morning he had already gone out."

Mr. Maren attempted some further questioning, but was unable longer to restrain the family's tongues; the story of Deluse's death and burial came out, greatly to the good minister's astonishment. "The explanation of your adventure is very simple," said Mr. Maren. "I don't believe old Deluse walks in his sleep—not in his present one—but you evidently dream in yours." And to this view of the matter Mr. Galbraith

BEHIND THE VEIL

was compelled reluctantly to assent. Nevertheless, a late hour of the next night found these two gentlemen, accompanied by a son of the minister, in the road in front of the Deluse old house. There was a light inside: it appeared now at one window and now at another. The three men advanced to the door. Just as they reached it there came from the interior a confusion of the most appalling sounds—the clash of weapons, steel against steel, sharp explosions as of firearms, shrieks of women, groans and curses of men in combat. The investigators stood a moment irresolute, frightened. Then Mr. Galbraith tried the door. It was fast. But the minister was a man of courage, a man, moreover, of Herculean strength. He retired a pace or two and rushed against the door, striking it with his right shoulder and bursting it from the hinges with a loud crash. In a moment the three were inside. Darkness and silence! The only sound was the beating of their own hearts.

Mr. Maren had provided himself with matches and a candle. With some difficulty, begotten of his excitement, he made a light, and they proceeded to explore the place, passing from room to room. Everything was in orderly arrangement, as it had been left by the Sheriff: nothing had been disturbed. A light coating of dust was everywhere. A back door was partly open, as if by neglect, and their first thought was that the authors of the awful revelry might have escaped. The door was opened and the light of the candle thrown through upon the ground. The expiring effort of the previous night's storm had been a light fall of snow; there were no footprints; the white surface was unbroken. They closed the door and entered the last room of the four which the house contained—that farthest from the road in an angle of the building. Here the candle in Mr. Maren's hand was suddenly extinguished as by a draught of air. Almost immediately followed the sound of a heavy fall, shaking the building. When the candle had been hastily relighted young Mr. Galbraith was seen prostrated on the floor at a little distance from the others. He was dead. In one hand the body grasped a heavy sack of coins, which later examination showed to be all of old Spanish mintage. Directly over the body a board had been torn from its fastenings in the wall, and from the cavity so disclosed it was evident that the bag had been taken.

Another inquest was held: another post-mortem examination failed to reveal a probable cause of death. Another verdict of "the visitation of God" left all at liberty to form their own conclusions. Mr. Maren contended that the young man died of excitement. What does the Society for Psychical Research think?

Mr. Maren died two years ago in Cleveland, O. Mr. Galbraith is living—or was living last June—at the Golden Eagle Hotel in Sacramento.

E (26 Aug. 1888): 9 (as by "A. G. B."). Reprinted (in part) in *Current Literature* 3, no. 6 (Dec. 1889): 528–29 (as "The Inexplicable"). Reprinted as "The Isle of Pines" (*CSTB* 273–79; *CW* 3.369–76) and "A Cold Greeting" (*CW* 3.331–34).

BEHIND THE VEIL

NOTES

The fictional nature of the narratives in this piece is suggested in *E* by a melodramatic illustration accompanying the first sentence, depicting a skull on a book, with a cobweb behind.

1. "Bodies of the Dead" [I] (p. 577).
2. The Society for Psychical Research was founded in the United Kingdom in 1882; an American branch was founded in 1885. Years later AB confessed to the hoax he played upon the society in "Ambrose Bierce Says: Not All Men Desire Immortality," *NYJ* (25 Apr. 1901): 14; *E* (26 June 1901): 14 (repr. *SD* 285): "A few years ago I was publishing in the San Francisco Examiner the most awful ghost stories that I could think out. With a hardy mendacity that I now blush to remember I gave names, dates and places with a minute particularity which so seemed to authenticate the narratives that I came near to a belief in some of them myself.

   "One day I got a letter from the Secretary of the Society for Psychical Research. He explained that the society was greatly interested in these remarkable occurrences and would be pleased to have further particulars, with such corroborative evidence as I might be willing to take the trouble to supply. I could have supplied the further particulars easily enough, but the corroborative evidence—that is where I was weak. Whether the society, doing the best it knew how without my assistance, published the narratives in its official records, or sadly excluded them as the work of one unworthy of belief, I have never sought to know."
3. Cf. AB's whimsical sketch "That Ghost of Mine" (*Ar,* 6 Apr. 1878; *SS* 131–33), in which he recounts (possibly with tongue in cheek) a similar agreement between himself and Tom Hood the Younger; shortly after Hood died in 1874, AB thought he saw his ghost.
4. AB had fought in the battle of Franklin (30 Nov. 1864), in which the Confederate Army of Tennessee unsuccessfully attempted to dislodge the Federal troops outside the town of Franklin, resulting in heavy casualties. See *SS* 55–62.
5. See "'A Bad Woman,'" p. 395 note 2.
6. Gallipolis is the seat of Gallia County in southern Ohio, directly south of Meigs County, where AB was born.
7. The Isla de Pinos is an island in the Caribbean Sea, sixty miles south of Cuba. Columbus discovered it in 1494; for the next three hundred years it was occupied by pirates and runaway slaves, until formal colonization began in 1827. In 1904 the Hay-Quesada Treaty confirmed Cuban sovereignty over the island. In the 1970s it was renamed Isla de la Juventad (Isle of Youth) because of the large number of boarding schools for third-world children established there.
8. For this solecism see *WR* 40.

BEHIND THE VEIL

MY FAVORITE MURDER

Having murdered my mother under circumstances of singular atrocity, I was arrested and put upon my trial, which lasted seven years. In charging the jury, the judge of the Court of Acquittal remarked that it was one of the most ghastly crimes that he had ever been called upon to explain away.

At this, my attorney rose and said:

"May it please your Honor, crimes are ghastly or agreeable only by comparison. If you were familiar with the details of my client's previous murder of his uncle you would discern in his later offense (if offense it may be called) something in the nature of tender forbearance and filial consideration for the feelings of the victim. The appalling ferocity of the former assassination was indeed inconsistent with any hypothesis but that of guilt; and had it not been for the fact that the honorable judge before whom he was tried was the president of a life insurance company that took risks on hanging, and in which my client held a policy, it is hard to see how he could decently have been acquitted. If your Honor would like to hear about it for instruction and guidance of your Honor's mind, this unfortunate man, my client, will consent to give himself the pain of relating it under oath."

The district attorney said: "Your Honor, I object. Such a statement would be in the nature of evidence, and the testimony in this case is closed. The prisoner's statement should have been introduced three years ago, in the spring of 1881."

"In a statutory sense," said the judge, "you are right, and in the Court of Objections and Technicalities you would get a ruling in your favor. But not in a Court of Acquittal. The objection is overruled."

"I except," said the district attorney.

"You cannot do that," the judge said. "I must remind you that in order to take an exception you must first get this case transferred for a time to the Court of Exceptions

on a formal motion duly supported by affidavits. A motion to that effect by your predecessor in office was denied by me during the first year of this trial. Mr. Clerk, swear
the prisoner."

The customary oath having been administered, I made the following statement,
which impressed the judge with so strong a sense of the comparative triviality of the
offense for which I was on trial that he made no further search for mitigating circumstances, but simply instructed the jury to acquit, and I left the court, without a stain
upon my reputation:

"I was born in 1856 in Kalamakee, Mich.,[1] of honest and reputable parents, one of
whom Heaven has mercifully spared to comfort me in my later years. In 1867 the
family came to California and settled near Nigger Head,[2] where my father opened a
road agency[3] and prospered beyond the dreams of avarice.[4] He was a reticent, saturnine man then, though his increasing years have now somewhat relaxed the austerity
of his disposition, and I believe that nothing but his memory of the sad event for
which I am now on trial prevents him from manifesting a genuine hilarity.

"Four years after we had set up the road agency an itinerant preacher came along,
and having no other way to pay for the night's lodging that we gave him, favored us
with an exhortation of such power that, praise God, we were all converted to religion.
My father at once sent for his brother, the Hon. William Ridley of Stockton, and on
his arrival turned over the agency to him, charging him nothing for the franchise nor
plant—the latter consisting of a Winchester rifle, a sawed-off shotgun and an assort-
ment of masks made out of flour sacks. The family then moved to Ghost Rock[5] and
opened a dance house. It was called 'The Saints' Rest Hurdy-Gurdy,' and the proceedings each night began with prayer. It was there that my now sainted mother, by her
grace in the dance, acquired the *sobriquet* of 'The Bucking Walrus.'

"In the fall of '75 I had occasion to visit Coyote, on the road to Mahala, and took
the stage at Ghost Rock. There were four other passengers. About three miles beyond
Nigger Head, persons whom I identified as my Uncle William and his two sons held
up the stage. Finding nothing in the express box, they went through the passengers. I
acted a most honorable part in the affair, placing myself in line with the others, holding up my hands and permitting myself to be deprived of forty dollars and a gold
watch. From my behavior no one could have suspected that I knew the gentlemen
who gave the entertainment. A few days later, when I went to Nigger Head and asked
for the return of my money and watch my uncle and cousins swore they knew nothing of the matter, and they affected a belief that my father and I had done the job ourselves in dishonest violation of commercial good faith. Uncle William even threatened
to retaliate by starting an opposition dance house at Ghost Rock. As 'The Saints' Rest'
had become rather unpopular, I saw that this would assuredly ruin it and prove a paying enterprise, so I told my uncle that I was willing to overlook the past if he would
take me into the scheme and keep the partnership a secret from my father. This fair

offer he rejected, and I then perceived that it would be better and more satisfactory if he were dead.

"My plans to that end were soon perfected, and communicating them to my dear parents I had the gratification of receiving their approval. My father said he was proud of me, and my mother promised that although her religion forbade her to assist in taking human life I should have the advantage of her prayers for my success. As a preliminary measure looking to my security in case of detection I made an application for membership in that powerful order, the Knights of Murder,[6] and in due course was received as a member of the Ghost Rock commandery.[7] On the day that my probation ended I was for the first time permitted to inspect the records of the order and learn who belonged to it—all the rites of initiation having been conducted in masks. Fancy my delight when, in looking over the roll of membership, I found the third name to be that of my uncle, who indeed was junior vice-chancellor of the order! Here was an opportunity exceeding my wildest dreams—to murder I could add insubordination and treachery. It was what my good mother would have called 'a special Providence.'

"At about this time something occurred which caused my cup of joy, already full, to overflow on all sides, a circular cataract of bliss. Three men, strangers in that locality, were arrested for the stage robbery in which I had lost my money and watch. They were brought to trial and, despite my efforts to clear them and fasten the guilt upon three of the most respectable and worthy citizens of Ghost Rock, convicted on the clearest proof. The murder would now be as wanton and reasonless as I could wish.

"One morning I shouldered my Winchester rifle, and going over to my uncle's house, near Nigger Head, asked my Aunt Mary, his wife, if he were at home, adding that I had come to kill him. My aunt replied with a peculiar smile that so many gentlemen called on that errand and were afterward carried away without having performed it that I must excuse her for doubting my good faith in the matter. She said I did not look as if I would kill anybody, so, as a proof of good faith I leveled my rifle and wounded a Chinaman who happened to be passing the house. She said she knew whole families that could do a thing of that kind, but Bill Ridley was a horse of another color. She said, however, that I would find him over on the other side of the creek in the sheep lot; and she added that she hoped the best man would win.

"My Aunt Mary was one of the most fair-minded women that I have ever met.

"I found my uncle down on his knees engaged in skinning a sheep. Seeing that he had neither gun nor pistol handy I had not the heart to shoot him, so I approached him, greeted him pleasantly and struck him a powerful blow on the head with the butt of my rifle. I have a very good delivery and Uncle William lay down on his side, then rolled over on his back, spread out his fingers and shivered. Before he could recover the use of his limbs I seized the knife that he had been using and cut his hamstrings. You know, doubtless, that when you sever the *tendo Achillis* the patient has no further use of his leg; it is just the same as if he had no leg. Well, I parted them both, and when he revived he was at my service. As soon as he comprehended the situation, he said:

"'Samuel, you have got the drop on me and can afford to be generous. I have only one thing to ask of you, and that is that you carry me to the house and finish me in the bosom of my family.'

"I told him I thought that a pretty reasonable request and I would do so if he would let me put him into a wheat sack; he would be easier to carry that way and if we were seen by the neighbors *en route* it would cause less remark. He agreed to that, and going to the barn I got a sack. This, however, did not fit him; it was too short and much wider than he; so I bent his legs, forced his knees up against his breast and got him into it that way, tying the sack above his head. He was a heavy man and I had all that I could do to get him on my back, but I staggered along for some distance until I came to a swing that some of the children had suspended to the branch of an oak. Here I laid him down and sat upon him to rest, and the sight of the rope gave me a happy inspiration. In twenty minutes my uncle, still in the sack, swung free to the sport of the wind.

"I had taken down the rope, tied one end tightly about the mouth of the bag, thrown the other across the limb and hauled him up about five feet from the ground. Fastening the other end of the rope also about the mouth of the sack, I had the satisfaction to see my uncle converted into a large, fine pendulum. I must add that he was not himself entirely aware of the nature of the change that he had undergone in his relation to the exterior world, though in justice to a good man's memory I ought to say that I do not think he would in any case have wasted much of my time in vain remonstrance.

"Uncle William had a ram that was famous in all that region as a fighter. It was in a state of chronic constitutional indignation. Some deep disappointment in early life had soured its disposition and it had declared war upon the whole world. To say that it would butt anything accessible is but faintly to express the nature and scope of its military activity: the universe was its antagonist; its method that of a projectile. It fought like the angels and devils, in mid-air, cleaving the atmosphere like a bird, describing a parabolic curve and descending upon its victim at just the exact angle of incidence to make the most of its velocity and weight. Its momentum, calculated in foot-tons, was something incredible. It had been seen to destroy a four year old bull by a single impact upon that animal's gnarly forehead. No stone wall had ever been known to resist its downward swoop; there were no trees tough enough to stay it; it would splinter them into matchwood and defile their leafy honors in the dust. This irascible and implacable brute—this incarnate thunderbolt—this monster of the upper deep, I had seen reposing in the shade of an adjacent tree, dreaming dreams of conquest and glory. It was with a view to summoning it forth to the field of honor that I suspended its master in the manner described.

"Having completed my preparations, I imparted to the avuncular pendulum a gentle oscillation, and retiring to cover behind a contiguous rock, lifted up my voice in a long rasping cry whose diminishing final note was drowned in a noise like that of a swearing cat, which emanated from the sack. Instantly that formidable sheep was upon its feet and had taken in the military situation at a glance. In a few moments it had approached, stamping, to within fifty yards of the swinging foeman, who, now retreating and anon advancing, seemed to invite the fray. Suddenly I saw the beast's head drop earthward as if depressed by the weight of its enormous horns; then a dim, white, wavy streak of sheep prolonged itself from that spot in a generally horizontal direction to within about four yards of a point immediately beneath the enemy. There it struck sharply upward, and before it had faded from my gaze at the place whence it had set out I heard a horrid thump and a piercing scream, and my poor uncle shot forward, with a slack rope higher than the limb to which he was attached. Here the rope tautened with a jerk, arresting his flight, and back he swung in a breathless curve to the other end of his arc. The ram had fallen, a heap of indistinguishable legs, wool and horns, but pulling itself together and dodging as its antagonist swept downward it retired at random, alternately shaking its head and stamping its fore-feet. When it had backed about the same distance as that from which it had delivered the assault it paused again, bowed its head as if in prayer for victory and again shot forward, dimly visible as before—a prolonging white streak with monstrous undulations, ending with a sharp ascension. Its course this time was at a right angle to its former one, and its impatience so great that it struck the enemy before he had nearly reached the lowest point of his arc. In consequence he went flying round and round in a horizontal circle whose radius was about equal to half the length of the rope, which I forgot to say was nearly twenty feet long. His shrieks, *crescendo* in approach and *diminuendo* in recession, made the rapidity of his revolution more obvious to the ear than to the eye. He had evidently not yet been struck in a vital spot. His posture in the sack and the distance from the ground at which he hung compelled the ram to operate upon his lower extremities and the end of his back. Like a plant that has struck its root into some poisonous mineral, my poor uncle was dying slowly upward.

"After delivering its second blow the ram had not again retired. The fever of battle burned hot in its heart; its brain was intoxicated with the wine of strife. Like a pugilist who in his rage forgets his skill and fights ineffectively at half-arm's length, the angry beast endeavored to reach its fleeting foe by awkward vertical leaps as he passed overhead, sometimes, indeed, succeeding in striking him feebly, but more frequently overthrown by its own misguided eagerness. But as the impetus was ex-hausted and the man's circles narrowed in scope and diminished in speed, bringing him nearer to the ground, these tactics produced better results, eliciting a superior quality of screams, which I greatly enjoyed.

MY FAVORITE MURDER

"Suddenly, as if the bugles had sung truce, the ram suspended hostilities and walked away, thoughtfully wrinkling and smoothing its great aquiline nose, and occasionally cropping a bunch of grass and slowly munching it. It seemed to have tired of war's alarms and resolved to beat the sword into a plowshare and cultivate the arts of peace.[8] Steadily it held its course away from the field of fame until it had gained a distance of nearly a quarter of a mile. There it stopped and stood with its rear to the foe, chewing its cud and apparently half asleep. I observed, however, an occasional slight turn of its head, as if its apathy were more affected than real.

"Meantime Uncle William's shrieks had abated with his motion, and nothing was heard from him but long, low moans, and at long intervals my name, uttered in pleading tones exceedingly grateful to my ear. Evidently the man had not the faintest notion of what was being done to him, and was inexpressibly terrified. When Death comes cloaked in mystery he is terrible indeed. Little by little my uncle's oscillations diminished, and finally he hung motionless. I went to him and was about to give him the *coup de grâce,* when I heard and felt a succession of smart shocks which shook the ground like a series of light earthquakes, and turning in the direction of the ram, saw a long cloud of dust approaching me with inconceivable rapidity and alarming effect! At a distance of some thirty yards away it stopped short, and from the near end of it rose into the air what I at first thought a great white bird. Its ascent was so smooth and easy and regular that I could not realize its extraordinary celerity, and was lost in admiration of its grace. To this day the impression remains that it was a slow, deliberate movement, the ram—for it was that animal—being upborne by some power other than its own impetus, and supported through the successive stages of its flight with infinite tenderness and care. My eyes followed its progress through the air with unspeakable pleasure, all the greater by contrast with my former terror of its approach by land. Onward and upward the noble animal sailed, its head bent down almost between its knees, its fore-feet thrown back, its hinder legs trailing to rear like the legs of a soaring heron.

"At a height of forty or fifty feet, as fond recollection presents it to view,[9] it attained its zenith and appeared to remain an instant stationary; then, tilting suddenly forward without altering the relative position of its parts, it shot downward on a steeper and steeper course with augmenting velocity, passed immediately above me with a noise like the rush of a cannon shot and struck my poor uncle almost squarely on the top of the head! So frightful was the impact that not only the man's neck was broken, but the rope too; and the body of the deceased, forced against the earth, was crushed to pulp beneath the awful front of that meteoric sheep! The concussion stopped all the clocks between Lone Hand[10] and Dutch Dan's, and Professor Davidson,[11] a distinguished authority in matters seismic, who happened to be in the vicinity, promptly explained that the vibrations were from north to southwest.

"Altogether, I cannot help thinking that in point of artistic atrocity my murder of Uncle William has seldom been excelled."

MY FAVORITE MURDER

E (16 September 1888): 9 (with subtitle: "How I Disposed of an Objectionable Relative"); *CSTB* 37–50; *CW* **8.147–62**. Reprinted in *Short Stories* 2, no. 1 (Aug. 1890): 49–56; *Anti-Philistine*, no. 4 (15 September 1897): 210–20 (as "My Favourite Murder"); *Goose-Quill* 1, no. 2 (Mar. 1900): 3–13; *Goose-Quill* 2, no. 1 (Apr. 1902): 18–33; *10 Story Book* (Jan. 1907) [not located]; *Saturday Night Lantern* 1, no. 4 (29 Mar. 1913): 116–20.

NOTES

Perhaps the most notorious of the set of four "Parenticide Club" tales, what should have been recognized from the first as a satire from its flamboyant title and broadly extravagant plot has been instead misread and misinterpreted, incredibly, as a serious expression of AB's misanthropic bitterness toward his family. For a fuller discussion of the set, including this tale, see *PA* 141–51.

1. Fictitious, although perhaps meant to evoke the actual Michigan city of Kalamazoo, cited in "A Leaf Blown In from Days to Be" (p. 1134).

2. In *E* the reading is "Nigger Tent," which was a way station in the Sierra Turnpike in Sierra County in central California. Nigger Head is fictitious.

3. *Road agent* is American slang for a highway robber. Its first usage, according to *DAE*, dates to 1863. Cf. "The Famous Gilson Bequest" (1878): "After a few tentative and resultless undertakings in the way of highway robbery—if one may venture to designate road-agency by so harsh a name" (p. 381).

4. The earliest source of this quotation occurs in Edward Moore (1712–57), *The Gamester* (1753), act 2, scene 7 ("I am rich beyond the dreams of avarice"). But AB probably derived it from Boswell's *Life of Johnson* (1791), under the date 6 April 1781: "rich, beyond the dreams of avarice."

5. Fictitious, but suggestive of a deserted mining camp. It was first cited in "A Holy Terror" (p. 409) and is mentioned again in "One of the Missing" (p. 525).

6. A parody of the Knights of Labor, like the "Knights of Leisure" cited in "'A Bubble Reputation,'" p. 454 note 1.

7. A "commandery" is "the name for a local branch or 'lodge' of a secret order, as the American order of so-called 'Knights Templars'" (*OED*).

8. A string of quotations. Cf. Thomas Hood (1799–1845), "Faithless Nellie Gray" (1826): "Ben Battle was a soldier bold, / And used to war's alarms"; Isa. 2:4: "and they shall beat their swords into ploughshares"; Andrew Marvell (1621–78), "A Horatian Ode upon Cromwel's Return from Ireland" (1650), l. 10: "The inglorious arts of peace."

9. Samuel Woodworth (1785–1842), "The Old Oaken Bucket" (1817), ll. 1–2: "How dear to this heart are the scenes of my childhood, / When fond recollection presents them to view!"

10. Also first cited in "A Holy Terror."

11. George Davidson (1825–1911), professor of geology at the University of California and author of many papers on the history and geology of California and on astronomy. He is the subject of an untitled fable by Bierce (*E,* 16 July 1893; *CF* no. 737).

A TOUGH TUSSLE

One night in the autumn of 1861 a man sat alone in the heart of a forest in western Virginia. The region was one of the wildest on the continent—the Cheat Mountain country.[1] There was no lack of people close at hand, however; within a mile of where the man sat was the now silent camp of a whole Federal brigade. Somewhere about— it might be still nearer—was a force of the enemy, the numbers unknown. It was this uncertainty as to its numbers and position that accounted for the man's presence in that lonely spot; he was a young officer of a Federal infantry regiment and his business there was to guard his sleeping comrades in the camp against a surprise. He was in command of a detachment of men constituting a picket-guard. These men he had stationed just at nightfall in an irregular line, determined by the nature of the ground, several hundred yards in front of where he now sat. The line ran through the forest, among the rocks and laurel thickets, the men fifteen or twenty paces apart, all in concealment and under injunction of strict silence and unremitting vigilance. In four hours, if nothing occurred, they would be relieved by a fresh detachment from the reserve now resting in care of its captain some distance away to the left and rear. Before stationing his men the young officer of whom we are writing had pointed out to his two sergeants the spot at which he would be found if it should be necessary to consult him, or if his presence at the front line should be required.

It was a quiet enough spot—the fork of an old wood-road, on the two branches of which, prolonging themselves deviously forward in the dim moonlight, the sergeants were themselves stationed, a few paces in rear of the line. If driven sharply back by a sudden onset of the enemy—the pickets are not expected to make a stand after firing— the men would come into the converging roads and naturally following them to their point of intersection could be rallied and "formed." In his small way the author of these dispositions was something of a strategist; if Napoleon had planned as intelligently at Waterloo he would have won that memorable battle and been overthrown later.

Second-Lieutenant Brainerd Byring was a brave and efficient officer, young and comparatively inexperienced as he was in the business of killing his fellow-men. He had enlisted in the very first days of the war as a private, with no military knowledge whatever, had been made first-sergeant of his company on account of his education and engaging manner, and had been lucky enough to lose his captain by a Confederate bullet; in the resulting promotions he had gained a commission.[2] He had been in several engagements, such as they were—at Philippi, Rich Mountain, Carrick's Ford and Greenbrier[3]—and had borne himself with such gallantry as not to attract the attention of his superior officers. The exhilaration of battle was agreeable to him, but the sight of the dead, with their clay faces, blank eyes and stiff bodies, which when not unnaturally shrunken were unnaturally swollen, had always intolerably affected him. He felt toward them a kind of reasonless antipathy that was something more than the physical and spiritual repugnance common to us all. Doubtless this feeling was due to his unusually acute sensibilities—his keen sense of the beautiful, which these hideous things outraged. Whatever may have been the cause, he could not look upon a dead body without a loathing which had in it an element of resentment. What others have respected as the dignity of death had to him no existence—was altogether unthinkable. Death was a thing to be hated. It was not picturesque, it had no tender and solemn side—a dismal thing, hideous in all its manifestations and suggestions. Lieutenant Byring was a braver man than anybody knew, for nobody knew his horror of that which he was ever ready to incur.

Having posted his men, instructed his sergeants and retired to his station, he seated himself on a log, and with senses all alert began his vigil. For greater ease he loosened his sword-belt and taking his heavy revolver from his holster laid it on the log beside him. He felt very comfortable, though he hardly gave the fact a thought, so intently did he listen for any sound from the front which might have a menacing significance—a shout, a shot or the footfall of one of his sergeants coming to apprise him of something worth knowing. From the vast, invisible ocean of moonlight overhead fell, here and there, a slender, broken stream that seemed to plash against the intercepting branches and trickle to earth, forming small white pools among the clumps of laurel. But these leaks were few and served only to accentuate the blackness of his environment, which his imagination found it easy to people with all manner of unfamiliar shapes, menacing, uncanny or merely grotesque.

He to whom the portentous conspiracy of night and solitude and silence in the heart of a great forest is not an unknown experience needs not to be told what another world it all is—how even the most commonplace and familiar objects take on another character. The trees group themselves differently; they draw closer together, as if in fear. The very silence has another quality than the silence of the day. And it is full of half-heard whispers—whispers that startle—ghosts of sounds long dead. There are living sounds, too, such as are never heard under other conditions: notes of strange night-birds, the cries of small animals in sudden encounters with stealthy foes or in their dreams, a rustling in the dead leaves—it may be the leap of a wood-rat, it may be the footfall of a panther. What caused the breaking of that twig?—what the low, alarmed twittering in that bushful of birds? There are sounds without a name, forms without substance, translations in space of objects which have not been seen to move, movements wherein nothing is observed to change its place. Ah, children of the sunlight and the gaslight, how little you know of the world in which you live!

Surrounded at a little distance by armed and watchful friends, Byring felt utterly alone. Yielding himself to the solemn and mysterious spirit of the time and place, he had forgotten the nature of his connection with the visible and audible aspects and phases of the night. The forest was boundless; men and the habitations of men did not exist. The universe was one primeval mystery of darkness, without form and void,[4] himself the sole, dumb questioner of its eternal secret. Absorbed in thoughts born of this mood, he suffered the time to slip away unnoted. Meantime the infrequent patches of white light lying amongst the tree-trunks had undergone changes of size, form and place. In one of them near by, just at the roadside, his eye fell upon an object that he had not previously observed. It was almost before his face as he sat; he could have sworn that it had not before been there. It was partly covered in shadow, but he could see that it was a human figure. Instinctively he adjusted the clasp of his sword-belt and laid hold of his pistol—again he was in a world of war, by occupation an assassin.

The figure did not move. Rising, pistol in hand, he approached. The figure lay upon its back, its upper part in shadow, but standing above it and looking down upon the face, he saw that it was a dead body. He shuddered and turned from it with a feeling of sickness and disgust, resumed his seat upon the log, and forgetting military prudence struck a match and lit a cigar. In the sudden blackness that followed the extinction of the flame he felt a sense of relief; he could no longer see the object of his aversion. Nevertheless, he kept his eyes in that direction until it appeared again with growing distinctness. It seemed to have moved a trifle nearer.

"Damn the thing!" he muttered. "What does it want?"

It did not appear to be in need of anything but a soul.

Byring turned away his eyes and began humming a tune, but he broke off in the middle of a bar and looked at the dead body. Its presence annoyed him, though he could hardly have had a quieter neighbor. He was conscious, too, of a vague, indefinable feeling that was new to him. It was not fear, but rather a sense of the supernatural—in which he did not at all believe.

"I have inherited it," he said to himself. "I suppose it will require a thousand ages—perhaps ten thousand—for humanity to outgrow this feeling. Where and when did it originate? Away back, probably, in what is called the cradle of the human race—the plains of Central Asia. What we inherit as a superstition our barbarous ancestors must have held as a reasonable conviction. Doubtless they believed themselves justified by facts whose nature we cannot even conjecture in thinking a dead body a malign thing endowed with some strange power of mischief, with perhaps a will and a purpose to exert it. Possibly they had some awful form of religion of which that was one of the chief doctrines, sedulously taught by their priesthood, as ours teach the immortality of the soul. As the Aryans moved slowly on, to and through the Caucasus passes, and spread over Europe, new conditions of life must have resulted in the formulation of new religions. The old belief in the malevolence of the dead body was lost from the creeds and even perished from tradition, but it left its heritage of terror, which is transmitted from generation to generation—is as much a part of us as are our blood and bones."

In following out his thought he had forgotten that which suggested it; but now his eye fell again upon the corpse. The shadow had now altogether uncovered it. He saw the sharp profile, the chin in the air, the whole face, ghastly white in the moonlight. The clothing was gray, the uniform of a Confederate soldier. The coat and waistcoat, unbuttoned, had fallen away on each side, exposing the white shirt. The chest seemed unnaturally prominent, but the abdomen had sunk in, leaving a sharp projection at the line of the lower ribs. The arms were extended, the left knee was thrust upward. The whole posture impressed Byring as having been studied with a view to the horrible.

"Bah!" he exclaimed; "he was an actor—he knows how to be dead."

He drew away his eyes, directing them resolutely along one of the roads leading to the front, and resumed his philosophizing where he had left off.

"It may be that our Central Asian ancestors had not the custom of burial. In that case it is easy to understand their fear of the dead, who really were a menace and an evil. They bred pestilences. Children were taught to avoid the places where they lay, and to run away if by inadvertence they came near a corpse. I think, indeed, I'd better go away from this chap."

He half rose to do so, then remembered that he had told his men in front and the officer in the rear who was to relieve him that he could at any time be found at that spot. It was a matter of pride, too. If he abandoned his post he feared they would think he feared the corpse. He was no coward and he was unwilling to incur anybody's ridicule. So he again seated himself, and to prove his courage looked boldly at the body. The right arm—the one farthest from him—was now in shadow. He could hardly see the hand which, he had before observed, lay at the root of a clump of laurel. There had been no change, a fact which gave him a certain comfort, he could not have said why. He did not at once remove his eyes; that which we do not wish to see has a strange fascination, sometimes irresistible. Of the woman who covers her eyes with her hands and looks between the fingers let it be said that the wits have dealt with her not altogether justly.

Byring suddenly became conscious of a pain in his right hand. He withdrew his eyes from his enemy and looked at it. He was grasping the hilt of his drawn sword so tightly that it hurt him. He observed, too, that he was leaning forward in a strained attitude—crouching like a gladiator ready to spring at the throat of an antagonist. His teeth were clenched and he was breathing hard. This matter was soon set right, and as his muscles relaxed and he drew a long breath he felt keenly enough the ludicrousness of the incident. It affected him to laughter. Heavens! what sound was that? what mindless devil was uttering an unholy glee in mockery of human merriment? He sprang to his feet and looked about him, not recognizing his own laugh.

He could no longer conceal from himself the horrible fact of his cowardice; he was thoroughly frightened! He would have run from the spot, but his legs refused their office; they gave way beneath him and he sat again upon the log, violently trembling. His face was wet, his whole body bathed in a chill perspiration. He could not even cry out. Distinctly he heard behind him a stealthy tread, as of some wild animal, and dared not look over his shoulder. Had the soulless living joined forces with the soulless dead?—was it an animal? Ah, if he could but be assured of that! But by no effort of will could he now unfix his gaze from the face of the dead man.

I repeat that Lieutenant Byring was a brave and intelligent man. But what would you have? Shall a man cope, single-handed, with so monstrous an alliance as that of night and solitude and silence and the dead,—while an incalculable host of his own ancestors shriek into the ear of his spirit their coward counsel, sing their doleful death-songs in his heart and disarm his very blood of all its iron? The odds are too great—courage was not made for so rough use as that.

One sole conviction now had the man in possession: that the body had moved. It lay nearer to the edge of its plot of light—there could be no doubt of it. It had also moved its arms, for, look, they are both in the shadow! A breath of cold air struck Byring full in the face; the boughs of trees above him stirred and moaned. A strongly defined shadow passed across the face of the dead, left it luminous, passed back upon it and left it half obscured. The horrible thing was visibly moving! At that moment a single shot rang out upon the picket-line—a lonelier and louder, though more distant, shot than ever had been heard by mortal ear! It broke the spell of that enchanted man; it slew the silence and the solitude, dispersed the hindering host from Central Asia and released his modern manhood. With a cry like that of some great bird pouncing upon its prey he sprang forward, hot-hearted for action!

Shot after shot now came from the front. There were shoutings and confusion, hoof-beats and desultory cheers. Away to the rear, in the sleeping camp, were a singing of bugles and grumble of drums. Pushing through the thickets on either side the roads came the Federal pickets, in full retreat, firing backward at random as they ran. A straggling group that had followed back one of the roads, as instructed, suddenly sprang away into the bushes as half a hundred horsemen thundered by them, striking wildly with their sabers as they passed. At headlong speed these mounted madmen shot past the spot where Byring had sat, and vanished round an angle of the road, shouting and firing their pistols. A moment later there was a roar of musketry, followed by dropping shots—they had encountered the reserve-guard in line; and back they came in dire confusion, with here and there an empty saddle and many a maddened horse, bullet-stung, snorting and plunging with pain. It was all over—"an affair of outposts."

The line was reëstablished with fresh men, the roll called, the stragglers were re-formed. The Federal commander with a part of his staff, imperfectly clad, appeared upon the scene, asked a few questions, looked exceedingly wise and retired. After standing at arms for an hour the brigade in camp "swore a prayer or two" and went to bed.

Early the next morning a fatigue-party, commanded by a captain and accompanied by a surgeon, searched the ground for dead and wounded. At the fork of the road, a little to one side, they found two bodies lying close together—that of a Federal officer and that of a Confederate private. The officer had died of a sword-thrust through the heart, but not, apparently, until he had inflicted upon his enemy no fewer than five dreadful wounds. The dead officer lay on his face in a pool of blood, the weapon still in his breast. They turned him on his back and the surgeon removed it.

"Gad!" said the captain—"It is Byring!"—adding, with a glance at the other, "They had a tough tussle."

The surgeon was examining the sword. It was that of a line officer of Federal infantry—exactly like the one worn by the captain. It was, in fact, Byring's own. The only other weapon discovered was an undischarged revolver in the dead officer's belt.

The surgeon laid down the sword and approached the other body. It was frightfully gashed and stabbed, but there was no blood. He took hold of the left foot and tried to straighten the leg. In the effort the body was displaced. The dead do not wish to be moved—it protested with a faint, sickening odor. Where it had lain were a few maggots, manifesting an imbecile activity.

The surgeon looked at the captain. The captain looked at the surgeon.

E (30 September 1888): 9 (with subtitle: "The Facts about Byring's Encounter with an Unknown"); *TSC* 123–37; *IML* 119–34; *CW* **3.106–21**.

NOTES

This carefully constructed tale incorporates a series of traps for unwary readers, all tending to underline how reason, which should be humanity's main protection against superstition, instead can leave someone fatally vulnerable to it. For a fuller analysis of the story, see *PA* 88–90.

1. One of AB's earliest battles following his enlistment in May 1861 was in the Cheat Mountain region of what later became West Virginia. An engagement occurred there on 10–14 September 1861, although an actual battle was never fought: the Confederates, led by Colonel Albert Rust, discovered that they were far outnumbered and withdrew without firing a shot. Earlier there had been some minor skirmishes between opposing picket-guards. AB participated in a reconnaissance mission at Cheat Mountain on 3 October (see *SS* 6–10).
2. AB had also enlisted at the outset of the war, but he did have some "military knowledge," having spent a year (1859–60) at the Kentucky Military Institute. Upon his reenlistment in late July, he was promoted to sergeant major.
3. The battle of Philippi occurred on 3 June 1861; that of Rich Mountain on 11 July; that of Carrick's (or Corrick's) Ford on 13 July; that of Greenbrier on 3 October. All the sites are in western Virginia. AB participated in the first three battles.
4. "And the earth was without form, and void" (Gen. 1:2).

WHITHER?

BEHIND THE VEIL.

One Who Had the Hardihood to Cross a Field—How to Lose a Bet—Snow as a Detective.

One morning in July, 1854, a planter named Williamson, living six miles from Selma, Alabama, was sitting, with his wife and a child, on the veranda of his dwelling.[1] Immediately in front of the house was a lawn, perhaps fifty yards in extent, between the house and "turnpike," or, as it was called, the "pike." Beyond this road lay a close-cropped pasture of some ten acres, level and without a tree, rock or any natural or artificial object on its surface. At the time, there was not even a domestic animal in the whole field. In another field, beyond the pasture, a dozen slaves were at work in charge of an overseer.

Throwing away the stump of a cigar, Mr. Williamson rose, saying "I forgot to tell Andrew about those horses." Andrew was the overseer.

Williamson strolled leisurely down the gravel walk, plucking a flower as he went, passed across the road and into the pasture, pausing a moment as he closed the gate leading into it, to great a passing neighbor, Arnold Wren, who lived on the adjoining plantation. Mr. Wren was in an open barouche with his son James, a lad of thirteen. When he had driven some two hundred yards from the point of meeting, Mr. Wren said to his son: "I forgot to tell Mr. Williamson about those horses."

Mr. Wren had sold Mr. Williamson some horses, which were to have been sent for that day, but for some reason not now remembered it would be inconvenient to deliver them until the morrow. The coachman was directed to drive back, and as the vehicle turned, Williamson was seen by all three, walking leisurely across the pasture. At that moment one of the coach horses stumbled and came near falling. It had no more than fairly recovered itself when James Wren cried: "Why, father, what has become of Mr. Williamson?"

It is not the purpose of this narrative to answer that question.

Mr. Wren's account of the matter, given under oath in the course of legal proceedings relating to the Williamson estate, here follows:

"My son's exclamation caused me to look toward the spot where I had seen the deceased (*sic*) an instant before, but he was not there, nor was he anywhere visible. I cannot say that, at the moment, I was greatly startled, not realizing the gravity of the occurrence, though I thought it singular. My son, however, was much astonished, and kept repeating his question in different forms until we arrived at the gate. My black boy Sam was similarly affected, even in a greater degree, but I reckon more by my son's manner than by anything he had himself observed. [This part of the testimony was stricken out.] As we got out of the carriage at the gate of the field, and while Sam was hanging (*sic*) the team to the fence, Mrs. Williamson, with her child in her arms and followed by several servants, came running down the walk in great excitement, crying: 'He is gone, he is gone! O God! what an awful thing!' and many other such exclamations, which I do not distinctly recollect. I got from them the impression that they related to something more than the mere disappearance of her husband, even if that had occurred before her eyes. Her manner was wild, but not more so, I think, than was natural under the circumstances. I have no reason to think she had at that time lost her mind. I have never since seen nor heard from Mr. Williamson."

This testimony was, as might have been expected, corroborated in almost every particular by the only other eye-witness (if that is a proper term), the lad James. Mrs. Williamson had lost her reason and the servants were, of course, not competent to testify. The boy James Wren had declared at first that he *saw* the disappearance, but there is nothing of this in his testimony given in court. None of the hands working in the field to which Williamson was going had seen him at all, and the most rigorous search of the entire plantation and adjoining country failed to afford a clew. The most monstrous and grotesque fictions, originating with the blacks, were current in that part of the State for many years, and probably are to this day; but what has been here related is all that is certainly known of the matter. The courts decided that Williamson was dead, and his estate was distributed according to law.

James Burne Worson was a shoemaker who lived in Leamington, Warwickshire, England.[2] He had a little shop in one of the by-ways leading off the road to Warwick.

In his humble sphere he was esteemed an honest man, although like many of his class in English towns he was somewhat addicted to drink. When in liquor he would make foolish wagers. On one of these too frequent occasions he was boasting of his prowess as a pedestrian and athlete, and the outcome was a match against nature. For a stake of one sovereign he undertook to run all the way to Coventry and back, a distance of something more than forty miles. This was on the 3d day of September in 1873. He set out at once, the man with whom he had made the bet—whose name is not recorded—accompanied by Barham Wise, a linen draper, and Natterville Briggs, a photographer, I think, following in a light cart or wagon.

For several miles Worson went on very well, at an easy gait, without apparent fatigue, for he had really great powers of endurance and was not sufficiently intoxicated to enfeeble them. The three men in the wagon kept a short distance in the rear, giving him occasional friendly "chaff" or encouragement, as the spirit moved them. Suddenly—in the middle of the roadway, not a dozen yards from them, and with their eyes full upon him—the man seemed to stumble, pitched headlong forward, uttered a terrible cry and vanished. He did not fall to the earth—he vanished before touching it. No trace of him was ever afterward discovered.

After remaining at and about the spot with aimless irresolution the three dumbfounded men returned to Leamington, told their astonishing story and were promptly taken into custody, pending an inquiry. But they were of good standing, had always been considered truthful, were entirely sober, and nothing ever transpired to discredit their sworn account of their extraordinary adventure; concerning the truth of which, nevertheless, public opinion was divided, throughout the United Kingdom. If they had something to conceal, their choice of means is certainly one of the most amazing ever made by sane human beings.

The family of Christian Ashmore consisted of his wife, his mother, two grown daughters and a son of sixteen years. They lived in Troy, N. Y., were well-to-do, respectable people and had many friends, some of whom, reading these lines, will doubtless learn for the first time the extraordinary fate of the young man. From Troy the Ashmores moved in 1871 or '2 to Richmond, Indiana, and a year or two later to the vicinity of Quincy, Ill., where Mr. Ashmore bought a farm and lived on it. At some little distance from the farmhouse was a spring with a constant flow of clear, cold water, whence the family derived its supply for domestic use at all seasons.

On the evening of the 9th of November in 1878, at about 9 o'clock, young Charles Ashmore left the family circle about the hearth, took a tin bucket and started toward the spring. As he did not return the family became uneasy, and going to the door by which he had left, his father called repeatedly without receiving an answer. He then lighted a lantern and, with the eldest daughter, Martha, who insisted on accompanying him, went in search. A light snow had fallen, obliterating the path, but making the young man's trail conspicuous; each footprint was plainly defined. After going a little more than half-way—perhaps seventy-five yards—the father, who was in advance, halted and, elevating his lantern stood peering intently into the darkness ahead. "What is the matter, father?" the girl asked.

This was the matter: the trail of the young man had abruptly ended, and all beyond was smooth, unbroken snow. The last footprints were as conspicuous as any in the line; the very nail-marks were distinctly visible on close inspection. Mr. Ashmore looked upward, shading his eyes with his hat held between them and the lantern. The stars were shining; there was not a cloud in the sky; he was denied the explanation which had suggested itself, doubtful as it would have been—a snowfall with a limit so plainly defined. Taking a wide circuit round the ultimate tracks, so as to leave them undisturbed for further examination, the man proceeded to the spring, the girl following, weak and terrified. Neither had spoken a word of what they had observed. The spring was covered with ice, hours old.

Returning to the house they noted the appearance of the snow on both sides of the trail its entire length. No tracks led away from it. The morning light showed nothing more. Smooth, spotless, absolutely unbroken, the shallow snow lay everywhere.

Four days later the grief-stricken mother herself went to the spring for water. She came back and related that in passing the spot where the footprints had ended she had heard the voice of her son and had been eagerly calling to him, wandering about the place, as she had fancied the voice to be now in one direction, then in another, until she was exhausted with fatigue and emotion. Questioned as to what the voice had said she was unable to say, yet averred that the words were perfectly distinct. In a moment the entire family was at the place, but nothing was heard, and the voice was believed to be a hallucination caused by the mother's great anxiety and her disordered nerves. But for months afterward, at irregular intervals of several days, the voice was heard by the various members of the family and by others. All declared it unmistakably the voice of Charles Ashmore; all agreed that it seemed to come from a great distance, faintly yet with perfect distinctness of articulation. Yet none could determine its direction, nor repeat its words. The intervals of silence grew longer and longer, the voice fainter and farther, and by midsummer it was heard no more.

Broken in health and spirit, Mr. Ashmore, with his aged mother and his still unmarried daughters, lives on the farm. The place has an uncanny reputation and has fallen into decay. If anybody knows the fate of Charles Ashmore it is probably his mother. She is dead.

————————

In connection with this subject of "mysterious disappearance"—of which every memory is stored with abundant example—it is pertinent to note the belief of the famous Dr. Hern of Leipsic;[3] not by way of explanation, unless the reader may choose to take it so, but because of its intrinsic interest as a singular speculation. This distinguished scientist has expounded his views in a book entitled *"Verschwinden und Seine Theorie,"* which has attracted some attention, "particularly," says one writer, "among the followers of Hegel and mathematicians who hold to the actual existence of a so-called non-Euclidean space—that is to say, of a space which has more dimensions than length, breadth and thickness—a space in which it would be possible to tie a knot in an endless cord and to turn a rubber ball inside out without 'a solution of its continuity,' or in other words, without breaking or cracking it."

Dr. Hern believes that in the visible world there are void places—*vacua,* and something more—holes, as it were, through which animate and inanimate objects may fall into the invisible world and be seen and heard no more. The theory is something like this: Space is pervaded by luminiferous—light-bearing—ether, which is a material thing—as much a substance as air or water, though almost infinitely more attenuated. All force, all forms of energy must be propagated in this; every process must take place in it which takes place at all. But let us suppose that cavities exist in this otherwise universal medium, as caverns exist in the earth, or cells in a Swiss cheese. In such a cavity there would be absolutely nothing. It would be such a vacuum as cannot be artificially produced; for if we pump the air from a receiver there remains the luminiferous ether. Through one of these cavities light could not pass, for there would be nothing to bear it. Sound could not proceed from it; nothing could be felt in it. It would not have a single one of the conditions necessary to the action of any of our senses. In such a void, in short, nothing whatever could occur. Now, in the words of the writer before quoted—the learned doctor himself nowhere puts it so concisely: "A man inclosed in such a closet could neither see nor be seen; neither hear nor be heard; neither feel nor be felt; neither live nor die, for both life and death are processes which can take place only where there is force, and in empty space no force could exist." Are these the awful conditions (some will ask) under which the parents of Charley Ross and Annie Mooney are to think of their children as existing, and doomed forever to exist?

Baldly and imperfectly as I have stated it, Dr. Hern's theory, in so far as it professes to be an adequate explanation of "mysterious disappearances," is open to many obvious objections; to fewer as he states it himself in the "spacious volubility" of his book. But even as expounded by its author it does not cover, and in fact is incompatible with, some incidents of the occurrences related in this article; for example, the sound of Charles Ashmore's voice. It is not my business to bring facts and theories into perfect affinity.

E (14 Oct. 1888): 9 (as by "A. G. B."). Reprinted (in part) in *Current Literature* 1, no. 6 (Dec. 1888): 508; 2, no. 2 (Feb. 1889): 150–51. Reprinted as "The Difficulty of Crossing a Field" (*CSTB* 309–12; *CW* 3.415–18), "An Unfinished Race" (*CSTB* 313–14; *CW* 3.419–20), "Charles Ashmore's Trail" (*CSTB* 315–20; *CW* 3.421–24), and "Science to the Front" (*CW* 3.424–27).

WHITHER?

This is another piece that solemnly relates narratives of the uncanny that AB either concocted or altered as entertaining hoaxes, much as "Bodies of the Dead," "Hither from Hades," and "Behind the Veil" do. Although the comments about non-Euclidean space show AB to have been aware of a recent development in mathematics, the discussion itself is not accurate and the conclusions drawn from it are either illogical or fallacious. Some hint of the hoaxing nature of the piece is suggested by the last two sentences.

1. It is possible that AB heard the anecdote recounted in this segment from his friend and colleague W. C. Morrow. Morrow was born in 1854 in Selma, Alabama, and his family owned slaves. As a boy Morrow was told many strange tales by an African American nurse; see his article, "Some Queer Experiences" (*Ar,* 21 Dec. 1891); reprinted in *The Monster Maker and Other Stories,* ed. S. T. Joshi and Stefan Dziemianowicz (Seattle: Midnight House, 2000), 293–97.

2. AB had lived in Leamington from April 1874 to June 1875.

3. Dr. Hern and his book are fictitious.

ONE OF TWINS

A Letter Found among the Papers of the Late
Mortimer Barr

You ask me if in my experience as one of a pair of twins I ever observed anything unaccountable by the natural laws with which we have acquaintance. As to that you shall judge; perhaps we have not all acquaintance with the same natural laws. You may know some that I do not, and what is to me unaccountable may be very clear to you.

You knew my brother John—that is, you knew him when you knew that I was not present; but neither you nor, I believe, any human being could distinguish between him and me if we chose to seem alike. Our parents could not; ours is the only instance of which I have any knowledge of so close resemblance as that. I speak of my brother John, but I am not at all sure that his name was not Henry and mine John. We were regularly christened, but afterward, in the very act of tattooing us with small distinguishing marks, the operator lost his reckoning; and although I bear upon my forearm a small "H" and he bore a "J," it is by no means certain that the letters ought not to have been transposed. During our boyhood our parents tried to distinguish us more obviously by our clothing and other simple devices, but we would so frequently exchange suits and otherwise circumvent the enemy that they abandoned all such ineffectual attempts, and during all the years that we lived together at home everybody recognized the difficulty of the situation and made the best of it by calling us both "Jehnry." I have often wondered at my father's forbearance in not branding us conspicuously upon our unworthy brows, but as we were tolerably good boys and used our power of embarrassment and annoyance with commendable moderation, we escaped the iron. My father was, in fact, a singularly good-natured man, and I think quietly enjoyed nature's practical joke.

Soon after we had come to California, and settled at San Jose (where the only good fortune that awaited us was our meeting with so kind a friend as you) the family, as you know, was broken up by the death of both my parents in the same week. My father died insolvent, and the homestead was sacrificed to pay his debts. My sisters returned to relatives in the East, but owing to your kindness John and I, then twenty-two years of age, obtained employment in San Francisco, in different quarters of the town. Circumstances did not permit us to live together, and we saw each other infrequently, sometimes not oftener than once a week. As we had few acquaintances in common, the fact of our extraordinary likeness was little known. I come now to the matter of your inquiry.

One day soon after we had come to this city I was walking down Market street late in the afternoon, when I was accosted by a well-dressed man of middle age, who after greeting me cordially said: "Stevens, I know, of course, that you do not go out much, but I have told my wife about you, and she would be glad to see you at the house. I have a notion, too, that my girls are worth knowing. Suppose you come out to-morrow at six and dine with us, *en famille;* and then if the ladies can't amuse you afterward I'll stand in with a few games of billiards."

This was said with so bright a smile and so engaging a manner that I had not the heart to refuse, and although I had never seen the man in my life I promptly replied: "You are very good, sir, and it will give me great pleasure to accept the invitation. Please present my compliments to Mrs. Margovan and ask her to expect me."

With a shake of the hand and a pleasant parting word the man passed on. That he had mistaken me for my brother was plain enough. That was an error to which I was accustomed and which it was not my habit to rectify unless the matter seemed important. But how had I known that this man's name was Margovan? It certainly is not a name that one would apply to a man at random, with a probability that it would be right. In point of fact, the name was as strange to me as the man.

The next morning I hastened to where my brother was employed and met him coming out of the office with a number of bills that he was to collect. I told him how I had "committed" him and added that if he didn't care to keep the engagement I should be delighted to continue the impersonation.

"That's queer," he said thoughtfully. "Margovan is the only man in the office here whom I know well and like. When he came in this morning and we had passed the usual greetings some singular impulse prompted me to say: 'Oh, I beg your pardon, Mr. Margovan, but I neglected to ask your address.' I got the address, but what under the sun I was to do with it, I did not know until now. It's good of you to offer to take the consequence of your impudence, but I'll eat that dinner myself, if you please."

He ate a number of dinners at the same place—more than were good for him, I may add without disparaging their quality; for he fell in love with Miss Margovan, proposed marriage to her and was heartlessly accepted.

Several weeks after I had been informed of the engagement, but before it had been convenient for me to make the acquaintance of the young woman and her family, I met one day on Kearny street a handsome but somewhat dissipated-looking man whom something prompted me to follow and watch, which I did without any scruple whatever. He turned up Geary street and followed it until he came to Union square. There he looked at his watch, then entered the square. He loitered about the paths for some time, evidently waiting for some one. Presently he was joined by a fashionably dressed and beautiful young woman and the two walked away up Stockton street, I following. I now felt the necessity of extreme caution, for although the girl was a stranger it seemed to me that she would recognize me at a glance. They made several turns from one street to another and finally, after both had taken a hasty look all about—which I narrowly evaded by stepping into a doorway—they entered a house of which I do not care to state the location. Its location was better than its character.

I protest that my action in playing the spy upon these two strangers was without assignable motive. It was one of which I might or might not be ashamed, according to my estimate of the character of the person finding it out. As an essential part of a narrative educed by your question it is related here without hesitancy or shame.

A week later John took me to the house of his prospective father-in-law, and in Miss Margovan, as you have already surmised, but to my profound astonishment, I recognized the heroine of that discreditable adventure. A gloriously beautiful heroine of a discreditable adventure I must in justice admit that she was; but that fact has only this importance: her beauty was such a surprise to me that it cast a doubt upon her identity with the young woman I had seen before; how could the marvelous fascination of her face have failed to strike me at that time? But no—there was no possibility of error; the difference was due to costume, light and general surroundings.

John and I passed the evening at the house, enduring, with the fortitude of long experience, such delicate enough banter as our likeness naturally suggested. When the young lady and I were left alone for a few minutes I looked her squarely in the face and said with sudden gravity:

"You, too, Miss Margovan, have a double: I saw her last Tuesday afternoon in Union square."

She trained her great gray eyes upon me for a moment, but her glance was a trifle less steady than my own and she withdrew it, fixing it on the tip of her shoe.

"Was she very like me?" she asked, with an indifference which I thought a little overdone.

"So like," said I, "that I greatly admired her, and being unwilling to lose sight of her I confess that I followed her until—Miss Margovan, are you sure that you understand?"

She was now pale, but entirely calm. She again raised her eyes to mine, with a look that did not falter.

"What do you wish me to do?" she asked. "You need not fear to name your terms. I accept them."

It was plain, even in the brief time given me for reflection, that in dealing with this girl ordinary methods would not do, and ordinary exactions were needless.

ONE OF TWINS

"Miss Margovan," I said, doubtless with something of the compassion in my voice that I had in my heart, "it is impossible not to think you the victim of some horrible compulsion. Rather than impose new embarrassments upon you I would prefer to aid you to regain your freedom."

She shook her head, sadly and hopelessly, and I continued, with agitation:

"Your beauty unnerves me. I am disarmed by your frankness and your distress. If you are free to act upon conscience you will, I believe, do what you conceive to be best; if you are not—well, Heaven help us all! You have nothing to fear from me but such opposition to this marriage as I can try to justify on—on other grounds."

These were not my exact words, but that was the sense of them, as nearly as my sudden and conflicting emotions permitted me to express it. I rose and left her without another look at her, met the others as they re-entered the room and said, as calmly as I could: "I have been bidding Miss Margovan good evening; it is later than I thought."

John decided to go with me. In the street he asked if I had observed anything singular in Julia's manner.

"I thought her ill," I replied; "that is why I left." Nothing more was said.

The next evening I came late to my lodgings. The events of the previous evening had made me nervous and ill; I had tried to cure myself and attain to clear thinking by walking in the open air, but I was oppressed with a horrible presentiment of evil— a presentiment which I could not formulate. It was a chill, foggy night; my clothing and hair were damp and I shook with cold. In my dressing-gown and slippers before a blazing grate of coals I was even more uncomfortable. I no longer shivered but shuddered—there is a difference. The dread of some impending calamity was so strong and dispiriting that I tried to drive it away by inviting a real sorrow—tried to dispel the conception of a terrible future by substituting the memory of a painful past. I recalled the death of my parents and endeavored to fix my mind upon the last sad scenes at their bedsides and their graves. It all seemed vague and unreal, as having occurred ages ago and to another person. Suddenly, striking through my thought and parting it as a tense cord is parted by the stroke of steel—I can think of no other comparison—I heard a sharp cry as of one in mortal agony! The voice was that of my brother and seemed to come from the street outside my window. I sprang to the window and threw it open. A street lamp directly opposite threw a wan and ghastly light upon the wet pavement and the fronts of the houses. A single policeman, with upturned collar, was leaning against a gatepost, quietly smoking a cigar. No one else was in sight. I closed the window and pulled down the shade, seated myself before the fire and tried to fix my mind upon my surroundings. By way of assisting, by performance of some familiar act, I looked at my watch; it marked half-past eleven. Again I heard that awful cry! It seemed in the room—at my side. I was frightened and for some moments had not the power to move. A few minutes later—I have no recollection of the intermediate time—I found myself hurrying along an unfamiliar street as fast as I could walk. I did not know where I was, nor whither I was going, but presently sprang up the steps of a house before which were two or three carriages and in which were moving lights and a subdued confusion of voices. It was the house of Mr. Margovan.

You know, good friend, what had occurred there. In one chamber lay Julia Margovan, hours dead by poison; in another John Stevens, bleeding from a pistol wound in the chest, inflicted by his own hand. As I burst into the room, pushed aside the physicians and laid my hand upon his forehead he unclosed his eyes, stared blankly, closed them slowly and died without a sign.

I knew no more until six weeks afterward, when I had been nursed back to life by your own saintly wife in your own beautiful home. All of that you know, but what you do not know is this—which, however, has no bearing upon the subject of your psychological researches—at least not upon that branch of them in which, with a delicacy and consideration all your own, you have asked for less assistance than I think I have given you:

One moonlight night several years afterward I was passing through Union square. The hour was late and the square deserted. Certain memories of the past naturally came into my mind as I came to the spot where I had once witnessed that fateful assignation, and with that unaccountable perversity which prompts us to dwell upon thoughts of the most painful character I seated myself upon one of the benches to indulge them. A man entered the square and came along the walk toward me. His hands were clasped behind him, his head was bowed; he seemed to observe nothing. As he approached the shadow in which I sat I recognized him as the man whom I had seen meet Julia Margovan years before at that spot. But he was terribly altered—gray, worn and haggard. Dissipation and vice were in evidence in every look; illness was no less apparent. His clothing was in disorder, his hair fell across his forehead in a derangement which was at once uncanny and picturesque. He looked fitter for restraint than liberty—the restraint of a hospital.

With no defined purpose I rose and confronted him. He raised his head and looked me full in the face. I have no words to describe the ghastly change that came over his own; it was a look of unspeakable terror—he thought himself eye to eye with a ghost. But he was a courageous man. "Damn you, John Stevens!" he cried, and lifting his trembling arm he dashed his fist feebly at my face and fell headlong upon the gravel as I walked away.

Somebody found him there, stone-dead. Nothing more is known of him, not even his name. To know of a man that he is dead should be enough.

E (28 Oct. 1888): 9 (with subtitle: "A Story Found among the Notes of a Scientist"); *CSTB* 195–205 (with subtitle: "A Letter Found among the Papers of a Deceased Physician"); *CW* 3.121–33.

ONE OF TWINS

NOTE

In this tale, AB shifts from the obviously supernatural to the paranormal, the gray area of phenomena, such as extrasensory perception, which cannot be presently explained by science but are not completely discounted, on the ground that it is conceivable that they may yet be verified. Even so, the degree of sympathetic communication between the brothers and the number of coincidences strains credulity. However, perhaps as important, if not more important, than the story's use of paranormal phenomena is its daring depiction of a loose woman from a respectable family. As was the case with "Killed at Resaca," AB advanced realism in giving readers a glimpse of a woman whose sexuality was not constrained by convention.

THE TAMTONIANS

SOME ACCOUNT OF POLITICS IN THE UNCANNY ISLANDS

In all my intercourse with the Tamtonians I was treated with the most distinguished consideration and no obstacles to a perfect understanding of their social and political life were thrown in my way. My enforced residence on the island was, however, too brief to enable me to master the whole subject as I would have liked, nor do the limits to which I am here restricted permit me to present more than a few of the salient features of Tamtonian political life.

The Government of Tamtonia is what is known in the language of the island as a *Cilbuper.* It differs radically from any form known in other parts of the world and is supposed to have been invented by an ancient chief of the race, named Natas, who was for many centuries after his death worshiped as a god, and whose memory is still held in profound veneration. The Government is of infinite complexity, its various functions distributed among as many officers as possible, the multiplication of places being regarded as of the highest importance, and not so much a means as an end. The Tamtonians seem to think that the highest good to which a human being can attain is the incumbency of an office; and in order that as many as possible may enjoy this advantage, they have as many offices as the country will support, and make the tenure very brief and in no way dependent on good conduct and intelligent administration of official duty. In truth, it occurs usually that a man is turned out of his office in favor of an inexperienced successor before he has himself acquired sufficient experience to perform the duties for which he was chosen with credit to himself or profit to the country. Owing to this incredible folly, the affairs of the island are generally mismanaged. Complaints are the rule, even from those who have had their way in the choice of officers. Of course there can be no such thing as a knowledge of the science of government among such a people, for it is to nobody's interest to acquire it by study of political history. There is, indeed, a prevalent belief that nothing worth knowing is to be learned from the history of other nations—not even from the history of their errors—such is this extraordinary people's national vanity! One of the most notable consequences of this universal voluntary ignorance is that Tamtonia is the home of all the discredited political and fiscal heresies from which many other nations, and especially our own, emancipated themselves centuries ago. They are there in vigorous growth and full flower, and believed to be of purely Tamtonian origin.

It needs hardly to be stated that in their personal affairs these people pursue an entirely different course, for if they did not there could be no profitable industries and professions among them and no property to tax for the support of their government. In his private business a Tamtonian has as high appreciation of fitness and experience as anybody, and having secured a good man keeps him in service as long as possible.

The ruler of the nation, whom they call a *Tnediserp,* is chosen every five years but may be re-chosen for five more. He is supposed to be selected by the people themselves, but in reality they have nothing to do with his selection. The method of choosing a man for Tnediserp is so strange that I doubt my ability to make it clear. The adult male population of the island divides itself into two or more *seitrap.**

Commonly there are three or four, but only two ever have any numerical strength, and none is ever strong morally or intellectually. All the members of each *ytrap* profess the same political opinions, which are provided for them by their leaders every five years and written down on pieces of paper so that they will not be forgotten. The moment that any Tamtonian has read his piece of paper, or *mroftalp,* he unhesitatingly adopts all the opinions that he finds written on it, sometimes as many as forty or fifty, although these may be altogether different from, or even antagonistic to, those with which he was supplied five years before and has been advocating ever since. It will be seen from this that the Tamtonian mind is a thing whose processes no American can hope to understand or even respect. It is instantaneously convinced without either fact or argument, and when these are afterward presented they only confirm it in its miraculous conviction; those which make against that conviction having an even stronger confirmatory power than the others. I have said any Tamtonian, but that is an overstatement. A few usually persist in thinking as they did before; or in altering their convictions in obedience to reason instead of authority, the same as our own people do; but they are at once assailed with the most opprobrious names, accused of treason and all

---

*The Tamtonian language forms its plurals most irregularly, but generally by inflecting the initial syllable of the word instead of the final. The language has a certain crude and primitive grammar, but in point of orthoepy is extremely difficult. With our letters I can hardly hope to give any accurate conception of its pronunciation. As nearly as possible I write its words as they sounded to my ear when carefully spoken for the purpose by intelligent natives. It is a harsh tongue.

THE TAMTONIANS

manner of crimes, pelted with mud and stones and in some instances deprived of their noses and ears by the public executioner, yet in no country is independence of thought so vaunted as a virtue, and in none is freedom of speech considered so obvious a natural right or so necessary to good government.

At the same time that each *ytrap* is supplied with its political opinions for the next five years, its leaders—who, I am told, all pursue the vocation of sharpening axes—name a man whom they wish chosen for the office of Tnediserp. He is usually an idiot from birth, the Tamtonians having a great veneration for such, believing them to be divinely inspired. Although few members of the *ytrap* have ever heard of him before, they at once believe him to have been long the most distinguished idiot in the country; and for the next few months they do little else than quote his words and point to his actions to prove that his idiocy is of entirely superior intensity to that of his opponent—a view that he himself, instructed by his discoverers, does and says all that he can to confirm. His inarticulate mumblings are everywhere repeated as utterances of profound wisdom, and the slaver that drools from his chin is carefully collected and shown to the people, evoking the wildest enthusiasm of his supporters. His opponents all this time are trying to blacken his character by the foulest conceivable falsehoods, some even going so far as to assert that he is not an idiot at all! It is generally agreed among them that if he were chosen to office the most dreadful disasters would ensue, and that, *therefore,* he will not be chosen.

To this last mentioned conviction, namely that the opposing candidate *(rehtot lacsar)* cannot possibly be chosen, I wish to devote a few words here, for it seems to me one of the most extraordinary phenomena of the human mind. It implies, of course, a profound belief in the wisdom of majorities and the error of minorities. This belief can and does in some mysterious way co-exist, in the Tamtonian understanding, with the deepest disgust and most earnest disapproval of a decision which a majority has made. It is of record, indeed, that one political *ytrap* sustained no fewer than six successive defeats by the choice of the man whom it regarded as infinitely inferior to its own, without at all impairing its conviction that the right side must win. In each recurring contest this *ytrap* was as sure that it would succeed as it had been in all the preceding ones—and sure *because* it was in the right! It has been held by some native observers that this conviction is not actually entertained, but only professed for the purpose of influencing the action of others; but this is disproved by the fact that even after the contest is decided, though the result is unknown—when nobody's action can have effect—the leaders (ax-sharpeners) continue earnestly to "claim" this province and that up to the very last moment of uncertainty, and the common people murder one another in the streets for the crime of doubting that the man is chosen whom the murderer chose to prefer. When the majority of a province has chosen one candidate and a majority of the nation another, the mental situation of the worthy Tamtonian is not over-easy of conception, but there can be no doubt that his faith in the wisdom of majorities remains unshaken.

THE TAMTONIANS

One of the two antagonistic idiots having been chosen as ruler, it is customary to speak of him as "the choice of the people," whereas it is obvious that, with the single exception of the corpse that is always put up with him to share his fortunes, he is the only man of whom it is certainly known that nearly one-half the people regard with loathing, as utterly unfit for the position. He is less certainly "the people's choice" than any other man in the country; for while it is known that a large body of his countrymen did not want him, it cannot be known how many really chose some other person but had no opportunity to make their choice known.

The Tamtonians are very proud of their form of government, which gives them so much power in selecting their rulers. This power consists in the privilege of choosing between two men whom they had no hand in selecting from among many millions, any one of whom they might have preferred to either. Yet every Tamtonian is as vain of possessing this incalculably small influence as if he were a very Warwick in making kings and a very Bismarck in using them. He gives himself as many airs and graces as would be appropriate to the display of an honest pin-feather upon the pope's-nose of a mooley peacock.

As already intimated, each congenital idiot whom the ax-grinders name for the office of Tnediserp has upon the "ticket" with him a dead man, who stands or falls with his leader. There is no way of voting for the idiot without voting for the corpse also, and *vice versa*. When one of these precious couples has been chosen the idiot in due time enters upon the duties of his office and the corpse is put into an ice chest and carefully preserved from decay. In case the idiot should himself become a corpse he is buried at once and the other body is then haled out of its ice to take his place. It is propped up in the seat of authority and duly instated in power. This is the signal for a general attack upon it. It is subjected to every kind of sacrilegious indignity, vituperated as a usurper and an "accident," struck with rotten eggs and dead cats, and undergoes the meanest misrepresentation. Its attitude in the chair, its fallen jaw, glazed eyes and degree of decomposition are caricatured and exaggerated out of all reason. Yet such as it is it must be endured for the unexpired term for which its predecessor was chosen. To guard against a possible interregnum, however, a law has recently been passed providing that if it should tumble out of the chair and be too rotten to set up again its clerks *(seiraterces)* are eligible to its place in a stated order of succession. Here we have the remarkable anomaly of the rulers of a "free" people actually appointing their potential successors!—a thing inexpressibly repugnant to all our ideas of popular government, but apparently regarded in Tamtonia as a matter of course.

During the few months intervening between the ax-men's selection of candidates and the people's choice between those selected (a period known as the *laitnediserp ngiapmac*) the Tamtonian character is seen at its worst. There is no infamy too great or too little for the partisans of the various candidates to commit and accuse their opponents of committing. While every one of them declares, and in his heart believes, that honest arguments have greater weight than dishonest; that falsehood reacts on the falsifier's cause; that appeals to passion and prejudice are as ineffectual as dishonorable, few have the strength and sense to deny themselves the luxury of all these methods and worse ones. The laws against bribery, made by themselves, are set at naught and those of civility and good breeding are forgotten. The best of friends quarrel and openly insult one another. The women, who know almost as little of the matters at issue as the men, take part in the abominable discussions; some even encouraging the general demoralization by showing themselves at the public meetings, sometimes actually putting themselves into uniform and marching in procession with banners, music and torchlights.

I feel that this last statement will be hardly understood without explanation. Among the agencies employed by the Tamtonians to prove that one set of candidates is better than another, or to show that one political policy is more likely than another to promote the general prosperity, a high place is accorded to colored rags, flames of fire, noises made upon brass instruments, inarticulate shouts, explosions of gunpowder and lines of men walking and riding through the streets in cheap and tawdry costumes more or less alike. Vast sums of money are expended to procure these convincing evidences of the personal worth of candidates and the political wisdom of ideas. It is very much as if a man should paint his nose pea-green and stand on his head to convince his neighbors that his pigs are fed on acorns. Of course the money subscribed for these various controversial devices is not all wasted: the greater part of it is pocketed by the ax-grinders by whom it is solicited, and who have invented the system. That they have invented it for their own benefit seems not to have occurred to the dupes who pay it. In the universal madness everybody believes whatever monstrous and obvious falsehood is told by the leaders of his own *ytrap*, and nobody listens for a moment to the exposures of their rascality. Reason has flown shrieking from the scene. Caution slumbers by the wayside with unbuttoned pocket: it is the opportunity of thieves!

With a view to abating somewhat the horrors of this recurring season of depravity, it has been proposed by several wise and decent Tamtonians to extend the term of office of the Tnediserp to six years instead of five, but the sharpeners of axes are too powerful to be overthrown. They have made the people believe that if the men whom the country chooses to rule it because it thinks them wise and good were permitted to rule it too long it would be impossible to displace them in punishment for their folly and wickedness. It is, indeed, far more likely that the term of office will be reduced to four years than extended to six. The effect can be no less than hideous!

In Tamtonia there is a current popular phrase dating from many centuries back and running this way: *Eht eciffo dluohs ķees eht nam, ton eht nam eht eciffo*—which may be translated thus: "No citizen ought to try to secure power for himself, but should be selected by others for his fitness to exercise it." The sentiment which this wise and decent phrase expresses has long ceased to have a place in the hearts of those who are everlastingly repeating it, but with regard to the office of Tnediserp it has still a remnant of the vitality of habit. But this is fast dying out, and a few years ago one of the congenital idiots who was a candidate for the highest dignity boldly broke the inhibition

THE TAMTONIANS

and made speeches to the people in advocacy of himself, all over the country. Even more recently another has uttered his preferences in much the same way, but with this difference: he did his speechmaking at his own home, the ax-grinders in his interest rounding up audiences for him and herding them before his own door. One of the two principal corpses, too, was galvanized into a kind of ghastly activity and became a talking automaton; but the other had been too long dead. In a few years more the decent tradition that a man should not blow his own horn will be dead in its application to the high office as it is to all the others, but the phrase will lose none of its currency for that. To the American mind nothing can be more shocking than the Tamtonian practice of openly soliciting political preferment and even paying money to assist in securing it. Such immodesty would be taken as proof of the offender's unfitness to exercise the power which he asks for or bear the dignity which, in demanding it, he belittles. Yet no Tamtonian ever refused to take the hand of a man guilty of such conduct, and there have been instances of fathers giving these greedy vulgarians the hands of their daughters in marriage and thereby assisting to perpetuate the species. The kind of government given by men who go about begging for the right to govern can be more easily imagined than endured. As one of the most celebrated of Tamtonian poets sarcastically says:

> Ill fares the land, to hastening ills a prey,
> Where statesmen rise by throwing shame away.[1]

In short, my readers, I cannot but think that when I swam away from the accursed island of Tamtonia I left behind me the most pestilent race of political rascals and ignoramuses that ever infested any country under the heavens; and I can never sufficiently thank the divine Powers who directed my course to this favored land of goodness, right reason, the blest abode of private worth and public morality— of conscience, liberty and common sense.

E (11 Nov. 1888): 9. Incorporated into "The Land Beyond the Blow."

NOTES

A thinly disguised satire on American politics. AB clearly intended the piece to shock readers when they recognize that the ludicrous practices and attitudes the narrator describes are only familiar American customs, just exaggerated in the telling.

1. The first line is from Oliver Goldsmith's *The Deserted Village* (1770), l. 51; the second is by AB.

THE CITY OF THE GONE AWAY

I was born of poor because honest parents, and until I was twenty-three years old never knew the possibilities of happiness latent in another person's coin. At that time Providence threw me into a deep sleep and revealed to me in a dream the folly of labor. "Behold," said a vision of a holy hermit, "the poverty and squalor of your lot and listen to the teachings of nature. You rise in the morning from your pallet of straw and go forth to your daily labor in the fields. The flowers nod their heads in friendly salutation as you pass. The lark greets you with a burst of song. The early sun sheds his temperate beams upon you, and from the dewy grass you inhale an atmosphere cool and grateful to your lungs. All Nature seems to salute you with the joy of a generous servant welcoming a faithful master. You are in harmony with her gentlest mood and your soul sings within you. You begin your daily task at the plow, hopeful that the noonday will fulfill the promise of the morn, maturing the charms of the landscape and confirming its benediction upon your spirit. You follow the plow until fatigue invokes repose, and seating yourself upon the earth at the end of your furrow you expect to enjoy in fullness the delights of which you did but taste.

"Alas! the sun has climbed into a brazen sky and his beams are become a torrent. The flowers have closed their petals, confining their perfume and denying their colors to the eye. Coolness no longer exhales from the grass: the dew has vanished and the dry surface of the fields repeats the fierce heat of the sky. No longer the birds of Heaven salute you with melody, but the jay harshly upbraids you from the edge of the copse. Unhappy man! all the gentle and healing ministrations of Nature are denied you in punishment of your sin. You have broken the First Commandment of the Natural Decalogue: you have labored!"

Awakening from my dream, I collected my few belongings, bade adieu to my erring parents and departed out of that land, pausing at the grave of my grandfather, who had been a priest, to take an oath that never again, Heaven helping me, would I earn an honest penny.

How long I traveled I know not, but I came at last to a great city by the sea, where I set up as a physician. The name of that place I do not now remember, for such were my activity and renown in my new profession that the Aldermen, moved by pressure of public opinion, altered it, and thenceforth the place was known as the City of the Gone Away. It is needless to say that I had no knowledge of medicine, but by securing the service of an eminent forger I obtained a diploma purporting to have been granted by the Royal Quackery of Charlatanic Empiricism at Hoodos, which, framed in immortelles and suspended by a bit of *crêpe* to a willow in front of my office, attracted the ailing in great numbers. In connection with my dispensary I conducted one of the largest undertaking establishments ever known, and as soon as my means permitted, purchased a wide tract of land and made it into a cemetery. I owned also some very profitable marble works on one side of the gateway to the cemetery, and on the other an extensive flower garden. My Mourner's Emporium was patronized by the beauty, fashion and sorrow of the city. In short, I was in a very prosperous way of business, and within a year was able to send for my parents and establish my old father very comfortably as a receiver of stolen goods—an act which I confess was saved from the reproach of filial gratitude only by my exaction of all the profits.

But the vicissitudes of fortune are avoidable only by practice of the sternest indigence: human foresight cannot provide against the envy of the gods and the tireless machinations of Fate. The widening circle of prosperity grows weaker as it spreads until the antagonistic forces which it has pushed back are made powerful by compression to resist and finally overwhelm. So great grew the renown of my skill in medicine that patients were brought to me from all the four quarters of the globe. Burdensome invalids whose tardiness in dying was a perpetual grief to their friends; wealthy testators whose legatees were desirous to come by their own; superfluous children of penitent parents and dependent parents of frugal children; wives of husbands ambitious to remarry and husbands of wives without standing in the courts of divorce— these and all conceivable classes of the surplus population were conducted to my dispensary in the City of the Gone Away. They came in incalculable multitudes.

Government agents brought me caravans of orphans, paupers, lunatics and all who had become a public charge. My skill in curing orphanism and pauperism was particularly acknowledged by a grateful parliament.

Naturally, all this promoted the public prosperity, for although I got the greater part of the money that strangers expended in the city, the rest went into the channels of trade, and I was myself a liberal investor, purchaser and employer, and a patron of the arts and sciences. The City of the Gone Away grew so rapidly that in a few years it had inclosed my cemetery, despite its own constant growth. In that fact lay the lion that rent me.

THE CITY OF THE GONE AWAY

The Aldermen declared my cemetery a public evil and decided to take it from me, remove the bodies to another place and make a park of it. I was to be paid for it and could easily bribe the appraisers to fix a high price, but for a reason which will appear the decision gave me little joy. It was in vain that I protested against the sacrilege of disturbing the holy dead, although this was a powerful appeal, for in that land the dead are held in religious veneration. Temples are built in their honor and a separate priesthood maintained at the public expense, whose only duty is performance of memorial services of the most solemn and touching kind. On four days in the year there is a Festival of the Good, as it is called, when all the people lay by their work or business and, headed by the priests, march in procession through the cemeteries, adorning the graves and praying in the temples. However bad a man's life may be, it is believed that when dead he enters into a state of eternal and inexpressible happiness. To signify a doubt of this is an offense punishable by death. To deny burial to the dead, or to exhume a buried body, except under sanction of law by special dispensation and with solemn ceremony, is a crime having no stated penalty because no one has ever had the hardihood to commit it.

All these considerations were in my favor, yet so well assured were the people and their civic officers that my cemetery was injurious to the public health that it was condemned and appraised, and with terror in my heart I received three times its value and began to settle up my affairs with all speed.

A week later was the day appointed for the formal inauguration of the ceremony of removing the bodies. The day was fine and the entire population of the city and surrounding country was present at the imposing religious rites. These were directed by the mortuary priesthood in full canonicals. There was propitiatory sacrifice in the Temples of the Once, followed by a processional pageant of great splendor, ending at the cemetery. The Great Mayor in his robe of state led the procession. He was armed with a golden spade and followed by one hundred male and female singers, clad all in white and chanting the Hymn to the Gone Away. Behind these came the minor priesthood of the temples, all the civic authorities, habited in their official apparel, each carrying a living pig as an offering to the gods of the dead. Of the many divisions of the line, the last was formed by the populace, with uncovered heads, sifting dust into their hair in token of humility. In front of the mortuary chapel in the midst of the necropolis, the Supreme Priest stood in gorgeous vestments, supported on each hand by a line of bishops and other high dignitaries of his prelacy, all frowning with the utmost austerity. As the Great Mayor paused in the Presence, the minor clergy, the civic authorities, the choir and populace closed in and encompassed the spot. The Great Mayor, laying his golden spade at the feet of the Supreme Priest, knelt in silence.

"Why comest thou here, presumptuous mortal?" said the Supreme Priest in clear, deliberate tones. "Is it thy unhallowed purpose with this implement to uncover the mysteries of death and break the repose of the Good?"

THE CITY OF THE GONE AWAY

The Great Mayor, still kneeling, drew from his robe a document with portentous seals: "Behold, O ineffable, thy servant, having warrant of his people, entreateth at thy holy hands the custody of the Good, to the end and purpose that they lie in fitter earth, by consecration duly prepared against their coming."

With that he placed in the sacerdotal hands the order of the Council of Aldermen decreeing the removal. Merely touching the parchment, the Supreme Priest passed it to the Head Necropolitan at his side, and raising his hands relaxed the severity of his countenance and exclaimed: "The gods comply."

Down the line of prelates on either side, his gesture, look and words were successively repeated. The Great Mayor rose to his feet, the choir began a solemn chant and, opportunely, a funeral car drawn by ten white horses with black plumes rolled in at the gate and made its way through the parting crowd to the grave selected for the occasion—that of a high official whom I had treated for chronic incumbency. The Great Mayor touched the grave with his golden spade (which he then presented to the Supreme Priest) and two stalwart diggers with iron ones set vigorously to work.

At that moment I was observed to leave the cemetery and the country; for a report of the rest of the proceedings I am indebted to my sainted father, who related it in a letter to me, written in jail the night before he had the irreparable misfortune to take the kink out of a rope.

As the workmen proceeded with their excavation, four bishops stationed themselves at the corners of the grave and in the profound silence of the multitude, broken otherwise only by the harsh grinding sound of spades, repeated continuously, one after another, the solemn invocations and responses from the Ritual of the Disturbed, imploring the blessed brother to forgive. But the blessed brother was not there. Full fathom two they mined for him in vain, then gave it up. The priests were visibly disconcerted, the populace was aghast, for that grave was indubitably vacant.

After a brief consultation with the Supreme Priest, the Great Mayor ordered the workmen to open another grave. The ritual was omitted this time until the coffin should be uncovered. There was no coffin, no body.

The cemetery was now a scene of the wildest confusion and dismay. The people shouted and ran hither and thither, gesticulating, clamoring, all talking at once, none listening. Some ran for spades, fire-shovels, hoes, sticks, anything. Some brought carpenters' adzes, even chisels from the marble works, and with these inadequate aids set to work upon the first graves they came to. Others fell upon the mounds with their bare hands, scraping away the earth as eagerly as dogs digging for marmots. Before nightfall the surface of the greater part of the cemetery had been upturned; every grave had been explored to the bottom and thousands of men were tearing away at the interspaces with as furious a frenzy as exhaustion would permit. As night came on torches were lighted, and in the sinister glare these frantic mortals, looking like a legion of fiends performing some unholy rite, pursued their disappointing work until they had devastated the entire area. But not a body did they find—not even a coffin.

THE CITY OF THE GONE AWAY

The explanation is exceedingly simple. An important part of my income had been derived from the sale of *cadavres* to medical colleges, which never before had been so well supplied, and which, in added recognition of my services to science, had all bestowed upon me diplomas, degrees and fellowships without number. But their demand for *cadavres* was unequal to my supply: by even the most prodigal extravagances they could not consume the one-half of the products of my skill as a physician. As to the rest, I had owned and operated the most extensive and thoroughly appointed soapworks in all the country. The excellence of my "Toilet Homoline" was attested by certificates from scores of the saintliest theologians, and I had one in autograph from Badelina Fatti the most famous living soaprano.[1]

E (2 Dec. 1888): 9 (as "The Gone Away: A Tale of Medical Science and Commercial Thrift"); *CW* **8**.52–62.

NOTES

A criticism of a society to which nothing is sacred and whose hypocrisy conceals its valuing of appearance over reality. The story bears some resemblances to "Oil of Dog" (p. 754) and AB's fierce contempt for such duplicity underlies the tale's humor of exaggeration. In its linking of medical malpractice and undertaking, he very likely touched on issues in the real world.

1. An allusion to Adelina Patti. See "The Miraculous Guest," p. 350 note 2.

CHICKAMAUGA

One sunny autumn afternoon a child strayed away from its rude home in a small field and entered a forest unobserved. It was happy in a new sense of freedom from control, happy in the opportunity of exploration and adventure; for this child's spirit, in bodies of its ancestors, had for thousands of years been trained to memorable feats of discovery and conquest—victories in battles whose critical moments were centuries, whose victors' camps were cities of hewn stone. From the cradle of its race it had conquered its way through two continents and passing a great sea had penetrated a third, there to be born to war and dominion as a heritage.

The child was a boy aged about six years, the son of a poor planter. In his younger manhood the father had been a soldier, had fought against naked savages and followed the flag of his country into the capital of a civilized race to the far South.[1] In the peaceful life of a planter the warrior-fire survived; once kindled, it is never extinguished. The man loved military books and pictures and the boy had understood enough to make himself a wooden sword, though even the eye of his father would hardly have known it for what it was. This weapon he now bore bravely, as became the son of an heroic race, and pausing now and again in the sunny space of the forest assumed, with some exaggeration, the postures of aggression and defense that he had been taught by the engraver's art. Made reckless by the ease with which he overcame invisible foes attempting to stay his advance, he committed the common enough military error of pushing the pursuit to a dangerous extreme, until he found himself upon the margin of a wide but shallow brook, whose rapid waters barred his direct advance against the flying foe that had crossed with illogical ease. But the intrepid victor was not to be baffled; the spirit of the race which had passed the great sea burned unconquerable in that small breast and would not be denied. Finding a place where some bowlders in the bed of the stream lay but a step or a leap apart, he made his way across and fell again upon the rear-guard of his imaginary foe, putting all to the sword.

Now that the battle had been won, prudence required that he withdraw to his base of operations. Alas; like many a mightier conqueror, and like one, the mightiest, he could not

> curb the lust for war,
> Nor learn that tempted Fate will leave the loftiest star.[2]

Advancing from the bank of the creek he suddenly found himself confronted with a new and more formidable enemy: in the path that he was following, sat, bolt upright, with ears erect and paws suspended before it, a rabbit! With a startled cry the child turned and fled, he knew not in what direction, calling with inarticulate cries for his mother, weeping, stumbling, his tender skin cruelly torn by brambles, his little heart beating hard with terror—breathless, blind with tears—lost in the forest! Then, for more than an hour, he wandered with erring feet through the tangled under-growth, till at last, overcome by fatigue, he lay down in a narrow space between two rocks, within a few yards of the stream and still grasping his toy sword, no longer a weapon but a companion, sobbed himself to sleep. The wood birds sang merrily above his head; the squirrels, whisking their bravery of tail, ran barking from tree to tree, unconscious of the pity of it, and somewhere far away was a strange, muffled thun-der, as if the partridges were drumming in celebration of Nature's victory over the son of her immemorial enslavers. And back at the little plantation, where white men and black were hastily searching the fields and hedges in alarm, a mother's heart was breaking for her missing child.

Hours passed, and then the little sleeper rose to his feet. The chill of the evening was in his limbs, the fear of the gloom in his heart. But he had rested, and he no longer wept. With some blind instinct which impelled to action he struggled through the undergrowth about him and came to a more open ground—on his right the brook, to the left a gentle acclivity studded with infrequent trees; over all, the gathering gloom of twilight. A thin, ghostly mist rose along the water. It frightened and repelled him; instead of recrossing, in the direction whence he had come, he turned his back upon it, and went forward toward the dark inclosing wood. Suddenly he saw before him a strange moving object which he took to be some large animal—a dog, a pig—he could not name it; perhaps it was a bear. He had seen pictures of bears, but knew noth-ing to their discredit and had vaguely wished to meet one. But something in form or movement of this object—something in the awkwardness of its approach—told him that it was not a bear, and curiosity was stayed by fear. He stood still and as it came slowly on gained courage every moment, for he saw that at least it had not the long, menacing ears of the rabbit. Possibly his impressionable mind was half conscious of something familiar in its shambling, awkward gait. Before it had approached near enough to resolve his doubts he saw that it was followed by another and another. To right and to left were many more; the whole open space about him was alive with them—all moving toward the brook.

CHICKAMAUGA

They were men. They crept upon their hands and knees. They used their hands only, dragging their legs. They used their knees only, their arms hanging idle at their sides. They strove to rise to their feet, but fell prone in the attempt. They did nothing naturally, and nothing alike, save only to advance foot by foot in the same direction. Singly, in pairs and in little groups, they came on through the gloom, some halting now and again while others crept slowly past them, then resuming their movement. They came by dozens and by hundreds; as far on either hand as one could see in the deepening gloom they extended and the black wood behind them appeared to be inexhaustible. The very ground seemed in motion toward the creek. Occasionally one who had paused did not again go on, but lay motionless. He was dead. Some, pausing, made strange gestures with their hands, erected their arms and lowered them again, clasped their heads; spread their palms upward, as men are sometimes seen to do in public prayer.

Not all of this did the child note; it is what would have been noted by an elder observer; he saw little but that these were men, yet crept like babes. Being men, they were not terrible, though unfamiliarly clad. He moved among them freely, going from one to another and peering into their faces with childish curiosity. All their faces were singularly white and many were streaked and gouted with red. Something in this—something too, perhaps, in their grotesque attitudes and movements— reminded him of the painted clown whom he had seen last summer in the circus, and he laughed as he watched them. But on and ever on they crept, these maimed and bleeding men, as heedless as he of the dramatic contrast between his laughter and their own ghastly gravity. To him it was a merry spectacle. He had seen his father's negroes creep upon their hands and knees for his amusement—had ridden them so, "making believe" they were his horses. He now approached one of these crawling figures from behind and with an agile movement mounted it astride. The man sank upon his breast, recovered, flung the small boy fiercely to the ground as an unbroken colt might have done, then turned upon him a face that lacked a lower jaw—from the upper teeth to the throat was a great red gap fringed with hanging shreds of flesh and splinters of bone. The unnatural prominence of nose, the absence of chin, the fierce eyes, gave this man the appearance of a great bird of prey crimsoned in throat and breast by the blood of its quarry. The man rose to his knees, the child to his feet. The man shook his fist at the child; the child, terrified at last, ran to a tree near by, got upon the farther side of it and took a more serious view of the situation. And so the clumsy multitude dragged itself slowly and painfully along in hideous pantomime—moved forward down the slope like a swarm of great black beetles, with never a sound of going—in silence profound, absolute.[3]

Instead of darkening, the haunted landscape began to brighten. Through the belt of trees beyond the brook shone a strange red light, the trunks and branches of the trees making a black lacework against it. It struck the creeping figures and gave them monstrous shadows, which caricatured their movements on the lit grass. It fell upon their faces, touching their whiteness with a ruddy tinge, accentuating the stains with which so many of them were freaked[4] and maculated. It sparkled on buttons and bits of metal in their clothing. Instinctively the child turned toward the growing splendor and moved down the slope with his horrible companions; in a few moments had passed the foremost of the throng—not much of a feat, considering his advantages. He placed himself in the lead, his wooden sword still in hand, and solemnly directed the march, conforming his pace to theirs and occasionally turning as if to see that his forces did not straggle. Surely such a leader never before had such a following.

Scattered about upon the ground now slowly narrowing by the encroachment of this awful march to water, were certain articles to which, in the leader's mind, were coupled no significant associations: an occasional blanket, tightly rolled lengthwise, doubled and the ends bound together with a string; a heavy knapsack here, and there a broken rifle—such things, in short, as are found in the rear of retreating troops, the "spoor" of men flying from their hunters. Everywhere near the creek, which here had a margin of lowland, the earth was trodden into mud by the feet of men and horses. An observer of better experience in the use of his eyes would have noticed that these footprints pointed in both directions; the ground had been twice passed over—in advance and in retreat. A few hours before, these desperate, stricken men, with their more fortunate and now distant comrades, had penetrated the forest in thousands. Their successive battalions, breaking into swarms and re-forming in lines, had passed the child on every side—had almost trodden on him as he slept. The rustle and murmur of their march had not awakened him. Almost within a stone's throw of where he lay they had fought a battle; but all unheard by him were the roar of the musketry, the shock of the cannon, "the thunder of the captains and the shouting."[5] He had slept through it all, grasping his little wooden sword with perhaps a tighter clutch in unconscious sympathy with his martial environment, but as heedless of the grandeur of the struggle as the dead who had died to make the glory.

The fire beyond the belt of woods on the farther side of the creek, reflected to earth from the canopy of its own smoke, was now suffusing the whole landscape. It transformed the sinuous line of mist to the vapor of gold. The water gleamed with dashes of red, and red, too, were many of the stones protruding above the surface. But that was blood; the less desperately wounded had stained them in crossing. On them, too, the child now crossed with eager steps; he was going to the fire. As he stood upon the farther bank he turned about to look at the companions of his march. The advance was arriving at the creek. The stronger had already drawn themselves to the brink and plunged their faces into the flood. Three or four who lay without motion appeared to have no heads. At this the child's eyes expanded with wonder; even his hospitable understanding could not accept a phenomenon implying such vitality as that. After slaking their thirst these men had not had the strength to back away from the water, nor to keep their heads above it. They were drowned. In rear of these, the open spaces of the forest showed the leader as many formless figures of his grim command as at first; but not nearly so many were in motion. He waved his cap for their encouragement and smilingly pointed with his weapon in the direction of the guiding light—a pillar of fire to this strange exodus.[6]

Confident of the fidelity of his forces, he now entered the belt of woods, passed through it easily in the red illumination, climbed a fence, ran across a field, turning now and again to coquet with his responsive shadow, and so approached the blazing ruin of a dwelling. Desolation everywhere! In all the wide glare not a living thing was visible. He cared nothing for that; the spectacle pleased, and he danced with glee in imitation of the wavering flames. He ran about, collecting fuel, but every object that he found was too heavy for him to cast in from the distance to which the heat limited his approach. In despair he flung in his sword—a surrender to the superior forces of Nature. His military career was at an end.

Shifting his position, his eyes fell upon some outbuildings which had an oddly familiar appearance, as if he had dreamed of them. He stood considering them with wonder, when suddenly the entire plantation, with its inclosing forest, seemed to turn as if upon a pivot. His little world swung half around; the points of the compass were reversed. He recognized the blazing building as his own home!

For a moment he stood stupefied by the power of the revelation, then ran with stumbling feet, making a half-circuit of the ruin. There, conspicuous in the light of the conflagration, lay the dead body of a woman—the white face turned upward, the hands thrown out and clutched full of grass, the clothing deranged, the long dark hair in tangles and full of clotted blood. The greater part of the forehead was torn away, and from the jagged hole the brain protruded, overflowing the temple, a frothy mass of gray, crowned with clusters of crimson bubbles—the work of a shell.[7]

The child moved his little hands, making wild, uncertain gestures. He uttered a series of inarticulate and indescribable cries—something between the chattering of an ape and the gobbling of a turkey—a startling, soulless, unholy sound, the language of a devil. The child was a deaf mute.

Then he stood motionless, with quivering lips, looking down upon the wreck.

E (20 Jan. 1889): 9; TSC 41–53; IML 36–48; **CW 2.46–57**. Reprinted in *Anti-Philistine*, no. 3 (15 Aug. 1897): 150–58.

NOTES

The battle of Chickamauga, like that of Shiloh, remained for Bierce an epitome of warfare. Two of his greatest works—his memoir, "A Little of Chickamauga," and this story—came out of it. The memoir (E, 24 Apr. 1898; SS 29–33) recounts the battle in conventional but gripping detail, and this story is justly famous as being one of his strongest and most eloquent antiwar statements. Perhaps no other work of his presents such a terrible indictment of the scheme of things. The boy as a symbol of the human race is described as "born to war and dominion," but the quotation from Byron (see note 2) warns that the lust for war is fated to disaster. A sense of doom thus hovers over the tale, which extends the theme of war from man versus man to the more encompassing venue of nature versus man. The boy, who cannot hear or speak, is a victim of nature from birth. Once it becomes evident that a battle is under way, first the wounded soldiers and then he are seen as victims of war. At the end of the story he and the soldiers are common victims who succumb to nature's elemental assault on them in the form of fire.

The soldiers are all stained—"maculated and freaked"—by warfare and are reduced to the status of animals that creep on all fours and crawl on their bellies. The boy has an additional stain: he comes from a slave-owning family. His riding of his family's slaves metaphorically recapitulates what the adults of his family did to their slaves, and his riding of the crawling soldier hints at the political and military consequences of slavery. Lincoln, in his second inaugural address, recognized slavery as the root cause of the Civil War and contemplated that the blood, suffering, and cost of the war might be a just scourging for the 250 years of the evils of slavery. In this story, AB also leaves open the possibility that the war might be enforcing some measure of equity but, unlike Lincoln, he does not propose humble submission to the grand purposes of a just and righteous Deity. Instead he sees war as unredeemingly inhumane and brutalizing in its impartial, incomprehensible, and awful violence.

1. During the Mexican War (1846–48), American troops besieged and captured many cities in Mexico, including Mexico City, which Gen. Winfield Scott entered on 14 September 1847 with an army of six thousand men.

2. Lord Byron (1788–1824), *Childe Harold's Pilgrimage* (1812), canto 3, stanza 38, referring to Napoleon.

3. Cf. "A Little of Chickamauga": "we finally retired in profound silence and dejection, unmolested" (*SS* 32).

4. In this sense "freak" means "to variegate; streak or fleck" (*C* [s.v. FREAK³]).

5. Cf. Job 39:25: "He saith among the trumpets, Ha, ha; and he smelleth the battle afar off, the thunder of the captains, and the shouting." A phrase much used by AB; see the essay "The Thunder of the Captains," *E* (3 Dec. 1899): 15.

6. Ex. 13:21: "And the Lord went before them by day in a pillar of a cloud, to lead them the way; and by night in a pillar of fire, to give them light; to go by day and night."

7. Cf. "What I Saw of Shiloh" (1874; *SS* 19): "He lay face upward, taking in his breath in convulsive, rattling snorts, and blowing it out in sputters of froth which crawled creamily down his cheeks, piling itself alongside his neck and ears. A bullet had clipped a groove in his skull, above the temple; from this the brain protruded in bosses, dropping off in flakes and strings. I had not previously known one could get on, even in this unsatisfactory fashion, with so little brain."

ONE OFFICER, ONE MAN

Captain Graffenreid stood at the head of his company. The regiment was not engaged. It formed a part of the front line-of-battle, which stretched away to the right with a visible length of nearly two miles through the open ground. The left flank was veiled by woods; to the right also the line was lost to sight, but it extended many miles. A hundred yards in rear was a second line; behind this, the reserve brigades and divisions in column. Batteries of artillery occupied the spaces between and crowned the low hills. Groups of horsemen—generals with their staffs and escorts, and field officers of regiments behind the colors—broke the regularity of the lines and columns. Numbers of these figures of interest had field-glasses at their eyes and sat motionless, stolidly scanning the country in front; others came and went at a slow canter, bearing orders. There were squads of stretcher-bearers, ambulances, wagon-trains with ammunition and officers' servants in rear of all—of all that was visible—for still in rear of these, along the roads, extended for many miles all that vast multitude of noncombatants who with their various *impedimenta* are assigned to the inglorious but important duty of supplying the fighters' many needs.

An army in line-of-battle awaiting attack, or preparing to deliver it, presents strange contrasts. At the front are precision, formality, fixity and silence. Toward the rear these characteristics are less and less conspicuous, and finally, in point of space, are lost altogether in confusion, motion and noise. The homogeneous becomes heterogeneous. Definition is lacking; repose is replaced by an apparently purposeless activity; harmony vanishes in hubbub, form in disorder. Commotion everywhere and ceaseless unrest. The men who do not fight are never ready.

From his position at the right of his company in the front rank, Captain Graffenreid had an unobstructed outlook toward the enemy. A half-mile of open and nearly level ground lay before him, and beyond it an irregular wood, covering a slight acclivity; not a human being anywhere visible. He could imagine nothing more peaceful than the appearance of that pleasant landscape with its long stretches of brown fields over which the atmosphere was beginning to quiver in the heat of the morning sun. Not a sound came from forest or field—not even the barking of a dog or the crowing of a cock at the half-seen plantation house on the crest among the trees. Yet every man in those miles of men knew that he and death were face to face.

Captain Graffenreid had never in his life seen an armed enemy, and the war in which his regiment was one of the first to take the field was two years old. He had had the rare advantage of a military education, and when his comrades had marched to the front he had been detached for administrative service at the capital of his State, where it was thought that he could be most useful. Like a bad soldier he protested, and like a good one obeyed. In close official and personal relations with the governor of his State, and enjoying his confidence and favor, he had firmly refused promotion and seen his juniors elevated above him. Death had been busy in his distant regiment; vacancies among the field officers had occurred again and again; but from a chivalrous feeling that war's rewards belonged of right to those who bore the storm and stress of battle he had held his humble rank and generously advanced the fortunes of others. His silent devotion to principle had conquered at last: he had been relieved of his hateful duties and ordered to the front, and now, untried by fire, stood in the van of battle in command of a company of hardy veterans, to whom he had been only a name, and that name a by-word. By none—not even by those of his brother officers in whose favor he had waived his rights—was his devotion to duty understood. They were too busy to be just; he was looked upon as one who had shirked his duty, until forced unwillingly into the field. Too proud to explain, yet not too insensible to feel, he could only endure and hope.

Of all the Federal Army on that summer morning none had accepted battle more joyously than Anderton Graffenreid. His spirit was buoyant, his faculties were riotous. He was in a state of mental exaltation and scarcely could endure the enemy's tardiness in advancing to the attack. To him this was opportunity—for the result he cared nothing. Victory or defeat, as God might will; in one or in the other he should prove himself a soldier and a hero; he should vindicate his right to the respect of his men and the companionship of his brother officers—to the consideration of his superiors. How his heart leaped in his breast as the bugle sounded the stirring notes of the "assembly"![1] With what a light tread, scarcely conscious of the earth beneath his feet, he strode forward at the head of his company, and how exultingly he noted the tactical dispositions which placed his regiment in the front line! And if perchance some memory came to him of a pair of dark eyes that might take on a tenderer light in reading the account of that day's doings, who shall blame him for the unmartial thought or count it a debasement of soldierly ardor?

Suddenly, from the forest a half-mile in front—apparently from among the upper branches of the trees, but really from the ridge beyond—rose a tall column of white smoke. A moment later came a deep, jarring explosion, followed—almost attended—

ONE OFFICER, ONE MAN

by a hideous rushing sound that seemed to leap forward across the intervening space with inconceivable rapidity, rising from whisper to roar with too quick a gradation for attention to note the successive stages of its horrible progression! A visible tremor ran along the lines of men; all were startled into motion. Captain Graffenreid dodged and threw up his hands to one side of his head, palms outward. As he did so he heard a keen, ringing report, and saw on a hillside behind the line a fierce roll of smoke and dust—the shell's explosion. It had passed a hundred feet to his left! He heard, or fancied he heard, a low, mocking laugh and turning in the direction whence it came saw the eyes of his first lieutenant fixed upon him with an unmistakable look of amusement. He looked along the line of faces in the front ranks. The men were laughing. At him? The thought restored the color to his bloodless face—restored too much of it. His cheeks burned with a fever of shame.

The enemy's shot was not answered: the officer in command at that exposed part of the line had evidently no desire to provoke a cannonade. For the forbearance Captain Graffenreid was conscious of a sense of gratitude. He had not known that the flight of a projectile was a phenomenon of so appalling character. His conception of war had already undergone a profound change, and he was conscious that his new feeling was manifesting itself in visible perturbation. His blood was boiling in his veins; he had a choking sensation and felt that if he had a command to give it would be inaudible, or at least unintelligible. The hand in which he held his sword trembled; the other moved automatically, clutching at various parts of his clothing. He found a difficulty in standing still and fancied that his men observed it. Was it fear? He feared it was.

From somewhere away to the right came, as the wind served, a low, intermittent murmur like that of ocean in a storm—like that of a distant railway train—like that of wind among the pines—three sounds so nearly alike that the ear, unaided by the judgment, cannot distinguish them one from another. The eyes of the troops were drawn in that direction; the mounted officers turned their field-glasses that way. Mingled with the sound was an irregular throbbing. He thought it, at first, the beating of his fevered blood in his ears; next, the distant tapping of a bass drum.

"The ball is opened on the right flank," said an officer.

Captain Graffenreid understood: the sounds were musketry and artillery. He nodded and tried to smile. There was apparently nothing infectious in the smile.

Presently a light line of blue smoke-puffs broke out along the edge of the wood in front, succeeded by a crackle of rifles. There were keen, sharp hissings in the air, terminating abruptly with a thump near by. The man at Captain Graffenreid's side dropped his rifle; his knees gave way and he pitched awkwardly forward, falling upon his face. Somebody shouted "Lie down!" and the dead man was hardly distinguishable from the living. It looked as if those few rifle-shots had slain ten thousand men. Only the field officers remained erect; their concession to the emergency consisted in dismounting and sending their horses to the shelter of the low hills immediately in rear.

ONE OFFICER, ONE MAN

Captain Graffenreid lay alongside the dead man, from beneath whose breast flowed a little rill of blood. It had a faint, sweetish odor that sickened him. The face was crushed into the earth and flattened. It looked yellow already, and was repulsive. Nothing suggested the glory of a soldier's death nor mitigated the loathsomeness of the incident. He could not turn his back upon the body without facing away from his company.

He fixed his eyes upon the forest, where all again was silent. He tried to imagine what was going on there—the lines of troops forming to attack, the guns being pushed forward by hand to the edge of the open. He fancied he could see their black muzzles protruding from the undergrowth, ready to deliver their storm of missiles—such missiles as the one whose shriek had so unsettled his nerves. The distension of his eyes became painful; a mist seemed to gather before them; he could no longer see across the field, yet would not withdraw his gaze lest he see the dead man at his side.

The fire of battle was not now burning very brightly in this warrior's soul. From inaction had come introspection. He sought rather to analyze his feelings than distinguish himself by courage and devotion. The result was profoundly disappointing. He covered his face with his hands and groaned aloud.

The hoarse murmur of battle grew more and more distinct upon the right; the murmur had, indeed, become a roar, the throbbing, a thunder. The sounds had worked round obliquely to the front; evidently the enemy's left was being driven back, and the propitious moment to move against the salient angle of his line would soon arrive. The silence and mystery in front were ominous; all felt that they boded evil to the assailants.

Behind the prostrate lines sounded the hoof-beats of galloping horses; the men turned to look. A dozen staff officers were riding to the various brigade and regimental commanders, who had remounted. A moment more and there was a chorus of voices, all uttering out of time the same words—"Attention, battalion!" The men sprang to their feet and were aligned by the company commanders. They awaited the word "forward"—awaited, too, with beating hearts and set teeth the gusts of lead and iron that were to smite them at their first movement in obedience to that word. The word was not given; the tempest did not break out. The delay was hideous, maddening! It unnerved like a respite at the guillotine.

Captain Graffenreid stood at the head of his company, the dead man at his feet. He heard the battle on the right—rattle and crash of musketry, ceaseless thunder of cannon, desultory cheers of invisible combatants. He marked ascending clouds of smoke from distant forests. He noted the sinister silence of the forest in front. These contrasting extremes affected the whole range of his sensibilities. The strain upon his nervous organization was insupportable. He grew hot and cold by turns. He panted like a dog, and then forgot to breathe until reminded by vertigo.

Suddenly he grew calm. Glancing downward, his eyes had fallen upon his naked sword, as he held it, point to earth. Foreshortened to his view, it resembled somewhat,

ONE OFFICER, ONE MAN

he thought, the short heavy blade of the ancient Roman. The fancy was full of suggestion, malign, fateful, heroic!

The sergeant in the rear rank, immediately behind Captain Graffenreid, now observed a strange sight. His attention drawn by an uncommon movement made by the captain—a sudden reaching forward of the hands and their energetic withdrawal, throwing the elbows out, as in pulling an oar—he saw spring from between the officer's shoulders a bright point of metal which prolonged itself outward, nearly a half-arm's length—a blade! It was faintly streaked with crimson, and its point approached so near to the sergeant's breast, and with so quick a movement, that he shrank backward in alarm. That moment Captain Graffenreid pitched heavily forward upon the dead man and died.

A week later the major-general commanding the left corps of the Federal Army submitted the following official report:

"SIR: I have the honor to report, with regard to the action of the 19th inst., that owing to the enemy's withdrawal from my front to reinforce his beaten left, my command was not seriously engaged. My loss was as follows: Killed, one officer, one man."

E (17 Feb. 1889): 9 (as "A Coward"); *CSTB* 51–60; **CW 2.197–208**.

NOTES

This story and others like it earned for AB the credit for bringing a new dimension of realism to war fiction. Unlike most of his predecessors, AB constructed his tales more from introspection than action. His realism consisted not so much of gory details as of the rendering of the true emotions and concerns of a soldier as he faced death.

Again, in this tale, AB explores the thin divide between bravery and cowardice, and the fact that reason may work against its possessor. Although the story was originally titled "A Coward" and the *E* version begins with the lines "I shall break down! I shall break down!" it is likely that the title change was made mainly because AB did not consider Graffenreid a coward. In a "Prattle" reply to a correspondent, he said of the story: "Observe that the inexperienced officer committed suicide because, from many symptoms, he *thought* himself cowardly. It is nowhere intimated that he was" (*E,* 27 May 1894). Support for this comment can be found in a sentence in the *E* version on those "many symptoms" that was dropped from the *CW* version: "These symptoms of excitement he interpreted as cowardice, and was filled with apprehensions of disgrace." In other words, Graffenreid's reactions to the imminence of action were normal feelings of excitement, but his inexperience and anxiety led him to misinterpret them. In addition, it was not death he feared, but disgrace.

Relatedly, AB consistently refused to make a blanket condemnation of suicide. Throughout his career, he displayed empathy for individuals whose suffering exceeded their strength to endure it. Another "Prattle" comment is relevant to Graffenreid's situation: "the soldier braves the danger of death; the suicide braves death itself" (*E,* 23 Apr. 1893). Possibly only someone who knew firsthand what an intelligent and introspective soul felt at the approach of battle could have written so understanding and tragic story as this.

1. Cf. "What I Saw of Shiloh" (1874; *SS* 12): "on the instant rose the sharp, clear notes of a bugle, caught up and repeated, and passed on by other bugles, until the level reaches of brown fields, the line of woods trending away to far hills, and the unseen valleys beyond were 'telling of the sound,' the farther, fainter strains half drowned in ringing cheers as the men ran to range themselves behind the stacks of arms. For this call was not the wearisome 'general' before which the tents go down; it was the exhilarating 'assembly,' which goes to the heart as wine and stirs the blood like the kisses of a beautiful woman. Who that has heard it calling to him above the grumble of great guns can forget the wild intoxication of its music?"

A HORSEMAN IN THE SKY

One sunny afternoon in the autumn of the year 1861 a soldier lay in a clump of laurel by the side of a road in western Virginia. He lay at full length upon his stomach, his feet resting upon the toes, his head upon the left forearm. His extended right hand loosely grasped his rifle. But for the somewhat methodical disposition of his limbs and a slight rhythmic movement of the cartridge-box at the back of his belt he might have been thought to be dead. He was asleep at his post of duty. But if detected he would be dead shortly afterward, death being the just and legal penalty of his crime.

The clump of laurel in which the criminal lay was in the angle of a road which after ascending southward a steep acclivity to that point turned sharply to the west, running along the summit for perhaps one hundred yards. There it turned southward again and went zigzagging downward through the forest. At the salient of that second angle was a large flat rock, jutting out northward, overlooking the deep valley from which the road ascended. The rock capped a high cliff; a stone dropped from its outer edge would have fallen sheer downward one thousand feet to the tops of the pines. The angle where the soldier lay was on another spur of the same cliff. Had he been awake he would have commanded a view, not only of the short arm of the road and the jutting rock, but of the entire profile of the cliff below it. It might well have made him giddy to look.

The country was wooded everywhere except at the bottom of the valley to the northward, where there was a small natural meadow, through which flowed a stream scarcely visible from the valley's rim. This open ground looked hardly larger than an ordinary door-yard, but was really several acres in extent. Its green was more vivid than that of the inclosing forest. Away beyond it rose a line of giant cliffs similar to those upon which we are supposed to stand in our survey of the savage scene, and through which the road had somehow made its climb to the summit. The configuration of the valley, indeed, was such that from this point of observation it seemed entirely shut in, and one could but have wondered how the road which found a way out of it had found a way into it, and whence came and whither went the waters of the stream that parted the meadow more than a thousand feet below.

No country is so wild and difficult but men will make it a theatre of war; concealed in the forest at the bottom of that military rat-trap, in which half a hundred men in possession of the exits might have starved an army to submission, lay five regiments of Federal infantry. They had marched all the previous day and night and were resting. At nightfall they would take to the road again, climb to the place where their unfaithful sentinel now slept, and descending the other slope of the ridge fall upon a camp of the enemy at about midnight. Their hope was to surprise it, for the road led to the rear of it. In case of failure, their position would be perilous in the extreme; and fail they surely would should accident or vigilance apprise the enemy of the movement.

II

The sleeping sentinel in the clump of laurel was a young Virginian named Carter Druse. He was the son of wealthy parents, an only child, and had known such ease and cultivation and high living as wealth and taste were able to command in the mountain country of western Virginia. His home was but a few miles from where he now lay. One morning he had risen from the breakfast-table and said, quietly but gravely: "Father, a Union regiment has arrived at Grafton.[1] I am going to join it."

The father lifted his leonine head, looked at the son a moment in silence and replied: "Well, go, sir, and whatever may occur do what you conceive to be your duty. Virginia, to which you are a traitor, must get on without you. Should we both live to the end of the war, we will speak further of the matter. Your mother, as the physician has informed you, is in a most critical condition; at the best she cannot be with us longer than a few weeks, but that time is precious. It would be better not to disturb her."

So Carter Druse, bowing reverently to his father, who returned the salute with a stately courtesy that masked a breaking heart, left the home of his childhood to go soldiering. By conscience and courage, by deeds of devotion and daring, he soon commended himself to his fellows and his officers; and it was to these qualities and to some knowledge of the country that he owed his selection for his present perilous duty at the extreme outpost. Nevertheless, fatigue had been stronger than resolution and he had fallen asleep. What good or bad angel came in a dream to rouse him from his state of crime, who shall say? Without a movement, without a sound, in the profound silence and the languor of the late afternoon, some invisible messenger of fate touched with unsealing finger the eyes of his consciousness—whispered into the ear of his spirit the mysterious awakening word which no human lips ever have spoken, no human memory ever has recalled. He quietly raised his forehead from his arm and

A HORSEMAN IN THE SKY

looked between the masking stems of the laurels, instinctively closing his right hand about the stock of his rifle.

His first feeling was a keen artistic delight. On a colossal pedestal, the cliff,—motionless at the extreme edge of the capping rock and sharply outlined against the sky,—was an equestrian statue of impressive dignity. The figure of the man sat the figure of the horse, straight and soldierly, but with the repose of a Grecian god carved in the marble which limits the suggestion of activity. The gray costume harmonized with its aërial background; the metal of accouterment and caparison was softened and subdued by the shadow; the animal's skin had no points of high light. A carbine strikingly foreshortened lay across the pommel of the saddle, kept in place by the right hand grasping it at the "grip"; the left hand, holding the bridle rein, was invisible. In silhouette against the sky the profile of the horse was cut with the sharpness of a cameo; it looked across the heights of air to the confronting cliffs beyond. The face of the rider, turned slightly away, showed only an outline of temple and beard; he was looking downward to the bottom of the valley. Magnified by its lift against the sky and by the soldier's testifying sense of the formidableness of a near enemy the group appeared of heroic, almost colossal, size.

For an instant Druse had a strange, half-defined feeling that he had slept to the end of the war and was looking upon a noble work of art reared upon that eminence to commemorate the deeds of an heroic past of which he had been an inglorious part. The feeling was dispelled by a slight movement of the group: the horse, without moving its feet, had drawn its body slightly backward from the verge; the man remained immobile as before. Broad awake and keenly alive to the significance of the situation, Druse now brought the butt of his rifle against his cheek by cautiously pushing the barrel forward through the bushes, cocked the piece, and glancing through the sights covered a vital spot of the horseman's breast. A touch upon the trigger and all would have been well with Carter Druse. At that instant the horseman turned his head and looked in the direction of his concealed foeman—seemed to look into his very face, into his eyes, into his brave, compassionate heart.

Is it then so terrible to kill an enemy in war—an enemy who has surprised a secret vital to the safety of one's self and comrades—an enemy more formidable for his knowledge than all his army for its numbers? Carter Druse grew pale; he shook in every limb, turned faint and saw the statuesque group before him as black figures, rising, falling, moving unsteadily in arcs of circles in a fiery sky. His hand fell away from his weapon, his head slowly dropped until his face rested on the leaves in which he lay. This courageous gentleman and hardy soldier was near swooning from intensity of emotion.

It was not for long; in another moment his face was raised from earth, his hands resumed their places on the rifle, his forefinger sought the trigger; mind, heart and eyes were clear, conscience and reason sound. He could not hope to capture that enemy; to alarm him would but send him dashing to his camp with his fatal news.

A HORSEMAN IN THE SKY

The duty of the soldier was plain: the man must be shot dead from ambush—without warning, without a moment's spiritual preparation, with never so much as an unspoken prayer, he must be sent to his account. But no—there is a hope; he may have discovered nothing—perhaps he is but admiring the sublimity of the landscape. If permitted, he may turn and ride carelessly away in the direction whence he came. Surely it will be possible to judge at the instant of his withdrawing whether he knows. It may well be that his fixity of attention—Druse turned his head and looked through the deeps of air downward, as from the surface to the bottom of a translucent sea. He saw creeping across the green meadow a sinuous line of figures of men and horses— some foolish commander was permitting the soldiers of his escort to water their beasts in the open, in plain view from a dozen summits!

Druse withdrew his eyes from the valley and fixed them again upon the group of man and horse in the sky, and again it was through the sights of his rifle. But this time his aim was at the horse. In his memory, as if they were a divine mandate, rang the words of his father at their parting: "Whatever may occur, do what you conceive to be your duty." He was calm now. His teeth were firmly but not rigidly closed; his nerves were as tranquil as a sleeping babe's—not a tremor affected any muscle of his body; his breathing, until suspended in the act of taking aim, was regular and slow. Duty had conquered; the spirit had said to the body: "Peace, be still."[2] He fired.

III

An officer of the Federal force, who in a spirit of adventure or in quest of knowledge had left the hidden bivouac in the valley, and with aimless feet had made his way to the lower edge of a small open space near the foot of the cliff, was considering what he had to gain by pushing his exploration further. At a distance of a quarter-mile before him, but apparently at a stone's throw, rose from its fringe of pines the gigantic face of rock, towering to so great a height above him that it made him giddy to look up to where its edge cut a sharp, rugged line against the sky. It presented a clean, vertical profile against a background of blue sky to a point half the way down, and of distant hills, hardly less blue, thence to the tops of the trees at its base. Lifting his eyes to the dizzy altitude of its summit the officer saw an astonishing sight—a man on horseback riding down into the valley through the air!

Straight upright sat the rider, in military fashion, with a firm seat in the saddle, a strong clutch upon the rein to hold his charger from too impetuous a plunge. From his bare head his long hair streamed upward, waving like a plume. His hands were concealed in the cloud of the horse's lifted mane. The animal's body was as level as if every hoof-stroke encountered the resistant earth. Its motions were those of a wild gallop, but even as the officer looked they ceased, with all the legs thrown sharply forward as in the act of alighting from a leap. But this was a flight!

Filled with amazement and terror by this apparition of a horseman in the sky—half believing himself the chosen scribe of some new Apocalypse, the officer was overcome by the intensity of his emotions; his legs failed him and he fell. Almost at the same instant he heard a crashing sound in the trees—a sound that died without an echo—and all was still.

The officer rose to his feet, trembling. The familiar sensation of an abraded shin recalled his dazed faculties. Pulling himself together he ran rapidly obliquely away from the cliff to a point distant from its foot; thereabout he expected to find his man; and thereabout he naturally failed. In the fleeting instant of his vision his imagination had been so wrought upon by the apparent grace and ease and intention of the marvelous performance that it did not occur to him that the line of march of aërial cavalry is directly downward, and that he could find the objects of his search at the very foot of the cliff. A half-hour later he returned to camp.

This officer was a wise man; he knew better than to tell an incredible truth. He said nothing of what he had seen. But when the commander asked him if in his scout he had learned anything of advantage to the expedition he answered:

"Yes, sir; there is no road leading down into this valley from the southward."

The commander, knowing better, smiled.

IV

After firing his shot, Private Carter Druse reloaded his rifle and resumed his watch. Ten minutes had hardly passed when a Federal sergeant crept cautiously to him on hands and knees. Druse neither turned his head nor looked at him, but lay without motion or sign of recognition.

"Did you fire?" the sergeant whispered.

"Yes."

"At what?"

"A horse. It was standing on yonder rock—pretty far out. You see it is no longer there. It went over the cliff."

The man's face was white, but he showed no other sign of emotion. Having answered, he turned away his eyes and said no more. The sergeant did not understand.

"See here, Druse," he said, after a moment's silence, "it's no use making a mystery. I order you to report. Was there anybody on the horse?"

"Yes."

"Well?"

"My father."

The sergeant rose to his feet and walked away. "Good God!" he said.

E (14 Apr. 1889): 9 (as "The Horseman in the Sky: An Incident of the Civil War"); *TSC* 9–20; *IML* 3–15; *CW* 2.15–26. Reprinted in *Short Stories* 4, no. 1 (Dec. 1890): 3–8 (as "The Horseman in the Sky"); *Current Literature* 18, no. 3 (September 1895): 258–59 (with subtitle: "The Sentry's Shot"); in *A Son of the Gods and A Horseman in the Sky* (San Francisco & New York: Paul Elder & Co., 1907), 27–47; *Current Opinion* 47, no. 3 (September 1909): 343–45; *Independent* (Kansas City) 25, no. 19 (1 July 1911): 10–11.

NOTES

This is one of AB's most outstanding and memorable stories. With less control, it could have been pathetic instead of tragic, but AB keeps it tightly focused on the irreconcilable issues at its heart: divided loyalties, duty versus love, and how the normally desirable possession of reason and character may turn a conflict of good qualities into tragedy. There are significant differences between the *E* and *CW* versions of the story, the main one being that *E* makes it clearer that the cost to Carter Druse of killing his father is that his mind is broken. For a fuller discussion of this story, see *PA* 105–12.

1. Grafton (now in West Virginia) was the site of one of the earliest battles of the Civil War: it was occupied by Federal troops on 30 May 1861. AB took part in the battle; see "A Bivouac of the Dead" (1903; *SS* 1–3); "Battlefields and Ghosts" (1904; *SS* 3–6), and "On a Mountain" (1909; *SS* 6–10).

2. Cf. Mark 4:39: "And he [Jesus] arose, and rebuked the wind, and said unto the sea, Peace, be still."

THE COUP DE GRÂCE

The fighting had been hard and continuous; that was attested by all the senses. The very taste of battle was in the air. All was now over; it remained only to succor the wounded and bury the dead—to "tidy up a bit," as the humorist of a burial squad put it. A good deal of "tidying up" was required. As far as one could see through the forest, among the splintered trees, lay wrecks of men and horses. Among them moved the stretcher-bearers, gathering and carrying away the few who showed signs of life. Most of the wounded had died of neglect while the right to minister to their wants was in dispute. It is an army regulation that the wounded must wait; the best way to care for them is to win the battle. It must be confessed that victory is a distinct advantage to a man requiring attention, but many do not live to avail themselves of it.

The dead were collected in groups of a dozen or a score and laid side by side in rows while the trenches were dug to receive them. Some, found at too great a distance from these rallying points, were buried where they lay. There was little attempt at identification, though in most cases, the burial parties being detailed to glean the same ground which they had assisted to reap, the names of the victorious dead were known and listed. The enemy's fallen had to be content with counting. But of that they got enough: many of them were counted several times, and the total, as given afterward in the official report of the victorious commander, denoted rather a hope than a result.

At some little distance from the spot where one of the burial parties had established its "bivouac of the dead,"[1] a man in the uniform of a Federal officer stood leaning against a tree. From his feet upward to his neck his attitude was that of weariness reposing; but he turned his head uneasily from side to side; his mind was apparently not at rest. He was perhaps uncertain in which direction to go; he was not likely to remain long where he was, for already the level rays of the setting sun straggled redly through the open spaces of the wood and the weary soldiers were quitting their task for the day. He would hardly make a night of it alone there among the dead. Nine men in ten whom you meet after a battle inquire the way to some fraction of the army—as if any one could know. Doubtless this officer was lost. After resting himself a moment he would presumably follow one of the retiring burial squads.

When all were gone he walked straight away into the forest toward the red west, its light staining his face like blood. The air of confidence with which he now strode along showed that he was on familiar ground; he had recovered his bearings. The dead on his right and on his left were unregarded as he passed. An occasional low moan from some sorely stricken wretch whom the relief-parties had not reached, and who would have to pass a comfortless night beneath the stars with his thirst to keep him company, was equally unheeded. What, indeed, could the officer have done, being no surgeon and having no water?

At the head of a shallow ravine, a mere depression of the ground, lay a small group of bodies. He saw, and swerving suddenly from his course walked rapidly toward them. Scanning each one sharply as he passed, he stopped at last above one which lay at a slight remove from the others, near a clump of small trees. He looked at it narrowly. It seemed to stir. He stooped and laid his hand upon its face. It screamed.

The officer was Captain Downing Madwell, of a Massachusetts regiment of infantry, a daring and intelligent soldier, an honorable man.

In the regiment were two brothers named Halcrow—Caffal and Creede Halcrow. Caffal Halcrow was a sergeant in Captain Madwell's company, and these two men, the sergeant and the captain, were devoted friends. In so far as disparity of rank, difference in duties and considerations of military discipline would permit they were commonly together. They had, indeed, grown up together from childhood. A habit of the heart is not easily broken off. Caffal Halcrow had nothing military in his taste nor disposition, but the thought of separation from his friend was disagreeable; he enlisted in the company in which Madwell was second-lieutenant. Each had taken two steps upward in rank, but between the highest non-commissioned and the lowest commissioned officer the gulf is deep and wide and the old relation was maintained with difficulty and a difference.

Creede Halcrow, the brother of Caffal, was the major of the regiment—a cynical, saturnine man, between whom and Captain Madwell there was a natural antipathy which circumstances had nourished and strengthened to an active animosity. But for the restraining influence of their mutual relation to Caffal these two patriots would doubtless have endeavored to deprive their country of each other's services.

At the opening of the battle that morning the regiment was performing outpost duty a mile away from the main army. It was attacked and nearly surrounded in the forest, but stubbornly held its ground. During a lull in the fighting, Major Halcrow came to Captain Madwell. The two exchanged formal salutes, and the major said: "Captain, the colonel directs that you push your company to the head of this ravine and hold your place there until recalled. I need hardly apprise you of the dangerous character of the movement, but if you wish, you can, I suppose, turn over the command to your first-lieutenant. I was not, however, directed to authorize the substitution; it is merely a suggestion of my own, unofficially made."

To this deadly insult Captain Madwell coolly replied:

"Sir, I invite you to accompany the movement. A mounted officer would be a conspicuous mark, and I have long held the opinion that it would be better if you were dead."

The art of repartee[2] was cultivated in military circles as early as 1862.

A half-hour later Captain Madwell's company was driven from its position at the head of the ravine, with a loss of one-third its number. Among the fallen was Sergeant Halcrow. The regiment was soon afterward forced back to the main line, and at the close of the battle was miles away. The captain was now standing at the side of his subordinate and friend.

Sergeant Halcrow was mortally hurt. His clothing was deranged; it seemed to have been violently torn apart, exposing the abdomen. Some of the buttons of his jacket had been pulled off and lay on the ground beside him and fragments of his other garments were strewn about. His leather belt was parted and had apparently been dragged from beneath him as he lay. There had been no great effusion of blood. The only visible wound was a wide, ragged opening in the abdomen. It was defiled with earth and dead leaves. Protruding from it was a loop of small intestine. In all his experience Captain Madwell had not seen a wound like this. He could neither conjecture how it was made nor explain the attendant circumstances—the strangely torn clothing, the parted belt, the besmirching of the white skin. He knelt and made a closer examination. When he rose to his feet, he turned his eyes in different directions as if looking for an enemy. Fifty yards away, on the crest of a low, thinly wooded hill, he saw several dark objects moving about among the fallen men—a herd of swine.[3] One stood with its back to him, its shoulders sharply elevated. Its forefeet were upon a human body, its head was depressed and invisible. The bristly ridge of its chine showed black against the red west. Captain Madwell drew away his eyes and fixed them again upon the thing which had been his friend.

The man who had suffered these monstrous mutilations was alive. At intervals he moved his limbs; he moaned at every breath. He stared blankly into the face of his friend and if touched screamed. In his giant agony he had torn up the ground on which he lay; his clenched hands were full of leaves and twigs and earth. Articulate speech was beyond his power; it was impossible to know if he were sensible to anything but pain. The expression of his face was an appeal; his eyes were full of prayer. For what?

There was no misreading that look; the captain had too frequently seen it in eyes of those whose lips had still the power to formulate it by an entreaty for death. Consciously or unconsciously, this writhing fragment of humanity, this type and example

THE COUP DE GRÂCE

of acute sensation, this handiwork of man and beast, this humble, unheroic Prometheus, was imploring everything, all, the whole non-ego, for the boon of oblivion. To the earth and the sky alike, to the trees, to the man, to whatever took form in sense or consciousness, this incarnate suffering addressed that silent plea.

For what, indeed? For that which we accord to even the meanest creature without sense to demand it, denying it only to the wretched of our own race: for the blessed release, the rite of uttermost compassion, the *coup de grâce*.[4]

Captain Madwell spoke the name of his friend. He repeated it over and over without effect until emotion choked his utterance. His tears plashed upon the livid face beneath his own and blinded himself. He saw nothing but a blurred and moving object, but the moans were more distinct than ever, interrupted at briefer intervals by sharper shrieks. He turned away, struck his hand upon his forehead and strode from the spot. The swine, catching sight of him, threw up their crimson muzzles, regarding him suspiciously a second, and then with a gruff, concerted grunt, raced away out of sight. A horse, its foreleg splintered by a cannon-shot, lifted its head sidewise from the ground and neighed piteously. Madwell stepped forward, drew his revolver and shot the poor beast between the eyes, narrowly observing its death-struggle, which, contrary to his expectation, was violent and long; but at last it lay still. The tense muscles of its lips, which had uncovered the teeth in a horrible grin, relaxed; the sharp, clean-cut profile took on a look of profound peace and rest.

Along the distant, thinly wooded crest to westward the fringe of sunset fire had now nearly burned itself out. The light upon the trunks of the trees had faded to a tender gray; shadows were in their tops, like great dark birds aperch. Night was coming and there were miles of haunted forest between Captain Madwell and camp. Yet he stood there at the side of the dead animal, apparently lost to all sense of his surroundings. His eyes were bent upon the earth at his feet; his left hand hung loosely at his side, his right still held the pistol. Presently he lifted his face, turned it toward his dying friend and walked rapidly back to his side. He knelt upon one knee, cocked the weapon, placed the muzzle against the man's forehead, and turning away his eyes pulled the trigger. There was no report. He had used his last cartridge for the horse.

The sufferer moaned and his lips moved convulsively. The froth that ran from them had a tinge of blood.

Captain Madwell rose to his feet and drew his sword from the scabbard. He passed the fingers of his left hand along the edge from hilt to point. He held it out straight before him, as if to test his nerves. There was no visible tremor of the blade; the ray of bleak skylight that it reflected was steady and true. He stooped and with his left hand tore away the dying man's shirt, rose and placed the point of the sword just over the heart. This time he did not withdraw his eyes. Grasping the hilt with both hands, he thrust downward with all his strength and weight. The blade sank into the man's body—through his body into the earth; Captain Madwell came near falling forward upon his work. The dying man drew up his knees and at the same time threw his right arm across his breast and grasped the steel so tightly that the knuckles of the hand visibly whitened. By a violent but vain effort to withdraw the blade the wound was enlarged; a rill of blood escaped, running sinuously down into the deranged clothing. At that moment three men stepped silently forward from behind the clump of young trees which had concealed their approach. Two were hospital attendants and carried a stretcher.

The third was Major Creede Halcrow.

E (30 June 1889): 9 (with subtitle: "An Uncanny Occurrence in the Chicahominy Woods"); *TSC* 139–49; *IML* 135–46; *CW* 2.122–32. Reprinted in *Short Stories* 6, no. 2 (May 1891): 138–43.

NOTES

This is one of AB's most controversial stories, confronting as it does the issue of mercy killing. As with other of his stories, "A Horseman in the Sky," for instance, AB does not allow his protagonist time to run through philosophical or religious rationales for an action. AB here advanced realism by forcing readers to come to grips with a situation in which a decision had to be made immediately on the basis of urgent facts and what was already in the mind and the gut. The story is an excellent example of how AB used literary art to articulate issues which he had faced on the battlefield and which continued to torment him.

Title: A finishing stroke, especially to kill a wounded animal or person. The French literally means "stroke of grace," or mercy.

1. Theodore O'Hara (1820–67), "The Bivouac of the Dead" (1847), l. 4. The poem was written to commemorate the Americans slain in the battle of Buena Vista (22–23 Feb. 1847). AB published a piece called "A Bivouac of the Dead," *CW* 11.395–98 (from "The Passing Show," *NYA,* 22 Nov. 1903).

2. Cf. *DD*: "REPARTEE, *n.* Prudent insult in retort. Practiced by gentlemen with a constitutional aversion to violence, but a strong disposition to offend."

3. The essay "On a Mountain" contains a scene in which swine are encountered feeding on dead soldiers (*SS* 10). The incident apparently affected AB deeply; this story is one of a few instances in his canon where he uses the situation of animals ravening on human corpses.

4. AB wrote on this subject in "On the Right to Kill the Sick," *NYJ* (1 Oct. 1899): 30; *E* (1 Oct. 1899): 14, and describes a situation from experience in "What I Saw of Shiloh" (*SS* 19).

TWO HAUNTED HOUSES

SOME STRANGE NARRATIVES FROM THE NOTE-BOOK
OF AN INVESTIGATOR

I.

John Easton Lord, of Coopertown, Pennsylvania, sold his house and lot in that town to William Burrill and moved with his family to the suburbs of Pittsburg. The Burrill family occupied the Coopertown house for nearly four years, then abandoned it—being unable to resell it—and occupied another, a half-mile away, which at first they rented and afterward bought. Here the widow of William Burrill and one maiden daughter were living as lately as 1884, which was the date of the writer's last knowledge of him.

At that time the old Lord dwelling, which had stood tenantless for years, had just been demolished, with many others, to make room for a new street. It had long had an uncanny reputation as a "haunted house," and although the skeptics were many, and repeated investigations had been made of the supernatural phenomena said to occur nightly within its walls, it was noticeable that even the most incredulous always spoke of them with gravity and no one in Coopertown attempted to discredit them by ridicule. The subject was universally regarded as worthy of serious discussion. There was reason enough, for one of the dismal traditions of the house—namely that no one could remain alone in it over night and keep both life and reason—had been twice confirmed in the most authenticating way. One hardy investigator had been found in the morning dead without a wound or assignable cause, and another person—a tramp who in all unconsciousness of the dwelling's history had stolen a lodging there—had rushed out at the gray of the morning incurably mad. That the house was haunted was open to honest doubt, but these somber passages in its annals had at least invested that proposition with a certain dignity which made it inaccessible to ridicule.

The manifestations, it appears, began on the 20th day of June, 1872, somewhat more than three years after the Burrill family moved into the house. On the evening of that day, at about 7 o'clock, while the family were sitting on the veranda after dinner, John Easton Lord, the former owner, came in at the gate, ascended the steps of the veranda, passed directly between Mr. and Mrs. Burrill and entered the house by the hall door. Mr. Burrill had risen to greet him, but the proffered hand had remained unheeded. By not so much as a look had Lord recognized any member of the family, to all of whom he was well known. He was immediately followed into the house by Burrill and his son, Parker Burrill, whose astonishment was great indeed at not finding their visitor. The only door by which he could have left the house was found securely locked, with the key inside, and all the windows were fastened excepting those opening on to the veranda. A search of the entire house resulted in nothing. Lord had not been seen by anybody else in town, and the incident was simply without an explanation. A letter to Pittsburg brought out the fact in reply that on the day of its occurrence John Easton Lord had been seven weeks dead.

From this time forward, until they left the house months afterward, the Burrill family appear to have suffered great annoyance and alarm from what were affirmed to be supernatural manifestations. The character of these is inexactly known; with a view to damaging their property as little as possible, all the members of the family preserved a discreet silence; but the most extravagant tales were bruited about, orally and through the local newspapers. It is needless to repeat them here: they were of the kind usually related of houses said to be "haunted." By the time the property had been condemned for a public use, appraised and paid for Mr. Burrill was dead, and the family scattered in distant parts of the country—all except the widow, who was in her dotage, and one elderly maiden daughter, whose austere silence on this subject was infrangible. There is ample and credible testimony, popular and professional, that when the family moved out of the house all were suffering acutely from insomnia and nervous prostration—from which, indeed, the youngest, a girl of seventeen, eventually died.

From voluminous notes of an investigation made by a competent inquirer in 1884 it is found that all, or nearly all, of the least incredible accounts of supernatural occurrences in and about the Lord house relate to the visible apparition of the late John Easton Lord. Most of the testimony as to that element has in it something approaching trustworthiness. If anything at all "out of the common" ever took place there, something which many cool-headed witnesses took to be the ghost of Lord habitually showed itself about the premises by night and sometimes by day. It was considered a malign spirit although in life Lord had been of a singularly amiable disposition.

When the house was pulled down and its site excavated for a new street a workman, beginning a trench from the cellar, uncovered a plain board box which appeared to have been thrust through an opening in the cellar wall into a hole behind it. The opening in the wall had been carefully bricked up so that the place was indistinguishable. The box contained the remains of a human being—a man. The body was little affected by decay, although the appearance of the box and the mould on the clothing indicated that a considerable period must have elapsed since the date of interment; several years, those said whose opinion had most weight. The face of the corpse had apparently undergone very little alteration, and on seeing it every acquaintance of the late Mr. Lord instantly pronounced the body his; but two reputable citizens of Coopertown went to Pittsburg and there found and identified the body of Lord in a cemetery at that city, the family having consented to the exhumation and an adult son of the deceased being present.

Despite the efforts of the officers of the law, assisted by many amateur detectives, working *con amore,* not the slightest clew to the identity of the dead, the manner of his taking off nor the mystery of his interment has ever been discovered. "Theories" were abundant enough while anybody cared to entertain them, but none were consonant with all the facts, nor even with the main ones here set down. The body was reburied in a public cemetery, and a stone without name or date marks the spot.

II.

On the road leading north from Manchester, in eastern Kentucky, to Booneville, twenty miles away, stood, in 1862, a wooden plantation-house of a somewhat better quality than most of the dwellings in that region. The house was destroyed by fire in the year following—probably by some stragglers from the retreating column of General George W. Morgan, when he was driven from Cumberland Gap to the Ohio river by General Kirby Smith.[1] At the time of its destruction it had for four or five years been vacant. The fields about it were overgrown with brambles, the fences gone, even the few negro quarters, and outhouses generally, fallen partly into ruin by neglect and pillage; for the negroes and poor whites of the vicinity found in the building and fences an abundant supply of fuel, of which they availed themselves without hesitation, openly and by daylight. By daylight alone; after nightfall no human being except passing strangers ever went near the place.

It was known as the "Spook House." That it was tenanted by evil spirits, visible, audible and active, no one in all that region doubted, any more than he doubted what he was told of Sundays by the traveling preacher. Its owner's opinion of the matter was unknown; he and his family had disappeared one night and no trace of them had ever been found. They left everything—household goods, clothing, provisions, the horses in the stable, the cows in the field, the negroes in the quarters—all as it stood; nothing was missing—except a man, a woman, three girls, a boy and a babe! It was not altogether surprising that a plantation where seven human beings could be simultaneously effaced and nobody the wiser should be thought to be under some monstrous curse and teeming with possibilities of evil.

One night in June, 1859, two citizens of Frankfort, Col. J. C. McArdle, a lawyer, and Judge Myron Veigh, of the State Militia, were driving from Booneville to Manchester. Their business was so important that they decided to push on despite the darkness and the mutterings of an approaching storm, which eventually broke upon them just as they arrived opposite the "Spook House." The lightning was so incessant that they easily found their way through the gateway and into a shed, where they unhitched their team, which they conducted into an adjacent stable and unharnessed by no other light than that of the heavens. They then went to the house, through the scourging rain, and knocked at all the doors without, however, eliciting any response. Attributing this to the continuous uproar of the thunder, they pushed at one of the doors, which yielded. They entered without further ceremony. That instant they were in darkness and silence absolute. Not a gleam of the lightning's unceasing blaze penetrated the windows or crevices; not a whisper of the awful tumult without reached them there. It was as if they had suddenly been stricken blind and deaf, and McArdle afterward said that for a moment he believed himself to have been killed by a stroke of lightning as he crossed the threshold. The rest of this adventure can as well be related in that gentleman's words, from the Frankfort *Gazette* of August 6, 1876:[2]

"When I had somewhat recovered from the dazing effect of the transition from uproar to silence, my first impulse was to reopen the door which I had closed, and from the knob of which I was not conscious of having removed my hand; I felt it distinctly, still in the clasp of my fingers. My notion was to ascertain by stepping again into the storm whether I had been deprived of sight and hearing. I turned the door-knob and pulled open the door. It led into another room! This apartment was suffused with a faint greenish light, the source of which I could not determine, making everything distinctly visible, though nothing was sharply defined. Everything, I say, but in truth the only objects within the blank stone walls of that room were human dead bodies. In number they were perhaps eight or ten—it may well be understood that I did not coolly count them. They were of various ages, or rather sizes, from infancy up, and of both sexes. All were prostrate on the floor in all kinds of attitudes, excepting one, the body, apparently, of a young woman, which sat up, her back supported by an angle of the wall. The babe was clasped in the arms of another and older woman. A half-grown lad lay face downward across the legs of a full-bearded man. One or two were nearly naked, and the hand of a young girl held the fragment of a gown which she had torn open at the breast. The bodies were in various stages of decay, all greatly shrunken in face and figure. Some were but little more than skeletons.

"While I stood stupefied with horror by this ghastly spectacle and still holding open the door by some unaccountable perversity my attention was diverted from the shocking scene and concerned itself with trifles and details. Perhaps my mind, with an instinct of self-preservation, sought relief in matters which would relax its dangerous tension. Among other things I observed that the door which I was holding open was of heavy iron plates riveted. Equidistant from each other and from the top and bottom three strong bolts protruded from the beveled edge. I turned the knob and they were retracted flush with the edge, released it, and they shot out. It was a spring lock. On the inside there was no knob, nor any kind of projection—all was a smooth surface of iron.

"While noting these things with an interest and attention which it now astonishes me to recall I felt myself thrust aside, and Judge Veigh, whom in the intensity and vicissitudes of my feelings I had altogether forgotten, pushed by me into the room. 'For God's sake,' I cried, 'do not go in there! Let us get out of this dreadful place!'

"He gave no heed to my entreaties, but (as fearless a gentleman as lived in all the South) walked quickly to the center of the room, knelt beside one of the bodies for a closer examination and tenderly raised its blackened and shriveled head in his hands. A strong sickening odor came through the doorway, completely overpowering me. My senses reeled; I felt myself falling, and in clutching at the edge of the door for support closed it with a sharp click!

"I remember no more: six weeks later I recovered my reason in a hotel at Manchester, whither I had been taken by strangers the next day. For all these weeks I had suffered from a nervous fever, attended with constant delirium. I had been found lying in the road several miles away from the house; but how I had escaped from it to get there I never knew. On recovery, or as soon as my physicians permitted me to talk, I inquired the fate of Judge Veigh, whom (to humor me, as I now know) they represented as well and at home. No one believed a word of my story, and who can wonder? And who can imagine my grief when, arriving at my home in Frankfort two months later, I learned that Judge Veigh had never been heard of since that night? I then regretted bitterly the pride which since the first few days after the recovery of my reason had forbidden me to repeat my discredited story and insist upon its truth. With all that subsequently occurred—the examination of the house; the failure to find any rooms corresponding to those which I have described; the attempt to have me adjudged insane, and my triumph over my accusers—the readers of the *Gazette* are entirely familiar. After all these years I am still confident that excavations which I have neither the legal right to undertake nor the wealth to make would disclose the secret of the disappearance of my unhappy friend, and possibly of the Butlers, former occupants and owners of the deserted and now destroyed house. I do not despair of yet bringing about such a research, and it is a source of deep grief to me that it has been delayed by the undeserved hostility and unwise incredulity of the family and friends of the late Judge Veigh."

Colonel J. C. McArdle died in Lexington, Ky., on the 15th day of September, 1882.

E (7 July 1889): 9. One section reprinted as "The Spook House" (*CW* 3.393–99). See also "A Doppelganger" (Appendix A).

NOTES

Included among the obviously fictional stories of AB's oeuvre are some few like this, which appear to be factual reports. They are included here because, despite appearances, they are almost certainly, from AB's point of view, works of fiction. Whether he made this story up out of whole cloth or merely reworked accounts of the popular topic of haunted houses he found in the newspapers that exchanged subscriptions with *E* is not presently known. One such article appeared in *E* on 2 July, just five days before AB's piece. As has been said before, AB did not believe in ghosts. In *DD* he defines a ghost as the "outward and visible sign of an inward fear."

It should be remembered that AB as a professional writer excelled in an unusually large range of subgenres of the short story. Ghost stories were very popular in his day and sold well, so it is not surprising that he wrote a few. Some ghost stories emphasize spookiness and terrifying incidents. Others follow the tradition of verisimilitude that goes back at least as far as Daniel Defoe's *A True Relation of the Apparition of Mrs. Veal* (1706). This account is in the latter tradition, but it also is consonant with the straight-faced hoaxes that AB was familiar with from his readings of the contemporary Sagebrush humorists of Nevada. Their specialty was to begin with something that was ludicrous because impossible or extremely improbable and to make it seem plausible with the use of persuasive details. But once readers allowed for the ludicrous to happen, they were at the mercy of the hoax.

1. In March 1862 Gen. George Washington Morgan (1820–93; USV) had been appointed to command the Seventh Division of the Army of the Ohio to take Cumberland Gap, an important mountain pass at the junction of Tennessee, Kentucky, and Virginia. Morgan's troops occupied the Gap in June but were forced to evacuate in September when Gen. Edmund Kirby Smith (1824–1893; CSA) and Gen. Braxton Bragg invaded Kentucky.

2. The newspaper is fictitious.

TWO HAUNTED HOUSES

THE SUITABLE SURROUNDINGS

THE NIGHT

One midsummer night a farmer's boy living about ten miles from the city of Cincinnati was following a bridle path through a dense and dark forest. He had lost himself while searching for some missing cows, and near midnight was a long way from home, in a part of the country with which he was unfamiliar. But he was a stout-hearted lad, and knowing his general direction from his home, he plunged into the forest without hesitation, guided by the stars. Coming into the bridle path, and observing that it ran in the right direction, he followed it.

The night was clear, but in the woods it was exceedingly dark. It was more by the sense of touch than by that of sight that the lad kept the path. He could not, indeed, very easily go astray; the undergrowth on both sides was so thick as to be almost impenetrable. He had gone into the forest a mile or more when he was surprised to see a feeble gleam of light shining through the foliage skirting the path on his left. The sight of it startled him and set his heart beating audibly.

"The old Breede house is somewhere about here," he said to himself. "This must be the other end of the path which we reach it by from our side. Ugh! what should a light be doing there?"

Nevertheless, he pushed on. A moment later he had emerged from the forest into a small, open space, mostly upgrown to brambles. There were remnants of a rotting fence. A few yards from the trail, in the middle of the "clearing," was the house from which the light came, through an unglazed window. The window had once contained glass, but that and its supporting frame had long ago yielded to missiles flung by hands of venturesome boys to attest alike their courage and their hostility to the supernatural; for the Breede house bore the evil reputation of being haunted. Possibly it was not, but even the hardiest skeptic could not deny that it was deserted—which in rural regions is much the same thing.

Looking at the mysterious dim light shining from the ruined window the boy remembered with apprehension that his own hand had assisted at the destruction. His penitence was of course poignant in proportion to its tardiness and inefficacy. He half expected to be set upon by all the unworldly and bodiless malevolences whom he had outraged by assisting to break alike their windows and their peace. Yet this stubborn lad, shaking in every limb, would not retreat. The blood in his veins was strong and rich with the iron of the frontiersman. He was but two removes from the generation that had subdued the Indian. He started to pass the house.

As he was going by he looked in at the blank window space and saw a strange and terrifying sight,—the figure of a man seated in the center of the room, at a table upon which lay some loose sheets of paper. The elbows rested on the table, the hands supporting the head, which was uncovered. On each side the fingers were pushed into the hair. The face showed dead-yellow in the light of a single candle a little to one side. The flame illuminated that side of the face, the other was in deep shadow. The man's eyes were fixed upon the blank window space with a stare in which an older and cooler observer might have discerned something of apprehension, but which seemed to the lad altogether soulless. He believed the man to be dead.

The situation was horrible, but not without its fascination. The boy stopped to note it all. He was weak, faint and trembling; he could feel the blood forsaking his face. Nevertheless, he set his teeth and resolutely advanced to the house. He had no conscious intention—it was the mere courage of terror. He thrust his white face forward into the illuminated opening. At that instant a strange, harsh cry, a shriek, broke upon the silence of the night—the note of a screech-owl. The man sprang to his feet, overturning the table and extinguishing the candle. The boy took to his heels.

THE DAY BEFORE

"Good-morning, Colston. I am in luck, it seems. You have often said that my commendation of your literary work was mere civility, and here you find me absorbed—actually merged—in your latest story in the *Messenger.* Nothing less shocking than your touch upon my shoulder would have roused me to consciousness."

"The proof is stronger than you seem to know," replied the man addressed: "so keen is your eagerness to read my story that you are willing to renounce selfish considerations and forego all the pleasure that you could get from it."

"I don't understand you," said the other, folding the newspaper that he held and putting it into his pocket. "You writers are a queer lot, anyhow. Come, tell me what I have done or omitted in this matter. In what way does the pleasure that I get, or might get, from your work depend on me?"

"In many ways. Let me ask you how you would enjoy your breakfast if you took it in this street car. Suppose the phonograph[1] so perfected as to be able to give you an entire opera,—singing, orchestration and all; do you think you would get much pleasure out of it if you turned it on at your office during business hours? Do you really care for a serenade by Schubert when you hear it fiddled by an untimely Italian on a morning ferryboat? Are you always cocked and primed for enjoyment? Do you keep every mood on tap, ready to any demand? Let me remind you, sir, that the story which you have done me the honor to begin as a means of becoming oblivious to the discomfort of this car is a ghost story!"

"Well?"

"Well! Has the reader no duties corresponding to his privileges? You have paid five cents for that newspaper. It is yours. You have the right to read it when and where you will. Much of what is in it is neither helped nor harmed by time and place and mood; some of it actually requires to be read at once—while it is fizzing. But my story is not of that character. It is not 'the very latest advices' from Ghostland. You are not expected to keep yourself *au courant* with what is going on in the realm of spooks. The stuff will keep until you have leisure to put yourself into the frame of mind appropriate to the sentiment of the piece—which I respectfully submit that you cannot do in a street car, even if you are the only passenger. The solitude is not of the right sort. An author has rights which the reader is bound to respect."

"For specific example?"

"The right to the reader's undivided attention. To deny him this is immoral. To make him share your attention with the rattle of a street car, the moving panorama of the crowds on the sidewalks, and the buildings beyond—with any of the thousands of distractions which make our customary environment—is to treat him with gross injustice. By God, it is infamous!"

The speaker had risen to his feet and was steadying himself by one of the straps hanging from the roof of the car. The other man looked up at him in sudden astonishment, wondering how so trivial a grievance could seem to justify so strong language. He saw that his friend's face was uncommonly pale and that his eyes glowed like living coals.

"You know what I mean," continued the writer, impetuously crowding his words—"you know what I mean, Marsh. My stuff in this morning's *Messenger* is plainly sub-headed 'A Ghost Story.' That is ample notice to all. Every honorable reader will understand it as prescribing by implication the conditions under which the work is to be read."

The man addressed as Marsh winced a trifle, then asked with a smile: "What conditions? You know that I am only a plain business man who cannot be supposed to understand such things. How, when, where should I read your ghost story?"

"In solitude—at night—by the light of a candle. There are certain emotions which a writer can easily enough excite—such as compassion or merriment. I can move you to tears or laughter under almost any circumstances. But for my ghost story to be effective you must be made to feel fear—at least a strong sense of the supernatural—and that is a difficult matter. I have a right to expect that if you read me at all you will give me a chance; that you will make yourself accessible to the emotion that I try to inspire."

THE SUITABLE SURROUNDINGS

The car had now arrived at its terminus and stopped. The trip just completed was its first for the day and the conversation of the two early passengers had not been interrupted. The streets were yet silent and desolate; the house tops were just touched by the rising sun. As they stepped from the car and walked away together Marsh narrowly eyed his companion, who was reported, like most men of uncommon literary ability, to be addicted to various destructive vices. That is the revenge which dull minds take upon bright ones in resentment of their superiority. Mr. Colston was known as a man of genius. There are honest souls who believe that genius is a mode of excess.[2] It was known that Colston did not drink liquor, but many said that he ate opium. Something in his appearance that morning—a certain wildness of the eyes, an unusual pallor, a thickness and rapidity of speech—were taken by Mr. Marsh to confirm the report. Nevertheless, he had not the self-denial to abandon a subject which he found interesting, however it might excite his friend.

"Do you mean to say," he began, "that if I take the trouble to observe your directions—place myself in the conditions that you demand: solitude, night and a tallow candle—you can with your ghostly work give me an uncomfortable sense of the supernatural, as you call it? Can you accelerate my pulse, make me start at sudden noises, send a nervous chill along my spine and cause my hair to rise?"

Colston turned suddenly and looked him squarely in the eyes as they walked. "You would not dare—you have not the courage," he said. He emphasized the words with a contemptuous gesture. "You are brave enough to read me in a street car, but—in a deserted house—alone—in the forest—at night! Bah! I have a manuscript in my pocket that would kill you."

Marsh was angry. He knew himself courageous, and the words stung him. "If you know such a place," he said, "take me there to-night and leave me your story and a candle. Call for me when I've had time enough to read it and I'll tell you the entire plot and—kick you out of the place."

That is how it occurred that the farmer's boy, looking in at an unglazed window of the Breede house, saw a man sitting in the light of a candle.

THE DAY AFTER

Late in the afternoon of the next day three men and a boy approached the Breede house from that point of the compass toward which the boy had fled the preceding night. The men were in high spirits; they talked very loudly and laughed. They made facetious and good-humored ironical remarks to the boy about his adventure, which evidently they did not believe in. The boy accepted their raillery with seriousness, making no reply. He had a sense of the fitness of things and knew that one who professes to have seen a dead man rise from his seat and blow out a candle is not a credible witness.

Arriving at the house and finding the door unlocked, the party of investigators entered without ceremony. Leading out of the passage into which this door opened was another on the right and one on the left. They entered the room on the left—the one which had the blank front window. Here was the dead body of a man.

It lay partly on one side, with the forearm beneath it, the cheek on the floor. The eyes were wide open; the stare was not an agreeable thing to encounter. The lower jaw had fallen; a little pool of saliva had collected beneath the mouth. An overthrown table, a partly burned candle, a chair and some paper with writing on it were all else that the room contained. The men looked at the body, touching the face in turn. The boy gravely stood at the head, assuming a look of ownership. It was the proudest moment of his life. One of the men said to him, "You're a good 'un"—a remark which was received by the two others with nods of acquiescence. It was Skepticism apologizing to Truth. Then one of the men took from the floor the sheet of manuscript and stepped to the window, for already the evening shadows were glooming the forest. The song of the whip-poor-will was heard in the distance and a monstrous beetle sped by the window on roaring wings and thundered away out of hearing. The man read:

THE MANUSCRIPT

"Before committing the act which, rightly or wrongly, I have resolved on and appearing before my Maker for judgment, I, James R. Colston, deem it my duty as a journalist to make a statement to the public. My name is, I believe, tolerably well known to the people as a writer of tragic tales,[3] but the somberest imagination never conceived anything so tragic as my own life and history. Not in incident: my life has been destitute of adventure and action. But my mental career has been lurid with experiences such as kill and damn. I shall not recount them here—some of them are written and ready for publication elsewhere. The object of these lines is to explain to whomsoever may be interested that my death is voluntary—my own act. I shall die at twelve o'clock on the night of the 15th of July—a significant anniversary to me, for it was on that day, and at that hour, that my friend in time and eternity, Charles Breede, performed his vow to me by the same act which his fidelity to our pledge now entails upon me. He took his life in his little house in the Copeton woods. There was the customary verdict of 'temporary insanity.'[4] Had I testified at that inquest—had I told all I knew, they would have called *me* mad!"

Here followed an evidently long passage which the man reading aloud read to himself only. The rest he read aloud:

"I have still a week of life in which to arrange my worldly affairs and prepare for the great change. It is enough, for I have but few affairs and it is now four years since death became an imperative obligation.

"I shall bear this writing on my body; the finder will please hand it to the coroner.

"JAMES R. COLSTON.

"P. S.—Willard Marsh, on this the fatal fifteenth day of July I hand you this manuscript, to be opened and read under the conditions agreed upon, and at the place which I designated. I forego my intention to keep it on my body to explain the manner of my death, which is not important. It will serve to explain the manner of yours. I am to call for you during the night to receive assurance that you have read the manuscript. You know me well enough to expect me. But, my friend, it *will be after twelve o'clock*. May God have mercy on our souls!

"J. R. C."

Before the man who was reading this manuscript had finished, the candle had been picked up and lighted. When the reader had done, he quietly thrust the paper against the flame and despite the protestations of the others held it until it was burnt to ashes. The man who did this, and who afterward placidly endured a severe reprimand from the coroner, was a son-in-law of the late Charles Breede. At the inquest nothing could elicit an intelligent account of what the paper had contained.

FROM "THE TIMES"

"Yesterday the Commissioners of Lunacy committed to the asylum Mr. James R. Colston, a writer of some local reputation, connected with the *Messenger.* It will be remembered that on the evening of the 15th inst. Mr. Colston was given into custody by one of his fellow-lodgers in the Baine House, who had observed him acting very suspiciously, baring his throat and whetting a razor—occasionally trying its edge by actually cutting through the skin of his arm, etc. On being handed over to the police, the unfortunate man made a desperate resistance, and has ever since been so violent that it has been necessary to keep him in a strait-jacket. Most of our esteemed contemporary's other writers are still at large."

E (14 July 1889): 10 (with subtitle: "Instruction by Example in the Art of Reading a Ghost Story"); *TSC* 227–40; *IML* 249–64; *CW* **2.350–63**. Reprinted in *Current Literature* 3, no. 5 (Nov. 1889): 438–39 (as "The Real Art of Reading a Ghost Story"); *Evening Sun* (New York) (26 Jan. 1897): 2 (as "Suitable Surroundings").

NOTES

Not just an antighost story, "The Suitable Surroundings" is important for its exposé of reason as being not only fallible but also potentially lethal to its possessor. Marsh exemplifies one of AB's favorite targets, the rationalistic protagonist. He becomes a victim because of overconfident pride in his rationalism and because he is as a result excessively open-minded. Ironically, from AB's perspective, the best defense against superstition is a *belief* that excludes it, for once the possibility of superstition is seriously entertained, persuasive arguments and "suitable surroundings" can combine to turn reason against reasonableness, and become self-defeating. The motif of reason's dangerous fallibility recurs with some frequency among AB's stories—for example, "The Haunted Valley," "A Tough Tussle," and "The Man and the Snake."

1. Thomas Edison invented the phonograph in 1877, but the first phonograph records were not sold until 1892.

2. Cf. "Prattle," *W*, no. 495 (23 Jan. 1886): 5: "Mad, quoth'a! The only man who is not altogether mad is he who is not altogether destitute of genius. What *is* genius? . . . In the first

place, I believe it to be in some degree a very common faculty. There are few, I fancy, but have been at times conscious of having solved a problem, struck out a bright thought or hit upon a felicitous expression, by some lightning process altogether unlike those customary methods whose deliberate action enables us to trace and record their steps—a process which takes the mind to its mark with as straight and incomprehensible a certainty as the flight of a homing pigeon. In most of us this is a rare phenomenon; in many it never occurs. Many experience but do not mark. But the man to whom this straight and sure process is habitual; in whom it is the natural and customary mental mode; who gets to his conclusions without the help of premises; who, like a master of the rifle, hits his mark without sighting; who is right automatically, he knows not how,—him we call, distinctively, a genius, particularly if his gift display itself in those things which arrest attention and address our sympathies, as art, literature and war."

3. Cf. AB's characterization of his stories in a later letter: "I consider tragedy not only a higher order of thing than comedy, but a thing which takes a stronger grip on attention and has a more lasting vogue—teste the continued fame of it in the instance of such men as Poe, and the wide contemporary 'popularity' in the instance of such as de Maupassant. . . . For me to write a yarn with none of the tragic in it would hardly be what you call 'breaking out in a new place'. In my first story-book are a few that haven't any of it, and in my second a half-dozen or more" (AB to Bailey Millard, 19 Jan. 1906, MS, Univ. of Oregon).

4. Cf. "Certain Fool Epigrams for Certain Foolish People," *NYA* (26 Aug. 1903): 14; *E* (3 Sept. 1903): 16: "There are two kinds of temporary insanity. One ends in suicide, the other in marriage."

THE AFFAIR AT
COULTER'S NOTCH

"Do you think, Colonel, that your brave Coulter would like to put one of his guns in here?" the general asked.

He was apparently not altogether serious; it certainly did not seem a place where any artillerist, however brave, would like to put a gun. The colonel thought that possibly his division commander meant good-humoredly to intimate that in a recent conversation between them Captain Coulter's courage had been too highly extolled.

"General," he replied warmly, "Coulter would like to put a gun anywhere within reach of those people," with a motion of his hand in the direction of the enemy.

"It is the only place," said the general. He was serious, then.

The place was a depression, a "notch," in the sharp crest of a hill. It was a pass, and through it ran a turnpike, which reaching this highest point in its course by a sinuous ascent through a thin forest made a similar, though less steep, descent toward the enemy. For a mile to the left and a mile to the right, the ridge, though occupied by Federal infantry lying close behind the sharp crest and appearing as if held in place by atmospheric pressure, was inaccessible to artillery. There was no place but the bottom of the notch, and that was barely wide enough for the roadbed. From the Confederate side this point was commanded by two batteries posted on a slightly lower elevation beyond a creek, and a half-mile away. All the guns but one were masked by the trees of an orchard; that one—it seemed a bit of impudence—was on an open lawn directly in front of a rather grandiose building, the planter's dwelling. The gun was safe enough in its exposure—but only because the Federal infantry had been forbidden to fire. Coulter's Notch—it came to be called so—was not, that pleasant summer afternoon, a place where one would "like to put a gun."

Three or four dead horses lay there sprawling in the road, three or four dead men in a trim row at one side of it, and a little back, down the hill. All but one were cavalrymen belonging to the Federal advance. One was a quartermaster. The general commanding the division and the colonel commanding the brigade, with their staffs and escorts, had ridden into the notch to have a look at the enemy's guns—which had straightway obscured themselves in towering clouds of smoke. It was hardly profitable to be curious about guns which had the trick of the cuttlefish, and the season of observation had been brief. At its conclusion—a short remove backward from where it began—occurred the conversation already partly reported. "It is the only place," the general repeated thoughtfully, "to get at them."

The colonel looked at him gravely. "There is room for only one gun, General—one against twelve."

"That is true—for only one at a time," said the commander with something like, yet not altogether like, a smile. "But then, your brave Coulter—a whole battery in himself."

The tone of irony was now unmistakable. It angered the colonel, but he did not know what to say. The spirit of military subordination is not favorable to retort, nor even to deprecation.

At this moment a young officer of artillery came riding slowly up the road attended by his bugler. It was Captain Coulter. He could not have been more than twenty-three years of age. He was of medium height, but very slender and lithe, and sat his horse with something of the air of a civilian. In face he was of a type singularly unlike the men about him; thin, high-nosed, gray-eyed, with a slight blond mustache, and long, rather straggling hair of the same color. There was an apparent negligence in his attire. His cap was worn with the visor a trifle askew; his coat was buttoned only at the sword-belt, showing a considerable expanse of white shirt, tolerably clean for that stage of the campaign. But the negligence was all in his dress and bearing; in his face was a look of intense interest in his surroundings. His gray eyes, which seemed occasionally to strike right and left across the landscape, like search-lights, were for the most part fixed upon the sky beyond the Notch; until he should arrive at the summit of the road there was nothing else in that direction to see. As he came opposite his division and brigade commanders at the roadside he saluted mechanically and was about to pass on. The colonel signed to him to halt.

"Captain Coulter," he said, "the enemy has twelve pieces over there on the next ridge. If I rightly understand the general, he directs that you bring up a gun and engage them."

There was a blank silence; the general looked stolidly at a distant regiment swarming slowly up the hill through rough undergrowth, like a torn and draggled cloud of blue smoke; the captain appeared not to have observed him. Presently the captain spoke, slowly and with apparent effort:

"On the next ridge, did you say, sir? Are the guns near the house?"

"Ah, you have been over this road before. Directly at the house."

"And it is—necessary—to engage them? The order is imperative?"

THE AFFAIR AT COULTER'S NOTCH

His voice was husky and broken. He was visibly paler. The colonel was astonished and mortified. He stole a glance at the commander. In that set, immobile face was no sign; it was as hard as bronze. A moment later the general rode away, followed by his staff and escort. The colonel, humiliated and indignant, was about to order Captain Coulter in arrest, when the latter spoke a few words in a low tone to his bugler, saluted and rode straight forward into the Notch, where, presently, at the summit of the road, his field-glass at his eyes, he showed against the sky, he and his horse, sharply defined and statuesque. The bugler had dashed down the road in the opposite direction at head-long speed[1] and disappeared behind a wood. Presently his bugle was heard singing in the cedars,[2] and in an incredibly short time a single gun with its caisson, each drawn by six horses and manned by its full complement of gunners, came bounding and banging up the grade in a storm of dust, unlimbered under cover, and was run forward by hand to the fatal crest among the dead horses. A gesture of the captain's arm, some strangely agile movements of the men in loading, and almost before the troops along the way had ceased to hear the rattle of the wheels, a great white cloud sprang forward down the slope, and with a deafening report the affair at Coulter's Notch had begun.

It is not intended to relate in detail the progress and incidents of that ghastly contest—a contest without vicissitudes, its alternations only different degrees of despair. Almost at the instant when Captain Coulter's gun blew its challenging cloud twelve answering clouds rolled upward from among the trees about the plantation house, a deep multiple report roared back like a broken echo, and thenceforth to the end the Federal cannoneers fought their hopeless battle in an atmosphere of living iron whose thoughts were lightnings and whose deeds were death.

Unwilling to see the efforts which he could not aid and the slaughter which he could not stay, the colonel ascended the ridge at a point a quarter of a mile to the left, whence the Notch, itself invisible, but pushing up successive masses of smoke, seemed the crater of a volcano in thundering eruption. With his glass he watched the enemy's guns, noting as he could the effects of Coulter's fire—if Coulter still lived to direct it. He saw that the Federal gunners, ignoring those of the enemy's pieces whose positions could be determined by their smoke only, gave their whole attention to the one that maintained its place in the open—the lawn in front of the house. Over and about that hardy piece the shells exploded at intervals of a few seconds. Some exploded in the house, as could be seen by thin ascensions of smoke from the breached roof. Figures of prostrate men and horses were plainly visible.

"If our fellows are doing so good work with a single gun," said the colonel to an aide who happened to be nearest, "they must be suffering like the devil from twelve. Go down and present the commander of that piece with my congratulations on the accuracy of his fire."

Turning to his adjutant-general he said, "Did you observe Coulter's damned reluctance to obey orders?"

"Yes, sir, I did."

THE AFFAIR AT COULTER'S NOTCH

"Well, say nothing about it, please. I don't think the general will care to make any accusations. He will probably have enough to do in explaining his own connection with this uncommon way of amusing the rear-guard of a retreating enemy."

A young officer approached from below, climbing breathless up the acclivity. Almost before he had saluted, he gasped out:

"Colonel, I am directed by Colonel Harmon to say that the enemy's guns are within easy reach of our rifles, and most of them visible from several points along the ridge."

The brigade commander looked at him without a trace of interest in his expression. "I know it," he said quietly.

The young adjutant was visibly embarrassed. "Colonel Harmon would like to have permission to silence those guns," he stammered.

"So should I," the colonel said in the same tone. "Present my compliments to Colonel Harmon and say to him that the general's orders for the infantry not to fire are still in force."

The adjutant saluted and retired. The colonel ground his heel into the earth and turned to look again at the enemy's guns.

"Colonel," said the adjutant-general, "I don't know that I ought to say anything, but there is something wrong in all this. Do you happen to know that Captain Coulter is from the South?"

"No; *was* he, indeed?"

"I heard that last summer the division which the general then commanded was in the vicinity of Coulter's home—camped there for weeks, and—"

"Listen!" said the colonel, interrupting with an upward gesture. "Do you hear *that?*"

"That" was the silence of the Federal gun. The staff, the orderlies, the lines of infantry behind the crest—all had "heard," and were looking curiously in the direction of the crater, whence no smoke now ascended except desultory cloudlets from the enemy's shells. Then came the blare of a bugle, a faint rattle of wheels; a minute later the sharp reports recommenced with double activity. The demolished gun had been replaced with a sound one.

"Yes," said the adjutant-general, resuming his narrative, "the general made the acquaintance of Coulter's family. There was trouble—I don't know the exact nature of it—something about Coulter's wife. She is a red-hot Secessionist, as they all are, except Coulter himself, but she is a good wife and high-bred lady. There was a complaint to army headquarters. The general was transferred to this division. It is odd that Coulter's battery should afterward have been assigned to it."

The colonel had risen from the rock upon which they had been sitting. His eyes were blazing with a generous indignation.

"See here, Morrison," said he, looking his gossiping staff officer straight in the face, "did you get that story from a gentleman or a liar?"

"I don't want to say how I got it, Colonel, unless it is necessary"—he was blushing a trifle—"but I'll stake my life upon its truth in the main."

THE AFFAIR AT COULTER'S NOTCH

The colonel turned toward a small knot of officers some distance away. "Lieutenant Williams!" he shouted.

One of the officers detached himself from the group and coming forward saluted, saying: "Pardon me, Colonel, I thought you had been informed. Williams is dead down there by the gun. What can I do, sir?"

Lieutenant Williams was the aide who had had the pleasure of conveying to the officer in charge of the gun his brigade commander's congratulations.

"Go," said the colonel, "and direct the withdrawal of that gun instantly. No—I'll go myself."

He strode down the declivity toward the rear of the Notch at a break-neck pace, over rocks and through brambles, followed by his little retinue in tumultuous disorder. At the foot of the declivity they mounted their waiting animals and took to the road at a lively trot, round a bend and into the Notch. The spectacle which they encountered there was appalling!

Within that defile, barely broad enough for a single gun, were piled the wrecks of no fewer than four. They had noted the silencing of only the last one disabled—there had been a lack of men to replace it quickly with another. The débris lay on both sides of the road; the men had managed to keep an open way between, through which the fifth piece was now firing. The men?—they looked like demons of the pit! All were hatless, all stripped to the waist, their reeking skins black with blotches of powder and spattered with gouts of blood. They worked like madmen, with rammer and cartridge, lever and lanyard. They set their swollen shoulders and bleeding hands against the wheels at each recoil and heaved the heavy gun back to its place. There were no commands; in that awful environment of whooping shot, exploding shells, shrieking fragments of iron and flying splinters of wood, none could have been heard. Officers, if officers there were, were indistinguishable; all worked together—each while he lasted—governed by the eye. When the gun was sponged,[3] it was loaded; when loaded, aimed and fired. The colonel observed something new to his military experience—something horrible and unnatural: the gun was bleeding at the mouth! In temporary default of water, the man sponging had dipped his sponge into a pool of comrade's blood. In all this work there was no clashing; the duty of the instant was obvious. When one fell, another, looking a trifle cleaner, seemed to rise from the earth in the dead man's tracks, to fall in his turn.

With the ruined guns lay the ruined men—alongside the wreckage, under it and atop of it; and back down the road—a ghastly procession!—crept on hands and knees such of the wounded as were able to move. The colonel—he had compassionately sent his cavalcade to the right about—had to ride over those who were entirely dead in order not to crush those who were partly alive. Into that hell he tranquilly held his way, rode up alongside the gun and, in the obscurity of the last discharge, tapped upon the cheek the man holding the rammer—who straightway fell, thinking himself killed. A fiend seven times damned sprang out of the smoke to take his place, but

THE AFFAIR AT COULTER'S NOTCH

paused and gazed up at the mounted officer with an unearthly regard, his teeth flash-ing between his black lips, his eyes, fierce and expanded, burning like coals beneath his bloody brow. The colonel made an authoritative gesture and pointed to the rear. The fiend bowed in token of obedience. It was Captain Coulter.

Simultaneously with the colonel's arresting sign, silence fell upon the whole field of action. The procession of missiles no longer streamed into that defile of death, for the enemy also had ceased firing. His army had been gone for hours, and the com-mander of his rear-guard, who had held his position perilously long in hope to silence the Federal fire, at that strange moment had silenced his own. "I was not aware of the breadth of my authority," said the colonel to anybody, riding forward to the crest to see what had really happened.

An hour later his brigade was in bivouac on the enemy's ground, and its idlers were examining, with something of awe, as the faithful inspect a saint's relics, a score of straddling dead horses and three disabled guns, all spiked. The fallen men had been carried away; their torn and broken bodies would have given too great satisfaction.

Naturally, the colonel established himself and his military family in the plantation house. It was somewhat shattered, but it was better than the open air. The furniture was greatly deranged and broken. Walls and ceilings were knocked away here and there, and a lingering odor of powder smoke was everywhere. The beds, the closets of women's clothing, the cupboards were not greatly damaged. The new tenants for a night made themselves comfortable, and the virtual effacement of Coulter's battery supplied them with an interesting topic.

During supper an orderly of the escort showed himself into the dining-room and asked permission to speak to the colonel.

"What is it, Barbour?" said that officer pleasantly, having overheard the request.

"Colonel, there is something wrong in the cellar; I don't know what—somebody's there. I was down there rummaging about."

"I will go down and see," said a staff officer, rising.

"So will I," the colonel said; "let the others remain. Lead on, orderly."

They took a candle from the table and descended the cellar stairs, the orderly in visible trepidation. The candle made but a feeble light, but presently, as they ad-vanced, its narrow circle of illumination revealed a human figure seated on the ground against the black stone wall which they were skirting, its knees elevated, its head bowed sharply forward. The face, which should have been seen in profile, was invisible, for the man was bent so far forward that his long hair concealed it; and, strange to relate, the beard, of a much darker hue, fell in a great tangled mass and lay along the ground at his side. They involuntarily paused; then the colonel, taking a candle from the orderly's shaking hand, approached the man and attentively consid-ered him. The long dark beard was the hair of a woman—dead. The dead woman clasped in her arms a dead babe. Both were clasped in the arms of the man, pressed against his breast, against his lips. There was blood in the hair of the woman; there

THE AFFAIR AT COULTER'S NOTCH

was blood in the hair of the man. A yard away, near an irregular depression in the beaten earth which formed the cellar's floor—a fresh excavation with a convex bit of iron, having jagged edges, visible in one of the sides—lay an infant's foot. The colonel held the light as high as he could. The floor of the room above was broken through, the splinters pointing at all angles downward. "This casemate is not bomb-proof," said the colonel gravely. It did not occur to him that his summing up of the matter had any levity in it.

They stood about the group awhile in silence; the staff officer was thinking of his unfinished supper, the orderly of what might possibly be in one of the casks on the other side of the cellar. Suddenly the man whom they had thought dead raised his head and gazed tranquilly into their faces. His complexion was coal black; the cheeks were apparently tattooed in irregular sinuous lines from the eyes downward. The lips, too, were white, like those of a stage negro. There was blood upon his forehead.

The staff officer drew back a pace, the orderly two paces.

"What are you doing here, my man?" said the colonel, unmoved.

"This house belongs to me, sir," was the reply, civilly delivered.

"To you? Ah, I see! And these?"

"My wife and child. I am Captain Coulter."

E (20 Oct. 1889): 13; *TSC* 105–21; ***CW* 2.105–21.**

NOTES

The title's word "affair" dryly understates the bleak tragedy of an individual who is broken by the requirement that he make an inhuman choice between conflicting loyalties. The choice is made even harder and more bitter by being occasioned by the personal malice of his commanding officer, whose order has no redeeming military value yet must be obeyed unquestioningly. This exposure of a military tyrant is another aspect of AB's realism that recounted instances of lives being thrown away needlessly by the whim, incompetence, or malice of commanding officers (see AB's memoir, "The Crime at Pickett's Mill" [*SS* 37–44]). In response to a reader's objection that Coulter might have protested, AB replied that not only would that have run counter to the principle of military subordination but that he "had chosen to write of an officer whose pride and sense of duty forbade him" to complain ("Prattle," *E* [26 June 1892]: 6). In other words, AB admits undertaking to depict believable human beings whose characters determine their choices. AB is not often compared with Hawthorne and Henry James, but on this point their artistic goals seem to coincide.

The story is additionally interesting because a likely source for it is "The Fortune of War," an anonymous anecdote of the Franco-Prussian War that was reprinted in *E* on 23 October 1887—two years before the story was written (see Appendix C). If this anecdote is the germ of the story, it decouples AB from the requirement that his war stories have some basis in his autobiography and is evidence that he freely created stories around ideas as well as memories. Indeed, other sources for this story are probably to be found in his reading of Stoic philosophy, about whose lessons he was ambivalent. Particularly appropriate, for instance, is this passage from Epictetus: "Never say of anything, 'I lost it,' but say, 'I gave it back.' Has your child died? It was given back. Has your estate been taken from you? Was not this also given back? But you say, 'He who took it from me is wicked.' What does it matter to you through whom the Giver asked it back? As long as He gives it to you, take care of it, but not as your own; treat it as passers-by treat an inn" (*Manual* 11, trans. P. E. Matheson; *The Stoic and Epicurean Philosophers,* ed. Whitney J. Oates, 470). The philosophy is lofty, but its demand on the human heart might have been too much for AB.

 This story was plagiarized and published in the *New York Evening Post* on 14 July 1893 under the title "At Clipper Gap." The theft was soon discovered, however, and the newspaper itself exposed the plagiarist. AB seems to have been content to let the matter rest there and not pursue it in court.

1. This edition restores the text of *E*, correcting an error in *CW*, whose faulty text reads at this point: "The bugler had dashed down the speed."
2. Possibly an allusion to Walt Whitman's "When Lilacs Last in the Dooryard Bloom'd" (1865): "Sing on, sing on . . . out of the cedars and pines" (ll. 99–101).
3. The cannon was sponged after every shot to quench any sparks that remained in the tube, as they could ignite the next cartridge.

THE AFFAIR AT COULTER'S NOTCH

THE GOLAMPIANS

SOME ACCOUNT OF A MOST EXTRAORDINARY PEOPLE.

From my former account of the Golampians,[1] their civilization (to call it so), their morals, manners and customs, I necessarily omitted much that is of interest to the foreign observer; nor can I hope now to supply more than a small part of it. They are so extraordinary a people, inhabiting so marvelous a country, that everything which the traveler sees, hears or experiences makes the liveliest and most lasting impression upon his mind, and the labor of a lifetime would be required to relate the observation of a year. The utmost that I can hope to do in this article, and any which may follow, is merely to glance at those matters in which the Golampians most conspicuously differ from our own people and in which they are therefore least worthy.

With a fatuousness hardly more credible than creditable, the Golampians deny the immortality of the soul. In all my stay in their country I found only one person who believed in a life "beyond the grave," as we should say, though as the Golampians eat their dead they would say "beyond the stomach." In testimony to the consolatory value of the sublime doctrine of another life I may say that this one believer had in this life a comparatively unsatisfactory lot, for in early youth he had been struck by a flying stone from a volcano and lost a considerable part of his brain.

I cannot better set forth the nature and extent of the Golampian error regarding this matter than by relating a conversation which occurred between me and one of the high officers of the King's household—a man whose proficiency in all the vices of antiquity, together with his service to the realm in determining the normal radius of curvature in cats' claws, had elevated him to the highest plane of political preferment. His name was Gnarmag-Zote.

"You tell me," said he, "that the soul is immaterial. Now, matter is that of which we can have knowledge through one or more of our senses. Of what is immaterial— not matter—we can gain no knowledge in that way. How, then, can we know of it?"

"By report, for example," I replied.

"Ah, but you do not understand my question," he went on with a smile of superiority which I found singularly irritating. "I said how can *we* know: the pronoun includes all mankind—the man who reports, as well as him to whom the report is made. The reporter, having only the same five senses as we, can himself have no knowledge to report."

Perceiving that he did not rightly apprehend my position I abandoned it and shifted the argument to another ground. "Consider," I said, "the analogous case of a thought. You will hardly call thought material, yet we know there are thoughts." "I beg your pardon, but we do not know that. Thought is not a thing, therefore cannot *be,* in any such sense as the hand is. We use the word 'thought' to designate the result of an action of the brain, precisely as we use the word speed to designate the result of an action of a horse's legs. But can it be said that speed exists in the same way as the legs which produce it exist, or in any way? Is it a thing?"

I was about to disdain to reply, when I saw an old man approaching, with bowed head and apparently in deep distress. As he drew near he saluted my distinguished interlocutor in the manner of the country, by putting out his tongue to its full extent and moving it slowly from side to side. Gnarmag-Zote acknowledged the civility by courteously spitting, and the old man, advancing, seated himself at the great officer's feet, saying: "Exalted sir, I have just lost my wife by death, and am in a most melancholy frame of mind. He who has mastered all the vices of the ancients and wrested from Nature the secret of the curvature of cats' claws can surely spare from his wisdom a few rays of philosophy to cheer an old man's gloom. Pray tell me what I shall do to assuage my grief."

The reader can perhaps faintly conceive my astonishment when Gnarmag-Zote gravely replied: "Commit suicide."

"Surely," I cried, "you would not have this honest fellow procure oblivion (since you think that death is nothing else) by so rash an act!"

"An act that Gnarmag-Zote advises," he said, coldly, "is not rash."

"But death," I said, "death, whatever it may be, is at least an end of life. This old man is now in sorrow almost insupportable. But a few days and it will be supportable; a few months and it will have become no more than a tender melancholy. At last it will disappear, and in the society of his friends, in the skill of his cook, the profits of avarice, the study of how to be querulous and in the pursuit of loquacity he will again experience the joys of age. Why for a present grief should he deprive himself of all future happiness?"

THE GOLAMPIANS

Gnarmag-Zote looked upon me with something like compassion. "My friend," said he, "guest of my sovereign and my country, know that under any circumstances, even those upon which true happiness is based and conditioned, death is preferable to life. The sum of miseries in any life (here in Golampia, at least) exceeds the sum of pleasures; but suppose that it did not. Imagine an existence in which happiness, of whatever intensity, was the rule and discomfort, of whatever moderation, the exception. Still there is some discomfort. There is none in death, for (as it is given to us to know) that is oblivion, annihilation. True, by dying one loses his happiness as well as his sorrows, but he is not conscious of the loss. Surely a loss of which one will never know and which, if it operate to make him less happy, at the same time takes from him the desire and capacity for happiness, cannot be an evil. That is so intelligently understood among us here in Golampia that suicide is very common, and our word for sufferer is the same as that for fool. If this good man had not been an idiot he would have taken his life long ago."

"If what you say of the blessing of death is true," I asked, smilingly, for I greatly prided myself on the ingenuity of my thought, "it is unnecessary to commit suicide through grief for the dead, for the more you love, the more glad you should be that the object of your affection has passed into so desirable a state as death."

"So we are—those of us who have cultivated philosophy, history and logic; but this poor fellow is still under the domination of feelings inherited from a million ignorant and superstitious ancestors—for Golampia was once as barbarous a country as your own. The most grotesque and frightful conceptions of death, and life after death, were current; and now many of even those whose understandings are emancipated bear upon their feelings the heavy chains of heredity."

"But," said I, "granting for the sake of the argument which I am about to build upon the concession"—I could not bring myself to use the idiotic and meaningless phrase, "for the sake of argument"—"that death, especially the death of a Golampian, is desirable, yet the act of dying, the transition state between living and being dead, may be accompanied by the most painful physical, and most terrifying mental, phenomena. The moment of dissolution may seem to the exalted sensibilities of the moribund a century of horrors."

The great man smiled again, with a more intolerable benignancy than before. "There is no such thing as dying," he said: "the 'transition state' is a creation of your fancy and an evidence of imperfect reason. One is at any time either alive or dead. The one condition cannot 'shade off' into the other. There is no gradation like that between waking and sleeping. By the way, do you recognize a certain resemblance between death and a dreamless sleep?"

"Yes—death as you conceive it to be."

"Well, does any one fear to go to sleep? Do we not seek it, court it, wish that it may be sound—that is to say, dreamless? We desire occasional annihilation—wish to be dead for eight and ten hours at a time. True, we expect to awake, but that expectation, while it may account for our alacrity in embracing sleep, cannot alter the character of the state that we cheerfully go into. Suppose we did *not* wake in the morning, never did wake! Would our mental and spiritual condition be in any respect different through all eternity from what it was during the first few hours? The man who loves to sleep yet hates to die might justly be granted everlasting life with everlasting insomnia."

Gnarmag-Zote paused and appeared to be lost in the profundity of his thoughts, but I could easily enough see that he was only taking breath. The old man whose grief had given this turn to the conversation had fallen asleep and was roaring in the nose like a beast. The rush of a river near by, as it poured up a hill from the ocean, and the shrill singing of several kinds of brilliant quadrupeds were the only other sounds audible. I waited deferentially for the great antiquarian, scientist and courtier to resume, amusing myself meantime by turning over the leaves of an official report by the Minister of War on a new and improved process for extracting thunder from snail slime. Presently the oracle spoke. "You have been born," he said, which was true. "There was, it follows, a time when you had not been born. As we reckon time, it was probably some millions of ages. Of this considerable period you are unable to remember one unhappy moment, and in point of fact there was none. To a Golampian that is entirely conclusive as to the relative values of consciousness and oblivion, existence and non-existence, life and death. This old man lying here at my feet is now, if not dreaming, as if he had never been born. Would not it be cruel and inhuman to wake him back to grief? Is it, then, kind to permit him to wake by the natural action of his own physical energies? I have given him the advice for which he asked. Believing it good advice and seeing him too irresolute to act it seems my clear duty to assist him."

Before I could interfere, even had I dared take the liberty to do so, Gnarmag-Zote struck the old man a terrible blow upon the head with his mace of office. The victim turned upon his back, spread his fingers, shivered convulsively and was dead.

"You need not be shocked," said the distinguished assassin, coolly; "I have but performed a sacred duty and religious rite. The religion (established first in this realm by King Skanghutch the sixty-second of that name) consists in the worship of Death. We have sacred books, some three thousand thick volumes, written by inspiration of Death himself, whom no mortal has ever seen, but who is described by our priests as having the figure of a very fat man with a red face and wearing an affable smile. In art he is commonly represented in the costume of a husbandman, sowing seeds.

"The priests and sacred books teach that death is the supreme and only good— that the chief duties of man are assassination and suicide. Conviction of these cardinal truths is universal among us, but I am sorry to say that many do not honestly live up to the faith. Most of us are commendably zealous in assassination, but slack and lukewarm in suicide. Some justify themselves in this half-hearted observance of the Law and imperfect submission to the spirit by arguing that if they destroy themselves their usefulness in destroying others will be greatly abridged. 'I find,' said one of our most illustrious writers, not without a certain force, it must be confessed, 'that I can slay

THE GOLAMPIANS

many more of others than I can of myself.' There are still others, more distinguished for faith than works, who reason that if A kills B, B cannot kill C. So it happens that although many Golampians die, mostly by the hands of others though some by their own, the country is never wholly depopulated."

"In my own country," said I, "is a sect holding somewhat Golampian views of the evil of life; and among them it is considered a sin to bestow it. The philosopher Schopenhauer taught the same doctrine, and many of our rulers have shown strong sympathetic leanings toward it by procuring the destruction of many of their own people and those of other nations in what are called wars."

"They are greatly to be commended," said Gnarmag-Zote, rising to intimate that the conversation was at an end. I respectfully stood on my head while he withdrew into his palace spitting politely and with unusual copiousness in acknowledgment. A few minutes later, but before I had left the spot, two lackeys in livery emerged from the door by which he had entered, and while one shouldered the body of the old man and carried it into the palace kitchen the other informed me that his Highness was graciously pleased to desire my company at dinner that evening. With many expressions of regret I declined the invitation. The fact is, my own cook had, I knew, a fine fat babe in the oven.[2]

E (24 Nov. 1889): 11. Reprinted in *Short Stories* 6, no. 3 (June 1891): 304–9. Reprinted as "An Interview with Gnarmag-Zote" in "The Land Beyond the Blow."

NOTES

The difficulty in closely tying AB's stories to his biography is exemplified by this story. In the midst of writing his powerful war stories, he was able to drastically shift moods and compose this relatively lighthearted satire. Its indebtedness to *Gulliver's Travels* is obvious, but other influences on the piece might be Samuel Johnson's *History of Rasselas, Prince of Abyssinia* (1759). Possible but less likely are several contemporary works of time travel, Edward Bellamy's *Looking Backward* (1888) and Twain's *Connecticut Yankee in King Arthur's Court* (1889). Although the story is mainly humorous, it is not entirely so. The subject of whether it is better to live or die was a serious one to AB and therefore receives serious and logical debate within the satire and is given serious treatment in later fiction. The fact that AB mocks both sides and ends the debate inconclusively suggests that he convinced himself that logic alone could not answer the question.

1. AB alludes to "Sons of the Fair Star" (p. 587).
2. Two possible allusions are involved here: one to Jonathan Swift's mordantly ironic essay "A Modest Proposal" (1729), and the other to the illustration on the title page of *FD*, which depicts a gentleman using long tongs to hold a baby over the flames of a stove.

A WATCHER BY THE DEAD

In an upper room of an unoccupied dwelling in the part of San Francisco known as North Beach[1] lay the body of a man, under a sheet. The hour was near nine in the evening; the room was dimly lighted by a single candle. Although the weather was warm, the two windows, contrary to the custom which gives the dead plenty of air, were closed and the blinds drawn down. The furniture of the room consisted of but three pieces—an arm-chair, a small reading-stand supporting the candle and a long kitchen table, supporting the body of the man. All these, as also the corpse, seemed to have been recently brought in, for an observer, had there been one, would have seen that all were free from dust, whereas everything else in the room was pretty thickly coated with it, and there were cobwebs in the angles of the walls.

Under the sheet the outlines of the body could be traced, even the features, these having that unnaturally sharp definition which seems to belong to faces of the dead, but is really characteristic of those only that have been wasted by disease. From the silence of the room one would rightly have inferred that it was not in the front of the house, facing a street. It really faced nothing but a high breast of rock, the rear of the building being set into a hill.

As a neighboring church clock was striking nine with an indolence which seemed to imply such an indifference to the flight of time that one could hardly help wondering why it took the trouble to strike at all, the single door of the room was opened and a man entered, advancing toward the body. As he did so the door closed, apparently of its own volition; there was a grating, as of a key turned with difficulty, and the snap of the lock bolt as it shot into its socket. A sound of retiring footsteps in the passage outside ensued, and the man was to all appearance a prisoner. Advancing to the table, he stood a moment looking down at the body; then with a slight shrug of the shoulders walked over to one of the windows and hoisted the blind. The darkness outside was absolute, the panes were covered with dust, but by wiping this away he could see that the window was fortified with strong iron bars crossing it within a few inches of the glass and imbedded in the masonry on each side. He examined the other window. It was the same. He manifested no great curiosity in the matter, did not even so much as raise the sash. If he was a prisoner he was apparently a tractable one. Having completed his examination of the room, he seated himself in the arm-chair, took a book from his pocket, drew the stand with its candle alongside and began to read.

The man was young—not more than thirty—dark in complexion, smooth-shaven, with brown hair. His face was thin and high-nosed, with a broad forehead and a "firmness" of the chin and jaw which is said by those having it to denote resolution. The eyes were gray and steadfast, not moving except with definitive purpose. They were now for the greater part of the time fixed upon his book, but he occasionally withdrew them and turned them to the body on the table, not, apparently, from any dismal fascination which under such circumstances it might be supposed to exercise upon even a courageous person, nor with a conscious rebellion against the contrary influence which might dominate a timid one. He looked at it as if in his reading he had come upon something recalling him to a sense of his surroundings. Clearly this watcher by the dead was discharging his trust with intelligence and composure, as became him.

After reading for perhaps a half-hour he seemed to come to the end of a chapter and quietly laid away the book. He then rose and taking the reading-stand from the floor carried it into a corner of the room near one of the windows, lifted the candle from it and returned to the empty fireplace before which he had been sitting.

A moment later he walked over to the body on the table, lifted the sheet and turned it back from the head, exposing a mass of dark hair and a thin face-cloth, beneath which the features showed with even sharper definition than before. Shading his eyes by interposing his free hand between them and the candle, he stood looking at his motionless companion with a serious and tranquil regard. Satisfied with his inspection, he pulled the sheet over the face again and returning to the chair, took some matches off the candlestick, put them in the side pocket of his sack-coat and sat down. He then lifted the candle from its socket and looked at it critically, as if calculating how long it would last. It was barely two inches long; in another hour he would be in darkness. He replaced it in the candlestick and blew it out.

II

In a physician's office in Kearny street three men sat about a table, drinking punch and smoking. It was late in the evening, almost midnight, indeed, and there had been no lack of punch. The gravest of the three, Dr. Helberson, was the host—it was in his rooms they sat. He was about thirty years of age; the others were even younger; all were physicians.

"The superstitious awe with which the living regard the dead," said Dr. Helberson, "is hereditary and incurable. One needs no more be ashamed of it than of the fact that he inherits, for example, an incapacity for mathematics, or a tendency to lie."

The others laughed. "Oughtn't a man to be ashamed to lie?" asked the youngest of the three, who was in fact a medical student not yet graduated.

"My dear Harper, I said nothing about that. The tendency to lie is one thing; lying is another."

"But do you think," said the third man, "that this superstitious feeling, this fear of the dead, reasonless as we know it to be, is universal? I am myself not conscious of it."

"Oh, but it is 'in your system' for all that," replied Helberson; "it needs only the right conditions—what Shakespeare calls the 'confederate season'²—to manifest itself in some very disagreeable way that will open your eyes. Physicians and soldiers are of course more nearly free from it than others."

"Physicians and soldiers!—why don't you add hangmen and headsmen? Let us have in all the assassin classes."

"No, my dear Mancher;³ the juries will not let the public executioners acquire sufficient familiarity with death to be altogether unmoved by it."

Young Harper, who had been helping himself to a fresh cigar at the sideboard, resumed his seat. "What would you consider conditions under which any man of woman born⁴ would become insupportably conscious of his share of our common weakness in this regard?" he asked, rather verbosely.

"Well, I should say that if a man were locked up all night with a corpse—alone—in a dark room—of a vacant house—with no bed covers to pull over his head—and lived through it without going altogether mad, he might justly boast himself not of woman born, nor yet, like Macduff, a product of Cæsarean section."⁵

"I thought you never would finish piling up conditions," said Harper, "but I know a man who is neither a physician nor a soldier who will accept them all, for any stake you like to name."

"Who is he?"

"His name is Jarette—a stranger here; comes from my town in New York. I have no money to back him, but he will back himself with loads of it."

"How do you know that?"

"He would rather bet than eat. As for fear—I dare say he thinks it some cutaneous disorder, or possibly a particular kind of religious heresy."

"What does he look like?" Helberson was evidently becoming interested.

"Like Mancher, here—might be his twin brother."

"I accept the challenge," said Helberson, promptly.

"Awfully obliged to you for the compliment, I'm sure," drawled Mancher, who was growing sleepy. "Can't I get into this?"

"Not against me," Helberson said. "I don't want *your* money."

A WATCHER BY THE DEAD

"All right," said Mancher; "I'll be the corpse."

The others laughed.

The outcome of this crazy conversation we have seen.

III

In extinguishing his meager allowance of candle Mr. Jarette's object was to preserve it against some unforeseen need. He may have thought, too, or half thought, that the darkness would be no worse at one time than another, and if the situation became insupportable it would be better to have a means of relief, or even release. At any rate it was wise to have a little reserve of light, even if only to enable him to look at his watch.

No sooner had he blown out the candle and set it on the floor at his side than he settled himself comfortably in the arm-chair, leaned back and closed his eyes, hoping and expecting to sleep. In this he was disappointed; he had never in his life felt less sleepy, and in a few minutes he gave up the attempt. But what could he do? He could not go groping about in absolute darkness at the risk of bruising himself—at the risk, too, of blundering against the table and rudely disturbing the dead. We all recognize their right to lie at rest, with immunity from all that is harsh and violent. Jarette almost succeeded in making himself believe that considerations of this kind restrained him from risking the collision and fixed him to the chair.

While thinking of this matter he fancied that he heard a faint sound in the direction of the table—what kind of sound he could hardly have explained. He did not turn his head. Why should he—in the darkness? But he listened—why should he not? And listening he grew giddy and grasped the arms of the chair for support. There was a strange ringing in his ears; his head seemed bursting; his chest was oppressed by the constriction of his clothing. He wondered why it was so, and whether these were symptoms of fear. Then, with a long and strong expiration, his chest appeared to collapse, and with the great gasp with which he refilled his exhausted lungs the vertigo left him and he knew that so intently had he listened that he had held his breath almost to suffocation. The revelation was vexatious; he arose, pushed away the chair with his foot and strode to the center of the room. But one does not stride far in darkness; he began to grope, and finding the wall followed it to an angle, turned, followed it past the two windows and there in another corner came into violent contact with the reading-stand, overturning it. It made a clatter that startled him. He was annoyed. "How the devil could I have forgotten where it was?" he muttered, and groped his way along the third wall to the fireplace. "I must put things to rights," said he, feeling the floor for the candle.

Having recovered that, he lighted it and instantly turned his eyes to the table, where, naturally, nothing had undergone any change. The reading-stand lay unobserved upon the floor: he had forgotten to "put it to rights." He looked all about the room, dispersing the deeper shadows by movements of the candle in his hand, and crossing over to the door tested it by turning and pulling the knob with all his strength. It did not yield and this seemed to afford him a certain satisfaction; indeed, he secured it more firmly by a bolt which he had not before observed. Returning to his chair, he looked at his watch; it was half-past nine. With a start of surprise he held the watch at his ear. It had not stopped. The candle was now visibly shorter. He again extinguished it, placing it on the floor at his side as before.

Mr. Jarette was not at his ease; he was distinctly dissatisfied with his surroundings, and with himself for being so. "What have I to fear?" he thought. "This is ridiculous and disgraceful; I will not be so great a fool." But courage does not come of saying, "I will be courageous," nor of recognizing its appropriateness to the occasion. The more Jarette condemned himself, the more reason he gave himself for condemnation; the greater the number of variations which he played upon the simple theme of the harmlessness of the dead, the more insupportable grew the discord of his emotions. "What!" he cried aloud in the anguish of his spirit, "what! shall I, who have not a shade of superstition in my nature—I, who have no belief in immortality—I, who know (and never more clearly than now) that the after-life is a dream of a desire⁶—shall I lose at once my bet, my honor and my self-respect, perhaps my reason, because certain savage ancestors dwelling in caves and burrows conceived the monstrous notion that the dead walk by night?—that———" Distinctly, unmistakably, Mr. Jarette heard behind him a light, soft sound of footfalls, deliberate, regular, successively nearer!

IV

Just before daybreak the next morning Dr. Helberson and his young friend Harper were driving slowly through the streets of North Beach in the doctor's coupé.

"Have you still the confidence of youth in the courage or stolidity of your friend?" said the elder man. "Do you believe that I have lost the wager?"

"I *know* you have," replied the other, with enfeebling emphasis.

"Well, upon my soul, I hope so."

It was spoken earnestly, almost solemnly. There was a silence for a few minutes.

"Harper," the doctor resumed, looking very serious in the shifting half-lights that entered the carriage as they passed the street lamps, "I don't feel altogether comfortable about this business. If your friend had not irritated me by the contemptuous manner in which he treated my doubt of his endurance—a purely physical quality—and by the cool incivility of his suggestion that the corpse be that of a physician, I should not have gone on with it. If anything should happen we are ruined, as I fear we deserve to be."

"What can happen? Even if the matter should be taking a serious turn, of which I am not at all afraid, Mancher has only to 'resurrect' himself and explain matters. With a genuine 'subject' from the dissecting-room, or one of your late patients, it might be different."

Dr. Mancher, then, had been as good as his promise; he was the "corpse."

Dr. Helberson was silent for a long time, as the carriage, at a snail's pace, crept along the same street it had traveled two or three times already. Presently he spoke:

"Well, let us hope that Mancher, if he has had to rise from the dead, has been discreet about it. A mistake in that might make matters worse instead of better."

"Yes," said Harper, "Jarette would kill him. But, Doctor"—looking at his watch as the carriage passed a gas lamp—"it is nearly four o'clock at last."

A moment later the two had quitted the vehicle and were walking briskly toward the long-unoccupied house belonging to the doctor in which they had immured Mr. Jarette in accordance with the terms of the mad wager. As they neared it they met a man running. "Can you tell me," he cried, suddenly checking his speed, "where I can find a doctor?"

"What's the matter?" Helberson asked, non-committal.

"Go and see for yourself," said the man, resuming his running.

They hastened on. Arrived at the house, they saw several persons entering in haste and excitement. In some of the dwellings near by and across the way the chamber windows were thrown up, showing a protrusion of heads. All heads were asking questions, none heeding the questions of the others. A few of the windows with closed blinds were illuminated; the inmates of those rooms were dressing to come down. Exactly opposite the door of the house that they sought a street lamp threw a yellow, insufficient light upon the scene, seeming to say that it could disclose a good deal more if it wished. Harper paused at the door and laid a hand upon his companion's arm. "It is all up with us, Doctor," he said in extreme agitation, which contrasted strangely with his free-and-easy words; "the game has gone against us all. Let's not go in there; I'm for lying low."

"I'm a physician," said Dr. Helberson, calmly; "there may be need of one."

They mounted the doorsteps and were about to enter. The door was open; the street lamp opposite lighted the passage into which it opened. It was full of men. Some had ascended the stairs at the farther end, and, denied admittance above, waited for better fortune. All were talking, none listening. Suddenly, on the upper landing there was a great commotion; a man had sprung out of a door and was breaking away from those endeavoring to detain him. Down through the mass of affrighted idlers he came, pushing them aside, flattening them against the wall on one side, or compelling them to cling to the rail on the other, clutching them by the throat, striking them savagely, thrusting them back down the stairs and walking over the fallen. His clothing was in disorder, he was without a hat. His eyes, wild and restless, had in them something more terrifying than his apparently superhuman strength. His face, smooth-shaven, was bloodless, his hair frost-white.

As the crowd at the foot of the stairs, having more freedom, fell away to let him pass Harper sprang forward. "Jarette! Jarette!" he cried.

Dr. Helberson seized Harper by the collar and dragged him back. The man looked into their faces without seeming to see them and sprang through the door, down the steps, into the street, and away. A stout policeman, who had had inferior success in conquering his way down the stairway, followed a moment later and started in pursuit, all the heads in the windows—those of women and children now—screaming in guidance.

The stairway being now partly cleared, most of the crowd having rushed down to the street to observe the flight and pursuit, Dr. Helberson mounted to the landing, followed by Harper. At a door in the upper passage an officer denied them admittance. "We are physicians," said the doctor, and they passed in. The room was full of men, dimly seen, crowded about a table. The newcomers edged their way forward and looked over the shoulders of those in the front rank. Upon the table, the lower limbs covered with a sheet, lay the body of a man, brilliantly illuminated by the beam of a bull's-eye lantern held by a policeman standing at the feet. The others, excepting those near the head—the officer himself—all were in darkness. The face of the body showed yellow, repulsive, horrible! The eyes were partly open and upturned and the jaw fallen; traces of froth defined the lips, the chin, the cheeks. A tall man, evidently a doctor, bent over the body with his hand thrust under the shirt front. He withdrew it and placed two fingers in the open mouth. "This man has been about six hours dead," said he. "It is a case for the coroner."

He drew a card from his pocket, handed it to the officer and made his way toward the door.

"Clear the room—out, all!" said the officer, sharply, and the body disappeared as if it had been snatched away, as shifting the lantern he flashed its beam of light here and there against the faces of the crowd. The effect was amazing! The men, blinded, confused, almost terrified, made a tumultuous rush for the door, pushing, crowding and tumbling over one another as they fled, like the hosts of Night before the shafts of Apollo. Upon the struggling, trampling mass the officer poured his light without pity and without cessation. Caught in the current, Helberson and Harper were swept out of the room and cascaded down the stairs into the street.

"Good God, Doctor! did I not tell you that Jarette would kill him?" said Harper, as soon as they were clear of the crowd.

"I believe you did," replied the other, without apparent emotion.

They walked on in silence, block after block. Against the graying east the dwellings of the hill tribes showed in silhouette. The familiar milk wagon was already astir in the streets; the baker's man would soon come upon the scene; the newspaper carrier was abroad in the land.[7]

"It strikes me, youngster," said Helberson, "that you and I have been having too much of the morning air lately. It is unwholesome; we need a change. What do you say to a tour in Europe?"

"When?"

"I'm not particular. I should suppose that four o'clock this afternoon would be early enough."

"I'll meet you at the boat," said Harper.

V

Seven years afterward these two men sat upon a bench in Madison Square, New York, in familiar conversation. Another man, who had been observing them for some time, himself unobserved, approached and, courteously lifting his hat from locks as white as frost, said: "I beg your pardon, gentlemen, but when you have killed a man by coming to life, it is best to change clothes with him, and at the first opportunity make a break for liberty."

Helberson and Harper exchanged significant glances. They were obviously amused. The former then looked the stranger kindly in the eye and replied:

"That has always been my plan. I entirely agree with you as to its advant—"

He stopped suddenly, rose and went white. He stared at the man, open-mouthed; he trembled visibly.

"Ah!" said the stranger, "I see that you are indisposed, Doctor. If you cannot treat yourself Dr. Harper can do something for you, I am sure."

"Who the devil are you?" said Harper, bluntly.

The stranger came nearer and, bending toward them, said in a whisper: "I call myself Jarette sometimes, but I don't mind telling you, for old friendship, that I am Dr. William Mancher."

The revelation brought Harper to his feet. "Mancher!" he cried; and Helberson added: "It is true, by God!"

"Yes," said the stranger, smiling vaguely, "it is true enough, no doubt."

He hesitated and seemed to be trying to recall something, then began humming a popular air. He had apparently forgotten their presence.

"Look here, Mancher," said the elder of the two, "tell us just what occurred that night—to Jarette, you know."

"Oh, yes, about Jarette," said the other. "It's odd I should have neglected to tell you—I tell it so often. You see I knew, by overhearing him talking to himself, that he was pretty badly frightened. So I couldn't resist the temptation to come to life and have a bit of fun out of him—I couldn't really. That was all right, though certainly I did not think he would take it so seriously; I did not, truly. And afterward—well, it was a tough job changing places with him, and then—damn you! you didn't let me out!"

Nothing could exceed the ferocity with which these last words were delivered. Both men stepped back in alarm.

"We?—why—why," Helberson stammered, losing his self-possession utterly, "we had nothing to do with it."

"Didn't I say you were Drs. Hell-born and Sharper?" inquired the man, laughing.

"My name is Helberson, yes; and this gentleman is Mr. Harper," replied the former, reassured by the laugh. "But we are not physicians now; we are—well, hang it, old man, we are gamblers."

And that was the truth.

"A very good profession—very good, indeed; and, by the way, I hope Sharper here paid over Jarette's money like an honest stakeholder. A very good and honorable profession," he repeated, thoughtfully, moving carelessly away; "but I stick to the old one. I am High Supreme Medical Officer of the Bloomingdale Asylum;[8] it is my duty to cure the superintendent."

E (29 Dec. 1889): 14 (as "The Watcher by the Dead"); *TSC* 165–85; *CW* **2.290–310**. Reprinted in *Short Stories* 1, no. 2 (July 1890): 234–44 (as "The Watcher by the Dead"); *Anti-Philistine*, no. 4 (15 September 1897): 239–52.

NOTES

AB combines in this somewhat melodramatic story his themes of reason and fear. The situation, similar to that of "The Suitable Surroundings," is reinforced by Jarette's dishonest pride in his rationalism and his denial of his own fear. This self-deception ironically makes him more rather than less susceptible to superstition and terror. The ending is perhaps flawed by the late manifestation of AB's detestation of doctors who treat life so lightly as to endanger it for a bet. In this case, AB drops them from medical status to their real level, that of gamblers.

1. See "A Providential Intimation," p. 293 note 3.
2. Shakespeare, *Hamlet*, 3.2.194.
3. In "The Fall of the Republic," AB mentions the fictitious *Decline and Fall of the American Republics* by "Mancher" (p. 556).
4. Job 14:1–2: "Man that is born of a woman is of few days, and full of trouble. He cometh forth like a flower, and is cut down: he fleeth also as a shadow, and continueth not."
5. Shakespeare, *Macbeth*, 5.3.15–16: "I bear a charmed life, which must not yield / To one of woman born."
6. Cf. "Prattle," *E* (9 September 1894): 6: "When God made the soul of Mr. Huntington He made also the soul of the grandest scalawag that He thought the world would endure. And then He found he had clay enough for but one body. The scalawag got it, and Mr. Huntington is the dream of a desire."
7. Possibly an ironic commentary on journalism as babble, through an allusion to Gen. 11:9: "Therefore is the name of it called Babel; because the Lord did there confound the language of all the earth: and from thence did the Lord scatter them abroad upon the face of all the earth."
8. The New York Lunatic Asylum was established in 1808 at Morningside Heights on the Upper West Side of Manhattan. One of the oldest institutions of its kind in the United States, it started out in the cellar of the north wing of New York Hospital but got its own structure in 1808. It was renamed the Bloomingdale Insane Asylum in 1821, and in 1894 it was moved to the Westchester division of the New York Hospital in White Plains.

THE MAJOR'S TALE

In the days of the Civil War practical joking had not, I think, fallen into that disrepute which characterizes it now. That, doubtless, was owing to our extreme youth—men were much younger than now, and evermore your very young man has a boisterous spirit, running easily to horse-play. You cannot think how young the men were in the early sixties! Why, the average age of the entire Federal Army was not more than twenty-five; I doubt if it was more than twenty-three, but not having the statistics on that point (if there are any) I want to be moderate: we will say twenty-five. It is true a man of twenty-five was in that heroic time a good deal more of a man than one of that age is now; you could see that by looking at him. His face had nothing of that unripeness so conspicuous in his successor. I never see a young fellow now without observing how disagreeably young he really is; but during the war we did not think of a man's age at all unless he happened to be pretty well along in life. In that case one could not help it, for the unloveliness of age assailed the human countenance then much earlier than now; the result, I suppose, of hard service—perhaps, to some extent, of hard drink, for, bless my soul! we did shed the blood of the grape and the grain abundantly during the war. I remember thinking General Grant, who could not have been more than forty, a pretty well preserved old chap, considering his habits.[1] As to men of middle age—say from fifty to sixty—why, they all looked fit to personate the Last of the Hittites, or the Madagascarene Methuselah, in a museum.[2] Depend upon it, my friends, men of that time were greatly younger than men are to-day, but looked much older. The change is quite remarkable.

I said that practical joking had not then gone out of fashion. It had not, at least, in the army; though possibly in the more serious life of the civilian it had no place except in the form of tarring and feathering an occasional "copperhead." You all know, I suppose, what a "copperhead" was, so I will go directly at my story without introductory remark, as is my way.[3]

It was a few days before the battle of Nashville.[4] The enemy had driven us up out of northern Georgia and Alabama. At Nashville we had turned at bay and fortified, while old Pap Thomas,[5] our commander, hurried down reinforcements and supplies from Louisville. Meantime Hood,[6] the Confederate commander, had partly invested us and lay close enough to have tossed shells into the heart of the town. As a rule he abstained—he was afraid of killing the families of his own soldiers, I suppose, a great many of whom had lived there.[7] I sometimes wondered what were the feelings of those fellows, gazing over our heads at their own dwellings, where their wives and children or their aged parents were perhaps suffering for the necessaries of life, and certainly (so their reasoning would run) cowering under the tyranny and power of the barbarous Yankees.

To begin, then, at the beginning, I was serving at that time on the staff of a division commander whose name I shall not disclose, for I am relating facts, and the person upon whom they bear hardest may have surviving relatives who would not care to have him traced. Our headquarters were in a large dwelling which stood just behind our line of works. This had been hastily abandoned by the civilian occupants, who had left everything pretty much as it was—had no place to store it, probably, and trusted that Heaven would preserve it from Federal cupidity and Confederate artillery. With regard to the latter we were as solicitous as they.

Rummaging about in some of the chambers and closets one evening, some of us found an abundant supply of lady-gear—gowns, shawls, bonnets, hats, petticoats and the Lord knows what; I could not at that time have named the half of it.[8] The sight of all this pretty plunder inspired one of us with what he was pleased to call an "idea," which, when submitted to the other scamps and scapegraces of the staff, met with instant and enthusiastic approval. We proceeded at once to act upon it for the undoing of one of our comrades.

Our selected victim was an aide, Lieutenant Haberton, so to call him. He was a good soldier—as gallant a chap as ever wore spurs; but he had an intolerable weakness: he was a lady-killer, and like most of his class, even in those days, eager that all should know it. He never tired of relating his amatory exploits, and I need not say how dismal that kind of narrative is to all but the narrator. It would be dismal even if sprightly and vivacious, for all men are rivals in woman's favor, and to relate your successes to another man is to rouse in him a dumb resentment, tempered by disbelief. You will not convince him that you tell the tale for his entertainment; he will hear nothing in it but an expression of your own vanity. Moreover, as most men, whether rakes or not, are willing to be thought rakes, he is very likely to resent a stupid and unjust inference which he suspects you to have drawn from his reticence in the matter of his own adventures—namely, that he has had none. If, on the other hand, he has had no scruple in the matter and his reticence is due to lack of opportunity to talk, or of nimbleness in taking advantage of it, why, then he will be surly because you "have the floor" when he wants it himself. There are, in short, no circumstances under

THE MAJOR'S TALE

which a man, even from the best of motives, or no motive at all, can relate his feats of love without distinctly lowering himself in the esteem of his male auditor; and herein lies a just punishment for such as kiss and tell. In my younger days I was myself not entirely out of favor with the ladies, and have a memory stored with much concerning them which doubtless I might put into acceptable narrative had I not undertaken another tale, and if it were not my practice to relate one thing at a time, going straight away to the end, without digression.

Lieutenant Haberton was, it must be confessed, a singularly handsome man with engaging manners. He was, I suppose, judging from the imperfect view-point of my sex, what women call "fascinating." Now, the qualities which make a man attractive to ladies entail a double disadvantage. First, they are of a sort readily discerned by other men, and by none more readily than by those who lack them. Their possessor, being feared by all these, is habitually slandered by them in self-defense. To all the ladies in whose welfare they deem themselves entitled to a voice and interest they hint at the vices and general unworth of the "ladies' man" in no uncertain terms, and to their wives relate without shame the most monstrous falsehoods about him. Nor are they restrained by the consideration that he is their friend; the qualities which have engaged their own admiration make it necessary to warn away those to whom the allurement would be a peril. So the man of charming personality, while loved by all the ladies who know him well, yet not too well, must endure with such fortitude as he may the consciousness that those others who know him only "by reputation" consider him a shameless reprobate, a vicious and unworthy man—a type and example of moral depravity. To name the second disadvantage entailed by his charms: he commonly is.

In order to get forward with our busy story (and in my judgment a story once begun should not suffer impedition) it is necessary to explain that a young fellow attached to our headquarters as an orderly was notably effeminate in face and figure. He was not more than seventeen and had a perfectly smooth face and large lustrous eyes, which must have been the envy of many a beautiful woman in those days. And how beautiful the women of those days were! and how gracious! Those of the South showed in their demeanor toward us Yankees something of *hauteur*, but, for my part, I found it less insupportable than the studious indifference with which one's attentions are received by the ladies of this new generation, whom I certainly think destitute of sentiment and sensibility.

This young orderly, whose name was Arman, we persuaded—by what arguments I am not bound to say—to clothe himself in female attire and personate a lady. When we had him arrayed to our satisfaction—and a charming girl he looked—he was conducted to a sofa in the office of the adjutant-general. That officer was in the secret, as indeed were all excepting Haberton and the general; within the awful dignity hedging the latter lay possibilities of disapproval which we were unwilling to confront.

THE MAJOR'S TALE

When all was ready I went to Haberton and said: "Lieutenant, there is a young woman in the adjutant-general's office. She is the daughter of the insurgent gentleman who owns this house, and has, I think, called to see about its present occupancy. We none of us know just how to talk to her, but we think perhaps you would say about the right thing—at least you will say things in the right way. Would you mind coming down?"

The lieutenant would not mind; he made a hasty toilet and joined me. As we were going along a passage toward the Presence we encountered a formidable obstacle— the general.

"I say, Broadwood," he said, addressing me in the familiar manner which meant that he was in excellent humor, "there's a lady in Lawson's office. Looks like a devilish fine girl—came on some errand of mercy or justice, no doubt. Have the goodness to conduct her to my quarters. I won't saddle you youngsters with *all* the business of this division," he added facetiously.

This was awkward; something had to be done.

"General," I said, "I did not think the lady's business of sufficient importance to bother you with it. She is one of the Sanitary Commission's nurses, and merely wants to see about some supplies for the smallpox hospital where she is on duty. I'll send her in at once."

"You need not mind," said the general, moving on; "I dare say Lawson will attend to the matter."

Ah, the gallant general! how little I thought, as I looked after his retreating figure and laughed at the success of my ruse, that within the week he would be "dead on the field of honor!"[9] Nor was he the only one of our little military household above whom gloomed the shadow of the death angel, and who might almost have heard "the beating of his wings."[10] On that bleak December morning a few days later, when from an hour before dawn until ten o'clock we sat on horseback on those icy hills, waiting for General Smith to open the battle miles away to the right, there were eight of us. At the close of the fighting there were three. There is now one. Bear with him yet a little while, oh, thrifty generation; he is but one of the horrors of war strayed from his era into yours. He is only the harmless skeleton at your feast and peace-dance, responding to your laughter and your footing it featly,[11] with rattling fingers and bobbing skull—albeit upon suitable occasion, with a partner of his choosing, he might do his little dance with the best of you.

As we entered the adjutant-general's office we observed that the entire staff was there. The adjutant-general himself was exceedingly busy at his desk. The commissary of subsistence played cards with the surgeon in a bay window. The rest were in several parts of the room, reading or conversing in low tones. On a sofa in a half-lighted nook of the room, at some distance from any of the groups, sat the "lady," closely veiled, her eyes modestly fixed upon her toes.

THE MAJOR'S TALE

"Madam," I said, advancing with Haberton, "this officer will be pleased to serve you if it is in his power. I trust that it is."

With a bow I retired to the farther corner of the room and took part in a conversation going on there, though I had not the faintest notion what it was about, and my remarks had no relevancy to anything under the heavens. A close observer would have noticed that we were all intently watching Haberton and only "making believe" to do anything else.

He was worth watching, too; the fellow was simply an *édition de luxe* of "Turvey-drop on Deportment."[12] As the "lady" slowly unfolded her tale of grievances against our lawless soldiery and mentioned certain instances of wanton disregard of property rights—among them, as to the imminent peril of bursting our sides we partly overheard, the looting of her own wardrobe—the look of sympathetic agony in Haberton's handsome face was the very flower and fruit of histrionic art. His deferential and assenting nods at her several statements were so exquisitely performed that one could not help regretting their unsubstantial nature and the impossibility of preserving them under glass for instruction and delight of posterity. And all the time the wretch was drawing his chair nearer and nearer. Once or twice he looked about to see if we were observing, but we were in appearance blankly oblivious to all but one another and our several diversions. The low hum of our conversation, the gentle tap-tap of the cards as they fell in play and the furious scratching of the adjutant-general's pen as he turned off countless pages of words without sense were the only sounds heard. No—there was another: at long intervals the distant boom of a heavy gun, followed by the approaching rush of the shot. The enemy was amusing himself.

On these occasions the lady was perhaps not the only member of that company who was startled, but she was startled more than the others, sometimes rising from the sofa and standing with clasped hands, the authentic portrait of terror and irresolution. It was no more than natural that Haberton should at these times reseat her with infinite tenderness, assuring her of her safety and regretting her peril in the same breath. It was perhaps right that he should finally possess himself of her gloved hand and a seat beside her on the sofa; but it certainly was highly improper for him to be in the very act of possessing himself of *both* hands when—boom, *whiz,* BANG!

We all sprang to our feet. A shell had crashed into the house and exploded in the room above us. Bushels of plaster fell among us. That modest and murmurous young lady sprang erect.

"Jumping Jee-rusalem!" she cried.

Haberton, who had also risen, stood as one petrified—as a statue of himself erected on the site of his assassination. He neither spoke, nor moved, nor once took his eyes off the face of Orderly Arman, who was now flinging his girl-gear right and left, exposing his charms in the most shameless way; while out upon the night and away over the lighted camps into the black spaces between the hostile lines rolled the billows of our inexhaustible laughter! Ah, what a merry life it was in the old heroic days when men had not forgotten how to laugh!

Haberton slowly came to himself. He looked about the room less blankly; then by degrees fashioned his visage into the sickliest grin that ever libeled all smiling. He shook his head and looked knowing.

"You can't fool *me!*" he said.

E (5 Jan. 1890): 12 (as "A Practical Joke: Major Broadwood Recalls the Heroic Past"; unsigned); *CSTB* 147–57; *CW* **8.63–75**.

NOTES

What keeps this story from being classified as a memoir, besides the narrator's reference to himself as "Broadwood" and the opening mention of practical jokes and horseplay, is its title. Although "Major" could be a reference to himself—he had been awarded a brevet commission as major years after he resigned from the army—the use of "Tale" appears to be a hint that what follows is fiction. AB almost always strictly observed the distinction between a true recollection which was factual only, and a fictional tale which incorporated autobiographical elements. Further, AB retained a fondness for hoaxes and practical jokes well into his career. That means that he cultivated the art of camouflaging a "stretcher" with plausible details.

1. Maj. Gen. (USV) Ulysses Simpson Grant (1822–85), a native of Ohio, West Point graduate, Mexican War veteran, commander of the Army of the Tennessee and the Middle Tennessee Department at Shiloh. He was known to be a heavy drinker.

2. An ironically extravagant way of saying that to young men, men of middle age all looked so old that they either seemed representations of an almost extinct race (Hittites) or incredibly ancient individuals who had survived in some remote corner of the world, e.g., a Methuselah who survived in a place like Madagascar.

3. During the Civil War, a "copperhead" was a term of abuse coined by Unionists to designate a Northerner who sympathized with the South.

4. For the battle of Nashville (15–16 Dec. 1864), in which AB fought, see "George Thurston," p. 423 note 3.

5. Maj. Gen. George Henry Thomas (1816–70), a Virginian and prewar captain who stayed loyal to the Union, was Rosecrans's second in command and commander of the XIV Corps at Chickamauga. For his leadership of the refugees and his own troops as rear-guard to the collapsing Federal army, he was known in the army before the battle as "Old Slow-Trot" and "Pap"; after as "The Rock of Chickamauga."

6. Lt. Gen. (CSA) John Bell Hood (1831–79), a prewar regular from Kentucky who had lost an arm at Gettysburg while commanding the attack on Little Round Top and a leg at Chickamauga only two months later, commanded a corps in Johnston's army on the Dallas Line.

7. AB dealt with the situation of soldiers firing on their own homes in "The Affair at Coulter's Notch" (p. 684).

8. Cf. *DD*: "CHEMISE, *n*. Don't know what it means."

9. See "Killed at Resaca," p. 512 note 3.

10. John Bright (1811–89), a member of the Peace Society who denounced the Crimean War (1854–56) as un-Christian, contrary to the principles of international free trade, and harmful to British interests, stated: "The Angel of Death has been abroad throughout the land; you may almost hear the beating of his wings." AB quotes this statement in an unsigned editorial in *W*, no. 525 (21 Aug. 1886): 5.

11. Shakespeare, *The Tempest*, 1.2.379: "Foot it featly here and there."

12. In Dickens's *Bleak House* (1852–53), the character Mr. Turveydrop is the model of deportment.

THE STORY OF A CONSCIENCE

Captain Parrol Hartroy stood at the advanced post of his picket-guard, talking in low tones with the sentinel. This post was on a turnpike which bisected the captain's camp, a half-mile in rear, though the camp was not in sight from that point. The officer was apparently giving the soldier certain instructions—was perhaps merely inquiring if all were quiet in front. As the two stood talking a man approached them from the direction of the camp, carelessly whistling, and was promptly halted by the soldier. He was evidently a civilian—a tall person, coarsely clad in the home-made stuff of yellow gray, called "butternut," which was men's only wear in the latter days of the Confederacy.[1] On his head was a slouch felt hat, once white, from beneath which hung masses of uneven hair, seemingly unacquainted with either scissors or comb. The man's face was rather striking; a broad forehead, high nose and thin cheeks, the mouth invisible in the full dark beard, which seemed as neglected as the hair. The eyes were large and had that steadiness and fixity of attention which so frequently mark a considering intelligence and a will not easily turned from its purpose—so say those physiognomists who have that kind of eyes.[2] On the whole, this was a man whom one would be likely to observe and be observed by. He carried a walking-stick freshly cut from the forest and his ailing cowskin boots were white with dust.

"Show your pass," said the Federal soldier, a trifle more imperiously perhaps than he would have thought necessary if he had not been under the eye of his commander, who with folded arms looked on from the roadside.

"'Lowed you'd rec'lect me, Gineral," said the wayfarer tranquilly, while producing the paper from the pocket of his coat. There was something in his tone—perhaps a faint suggestion of irony—which made his elevation of his obstructor to exalted rank less agreeable to that worthy warrior than promotion is commonly found to be.

"You-all have to be purty pertickler, I reckon," he added, in a more conciliatory tone, as if in half-apology for being halted.

Having read the pass, with his rifle resting on the ground, the soldier handed the document back without a word, shouldered his weapon and returned to his commander. The civilian passed on in the middle of the road, and when he had penetrated the circumjacent Confederacy a few yards resumed his whistling and was soon out of sight beyond an angle in the road, which at that point entered a thin forest. Suddenly the officer undid his arms from his breast, drew a revolver from his belt and sprang forward at a run in the same direction, leaving his sentinel in gaping astonishment at his post. After making to the various visible forms of nature a solemn promise to be damned, that gentleman resumed the air of stolidity which is supposed to be appropriate to a state of alert military attention.

II

Captain Hartroy held an independent command. His force consisted of a company of infantry, a squadron of cavalry and a section of artillery, detached from the army to which they belonged, to defend an important defile in the Cumberland Mountains in Tennessee.[3] It was a field officer's command held by a line officer promoted from the ranks, where he had quietly served until "discovered." His post was one of exceptional peril; its defense entailed a heavy responsibility and he had wisely been given corresponding discretionary powers, all the more necessary because of his distance from the main army, the precarious nature of his communications and the lawless character of the enemy's irregular troops infesting that region. He had strongly fortified his little camp, which embraced a village of a half-dozen dwellings and a country store, and had collected a considerable quantity of supplies. To a few resident civilians of known loyalty, with whom it was desirable to trade, and of whose services in various ways he sometimes availed himself, he had given written passes admitting them within his lines. It is easy to understand that an abuse of this privilege in the interest of the enemy might entail serious consequences. Captain Hartroy had made an order to the effect that any one so abusing it would be summarily shot.

While the sentinel had been examining the civilian's pass the captain had eyed the latter narrowly. He thought his appearance familiar and had at first no doubt of having given him the pass which had satisfied the sentinel. It was not until the man had got out of sight and hearing that his identity was disclosed by a revealing light from memory. With soldierly promptness of decision the officer had acted on the revelation.

III

To any but a singularly self-possessed man the apparition of an officer of the military forces, formidably clad, bearing in one hand a sheathed sword and in the other a cocked revolver, and rushing in furious pursuit, is no doubt disquieting to a high degree; upon the man to whom the pursuit was in this instance directed it appeared to have no other effect than somewhat to intensify his tranquility. He might easily enough have escaped into the forest to the right or the left, but chose another course of action—turned and quietly faced the captain, saying as he came up: "I reckon ye must have something to say to me, which ye disremembered. What mout it be, neighbor?"

But the "neighbor" did not answer, being engaged in the unneighborly act of covering him with a cocked pistol.

"Surrender," said the captain as calmly as a slight breathlessness from exertion would permit, "or you die."

There was no menace in the manner of this demand; that was all in the matter and in the means of enforcing it. There was, too, something not altogether reassuring in the cold gray eyes that glanced along the barrel of the weapon. For a moment the two men stood looking at each other in silence; then the civilian, with no appearance of fear—with as great apparent unconcern as when complying with the less austere demand of the sentinel—slowly pulled from his pocket the paper which had satisfied that humble functionary and held it out, saying:

"I reckon this 'ere parss from Mister Hartroy is——"

"The pass is a forgery," the officer said, interrupting. "I am Captain Hartroy—and you are Dramer Brune."[4]

It would have required a sharp eye to observe the slight pallor of the civilian's face at these words, and the only other manifestation attesting their significance was a voluntary relaxation of the thumb and fingers holding the dishonored paper, which, falling to the road, unheeded, was rolled by a gentle wind and then lay still, with a coating of dust, as in humiliation for the lie that it bore. A moment later the civilian, still looking unmoved into the barrel of the pistol, said:

"Yes, I am Dramer Brune, a Confederate spy, and your prisoner. I have on my person, as you will soon discover, a plan of your fort and its armament, a statement of the distribution of your men and their number, a map of the approaches, showing the positions of all your outposts. My life is fairly yours, but if you wish it taken in a more formal way than by your own hand, and if you are willing to spare me the indignity of marching into camp at the muzzle of your pistol, I promise you that I will neither resist, escape nor remonstrate, but will submit to whatever penalty may be imposed."

The officer lowered his pistol, uncocked it, and thrust it into its place in his belt. Brune advanced a step, extending his right hand.

"It is the hand of a traitor and a spy," said the officer coldly, and did not take it. The other bowed.

"Come," said the captain, "let us go to camp; you shall not die until to-morrow morning."

He turned his back upon his prisoner, and these two enigmatical men retraced their steps and soon passed the sentinel, who expressed his general sense of things by a needless and exaggerated salute to his commander.

THE STORY OF A CONSCIENCE

IV

Early on the morning after these events the two men, captor and captive, sat in the tent of the former. A table was between them on which lay, among a number of letters, official and private, which the captain had written during the night, the incriminating papers found upon the spy. That gentleman had slept through the night in an adjoining tent, unguarded. Both, having breakfasted, were now smoking.

"Mr. Brune," said Captain Hartroy, "you probably do not understand why I recognized you in your disguise, nor how I was aware of your name."

"I have not sought to learn, Captain," the prisoner said with quiet dignity.

"Nevertheless I should like you to know—if the story will not offend. You will perceive that my knowledge of you goes back to the autumn of 1861. At that time you were a private in an Ohio regiment—a brave and trusted soldier. To the surprise and grief of your officers and comrades you deserted and went over to the enemy. Soon afterward you were captured in a skirmish, recognized, tried by court-martial and sentenced to be shot. Awaiting the execution of the sentence you were confined, unfettered, in a freight car standing on a side track of a railway."

"At Grafton, Virginia," said Brune, pushing the ashes from his cigar with the little finger of the hand holding it, and without looking up.

"At Grafton, Virginia," the captain repeated. "One dark and stormy night a soldier who had just returned from a long, fatiguing march was put on guard over you. He sat on a cracker box inside the car, near the door, his rifle loaded and the bayonet fixed. You sat in a corner and his orders were to kill you if you attempted to rise."

"But if I *asked* to rise he might call the corporal of the guard."

"Yes. As the long silent hours wore away the soldier yielded to the demands of nature: he himself incurred the death penalty by sleeping at his post of duty."

"You did."

"What! you recognize me? you have known me all along?"

The captain had risen and was walking the floor of his tent, visibly excited. His face was flushed, the gray eyes had lost the cold, pitiless look which they had shown when Brune had seen them over the pistol barrel; they had softened wonderfully.

"I knew you," said the spy, with his customary tranquility, "the moment you faced me, demanding my surrender. In the circumstances it would have been hardly becoming in me to recall these matters. I am perhaps a traitor, certainly a spy; but I should not wish to seem a suppliant."

The captain had paused in his walk and was facing his prisoner. There was a singular huskiness in his voice as he spoke again.

"Mr. Brune, whatever your conscience may permit you to be, you saved my life at what you must have believed the cost of your own. Until I saw you yesterday when halted by my sentinel I believed you dead—thought that you had suffered the fate which through my own crime you might easily have escaped. You had only to step from the car and leave me to take your place before the firing-squad. You had a divine compassion. You pitied my fatigue. You let me sleep, watched over me, and as the time drew near for the relief-guard to come and detect me in my crime, you gently waked me. Ah, Brune, Brune, that was well done—that was great—that———"

The captain's voice failed him; the tears were running down his face and sparkled upon his beard and his breast. Resuming his seat at the table, he buried his face in his arms and sobbed. All else was silence.

Suddenly the clear warble of a bugle was heard sounding the "assembly." The captain started and raised his wet face from his arms; it had turned ghastly pale. Outside, in the sunlight, were heard the stir of the men falling into line; the voices of the sergeants calling the roll; the tapping of the drummers as they braced their drums. The captain spoke again:

"I ought to have confessed my fault in order to relate the story of your magnanimity; it might have procured you a pardon. A hundred times I resolved to do so, but shame prevented. Besides, your sentence was just and righteous. Well, Heaven forgive me! I said nothing, and my regiment was soon afterward ordered to Tennessee and I never heard about you."

"It was all right, sir," said Brune, without visible emotion; "I escaped and returned to my colors—the Confederate colors. I should like to add that before deserting from the Federal service I had earnestly asked a discharge, on the ground of altered convictions. I was answered by punishment."

"Ah, but if I had suffered the penalty of my crime—if you had not generously given me the life that I accepted without gratitude you would not be again in the shadow and imminence of death."

The prisoner started slightly and a look of anxiety came into his face. One would have said, too, that he was surprised. At that moment a lieutenant, the adjutant, appeared at the opening of the tent and saluted. "Captain," he said, "the battalion is formed."

Captain Hartroy had recovered his composure. He turned to the officer and said: "Lieutenant, go to Captain Graham and say that I direct him to assume command of the battalion and parade it outside the parapet. This gentleman is a deserter and a spy; he is to be shot to death in the presence of the troops. He will accompany you, unbound and unguarded."

While the adjutant waited at the door the two men inside the tent rose and exchanged ceremonious bows, Brune immediately retiring.

Half an hour later an old negro cook, the only person left in camp except the commander, was so startled by the sound of a volley of musketry that he dropped the kettle that he was lifting from a fire. But for his consternation and the hissing which the contents of the kettle made among the embers, he might also have heard, nearer at hand, the single pistol shot with which Captain Hartroy renounced the life which in conscience he could no longer keep.

THE STORY OF A CONSCIENCE

In compliance with the terms of a note that he left for the officer who succeeded him in command, he was buried, like the deserter and spy, without military honors; and in the solemn shadow of the mountain which knows no more of war the two sleep well in long-forgotten graves.

E (1 June 1890): 11–12 (as "Dramer Brune, Deserter: A War Memory of the Cumberland Mountains"); *CSTB* 121–33; **CW 2.165–77**.

NOTES

Morally speaking, Hartroy and Brune are almost mirror images of each other. Both are men of honor, both are humane, and both share the same austere conceptions of duty and justice. In this story the same qualities of idealism that make them admirable individuals are warped by the circumstance of warfare to make them not only enemies but victims of identical codes of honor. This story is thus a tragic parable of civil war in which the same virtues, pitted against themselves, destroy each other.

1. The official color of the Confederate cotton uniform was a dull gray. When the South was virtually cut off from all supply sources by late 1862, it began to issue of a new homespun uniform made of cheap durable cloth dyed with oil of walnut or butternut trees. The nickname "butternut" came from anti-Yankee farmers of Ohio, Illinois, and Indiana who had sided with the South and had been wearing the homespun cloth for the previous fifty years. The butternut uniform made its first appearance at the battle of South Mountain (14 September 1862), when hundreds of the Confederate dead were seen to be wearing the new coarse uniform.

2. Cf. "Prattle," *E* (9 Aug. 1896): 6: "Every physiognomist, from Lavater down, takes his own face as the highest type and judges the mental and moral excellence of other persons by that convenient standard. I once knew a bullet-headed chap who, in the same spirit, described a well-known author as having 'a weak overgrowth of the head.'"

3. Perhaps a reference to the Cumberland Gap; see "Two Haunted Houses," p. 676 note 1.

4. Scopas Brune and Conmore Apel Brume are fictitious authors of verses "quoted" in *DD*.

5. See "A Horseman in the Sky," p. 665 note 1.

THE MAN AND THE SNAKE

It is of veritabyll report, and attested of so many that there be nowe of wyse and learned none to gaynsaye it, that ye serpente hys eye hath a magnetick propertie that whosoe falleth into its svasion is drawn forwards in despyte of his wille, and perisheth miserabyll by ye creature hys byte.

Stretched at ease upon a sofa, in gown and slippers, Harker Brayton smiled as he read the foregoing sentence in old Morryster's *Marvells of Science.*[1] "The only marvel in the matter," he said to himself, "is that the wise and learned in Morryster's day should have believed such nonsense as is rejected by most of even the ignorant in ours."

A train of reflection followed—for Brayton was a man of thought—and he unconsciously lowered his book without altering the direction of his eyes. As soon as the volume had gone below the line of sight, something in an obscure corner of the room recalled his attention to his surroundings. What he saw, in the shadow under his bed, was two small points of light, apparently about an inch apart. They might have been reflections of the gas jet above him, in metal nail heads; he gave them but little thought and resumed his reading. A moment later something—some impulse which it did not occur to him to analyze—impelled him to lower the book again and seek for what he saw before. The points of light were still there. They seemed to have become brighter than before, shining with a greenish lustre that he had not at first observed. He thought, too, that they might have moved a trifle—were somewhat nearer. They were still too much in shadow, however, to reveal their nature and origin to an indolent attention, and again he resumed his reading. Suddenly something in the text suggested a thought that made him start and drop the book for the third time to the side of the sofa, whence, escaping from his hand, it fell sprawling to the floor, back upward. Brayton, half-risen, was staring intently into the obscurity beneath the bed, where the points of light shone with, it seemed to him, an added fire. His attention was now fully aroused, his gaze eager and imperative. It disclosed, almost directly under the foot-rail of the bed, the coils of a large serpent—the points of light were its eyes! Its horrible head, thrust flatly forth from the innermost coil and resting upon the outermost, was directed straight toward him, the definition of the wide, brutal jaw and the idiot-like forehead serving to show the direction of its malevolent gaze. The eyes were no longer merely luminous points; they looked into his own with a meaning, a malign significance.

II

A snake in a bedroom of a modern city dwelling of the better sort is, happily, not so common a phenomenon as to make explanation altogether needless. Harker Brayton, a bachelor of thirty-five, a scholar, idler and something of an athlete, rich, popular and of sound health, had returned to San Francisco from all manner of remote and unfamiliar countries. His tastes, always a trifle luxurious, had taken on an added exuberance from long privation; and the resources of even the Castle Hotel being inadequate to their perfect gratification, he had gladly accepted the hospitality of his friend, Dr. Druring, the distinguished scientist. Dr. Druring's house, a large, old-fashioned one in what is now an obscure quarter of the city, had an outer and visible aspect of proud reserve. It plainly would not associate with the contiguous elements of its altered environment, and appeared to have developed some of the eccentricities which come of isolation. One of these was a "wing," conspicuously irrelevant in point of architecture, and no less rebellious in matter of purpose; for it was a combination of laboratory, menagerie and museum. It was here that the doctor indulged the scientific side of his nature in the study of such forms of animal life as engaged his interest and comforted his taste— which, it must be confessed, ran rather to the lower types. For one of the higher nimbly and sweetly to recommend itself unto his gentle senses it had at least to retain certain rudimentary characteristics allying it to such "dragons of the prime"[2] as toads and snakes. His scientific sympathies were distinctly reptilian; he loved nature's vulgarians and described himself as the Zola of zoology. His wife and daughters not having the advantage to share his enlightened curiosity regarding the works and ways of our ill-starred fellow-creatures, were with needless austerity excluded from what he called the Snakery and doomed to companionship with their own kind, though to soften the rigors of their lot he had permitted them out of his great wealth to outdo the reptiles in the gorgeousness of their surroundings and to shine with a superior splendor.

Architecturally and in point of "furnishing" the Snakery had a severe simplicity befitting the humble circumstances of its occupants, many of whom, indeed, could not safely have been intrusted with the liberty that is necessary to the full enjoyment of luxury, for they had the troublesome peculiarity of being alive. In their own apartments, however, they were under as little personal restraint as was compatible with their protection from the baneful habit of swallowing one another; and, as Brayton had thoughtfully been apprised, it was more than a tradition that some of them had at divers times been found in parts of the premises where it would have embarrassed them to explain their presence. Despite the Snakery and its uncanny associations—to which, indeed, he gave little attention—Brayton found life at the Druring mansion very much to his mind.

III

Beyond a smart shock of surprise and a shudder of mere loathing Mr. Brayton was not greatly affected. His first thought was to ring the call bell and bring a servant; but although the bell cord dangled within easy reach he made no movement toward it; it had occurred to his mind that the act might subject him to the suspicion of fear, which he certainly did not feel. He was more keenly conscious of the incongruous nature of the situation than affected by its perils; it was revolting, but absurd.

The reptile was of a species with which Brayton was unfamiliar. Its length he could only conjecture; the body at the largest visible part seemed about as thick as his forearm. In what way was it dangerous, if in any way? Was it venomous? Was it a constrictor? His knowledge of nature's danger signals did not enable him to say; he had never deciphered the code.

If not dangerous the creature was at least offensive. It was *de trop*—"matter out of place"³—an impertinence. The gem was unworthy of the setting. Even the barbarous taste of our time and country, which had loaded the walls of the room with pictures, the floor with furniture and the furniture with bric-a-brac, had not quite fitted the place for this bit of the savage life of the jungle. Besides—insupportable thought!—the exhalation of its breath mingled with the atmosphere which he himself was breathing.

These thoughts shaped themselves with greater or less definition in Brayton's mind and begot action. The process is what we call consideration and decision. It is thus that we are wise and unwise. It is thus that the withered leaf in an autumn breeze shows greater or less intelligence than its fellows, falling upon the land or upon the lake. The secret of human action is an open one: something contracts our muscles. Does it matter if we give to the preparatory molecular changes the name of will?

Brayton rose to his feet and prepared to back softly away from the snake, without disturbing it if possible, and through the door. Men retire so from the presence of the great, for greatness is power and power is a menace. He knew that he could walk backward without error. Should the monster follow, the taste which had plastered the walls with paintings had consistently supplied a rack of murderous Oriental weapons from which he could snatch one to suit the occasion. In the mean time the snake's eyes burned with a more pitiless malevolence than before.

Brayton lifted his right foot free of the floor to step backward. That moment he felt a strong aversion to doing so.

"I am accounted brave," he thought; "is bravery, then, no more than pride? Because there are none to witness the shame shall I retreat?"

He was steadying himself with his right hand upon the back of a chair, his foot suspended.

THE MAN AND THE SNAKE

"Nonsense!" he said aloud; "I am not so great a coward as to fear to seem to myself afraid."

He lifted the foot a little higher by slightly bending the knee and thrust it sharply to the floor—an inch in front of the other! He could not think how that occurred. A trial with the left foot had the same result; it was again in advance of the right. The hand upon the chair back was grasping it; the arm was straight, reaching somewhat backward. One might have said that he was reluctant to lose his hold. The snake's malignant head was still thrust forth from the inner coil as before, the neck level. It had not moved, but its eyes were now electric sparks, radiating an infinity of luminous needles.

The man had an ashy pallor. Again he took a step forward, and another, partly dragging the chair, which when finally released fell upon the floor with a crash. The man groaned; the snake made neither sound nor motion, but its eyes were two dazzling suns. The reptile itself was wholly concealed by them. They gave off enlarging rings of rich and vivid colors, which at their greatest expansion successively vanished like soap-bubbles; they seemed to approach his very face, and anon were an immeasurable distance away. He heard, somewhere, the continuous throbbing of a great drum, with desultory bursts of far music, inconceivably sweet, like the tones of an æolian harp. He knew it for the sunrise melody of Memnon's statue,[4] and thought he stood in the Nileside reeds hearing with exalted sense that immortal anthem through the silence of the centuries.

The music ceased; rather, it became by insensible degrees the distant roll of a retreating thunder-storm. A landscape, glittering with sun and rain, stretched before him, arched with a vivid rainbow framing in its giant curve a hundred visible cities. In the middle distance a vast serpent, wearing a crown, reared its head out of its voluminous convolutions and looked at him with his dead mother's eyes. Suddenly this enchanting landscape seemed to rise swiftly upward like the drop scene at a theatre, and vanished in a blank. Something struck him a hard blow upon the face and breast. He had fallen to the floor; the blood ran from his broken nose and his bruised lips. For a time he was dazed and stunned, and lay with closed eyes, his face against the floor. In a few moments he had recovered, and then knew that this fall, by withdrawing his eyes, had broken the spell that held him. He felt that now, by keeping his gaze averted, he would be able to retreat. But the thought of the serpent within a few feet of his head, yet unseen—perhaps in the very act of springing upon him and throwing its coils about his throat—was too horrible! He lifted his head, stared again into those baleful eyes and was again in bondage.

The snake had not moved and appeared somewhat to have lost its power upon the imagination; the gorgeous illusions of a few moments before were not repeated. Beneath that flat and brainless brow its black, beady eyes simply glittered as at first with an expression unspeakably malignant. It was as if the creature, assured of its triumph, had determined to practice no more alluring wiles.

THE MAN AND THE SNAKE

Now ensued a fearful scene. The man, prone upon the floor, within a yard of his enemy, raised the upper part of his body upon his elbows, his head thrown back, his legs extended to their full length. His face was white between its stains of blood; his eyes were strained open to their uttermost expansion. There was froth upon his lips; it dropped off in flakes. Strong convulsions ran through his body, making almost serpentile undulations. He bent himself at the waist, shifting his legs from side to side. And every moment left him a little nearer to the snake. He thrust his hands forward to brace himself back, yet constantly advanced upon his elbows.

IV

Dr. Druring and his wife sat in the library. The scientist was in rare good humor.

"I have just obtained by exchange with another collector," he said, "a splendid specimen of the *ophiophagus*."[5]

"And what may that be?" the lady inquired with a somewhat languid interest.

"Why, bless my soul, what profound ignorance! My dear, a man who ascertains after marriage that his wife does not know Greek is entitled to a divorce. The *ophiophagus* is a snake that eats other snakes."

"I hope it will eat all yours," she said, absently shifting the lamp. "But how does it get the other snakes? By charming them, I suppose."

"That is just like you, dear," said the doctor, with an affectation of petulance. "You know how irritating to me is any allusion to that vulgar superstition about a snake's power of fascination."

The conversation was interrupted by a mighty cry, which rang through the silent house like the voice of a demon shouting in a tomb! Again and yet again it sounded, with terrible distinctness. They sprang to their feet, the man confused, the lady pale and speechless with fright. Almost before the echoes of the last cry had died away the doctor was out of the room, springing up the stairs two steps at a time. In the corridor in front of Brayton's chamber he met some servants who had come from the upper floor. Together they rushed at the door without knocking. It was unfastened and gave way. Brayton lay upon his stomach on the floor, dead. His head and arms were partly concealed under the foot rail of the bed. They pulled the body away, turning it upon the back. The face was daubed with blood and froth, the eyes were wide open, staring—a dreadful sight!

"Died in a fit," said the scientist, bending his knee and placing his hand upon the heart. While in that position, he chanced to look under the bed. "Good God!" he added, "how did this thing get in here?"

He reached under the bed, pulled out the snake and flung it, still coiled, to the center of the room, whence with a harsh, shuffling sound it slid across the polished floor till stopped by the wall, where it lay without motion. It was a stuffed snake; its eyes were two shoe buttons.

THE MAN AND THE SNAKE

E (29 June 1890): 11–12; *TSC* 187–99; *IML* 206–19; **CW 2.311–23**. Reprinted in Julian Hawthorne, ed., *Library of the World's Best Mystery and Detective Stories: American* (New York: Review of Reviews, 1907), 103–11; in Julian Hawthorne, ed., *The Lock and Key Library* (New York: Review of Reviews, 1909), 9:103–11.

NOTES

Sensational stories about the power snakes supposedly had to charm humans were in style in late-nineteenth century newspapers. Between 24 March and 6 June 1889 alone, *E* printed six articles on the subject and one of them, "Catalina" (5 May), has some similarities to the AB's tale. It is also possible that AB appropriated the story line from another source, and Carey McWilliams reports that AB's tale was definitely appropriated by Harris Merton Lyon in his short story, "An Unused Rattlesnake" (*Ambrose Bierce* 182). In any case, the tale appears to capitalize on the popularity of this topic, although AB puts his own ironic spin on it. As in other stories, he again targets a rationalistic protagonist too proud of his reason. But by making a stuffed snake the agent of Brayton's fatal terror, AB undercuts the supposed power of snakes while he puts the blame where it belongs, on the weakness of the human mind. M. E. Grenander gives prominence to this story in her persuasive explanation of AB's development of stories of "ironical terror" (*Ambrose Bierce* 93–99).

1. Morryster is fictitious. As AB noted in "Prattle," *E* (6 July 1890): 6: "*Morryster's Marvells of Science* can certainly not be obtained in the 'book market.'" AB also mentioned Morryster's *Trauvells in yͤ Easte* in *DD* (s.v. "TREE").

2. Tennyson, *In Memoriam: A. H. H.* (1850), 56.22.

3. The lawyer John Chipman Gray (1839–1915) said that "dirt is only matter out of place; and what is a blot on the escutcheon of the Common Law may be a jewel in the crown of the Social Republic." See *Restraints on the Alienation of Property* (Boston: Soule & Bugbee, 1883).

4. In Greek myth, Memnon was the son of Tithonus and Eos (Dawn). He became a major object of worship in Pharaonic Egypt. An immense statue of Memnon near Thebes, when broken, emitted sounds upon the rising of the sun.

5. *Ophiophagus* denotes an actual genus of venomous snakes allied to the cobra, chiefly dwelling in India, which feed on other snakes. Cf. "Prattle," *Ar* 2, no. 11 (23 Mar. 1878): 9 (unsigned): "The man of wise œsophagus / Is not an ophiophagus."

THE MAN AND THE SNAKE

AN OCCURRENCE AT
OWL CREEK BRIDGE

A man stood upon a railroad bridge in northern Alabama, looking down into the swift water twenty feet below. The man's hands were behind his back, the wrists bound with a cord. A rope closely encircled his neck. It was attached to a stout cross-timber above his head and the slack fell to the level of his knees.[1] Some loose boards laid upon the sleepers supporting the metals of the railway supplied a footing for him and his executioners—two private soldiers[2] of the Federal army, directed by a sergeant who in civil life may have been a deputy sheriff. At a short remove upon the same temporary platform was an officer in the uniform of his rank, armed. He was a captain. A sentinel at each end of the bridge stood with his rifle in the position known as "support," that is to say, vertical in front of the left shoulder, the hammer resting on the forearm thrown straight across the chest—a formal and unnatural position, enforcing an erect carriage of the body. It did not appear to be the duty of these two men to know what was occurring at the center of the bridge; they merely blockaded the two ends of the foot planking that traversed it.

Beyond one of the sentinels nobody was in sight; the railroad ran straight away into a forest for a hundred yards, then, curving, was lost to view. Doubtless there was an outpost farther along. The other bank of the stream was open ground—a gentle acclivity topped with a stockade of vertical tree trunks, loopholed for rifles, with a single embrasure through which protruded the muzzle of a brass cannon commanding the bridge. Midway of the slope between bridge and fort were the spectators—a single company of infantry in line, at "parade rest," the butts of the rifles on the ground, the barrels inclining slightly backward against the right shoulder, the hands crossed upon the stock. A lieutenant stood at the right of the line, the point of his sword upon the ground, his left hand resting upon his right. Excepting the group of four at the center of the bridge, not a man moved. The company faced the bridge, staring stonily, motionless. The sentinels, facing the banks of the stream, might have been statues to adorn the bridge. The captain stood with folded arms, silent, observing the work of his subordinates, but making no sign. Death is a dignitary who when he comes announced is to be received with formal manifestations of respect, even by those most familiar with him. In the code of military etiquette silence and fixity are forms of deference.

The man who was engaged in being hanged was apparently about thirty-five years of age. He was a civilian, if one might judge from his habit, which was that of a planter.[3] His features were good—a straight nose, firm mouth, broad forehead, from which his long, dark hair was combed straight back, falling behind his ears to the collar of his well-fitting frock-coat. He wore a mustache and pointed beard, but no whiskers; his eyes were large and dark gray, and had a kindly expression which one would hardly have expected in one whose neck was in the hemp. Evidently this was no vulgar assassin. The liberal military code makes provision for hanging many kinds of persons, and gentlemen are not excluded.

The preparations being complete, the two private soldiers stepped aside and each drew away the plank upon which he had been standing. The sergeant turned to the captain, saluted and placed himself immediately behind that officer, who in turn moved apart one pace. These movements left the condemned man and the sergeant standing on the two ends of the same plank, which spanned three of the cross-ties of the bridge. The end upon which the civilian stood almost, but not quite, reached a fourth. This plank had been held in place by the weight of the captain; it was now held by that of the sergeant. At a signal from the former the latter would step aside, the plank would tilt and the condemned man go down between two ties. The arrangement commended itself to his judgment as simple and effective. His face had not been covered nor his eyes bandaged. He looked a moment at his "unsteadfast footing,"[4] then let his gaze wander to the swirling water of the stream racing madly beneath his feet. A piece of dancing driftwood caught his attention and his eyes followed it down the current. How slowly it appeared to move! What a sluggish stream!

He closed his eyes in order to fix his last thoughts upon his wife and children. The water, touched to gold by the early sun, the brooding mists under the banks at some distance down the stream, the fort, the soldiers, the piece of drift—all had distracted him. And now he became conscious of a new disturbance. Striking through the thought of his dear ones was a sound which he could neither ignore nor understand, a sharp, distinct, metallic percussion like the stroke of a blacksmith's hammer upon the anvil; it had the same ringing quality. He wondered what it was, and whether immeasurably distant or near by—it seemed both. Its recurrence was regular, but as slow as the tolling of a death knell. He awaited each stroke with impatience and—he knew not why—apprehension. The intervals of silence grew progressively longer; the delays became maddening. With their greater infrequency the sounds increased in strength and sharpness. They hurt his ear like the thrust of a knife; he feared he would shriek. What he heard was the ticking of his watch.

He unclosed his eyes and saw again the water below him. "If I could free my hands," he thought, "I might throw off the noose and spring into the stream. By diving I could evade the bullets and, swimming vigorously, reach the bank, take to the woods and get away home. My home, thank God, is as yet outside their lines; my wife and little ones are still beyond the invader's farthest advance."

As these thoughts, which have here to be set down in words, were flashed into the doomed man's brain rather than evolved from it the captain nodded to the sergeant. The sergeant stepped aside.

II

Peyton Farquhar was a well-to-do planter, of an old and highly respected Alabama family. Being a slave owner and like other slave owners a politician he was naturally an original secessionist[5] and ardently devoted to the Southern cause. Circumstances of an imperious nature, which it is unnecessary to relate here, had prevented him from taking service with the gallant army that had fought the disastrous campaigns ending with the fall of Corinth,[6] and he chafed under the inglorious restraint, longing for the release of his energies, the larger life of the soldier, the opportunity for distinction. That opportunity, he felt, would come, as it comes to all in war time. Meanwhile he did what he could. No service was too humble for him to perform in aid of the South, no adventure too perilous for him to undertake if consistent with the character of a civilian who was at heart a soldier, and who in good faith and without too much qualification assented to at least a part of the frankly villainous dictum that all is fair in love and war.[7]

One evening while Farquhar and his wife were sitting on a rustic bench near the entrance to his grounds, a gray-clad soldier rode up to the gate and asked for a drink of water. Mrs. Farquhar was only too happy to serve him with her own white hands. While she was fetching the water her husband approached the dusty horseman and inquired eagerly for news from the front.

"The Yanks are repairing the railroads," said the man, "and are getting ready for another advance. They have reached the Owl Creek bridge, put it in order and built a stockade on the north bank. The commandant has issued an order, which is posted everywhere, declaring that any civilian caught interfering with the railroad, its bridges, tunnels or trains will be summarily hanged. I saw the order."

"How far is it to the Owl Creek bridge?" Farquhar asked.

"About thirty miles."

"Is there no force on this side the creek?"

"Only a picket post half a mile out, on the railroad, and a single sentinel at this end of the bridge."

"Suppose a man—a civilian and student of hanging—should elude the picket post and perhaps get the better of the sentinel," said Farquhar, smiling, "what could he accomplish?"

The soldier reflected. "I was there a month ago," he replied. "I observed that the flood of last winter had lodged a great quantity of driftwood against the wooden pier at this end of the bridge. It is now dry and would burn like tow."

The lady had now brought the water, which the soldier drank. He thanked her ceremoniously, bowed to her husband and rode away. An hour later, after nightfall, he repassed the plantation, going northward in the direction from which he had come. He was a Federal scout.

III

As Peyton Farquhar fell straight downward through the bridge he lost consciousness and was as one already dead. From this state he was awakened—ages later, it seemed to him—by the pain of a sharp pressure upon his throat, followed by a sense of suffocation. Keen, poignant agonies seemed to shoot from his neck downward through every fibre of his body and limbs. These pains appeared to flash along well-defined lines of ramification and to beat with an inconceivably rapid periodicity. They seemed like streams of pulsating fire heating him to an intolerable temperature. As to his head, he was conscious of nothing but a feeling of fullness—of congestion. These sensations were unaccompanied by thought. The intellectual part of his nature was already effaced; he had power only to feel, and feeling was torment. He was conscious of motion. Encompassed in a luminous cloud, of which he was now merely the fiery heart, without material substance, he swung through unthinkable arcs of oscillation, like a vast pendulum. Then all at once, with terrible suddenness, the light about him shot upward with the noise of a loud plash; a frightful roaring was in his ears, and all was cold and dark. The power of thought was restored; he knew that the rope had broken and he had fallen into the stream. There was no additional strangulation; the noose about his neck was already suffocating him and kept the water from his lungs. To die of hanging at the bottom of a river!—the idea seemed to him ludicrous. He opened his eyes in the darkness and saw above him a gleam of light, but how distant, how inaccessible! He was still sinking, for the light became fainter and fainter until it was a mere glimmer. Then it began to grow and brighten, and he knew that he was rising toward the surface—knew it with reluctance, for he was now very comfortable. "To be hanged and drowned," he thought, "that is not so bad; but I do not wish to be shot. No; I will not be shot; that is not fair."

He was not conscious of an effort, but a sharp pain in his wrist apprised him that he was trying to free his hands. He gave the struggle his attention, as an idler might observe the feat of a juggler, without interest in the outcome. What splendid effort!—what magnificent, what superhuman strength! Ah, that was a fine endeavor! Bravo!

The cord fell away; his arms parted and floated upward, the hands dimly seen on each side in the growing light. He watched them with a new interest as first one and then the other pounced upon the noose at his neck. They tore it away and thrust it fiercely aside, its undulations resembling those of a water-snake. "Put it back, put it back!" He thought he shouted these words to his hands, for the undoing of the noose had been succeeded by the direst pang that he had yet experienced. His neck ached horribly; his brain was on fire; his heart, which had been fluttering faintly, gave a great leap, trying to force itself out at his mouth. His whole body was racked and wrenched with an insupportable anguish! But his disobedient hands gave no heed to the command. They beat the water vigorously with quick, downward strokes, forcing him to the surface. He felt his head emerge; his eyes were blinded by the sunlight; his chest expanded convulsively, and with a supreme and crowning agony his lungs engulfed a great draught of air, which instantly he expelled in a shriek!

He was now in full possession of his physical senses. They were, indeed, preternaturally keen and alert. Something in the awful disturbance of his organic system had so exalted and refined them that they made record of things never before perceived. He felt the ripples upon his face and heard their separate sounds as they struck. He looked at the forest on the bank of the stream, saw the individual trees, the leaves and the veining of each leaf—saw the very insects upon them: the locusts, the brilliant-bodied flies, the gray spiders stretching their webs from twig to twig. He noted the prismatic colors in all the dewdrops upon a million blades of grass. The humming of the gnats that danced above the eddies of the stream, the beating of the dragon-flies' wings, the strokes of the water-spiders' legs, like oars which had lifted their boat—all these made audible music. A fish slid along beneath his eyes and he heard the rush of its body parting the water.

He had come to the surface facing down the stream; in a moment the visible world seemed to wheel slowly round, himself the pivotal point, and he saw the bridge, the fort, the soldiers upon the bridge, the captain, the sergeant, the two privates, his executioners. They were in silhouette against the blue sky. They shouted and gesticulated, pointing at him. The captain had drawn his pistol, but did not fire; the others were unarmed. Their movements were grotesque and horrible, their forms gigantic.

Suddenly he heard a sharp report and something struck the water smartly within a few inches of his head, spattering his face with spray. He heard a second report, and saw one of the sentinels with his rifle at his shoulder, a light cloud of blue smoke rising from the muzzle. The man in the water saw the eye of the man on the bridge gazing into his own through the sights of the rifle. He observed that it was a gray eye and remembered having read that gray eyes were keenest, and that all famous marksmen had them. Nevertheless, this one had missed.

A counter-swirl had caught Farquhar and turned him half round; he was again looking at the forest on the bank opposite the fort. The sound of a clear, high voice in

AN OCCURRENCE AT OWL CREEK BRIDGE

a monotonous singsong now rang out behind him and came across the water with a distinctness that pierced and subdued all other sounds, even the beating of the ripples in his ears. Although no soldier, he had frequented camps enough to know the dread significance of that deliberate, drawling, aspirated chant; the lieutenant on shore was taking a part in the morning's work. How coldly and pitilessly—with what an even, calm intonation, presaging, and enforcing tranquility in the men—with what accurately measured intervals fell those cruel words:

"Attention, company! . . . Shoulder arms! . . . Ready! . . . Aim! . . . Fire!"

Farquhar dived—dived as deeply as he could. The water roared in his ears like the voice of Niagara, yet he heard the dulled thunder of the volley and, rising again toward the surface, met shining bits of metal, singularly flattened, oscillating slowly downward. Some of them touched him on the face and hands, then fell away, continuing their descent. One lodged between his collar and neck; it was uncomfortably warm and he snatched it out.

As he rose to the surface, gasping for breath, he saw that he had been a long time under water; he was perceptibly farther down stream—nearer to safety. The soldiers had almost finished reloading; the metal ramrods flashed all at once in the sunshine as they were drawn from the barrels, turned in the air, and thrust into their sockets. The two sentinels fired again, independently and ineffectually.

The hunted man saw all this over his shoulder; he was now swimming vigorously with the current. His brain was as energetic as his arms and legs; he thought with the rapidity of lightning.

"The officer," he reasoned, "will not make that martinet's error a second time. It is as easy to dodge a volley as a single shot. He has probably already given the command to fire at will. God help me, I cannot dodge them all!"

An appalling plash within two yards of him was followed by a loud, rushing sound, *diminuendo,* which seemed to travel back through the air to the fort and died in an explosion which stirred the very river to its deeps! A rising sheet of water curved over him, fell down upon him, blinded him, strangled him! The cannon had taken a hand in the game. As he shook his head free from the commotion of the smitten water he heard the deflected shot humming through the air ahead, and in an instant it was cracking and smashing the branches in the forest beyond.

"They will not do that again," he thought; "the next time they will use a charge of grape.[8] I must keep my eye upon the gun; the smoke will apprise me—the report arrives too late; it lags behind the missile. That is a good gun."

Suddenly he felt himself whirled round and round—spinning like a top. The water, the banks, the forest, the now distant bridge, fort and men—all were commingled and blurred. Objects were represented by their colors only; circular horizontal streaks of color—that was all he saw. He had been caught in a vortex and was being whirled on with a velocity of advance and gyration that made him giddy and sick. In

AN OCCURRENCE AT OWL CREEK BRIDGE

a few moments he was flung upon the gravel at the foot of the left bank of the stream—the southern bank—and behind a projecting point which concealed him from his enemies. The sudden arrest of his motion, the abrasion of one of his hands on the gravel, restored him, and he wept with delight. He dug his fingers into the sand, threw it over himself in handfuls and audibly blessed it. It looked like diamonds, rubies, emeralds; he could think of nothing beautiful which it did not resemble. The trees upon the bank were giant garden plants; he noted a definite order in their arrangement, inhaled the fragrance of their blooms. A strange, roseate light shone through the spaces among their trunks and the wind made in their branches the music of æolian harps. He had no wish to perfect his escape—was content to remain in that enchanting spot until retaken.

A whiz and rattle of grapeshot among the branches high above his head roused him from his dream. The baffled cannoneer had fired him a random farewell. He sprang to his feet, rushed up the sloping bank and plunged into the forest.

All that day he traveled, laying his course by the rounding sun. The forest seemed interminable; nowhere did he discover a break in it, not even a woodman's road. He had not known that he lived in so wild a region. There was something uncanny in the revelation.

By nightfall he was fatigued, footsore, famishing. The thought of his wife and children urged him on. At last he found a road which led him in what he knew to be the right direction. It was as wide and straight as a city street, yet it seemed untraveled. No fields bordered it, no dwelling anywhere. Not so much as the barking of a dog suggested human habitation. The black bodies of the trees formed a straight wall on both sides, terminating on the horizon in a point, like a diagram in a lesson in perspective. Overhead, as he looked up through this rift in the wood, shone great golden stars looking unfamiliar and grouped in strange constellations. He was sure they were arranged in some order which had a secret and malign significance. The wood on either side was full of singular noises, among which—once, twice and again—he distinctly heard whispers in an unknown tongue.

His neck was in pain and lifting his hand to it he found it horribly swollen. He knew that it had a circle of black where the rope had bruised it. His eyes felt congested; he could no longer close them. His tongue was swollen with thirst; he relieved its fever by thrusting it forward from between his teeth into the cold air. How softly the turf had carpeted the untraveled avenue—he could no longer feel the roadway beneath his feet!

Doubtless, despite his suffering, he had fallen asleep while walking, for now he sees another scene—perhaps he has merely recovered from a delirium. He stands at the gate of his own home. All is as he left it, and all bright and beautiful in the morning sunshine. He must have traveled the entire night. As he pushes open the gate and passes up the wide white walk, he sees a flutter of female garments; his wife, looking

AN OCCURRENCE AT OWL CREEK BRIDGE

fresh and cool and sweet, steps down from the veranda to meet him. At the bottom of the steps she stands waiting, with a smile of ineffable joy, an attitude of matchless grace and dignity. Ah, how beautiful she is! He springs forward with extended arms. As he is about to clasp her he feels a stunning blow upon the back of the neck; a blinding white light blazes all about him with a sound like the shock of a cannon—then all is darkness and silence!

Peyton Farquhar was dead; his body, with a broken neck, swung gently from side to side beneath the timbers of the Owl Creek bridge.[9]

E (13 July 1890): 11–12 (as "An Occurence [*sic*] at Owl Creek Bridge"); *TSC* 21–39; *IML* 16–35; **CW 2.27–45**. Reprinted in *Current Literature* 21, no. 3 (Mar. 1897): 237–39; *Novel Magazine* [London], no. 2 (May 1905): 153–57; in William J. Dawson and Coningsby W. Dawson, eds., *The Great English Short-Story Writers* (New York: Harper & Brothers, 1910), 2:29–41; *T.P.'s Magazine* 2, no. 8 (May 1911): 229–34; *Neale's Monthly* 3, no. 1 (Jan. 1914): 33–38.

NOTES

"Owl Creek" is AB's masterpiece. From the understated "an occurrence" of the title to the starkness of the last line, it is a virtuoso achievement of irony, expressed in levels ranging from the apparent to the most subtle. It is the quintessence of everything that preceded it in AB's life: his reading and contemplation, and the lessons of his writing career as well as those of his war experiences. Editorial changes he made to the story between *E* and *CW* have resulted in a very spare and pointed text, and necessitate close attention. The story is a hoax in the tradition of Jonathan Swift and Mark Twain; it allows readers to deceive themselves but it does this in order to instruct them about dangerous pitfalls in human nature and reason. Readers—in effect, all of us—who initially misread Farquhar as the hero of the story put their feet on a path that leads to the shocking conclusion, but the path requires readers to choose it repeatedly. Stephen Crane did not overstate the case when he praised it: "Nothing better exists. That story has everything" (letter to Richard Harding Davis, cited in *Stephen Crane: Letters,* ed. R. W. Stallman and Lillian Gilkes [New York: New York University Press, 1960], 139–40 n. 94). In separate essays David M. Owens describes how AB manipulated both local topography and the location of a railroad to serve fictional needs, and F. J. Logan situates AB's ironic use of a paradox of Zeno at the philosophical center of the story. For an extended analysis of the tale, see *PA*, 113–35.

1. AB describes what was called strap-rail construction, common in the antebellum South. It consisted simply of stout timbers where the rails were joined by ties (also called sleepers in light construction) with a strap of iron on top of the timbers to bear the load of the engine and cars. It was fast to build and relatively inexpensive, but could not bear as much load as conventional railways common in the North.

2. Or privates; a grammatically correct usage in the nineteenth century.

3. "Planter" is distinct from "farmer." The former profession, common in the South, used agriculture to gain wealth without regard to soil conservation, pesticides, or other scientific methods of cultivation becoming popular in the industrial world. The farmer, as the term was developed, practiced what was then known about crop rotation, soil-conserving

tilling methods, and practical soil chemistry and husbandry. Both were well known in the antebellum South, but the planter was more likely to be wealthy, with several pieces of land served by slaves in a plantation, rather than a farm.

4. Shakespeare, *1 Henry IV*, 1.3.193.

5. The Alabama state convention adopted an ordinance to secede from the Union on 11 January 1861. It was the third state (after Mississippi and Florida) to secede.

6. Corinth, Mississippi, was first occupied by Federal troops in early June 1862 after being abandoned by Beauregard's Army of Tennessee. Cf. "What I Saw of Shiloh": "The town of Corinth was a wretched place—the capital of a swamp. It is a two days' march west of the Tennessee River, which here and for a hundred and fifty miles farther, to where it falls into the Ohio at Paducah, runs nearly north. It is navigable to this point—that is to say, to Pittsburg Landing [i.e., Shiloh], where Corinth got to it by a road worn through a thickly wooded country seamed with ravines and bayous, rising nobody knows where and running into the river under sylvan arches heavily draped with Spanish moss. In some places they were obstructed by fallen trees. The Corinth road was at certain seasons a branch of the Tennessee River. Its mouth was Pittsburg Landing. Here in 1862 were some fields and a house or two; now there are a national cemetery and other improvements" (*SS* 12).

7. The first citation of the expression in this exact form ("All's fair in love and war") appears in Francis Edward Smedley (1818–64), *Frank Fairleigh* (1850), chap. 50.

8. Grapeshot was being replaced in field artillery by shell and canister before the Civil War, and some authorities claim it was not used in field pieces during the Civil War. However, the term had been common among soldiers for generations to describe any multiple-projectile artillery round.

9. In *E,* an important phrase follows "with a broken neck": "and suspended by as stout a rope as ever rewarded the zeal of a civilian patriot in war-time."

AN OCCURRENCE AT OWL CREEK BRIDGE

THE REALM OF THE UNREAL

For a part of the distance between Auburn and Newcastle[1] the road—first on one side of a creek and then on the other—occupies the whole bottom of the ravine, being partly cut out of the steep hillside, and partly built up with bowlders removed from the creek-bed by the miners. The hills are wooded, the course of the ravine is sinuous. In a dark night careful driving is required in order not to go off into the water. The night that I have in memory was dark, the creek a torrent, swollen by a recent storm. I had driven up from Newcastle and was within about a mile of Auburn in the darkest and narrowest part of the ravine, looking intently ahead of my horse for the roadway. Suddenly I saw a man almost under the animal's nose, and reined in with a jerk that came near setting the creature upon its haunches.

"I beg your pardon," I said; "I did not see you, sir."

"You could hardly be expected to see me," the man replied civilly, approaching the side of the vehicle; "and the noise of the creek prevented my hearing you."

I at once recognized the voice, although five years had passed since I had heard it. I was not particularly well pleased to hear it now.

"You are Dr. Dorrimore, I think," said I.

"Yes; and you are my good friend Mr. Manrich. I am more than glad to see you—the excess," he added, with a light laugh, "being due to the fact that I am going your way, and naturally expect an invitation to ride with you."

"Which I extend with all my heart."

That was not altogether true.

Dr. Dorrimore thanked me as he seated himself beside me, and I drove cautiously forward, as before. Doubtless it is fancy, but it seems to me now that the remaining distance was made in a chill fog; that I was uncomfortably cold; that the way was longer than ever before, and the town, when we reached it, cheerless, forbidding and desolate. It must have been early in the evening, yet I do not recollect a light in any of the houses nor a living thing in the streets. Dorrimore explained at some length how he happened to be there, and where he had been during the years that had elapsed since I had seen him. I recall the fact of the narrative, but none of the facts narrated. He had been in foreign countries and had returned—this is all that my memory retains, and this I already knew. As to myself I cannot remember that I spoke a word, though doubtless I did. Of one thing I am distinctly conscious: the man's presence at my side was strangely distasteful and disquieting—so much so that when I at last pulled up under the lights of the Putnam House[2] I experienced a sense of having escaped some spiritual peril of a nature peculiarly forbidding. This sense of relief was somewhat modified by the discovery that Dr. Dorrimore was living at the same hotel.

II

In partial explanation of my feelings regarding Dr. Dorrimore I will relate briefly the circumstances under which I had met him some years before. One evening a half-dozen men of whom I was one were sitting in the library of the Bohemian Club in San Francisco.[3] The conversation had turned to the subject of sleight-of-hand and the feats of the *prestidigitateurs,* one of whom was then exhibiting at a local theatre.

"These fellows are pretenders in a double sense," said one of the party; "they can do nothing which it is worth one's while to be made a dupe by. The humblest wayside juggler in India could mystify them to the verge of lunacy."

"For example, how?" asked another, lighting a cigar.

"For example, by all their common and familiar performances—throwing large objects into the air which never come down; causing plants to sprout, grow visibly and blossom, in bare ground chosen by spectators; putting a man into a wicker basket, piercing him through and through with a sword while he shrieks and bleeds, and then—the basket being opened nothing is there; tossing the free end of a silken ladder into the air, mounting it and disappearing."

"Nonsense!" I said, rather uncivilly, I fear. "You surely do not believe such things?"

"Certainly not: I have seen them too often."

"But I do," said a journalist of considerable local fame as a picturesque reporter. "I have so frequently related them that nothing but observation could shake my conviction. Why, gentlemen, I have my own word for it."

Nobody laughed—all were looking at something behind me. Turning in my seat I saw a man in evening dress who had just entered the room. He was exceedingly dark, almost swarthy, with a thin face, black-bearded to the lips, an abundance of coarse black hair in some disorder, a high nose and eyes that glittered with as soulless an expression as those of a cobra. One of the group rose and introduced him as Dr. Dorrimore, of Calcutta. As each of us was presented in turn he acknowledged the fact with a profound bow in the Oriental manner, but with nothing of Oriental gravity.

THE REALM OF THE UNREAL

His smile impressed me as cynical and a trifle contemptuous. His whole demeanor I can describe only as disagreeably engaging.

His presence led the conversation into other channels. He said little—I do not recall anything of what he did say. I thought his voice singularly rich and melodious, but it affected me in the same way as his eyes and smile. In a few minutes I rose to go. He also rose and put on his overcoat.

"Mr. Manrich," he said, "I am going your way."

"The devil you are!" I thought. "How do you know which way I am going?" Then I said, "I shall be pleased to have your company."

We left the building together. No cabs were in sight, the street cars had gone to bed, there was a full moon and the cool night air was delightful; we walked up the California street hill. I took that direction thinking he would naturally wish to take another, toward one of the hotels.

"You do not believe what is told of the Hindu jugglers," he said abruptly.

"How do you know that?" I asked.

Without replying he laid his hand lightly upon my arm and with the other pointed to the stone sidewalk directly in front. There, almost at our feet, lay the dead body of a man, the face upturned and white in the moonlight! A sword whose hilt sparkled with gems stood fixed and upright in the breast; a pool of blood had collected on the stones of the sidewalk.

I was startled and terrified—not only by what I saw, but by the circumstances under which I saw it. Repeatedly during our ascent of the hill my eyes, I thought, had traversed the whole reach of that sidewalk, from street to street. How could they have been insensible to this dreadful object now so conspicuous in the white moonlight?

As my dazed faculties cleared I observed that the body was in evening dress; the overcoat thrown wide open revealed the dress-coat, the white tie, the broad expanse of shirt front pierced by the sword. And—horrible revelation!—the face, except for its pallor, was that of my companion! It was to the minutest detail of dress and feature Dr. Dorrimore himself. Bewildered and horrified, I turned to look for the living man. He was nowhere visible, and with an added terror I retired from the place, down the hill in the direction whence I had come. I had taken but a few strides when a strong grasp upon my shoulder arrested me. I came near crying out with terror: the dead man, the sword still fixed in his breast, stood beside me! Pulling out the sword with his disengaged hand, he flung it from him, the moonlight glinting upon the jewels of its hilt and the unsullied steel of its blade. It fell with a clang upon the sidewalk ahead and—vanished! The man, swarthy as before, relaxed his grasp upon my shoulder and looked at me with the same cynical regard that I had observed on first meeting him. The dead have not that look—it partly restored me, and turning my head backward, I saw the smooth white expanse of sidewalk, unbroken from street to street.

"What is all this nonsense, you devil?" I demanded, fiercely enough, though weak and trembling in every limb.

THE REALM OF THE UNREAL

"It is what some are pleased to call jugglery," he answered, with a light, hard laugh. He turned down Dupont street and I saw him no more until we met in the Auburn ravine.

III

On the day after my second meeting with Dr. Dorrimore I did not see him: the clerk in the Putnam House explained that a slight illness confined him to his rooms. That afternoon at the railway station I was surprised and made happy by the unexpected arrival of Miss Margaret Corray and her mother, from Oakland.

This is not a love story. I am no story-teller, and love as it is cannot be portrayed in a literature dominated and enthralled by the debasing tyranny which "sentences letters"[4] in the name of the Young Girl. Under the Young Girl's blighting reign—or rather under the rule of those false Ministers of the Censure who have appointed themselves to the custody of her welfare—love

> veils her sacred fires,
> And, unaware, Morality expires,[5]

famished upon the sifted meal and distilled water of a prudish purveyance.

Let it suffice that Miss Corray and I were engaged in marriage. She and her mother went to the hotel at which I lived, and for two weeks I saw her daily. That I was happy needs hardly be said; the only bar to my perfect enjoyment of those golden days was the presence of Dr. Dorrimore, whom I had felt compelled to introduce to the ladies.

By them he was evidently held in favor. What could I say? I knew absolutely nothing to his discredit. His manners were those of a cultivated and considerate gentleman; and to women a man's manner is the man. On one or two occasions when I saw Miss Corray walking with him I was furious, and once had the indiscretion to protest. Asked for reasons, I had none to give and fancied I saw in her expression a shade of contempt for the vagaries of a jealous mind. In time I grew morose and consciously disagreeable, and resolved in my madness to return to San Francisco the next day. Of this, however, I said nothing.

IV

There was at Auburn an old, abandoned cemetery. It was nearly in the heart of the town, yet by night it was as gruesome a place as the most dismal of human moods could crave. The railings about the plats were prostrate, decayed or altogether gone. Many of the graves were sunken, from others grew sturdy pines, whose roots had committed unspeakable sin. The headstones were fallen and broken across; brambles overran the ground; the fence was mostly gone, and cows and pigs wandered there at will; the place was a dishonor to the living, a calumny on the dead, a blasphemy against God.

The evening of the day on which I had taken my madman's resolution to depart in anger from all that was dear to me found me in that congenial spot. The light of

THE REALM OF THE UNREAL

the half moon fell ghostly through the foliage of trees in spots and patches, revealing much that was unsightly, and the black shadows seemed conspiracies withholding to the proper time revelations of darker import. Passing along what had been a gravel path, I saw emerging from shadow the figure of Dr. Dorrimore. I was myself in shadow, and stood still with clenched hands and set teeth, trying to control the impulse to leap upon and strangle him. A moment later a second figure joined him and clung to his arm. It was Margaret Corray!

I cannot rightly relate what occurred. I know that I sprang forward, bent upon murder; I know that I was found in the gray of the morning, bruised and bloody, with finger marks upon my throat. I was taken to the Putnam House, where for days I lay in a delirium. All this I know, for I have been told. And of my own knowledge I know that when consciousness returned with convalescence I sent for the clerk of the hotel.

"Are Mrs. Corray and her daughter still here?" I asked.

"What name did you say?"

"Corray."

"Nobody of that name has been here."

"I beg you will not trifle with me," I said petulantly. "You see that I am all right now; tell me the truth."

"I give you my word," he replied with evident sincerity, "we have had no guests of that name."

His words stupefied me. I lay for a few moments in silence; then I asked: "Where is Dr. Dorrimore?"

"He left on the morning of your fight and has not been heard of since. It was a rough deal he gave you."

V

Such are the facts of this case. Margaret Corray is now my wife. She has never seen Auburn, and during the weeks whose history as it shaped itself in my brain I have endeavored to relate, was living at her home in Oakland, wondering where her lover was and why he did not write. The other day I saw in the Baltimore *Sun* the following paragraph:

"Professor Valentine Dorrimore, the hypnotist, had a large audience last night. The lecturer, who has lived most of his life in India, gave some marvelous exhibitions of his power, hypnotizing any one who chose to submit himself to the experiment, by merely looking at him. In fact, he twice hypnotized the entire audience (reporters alone exempted), making all entertain the most extraordinary illusions. The most valuable feature of the lecture was the disclosure of the methods of the Hindu jugglers in their famous performances, familiar in the mouths of travelers. The professor declares that these thaumaturgists[6] have acquired such skill in the art which he learned at their feet that they perform their miracles by simply throwing the 'spectators' into a state of hypnosis and telling them what to see and hear. His assertion that a peculiarly susceptible subject may be kept in the realm of the unreal for weeks, months, and even years, dominated by whatever delusions and hallucinations the operator may from time to time suggest, is a trifle disquieting."

E (20 July 1890): 11–12 (as "In the Realm of the Unreal"); *CSTB* 249–62; ***CW*** **3.255–67.** Reprinted in *Anti-Philistine*, no. 4 (15 September 1897): 258–67.

NOTES

Hypnosis, like ghosts, snakes, and haunted houses, was another topic dear to popular taste in the late nineteenth century. It is virtually impossible to hypnotize anyone as the narrator, Manrich, claimed to be hypnotized, and it is impossible to hypnotize an entire audience, as Dr. Dorrimore is said to have done. AB knew this, so this story is a tour de force of sensationalism, an exercise, as the title admits, in unreality.

1. Auburn and Newcastle are towns in Plaçer County, in central California, about four miles apart. AB lived in Auburn for most of 1884 and 1885; his opinion of the town can be gauged by the acerbic poem "The Perverted Village" (1884; *CW* 5.148–49).

2. The Putnam House on Lincoln Way in Auburn was built in 1880. In 1900 it changed hands and became the Conroy House. It burned down in 1912, and another hotel was built on the same location.

3. The Bohemian Club, originally located on Pine Street (after the 1906 earthquake at 624 Taylor Street), was (and is) one of the most prestigious of the social clubs in San Francisco. The journalist James F. Bowman (d. 1882), with the help of AB and others, founded the club around 1872; AB served as its secretary in 1876–77 but later resigned because he felt the club was too sycophantic to royal and noble visitors from overseas. He later defined Bohemia unflatteringly as "the tap-room of a wayside inn on the road from Bœotia to Philistia." "Small Contributions," *Co* 16, no. 4 (September 1908): 445. "A Story at the Club" was originally titled "Told at the Bohemian Club."

4. Lord Byron, *English Bards and Scotch Reviewers* (1809): "In soul so like, so merciful, yet just, / Some think that Satan has resign'd his trust, / And given the spirit to the world again, / To sentence letters, as he sentenced men" (ll. 440–43). AB's criticism of the "false ministers" is aimed directly at William Dean Howells, at this time editor of the *Atlantic Monthly* and the main advocate of literary realism (see "The Great Strike of 1895," note 1). As Howells conceived it, realism should narrate life as experienced by common people, but not recount experiences or use language that might bring pain or shame to readers who were young women. AB detested this notion of realism and scornfully referred to Howells as "Miss Nancy." One of his own views of what literature might do was expressed in TC, *NL* 22, no. 6 (9 Mar. 1872): 9 (unsigned): "—Satire should be not like a saw, but a sword; it should cut, not mangle.—*Exchange.* [It was not long ago that the *Atlantic* gravely praised somebody's satire, because it was 'so subtle as to leave a half doubt of its intent!' What a jackass-taste is this. Gad! if Miss Nancy is going to 'sentence letters' much longer, there will be little tatting made. Let us mangle!"

5. Alexander Pope, *The Dunciad* (1742), 4.649–50: "*Religion* blushing, veils her sacred fires, / And unawares *Morality* expires."

6. I.e., magicians.

THE REALM OF THE UNREAL

HIS WATERLOO

WHY HE IS NOT TO BE COMMISSIONER OF DEAD DOGS.

————

HOLOBOM[1] IN THE CAVE OF ADULLAM.[2]

————

THE INSIDE HISTORY OF THE LATE
CONVENTION—THE KNIFE AS A POLITICAL POWER.

Since returning from the Sacramento convention,[3] I have been so frequently impor-
tuned by my personal and political friends to explain my failure to secure the nomination of Commissioner of Dead Dogs on Vacant Lots, that I deem it my duty pub-
licly to state some of the causes leading to my defeat. My fitness for the position is, I
believe, not seriously questioned by any one. Political animosity has not yet reached
that extreme; its fires burn with a less unholy heat than that. I was beaten by smoother
and more secret methods.

   With the Alameda county delegation solid in my favor and a promise of support
from Trinity and Alpine counties, I went before the convention with a stronger backing than any competitor excepting General Salomon[4] of San Francisco, who by the
basest intrigues had secured the support of the Hon. Edward Curtis.[5] Mr. Curtis is a
Democrat, and was not a delegate, but he is a man of truly imperial influence because
he is so good. That he enrolled himself under the banner of General Salomon is nothing to his discredit, morally, for the General had promised him that if nominated and
elected he would appoint Mr. Curtis's aged grandfather Deputy Deodorizer[6] from the
Sixteenth District—which does not contain a single dead dog. Mr. Curtis's error was

in believing that General Salomon would keep his word—which, indeed, is hardly worth keeping.

On arriving at Sacramento I naturally sought out Governor Waterman,[7] whom I considered the head of the Republican party in this State. I found that illustrious man plunged in the deepest dejection.

"Your Excellency," I said, "I have come to solicit your influence. Heaven has been pleased to put it into the hearts of my friends that I would acceptably discharge the duties of Commissioner of Dead Dogs on Vacant Lots. You can aid me. One blast upon your bugle horn were worth ten thousand men."[8]

The Governor, who seemed deeply touched, blew his nose both loud and shrill.

"You misunderstand me," said I. "What I have the honor to request is that you write a letter to the San Bernardino delegation, saying that you should *so* like to see me defeated. You see what that has done for Markham!"

His Excellency rose from the gubernatorial chair with some difficulty; not having been made to measure, it fitted him not wisely but too well.[9] He grasped my hand.

"Mr. Holobom," said he, in a voice husky with emotion, "you are an honest, outspoken man, whom it will be a pleasure to serve. I will write the letter at once, and give it out for publication. The welfare of the people is the supreme law—I shall ask but one favor in return. A neighbor of mine aspires to the nomination of State Undertaker. His qualifications are first class; he is my cousin's brother-in-law. By supporting him your friends will—"

The Governor's remarks were cut short by a terrible uproar in the adjoining room—howls and screams of rage, as of a panther in its last strong agony, mingled with sounds of smashing furniture and grating teeth. "The Bornekillo is unhappy," said an attendant, entering, "it is the day for cutting his claws."

But that, as Rudyard Kipling would say, is another story.[10]

Returning to my headquarters at the Double Eagle Hotel in order to instruct my supporters in the interest of the Governor's cousin's brother-in-law, I had the misfortune to attract the attention of Mr. Arthur McEwen,[11] the well-known journalist, and in the next morning's *Examiner* I read the following statement over his signature:

"Mr. Jamrach Holobom, who is here figuring around for Commissioner of Dead Dogs on Vacant Lots, seeking to wrest that honor from the battle-saved veteran, General Salomon, the hero of Appomatum, is one of the most prominent scoundrels in the Golden West. Born in Opodeldoc[12] in 1834, of illegitimate parents, he received an epidemical education and for some years filled with great credit the Chair of Civic Chicanery in the Indiana State University at Cuticura.[13] He is a pensioner of the late war, having been seriously injured by his feet becoming entangled in the border line while crossing hastily into Canada to escape conscription. In 1871 he was appointed to a vacancy in the Nebraska State Prison, but resigned with a three-cornered file to accept a position in the Denver chain-gang. His career in California has been an example to

HIS WATERLOO

American youth, and his baldness will long survive him. He is a fervent Republican, and has entirely recovered from the delirium tremens, whereas his brother was hanged in the early 60's. Gifted with an infamous ability, and adorned with all the vices of his time; fat, ferocious and irresolute; studious to pocket and diligent to retain, this beacon statesman of the Barbary Coast[14] burns with a peculiar glory and casts a wide and tender light which softens down the hoar austerity of things considerably. His nomination as Commissioner of Dead Dogs would be acceptable on Fame's eternal dumping ground,[15] and ratified with effluvium."

Professor Kowalsky, who was trying to graft his uncle on to the ticket as Clerk of the Court of Acquittals, denounced me in open convention as an enemy of the liberal arts and struck at me with a cuspidor. The delegation from Alpine county, who in his youth had himself been a libeler of distinction, fell away from me and put up his nephew for the place which I sought. In short, I was knifed until I would not have held alfalfa; and when my name was presented to the convention by my aunt's stepson, it provoked the profoundest silence that ever echoed through that historic chamber. The upshot was that General Salomon was nominated by acclamation as Commissioner of Dead Dogs on Vacant Lots. That is how I am not in it. That is how the Republican party of this sovereign commonwealth went to the demnition bowwows.[16] That is why, if you peep into the Cave of Adullam, you will dimly discern, squatted alongside R. W. Waterman and Marcus D. Boruck,[17] the mortal part of

JAMRACH HOLOBOM.

OT (16 Aug. 1890): 1.

NOTES

Previously unreprinted, this broad farce is a send up of the recent Republican State Convention, and in the process AB manages to skewer many of the local political figures he most despised.

1. Jamrach Holobom, described as a professor at the fictitious University of Oshkosh, Wisconsin ("Prattle," *E* [9 Aug. 1896]: 6), is the "author" of *The Brass-Headed Whale,* two articles entitled "How Not to Eat" (n.d.), and the poems "At the Close of the Canvass," "To the Grove Side," and "Election Day" (early verses by AB from *W* that he reprinted in "The Passing Show"), as well as four verse contributions, some epigrams, and a "translation" of "Dies Irae" in *DD*.

2. The Cave of Adullam was the place where David fled from Saul, with a band of four hundred men, all of whom were in distress, in debt, and discontented (1 Sam. 22:1–2). AB was always scornful when he alluded to the Cave of Adullam or to Adullamites.

3. The Republican State Convention was held in Sacramento on 12–14 August 1890, during which Henry Harrison Markham (1841–1923) was nominated for governor. Markham won the election of 1890, serving one term (1891–95).

4. AB excoriated Brig. Gen. Edward S. Salomon (1836–1913) in his columns (see the poem "To E. S. Salomon: Who in a Memorial Day oration protested bitterly against decorating the graves of Confederate dead," *E* [8 Oct. 1903]: 16). President U. S. Grant appointed

Salomon governor of Washington Territory in 1869. After his term, he settled in San Francisco, where he practiced law. A notable veterans' leader, he became California state president of the Grand Army of the Republic in 1887, and he was elected to the state assembly as a Republican in November 1888.

5. Edward Curtis was a senator in the California state legislature in 1869–71.

6. Cf. the "deodorizer of dead dogs" in "A Revolt of the Gods" (p. 449).

7. Robert Whitney Waterman (1826–91) was elected lieutenant governor of California in 1886 but ascended to the governorship on 13 September 1887 when Gov. Washington Bartlett died in office. AB wrote numerous satirical verses and columns about Waterman during his term.

8. Adapted from Sir Walter Scott's *The Lady of the Lake* (1810), canto 6, stanza 18: "One blast upon his bugle-horn / Were worth a thousand men!"

9. An adaptation of Shakespeare's "Of one that lov'd not wisely but too well" (*Othello* 5.2.344).

10. A frequent tag in Rudyard Kipling's stories; see, e.g., "Watches of the Night," in *Plain Tales from the Hills* (London: Macmillan, 1890), 83.

11. Arthur McEwen was a longtime editorial writer for *E*. He and AB would tangle later, in 1895 in an argument that did credit to neither man and distressed many of their common friends. See the anonymous article "Bierce and McEwen," *E* (11 Nov. 1895): 6, and *SS* 211–14.

12. Opodeldoc is the name of a liniment invented by Paracelsus, containing powdered soap, camphor, oil of rosemary, alcohol, and water. The protagonist of Edgar Allan Poe's "The Literary Life of Thingum Bob, Esq." (1844) uses "Oppodeldoc" as a pseudonym.

13. Cuticura was among the very first medicated soaps to be sold commercially in North America, originating circa 1865.

14. The Barbary Coast was a rough-and-tumble region in San Francisco at the southern foot of Telegraph Hill, full of gambling dens, brothels, and saloons.

15. Cf. *DD*: "OBLIVION, *n*. The state or condition in which the wicked cease from struggling and the dreary are at rest. Fame's eternal dumping ground."

16. Cf. Dickens, *Nicholas Nickleby* (1838–39): "He has gone to the demnition bow-wows" (chap. 64).

17. Marcus D. Boruck (1833?–95) was the personal secretary of Senator Waterman. AB frequently criticized him for high-handedness.

HIS WATERLOO

THE MIDDLE TOE OF
THE RIGHT FOOT

It is well known that the old Manton house is haunted. In all the rural district near about, and even in the town of Marshall, a mile away, not one person of unbiased mind entertains a doubt of it; incredulity is confined to those opinionated persons who will be called "cranks" as soon as the useful word shall have penetrated the intellectual demesne of the Marshall *Advance*.[1] The evidence that the house is haunted is of two kinds: the testimony of disinterested witnesses who have had ocular proof, and that of the house itself. The former may be disregarded and ruled out on any of the various grounds of objection which may be urged against it by the ingenious; but facts within the observation of all are material and controlling.

In the first place, the Manton house has been unoccupied by mortals for more than ten years, and with its outbuildings is slowly falling into decay—a circumstance which in itself the judicious will hardly venture to ignore. It stands a little way off the loneliest reach of the Marshall and Harriston road, in an opening which was once a farm and is still disfigured with strips of rotting fence and half covered with brambles overrunning a stony and sterile soil long unacquainted with the plow. The house itself is in tolerably good condition, though badly weather-stained and in dire need of attention from the glazier, the smaller male population of the region having attested in the manner of its kind its disapproval of dwellings without dwellers. It is two stories in height, nearly square, its front pierced by a single doorway flanked on each side by a window boarded up to the very top. Corresponding windows above, not protected, serve to admit light and rain to the rooms of the upper floor. Grass and weeds grow pretty rankly all about, and a few shade trees, somewhat the worse for wind, and leaning all in one direction, seem to be making a concerted effort to run away. In short, as the Marshall town humorist explained in the columns of the *Advance,* "the proposition that the Manton house is badly haunted is the only logical conclusion from the premises." The fact that in this dwelling Mr. Manton thought it expedient one night some ten years ago to rise and cut the throats of his wife and two small children, removing at once to another part of the country, has no doubt done its share in directing public attention to the fitness of the place for supernatural phenomena.

To this house, one summer evening, came four men in a wagon. Three of them promptly alighted, and the one who had been driving hitched the team to the only remaining post of what had been a fence. The fourth remained seated in the wagon. "Come," said one of his companions, approaching him, while the others moved away in the direction of the dwelling—"this is the place."

The man addressed did not move. "By God!" he said harshly, "this is a trick, and it looks to me as if you were in it."

"Perhaps I am," the other said, looking him straight in the face and speaking in a tone which had something of contempt in it. "You will remember, however, that the choice of place was with your own assent left to the other side. Of course if you are afraid of spooks——"

"I am afraid of nothing," the man interrupted with another oath, and sprang to the ground. The two then joined the others at the door, which one of them had already opened with some difficulty, caused by rust of lock and hinge. All entered. Inside it was dark, but the man who had unlocked the door produced a candle and matches and made a light. He then unlocked a door on their right as they stood in the passage. This gave them entrance to a large, square room that the candle but dimly lighted. The floor had a thick carpeting of dust, which partly muffled their footfalls. Cobwebs were in the angles of the walls and depended from the ceiling like strips of rotting lace, making undulatory movements in the disturbed air. The room had two windows in adjoining sides, but from neither could anything be seen except the rough inner surfaces of boards a few inches from the glass. There was no fireplace, no furniture; there was nothing: besides the cobwebs and the dust, the four men were the only objects there which were not a part of the structure.

Strange enough they looked in the yellow light of the candle. The one who had so reluctantly alighted was especially spectacular—he might have been called sensational. He was of middle age, heavily built, deep chested and broad shouldered. Looking at his figure, one would have said that he had a giant's strength; at his features, that he would use it like a giant. He was clean shaven, his hair rather closely cropped and gray. His low forehead was seamed with wrinkles above the eyes, and over the nose these became vertical. The heavy black brows followed the same law, saved from meeting only by an upward turn at what would otherwise have been the point of contact. Deeply sunken beneath these, glowed in the obscure light a pair of eyes of uncertain color, but obviously enough too small. There was something forbidding in their expression, which was not bettered by the cruel mouth and wide jaw. The nose was well enough, as noses go; one does not expect much of noses. All that was sinister in the man's face seemed accentuated by an unnatural pallor—he appeared altogether bloodless.

THE MIDDLE TOE OF THE RIGHT FOOT

The appearance of the other men was sufficiently commonplace: they were such persons as one meets and forgets that he met. All were younger than the man described, between whom and the eldest of the others, who stood apart, there was apparently no kindly feeling. They avoided looking at each other.

"Gentlemen," said the man holding the candle and keys, "I believe everything is right. Are you ready, Mr. Rosser?"

The man standing apart from the group bowed and smiled.

"And you, Mr. Grossmith?"

The heavy man bowed and scowled.

"You will be pleased to remove your outer clothing."

Their hats, coats, waistcoats and neckwear were soon removed and thrown outside the door, in the passage. The man with the candle now nodded, and the fourth man—he who had urged Grossmith to leave the wagon—produced from the pocket of his overcoat two long, murderous-looking bowie-knives, which he drew now from their leather scabbards.

"They are exactly alike," he said, presenting one to each of the two principals—for by this time the dullest observer would have understood the nature of this meeting. It was to be a duel to the death.

Each combatant took a knife, examined it critically near the candle and tested the strength of blade and handle across his lifted knee. Their persons were then searched in turn, each by the second of the other.

"If it is agreeable to you, Mr. Grossmith," said the man holding the light, "you will place yourself in that corner."

He indicated the angle of the room farthest from the door, whither Grossmith retired, his second parting from him with a grasp of the hand which had nothing of cordiality in it. In the angle nearest the door Mr. Rosser stationed himself, and after a whispered consultation his second left him, joining the other near the door. At that moment the candle was suddenly extinguished, leaving all in profound darkness. This may have been done by a draught from the opened door; whatever the cause, the effect was startling.

"Gentlemen," said a voice which sounded strangely unfamiliar in the altered condition affecting the relations of the senses—"gentlemen, you will not move until you hear the closing of the outer door."

A sound of trampling ensued, then the closing of the inner door; and finally the outer one closed with a concussion which shook the entire building.

A few minutes afterward a belated farmer's boy met a light wagon which was being driven furiously toward the town of Marshall. He declared that behind the two figures on the front seat stood a third, with its hands upon the bowed shoulders of the others, who appeared to struggle vainly to free themselves from its grasp. This figure, unlike the others, was clad in white, and had undoubtedly boarded the wagon as it passed the haunted house. As the lad could boast a considerable former experience

THE MIDDLE TOE OF THE RIGHT FOOT

with the supernatural thereabouts his word had the weight justly due to the testimony of an expert. The story (in connection with the next day's events) eventually appeared in the *Advance,* with some slight literary embellishments and a concluding intimation that the gentlemen referred to would be allowed the use of the paper's columns for their version of the night's adventure. But the privilege remained without a claimant.

II

The events that led up to this "duel in the dark" were simple enough. One evening three young men of the town of Marshall were sitting in a quiet corner of the porch of the village hotel, smoking and discussing such matters as three educated young men of a Southern village would naturally find interesting. Their names were King, Sancher and Rosser. At a little distance, within easy hearing, but taking no part in the conversation, sat a fourth. He was a stranger to the others. They merely knew that on his arrival by the stage-coach that afternoon he had written in the hotel register the name Robert Grossmith. He had not been observed to speak to any one except the hotel clerk. He seemed, indeed, singularly fond of his own company—or, as the *personnel* of the *Advance* expressed it, "grossly addicted to evil associations."[2] But then it should be said in justice to the stranger that the *personnel* was himself of a too convivial disposition fairly to judge one differently gifted, and had, moreover, experienced a slight rebuff in an effort at an "interview."

"I hate any kind of deformity in a woman," said King, "whether natural or—acquired. I have a theory that any physical defect has its correlative mental and moral defect."

"I infer, then," said Rosser gravely, "that a lady lacking the moral advantage of a nose would find the struggle to become Mrs. King an arduous enterprise."

"Of course you may put it that way," was the reply; "but, seriously, I once threw over a most charming girl on learning quite accidentally that she had suffered amputation of a toe. My conduct was brutal if you like, but if I had married that girl I should have been miserable for life and should have made her so."

"Whereas," said Sancher, with a light laugh, "by marrying a gentleman of more liberal views she escaped with a parted throat."

"Ah, you know to whom I refer. Yes, she married Manton, but I don't know about his liberality; I'm not sure but he cut her throat because he discovered that she lacked that excellent thing in woman, the middle toe of the right foot."

"Look at that chap!" said Rosser in a low voice, his eyes fixed upon the stranger.

"That chap" was obviously listening intently to the conversation.

"Damn his impudence!" muttered King—"what ought we to do?"

"That's an easy one," Rosser replied, rising. "Sir," he continued, addressing the stranger, "I think it would be better if you would remove your chair to the other end of the veranda. The presence of gentlemen is evidently an unfamiliar situation to you."

The man sprang to his feet and strode forward with clenched hands, his face white with rage. All were now standing. Sancher stepped between the belligerents.

THE MIDDLE TOE OF THE RIGHT FOOT

"You are hasty and unjust," he said to Rosser; "this gentleman has done nothing to deserve such language."

But Rosser would not withdraw a word. By the custom of the country and the time there could be but one outcome to the quarrel.

"I demand the satisfaction due to a gentleman," said the stranger, who had become more calm. "I have not an acquaintance in this region. Perhaps you, sir," bowing to Sancher, "will be kind enough to represent me in this matter."

Sancher accepted the trust—somewhat reluctantly it must be confessed, for the man's appearance and manner were not at all to his liking. King, who during the colloquy had hardly removed his eyes from the stranger's face and had not spoken a word, consented with a nod to act for Rosser, and the upshot of it was that, the principals having retired, a meeting was arranged for the next evening. The nature of the arrangements has been already disclosed. The duel with knives in a dark room was once a commoner feature of Southwestern life than it is likely to be again.[3] How thin a veneering of "chivalry" covered the essential brutality of the code under which such encounters were possible we shall see.

III

In the blaze of a midsummer noonday the old Manton house was hardly true to its traditions. It was of the earth, earthy.[4] The sunshine caressed it warmly and affectionately, with evident disregard of its bad reputation. The grass greening all the expanse in its front seemed to grow, not rankly, but with a natural and joyous exuberance, and the weeds blossomed quite like plants. Full of charming lights and shadows and populous with pleasant-voiced birds, the neglected shade trees no longer struggled to run away, but bent reverently beneath their burden of sun and song. Even in the glassless upper windows was an expression of peace and contentment, due to the light within. Over the stony fields the visible heat danced with a lively tremor incompatible with the gravity which is an attribute of the supernatural.

Such was the aspect under which the place presented itself to Sheriff Adams and two other men who had come out from Marshall to look at it. One of these men was Mr. King, the sheriff's deputy; the other, whose name was Brewer, was a brother of the late Mrs. Manton. Under a beneficent law of the State relating to property which has been for a certain period abandoned by an owner whose residence cannot be ascertained, the sheriff was legal custodian of the Manton farm and appurtenances thereunto belonging. His present visit was in mere perfunctory compliance with some order of a court in which Mr. Brewer had an action to get possession of the property as heir to his deceased sister. By a mere coincidence, the visit was made on the day after the night that Deputy King had unlocked the house for another and very different purpose. His presence now was not of his own choosing: he had been ordered to accompany his superior and at the moment could think of nothing more prudent than simulated alacrity in obedience to the command.

THE MIDDLE TOE OF THE RIGHT FOOT

Carelessly opening the front door, which to his surprise was not locked, the sheriff was amazed to see, lying on the floor of the passage into which it opened, a confused heap of men's apparel. Examination showed it to consist of two hats, and the same number of coats, waistcoats and scarves, all in a remarkably good state of preservation, albeit somewhat defiled by the dust in which they lay. Mr. Brewer was equally astonished, but Mr. King's emotion is not of record. With a new and lively interest in his own actions the sheriff now unlatched and pushed open the door on the right, and the three entered. The room was apparently vacant—no; as their eyes became accustomed to the dimmer light something was visible in the farthest angle of the wall. It was a human figure— that of a man crouching close in the corner. Something in the attitude made the intruders halt when they had barely passed the threshold. The figure more and more clearly defined itself. The man was upon one knee, his back in the angle of the wall, his shoulders elevated to the level of his ears, his hands before his face, palms outward, the fingers spread and crooked like claws; the white face turned upward on the retracted neck had an expression of unutterable fright, the mouth half open, the eyes incredibly expanded. He was stone dead. Yet, with the exception of a bowie-knife, which had evidently fallen from his own hand, not another object was in the room.

In the thick dust that covered the floor were some confused footprints near the door and along the wall through which it opened. Along one of the adjoining walls, too, past the boarded-up windows, was the trail made by the man himself in reaching his corner. Instinctively in approaching the body the three men followed that trail. The sheriff grasped one of the outthrown arms; it was as rigid as iron, and the application of a gentle force rocked the entire body without altering the relation of its parts. Brewer, pale with excitement, gazed intently into the distorted face. "God of mercy!" he suddenly cried, "it is Manton!"

"You are right," said King, with an evident attempt at calmness: "I knew Manton. He then wore a full beard and his hair long, but this is he."

He might have added: "I recognized him when he challenged Rosser. I told Rosser and Sancher who he was before we played him this horrible trick. When Rosser left this dark room at our heels, forgetting his outer clothing in the excitement, and driving away with us in his shirt sleeves—all through the discreditable proceedings we knew whom we were dealing with, murderer and coward that he was!"

But nothing of this did Mr. King say. With his better light he was trying to penetrate the mystery of the man's death. That he had not once moved from the corner where he had been stationed; that his posture was that of neither attack nor defense; that he had dropped his weapon; that he had obviously perished of sheer horror of something that he *saw*—these were circumstances which Mr. King's disturbed intelligence could not rightly comprehend.

Groping in intellectual darkness for a clew to his maze of doubt, his gaze, directed mechanically downward in the way of one who ponders momentous matters, fell upon something which, there, in the light of day and in the presence of living companions,

THE MIDDLE TOE OF THE RIGHT FOOT

affected him with terror. In the dust of years that lay thick upon the floor—leading from the door by which they had entered, straight across the room to within a yard of Manton's crouching corpse—were three parallel lines of footprints—light but definite impressions of bare feet, the outer ones those of small children, the inner a woman's. From the point at which they ended they did not return; they pointed all one way. Brewer, who had observed them at the same moment, was leaning forward in an attitude of rapt attention, horribly pale.

"Look at that!" he cried, pointing with both hands at the nearest print of the woman's right foot, where she had apparently stopped and stood. "The middle toe is missing—it was Gertrude!"

Gertrude was the late Mrs. Manton, sister to Mr. Brewer.

E (17 Aug. 1890): 11–12; *TSC* 259–75; *IML* 283–300; *CW* **3.235–51**.

NOTES

Like "The Realm of the Unreal," another suspenseful tale dependent on a sensational supernatural ending.

1. In *E* (see "Selected Textual Variants") the tale was identified as taking place in Missouri. There is in fact a city named Marshall, the county seat of Saline County in west-central Missouri, founded in 1839. The *Marshall Advance,* however, is fictitious.

2. Cf. AB's famous definition in *DD*: "ALONE, *adj.* In bad company."

3. Cf. "Prattle," *E* (18 Nov. 1888): 4: "One incident of the recent dark-room duel with bowie-knives, in Birmingham, Alabama, was of a character tending, it is to be feared, to bring such contests into undeserved discredit. The survivor and victor on being released from the room of honor ran furiously down the street, covered with gore as he was, to a store kept by an inoffensive negro and attacked him with all his remaining ferocity. In self-defense the negro was compelled to kill him. No doubt the sight of an antagonist clearly visible, and even conspicuous by reason of his color, constituted a powerful temptation after the events of the preceding half hour—a consideration to which, doubtless, the negro was insufficiently sensible—but forbearance is a virtue which should accompany valor, and if the victor in an affair of honor cannot abstain from attacks upon non-combatants, he proves himself to have been unfit to fight at all. The deceased was clearly no gentleman, and if the other deceased had known in time the character of him to whom he was invited to give satisfaction he would have been almost justified in refusing it. If the deplorable occurrence have the effect of surrounding the duel *in camera obscura* with more stringent regulations for the safety of outsiders the party to the third part will not have saved his own life in vain."

4. Cf. 1 Cor. 15:47: "The first man is of the earth, earthy." AB parodied this in criticizing the homespun verse of James Whitcomb Riley: "Blackburn Harte . . . thinks Riley good *because* he is 'of the people,' peoply" (letter to Blanche Partington, 9 Jan. 1893; *MMM* 30).

BURBANK'S CRIME

A CAMPAIGN STRATAGEM DEFEATED.

A FLATTENED FATHER—A FAT OFFICE IN DISPUTE—THE NIGHT BEFORE
BURBANK WAS STRETCHED.

Before the hour of three tomorrow afternoon Burbank Jabsley will have become no
more. Lamentable calamity!—I am Burbank Jabsley. This is my confession; I write it
in the presence of the death watch, who lies drunk and snoring in the corner of my
cell. A sound of hammering comes from the jail yard where the carpenters are erecting my scaffold. Why should I not tell the truth?—my father, who is unfortunately
dead, will never know, but that good old man whose affectionate care I shall remember to the latest hour of my life, taught me from early infancy that a profitless falsehood was hardly better than no falsehood at all. In this supreme crisis of my political
career I will honor his memory by a single instance of obedience, for the truth can neither hurt nor help him.

In 1888 the Republican County Convention of Coyote county[1] nominated my
father for Collector of the Cat Tax. It was a strong nomination; my father had already
an honorable record. He had served two terms in the Board of Supervisors and one in
the penitentiary. He had endeared himself to all sorts and conditions of men by shooting the Judge of the Superior Court in self-defense, that gentleman being about to
issue a warrant for his arrest. It was a fearless act, for which he was tried without the

formality of arrest in the Court of Technicalities and Exceptions[2] and acquitted through a default of the Judge and Prosecuting Attorney, who clung to life, and when the case was called went fishing. Still further to augment his popularity, my father had the forethought to discharge all the Chinamen employed in his factory making currant jelly, and hired the Republican County Committee. A donation of twenty boxes of prunes from an orchard adjoining his own to the Home for the Indigent Vicious completed the edifice of his political solidity and made the Democratic heart exceedingly dark. It was from the Cat Tax that the Democrats of Coyote county had paid their campaign expenses ever since they had imposed it seven years before; loss of the Collectorship might entail a permanent exclusion from the seats of power. The loafers and fishers of the party rose as one man, and, with lifted arms, swore that it should not be.

In its extremity the Coyote Democracy turned to me: through the Chairman of the County Committee a proposal was made that I run against my father. It was to be a campaign of calumniation, the chairman explained, showing me a formal resolution to that effect, and he assumed that I knew more damaging facts against the opposing candidate than there was now time to invent: would I stand in and save the country?

"Of course," he added, "we understand the delicacy of your position: you have always been a Republican yourself, and—"

"I do not see what that has to do with it," I said; "a man's political interests are his own affair. The delicacy of my position is that the old man is intolerably handy with a gun."

"There are in the county of Coyote," said the chairman, consulting a pocket notebook, and apparently oblivious to what I had put forth, "765,040 cats, and the tax is 50 cents a head. The expenses of collection are heavy, but the present Collector, a most efficient officer, turned into the county treasury last year $345."

"Say no more," said I. "The nomination is accepted and I will address my fellow-citizens upon the issues of the day."

But I was none the less determined that the campaign of calumniation should not ensue.

Near our house in the town of Jayhawk[3] (the county seat) was a large hotel, built on three sides of a quadrangle, which was overlooked by no fewer than 150 bedroom windows. One dark night, just before my formal nomination was to have taken place, I inveigled my dear father into that court on a pretense of needing his assistance as "booster" in a burglary. He cheerfully accompanied me, and at an opportune moment I produced a noose from beneath my coat, whipped it over his head and arms and to his surprise soon had him bound fast and securely gagged. I left him lying in the middle of the court and going back to my lodging soon returned with two large Tomcats which I had previously tied together by the hind legs and muffled in two gunny-sacks. I now unsacked them and threw them carelessly across a clothes line directly above my poor father, as he lay helpless on the cold, cold ground.[4] They at once locked one another in deadly embrace and exalted their voices in war cries of the most terrifying nature, as I hastily retreated to a sheltered angle of the court to observe the effect of my political stratagem.

I need not distress myself by minute relation of what occurred; it is sufficient to say that when morning dawned my poor father was the bottom fact of a prodigious cone of beer bottles, bootjacks and other volatile property cast from the circumambient dormitories, and that the cats were not in it at all—they had simply suffered disintegration and pervaded space as a barely palpable crimson mist beneath a rising cloud of thin, fleecy exhalation of fur.

An hour later, when the servants of the hotel had removed the vast superstructure of missiles from the author of my being, they carried the body into the hotel office and spread it carefully upon the floor. I had just entered from another direction and was standing over it with simulated curiosity, when the clerk descended a stairway.

"Ah, good morning, Jabsley," he said, approaching the body; "what have we here?"

"It seems to be a map of South America," said I.

My connection with the affair was unfortunately discovered, and not only did I lose the nomination for Collector of the Cat Tax, but I was arrested and hauled before the Court of Commitment and Conviction, the Judge of which is a Republican. I am to be hanged tomorrow and it looks as if the next election would go against us.

OT (20 Sept. 1890): 1.

NOTES

Another unreprinted tale that, although superficially in the manner of the stories in "The Parenticide Club," is (like "His Waterloo") one of AB's more pungent satires on the corruption of California politics.

1. Coyote County, presumably in California, is fictitious. Cf. the use of the fictitious town of Coyote in "My Favorite Murder" (p. 612).
2. Cf. the Court of Objections and Technicalities in "My Favorite Murder."
3. Cf. the earlier uses of fictitious town of Jayhawk in "His Railway," "Corrupting the Press," and "Jupiter Doke, Brigadier-General"; each of them used to suggest an element of crude rusticity in their inhabitants.
4. Stephen Foster (1826–64), "Massa's in de Cold, Cold Ground" (1852).

BURBANK'S CRIME

OIL OF DOG

My name is Boffer Bings.[1] I was born of honest parents in one of the humbler walks of life, my father being a manufacturer of dog-oil and my mother having a small studio in the shadow of the village church, where she disposed of unwelcome babes. In my boyhood I was trained to habits of industry; I not only assisted my father in procuring dogs for his vats, but was frequently employed by my mother to carry away the débris of her work in the studio. In performance of this duty I sometimes had need of all my natural intelligence for all the law officers of the vicinity were opposed to my mother's business. They were not elected on an opposition ticket, and the matter had never been made a political issue; it just happened so. My father's business of making dog-oil was, naturally, less unpopular, though the owners of missing dogs sometimes regarded him with suspicion, which was reflected, to some extent, upon me. My father had, as silent partners, all the physicians of the town, who seldom wrote a prescription which did not contain what they were pleased to designate as *Ol. can.*[2] It is really the most valuable medicine ever discovered. But most persons are unwilling to make personal sacrifices for the afflicted, and it was evident that many of the fattest dogs in town had been forbidden to play with me—a fact which pained my youthful sensibilities, and at one time came near driving me to become a pirate.

Looking back upon those days, I cannot but regret, at times, that by indirectly bringing my beloved parents to their death I was the author of misfortunes profoundly affecting my future.

One evening while passing my father's oil factory with the body of a foundling from my mother's studio I saw a constable who seemed to be closely watching my movements. Young as I was, I had learned that a constable's acts, of whatever apparent character, are prompted by the most reprehensible motives, and I avoided him by dodging into the oilery by a side door which happened to stand ajar. I locked it at once and was alone with my dead. My father had retired for the night. The only light in the place came from the furnace, which glowed a deep, rich crimson under one of the vats, casting ruddy reflections on the walls. Within the cauldron the oil still rolled in indolent ebullition, occasionally pushing to the surface a piece of dog. Seating myself to wait for the constable to go away, I held the naked body of the foundling in my lap and tenderly stroked its short, silken hair. Ah, how beautiful it was! Even at that early age I was passionately fond of children, and as I looked upon this cherub I could almost find it in my heart to wish that the small, red wound upon its breast—the work of my dear mother—had not been mortal.

It had been my custom to throw the babes into the river which Nature had thoughtfully provided for the purpose,[3] but that night I did not dare to leave the oilery for fear of the constable. "After all," I said to myself, "it cannot greatly matter if I put it into this cauldron. My father will never know the bones from those of a puppy, and the few deaths which may result from administering another kind of oil for the incomparable *ol. can.* are not important in a population which increases so rapidly." In short, I took the first step in crime and brought myself untold sorrow by casting the babe into the cauldron.

The next day, somewhat to my surprise, my father, rubbing his hands with satisfaction, informed me and my mother that he had obtained the finest quality of oil that was ever seen; that the physicians to whom he had shown samples had so pronounced it. He added that he had no knowledge as to how the result was obtained; the dogs had been treated in all respects as usual, and were of an ordinary breed. I deemed it my duty to explain—which I did, though palsied would have been my tongue if I could have foreseen the consequences. Bewailing their previous ignorance of the advantages of combining their industries, my parents at once took measures to repair the error. My mother removed her studio to a wing of the factory building and my duties in connection with the business ceased; I was no longer required to dispose of the bodies of the small superfluous, and there was no need of alluring dogs to their doom, but my father discarded them altogether, though they still had an honorable place in the name of the oil. So suddenly thrown into idleness, I might naturally have been expected to become vicious and dissolute, but I did not. The holy influence of my dear mother was ever about me to protect me from the temptations which beset youth, and my father was a deacon in a church. Alas, that through my fault these estimable persons should have come to so bad an end!

Finding a double profit in her business, my mother now devoted herself to it with a new assiduity. She removed not only superfluous and unwelcome babes to order, but went out into the highways and byways, gathering in children of a larger growth, and even such adults as she could entice to the oilery. My father, too, enamored of the superior quality of oil produced, purveyed for his vats with diligence and zeal. The conversion of their neighbors into dog-oil became, in short, the one passion of their lives—an absorbing and overwhelming greed took possession of their souls and served them in place of a hope in Heaven—by which, also, they were inspired.

OIL OF DOG

So enterprising had they now become that a public meeting was held and resolutions passed severely censuring them. It was intimated by the chairman that any further raids upon the population would be met in a spirit of hostility. My poor parents left the meeting broken-hearted, desperate and, I believe, not altogether sane. Anyhow, I deemed it prudent not to enter the oilery with them that night, but slept outside in a stable.

At about midnight some mysterious impulse caused me to rise and peer through a window into the furnace-room, where I knew my father now slept. The fires were burning as brightly as if the following day's harvest had been expected to be abundant. One of the large cauldrons was slowly "walloping" with a mysterious appearance to self-restraint, as if it bided its time to put forth its full energy. My father was not in bed; he had risen in his nightclothes and was preparing a noose in a strong cord. From the looks which he cast at the door of my mother's bedroom I knew too well the purpose that he had in mind. Speechless and motionless with terror, I could do nothing in prevention or warning. Suddenly the door of my mother's apartment was opened, noiselessly, and the two confronted each other, both apparently surprised. The lady, also, was in her nightclothes, and she held in her right hand the tool of her trade, a long, narrow-bladed dagger.

She, too, had been unable to deny herself the last profit which the unfriendly action of the citizens and my absence had left her. For one instant they looked into each other's blazing eyes and then sprang together with indescribable fury. Round and round the room they struggled, the man cursing, the woman shrieking, both fighting like demons—she to strike him with the dagger, he to strangle her with his great bare hands. I know not how long I had the unhappiness to observe this disagreeable instance of domestic infelicity, but at last, after a more than usually vigorous struggle, the combatants suddenly moved apart.

My father's breast and my mother's weapon showed evidences of contact. For another instant they glared at each other in the most unamiable way; then my poor, wounded father, feeling the hand of death upon him, leaped forward, unmindful of resistance, grasped my dear mother in his arms, dragged her to the side of the boiling cauldron, collected all his failing energies and sprang in with her! In a moment, both had disappeared and were adding their oil to that of the committee of citizens who had called the day before with an invitation to the public meeting.

Convinced that these unhappy events closed to me every avenue to an honorable career in that town, I removed to the famous city of Otumwee,[4] where these memoirs are written with a heart full of remorse for a heedless act entailing so dismal a commercial disaster.

OT (11 Oct. 1890): 1 (as "The Oil of Dog: A Tragic Episode in the Life of an Eminent Educator"); *CW* 8.163–70.

NOTES

One of the four "Parenticide Club" tales. For an analysis of this and the other stories in the series, see *PA* 141–51.

1. In the original appearance, the narrator's name was Joram Turmore (see "The Widower Turmore" [p. 758]).

2. Not *oleum cannabis* (oil of hemp; a greenish oil used as a demulcent and protective), but *oleum canis*.

3. This is one of AB's favorite satirical barbs against those who asserted the argument from design, as in *DD*: "ADAM'S APPLE, *n.* A protuberance on the throat of a man, thoughtfully provided by Nature to keep the rope in place."

4. Cf. the use of Otamwee in "Kingdom of Tortirra" (see p. 576 note 4).

THE WIDOWER TURMORE

The circumstances under which Joram Turmore[1] became a widower have never been popularly understood. I know them, naturally, for I am Joram Turmore; and my wife, the late Elizabeth Mary Turmore, is by no means ignorant of them; but although she doubtless relates them, yet they remain a secret, for not a soul has ever believed her.

When I married Elizabeth Mary Johnin she was very wealthy, otherwise I could hardly have afforded to marry, for I had not a cent, and Heaven had not put into my heart any intention to earn one. I held the Professorship of Cats in the University of Graymaulkin,[2] and scholastic pursuits had unfitted me for the heat and burden of business or labor. Moreover, I could not forget that I was a Turmore—a member of a family whose motto from the time of William of Normandy has been *Laborare est errare*.[3] The only known infraction of the sacred family tradition occurred when Sir Aldebaran Turmore de Peters-Turmore, an illustrious master burglar of the seventeenth century, personally assisted at a difficult operation undertaken by some of his workmen. That blot upon our escutcheon cannot be contemplated without the most poignant mortification.

My incumbency of the Chair of Cats in the Graymaulkin University had not, of course, been marked by any instance of mean industry. There had never, at any one time, been more than two students of the Noble Science, and by merely repeating the manuscript lectures of my predecessor, which I had found among his effects (he died at sea on his way to Malta)[4] I could sufficiently sate their famine for knowledge without really earning even the distinction which served in place of salary.

Naturally, under the straitened circumstances, I regarded Elizabeth Mary as a kind of special Providence. She unwisely refused to share her fortune with me, but for that I cared nothing; for, although by the laws of that country (as is well known) a wife has control of her separate property during her life, it passes to the husband at her death; nor can she dispose of it otherwise by will. The mortality among wives is considerable, but not excessive.

Having married Elizabeth Mary and, as it were, ennobled her by making her a Turmore, I felt that the manner of her death ought, in some sense, to match her social distinction. If I should remove her by any of the ordinary marital methods I should incur a just reproach, as one destitute of a proper family pride. Yet I could not hit upon a suitable plan.

In this emergency I decided to consult the Turmore archives, a priceless collection of documents, comprising the records of the family from the time of its founder in the seventh century of our era. I knew that among these sacred muniments I should find detailed accounts of all the principal murders committed by my sainted ancestors for forty generations. From that mass of papers I could hardly fail to derive the most valuable suggestions.

The collection contained also most interesting relics. There were patents of nobility granted to my forefathers for daring and ingenious removals of pretenders to thrones, or occupants of them; stars, crosses and other decorations attesting services of the most secret and unmentionable character; miscellaneous gifts from the world's greatest conspirators, representing an intrinsic money value beyond computation. There were robes, jewels, swords of honor and every kind of "testimonials of esteem"; a king's skull fashioned into a wine cup; the title deeds to vast estates, long alienated by confiscation, sale or abandonment; an illuminated breviary that had belonged to Sir Aldebaran Turmore de Peters-Turmore of accursed memory; embalmed ears of several of the family's most renowned enemies; the small intestine of a certain unworthy Italian statesman inimical to Turmores, which, twisted into a jumping rope, had served the youth of six kindred generations—mementoes and souvenirs precious beyond the appraisals of imagination, but by the sacred mandates of tradition and sentiment forever inalienable by sale or gift.

As the head of the family, I was custodian of all these priceless heirlooms, and for their safe keeping had constructed in the basement of my dwelling a strong-room of massive masonry, whose solid stone walls and single iron door could defy alike the earthquake's shock, the tireless assaults of Time and Cupidity's unholy hand.

To this thesaurus of the soul, redolent of sentiment and tenderness, and rich in suggestions of crime, I now repaired for hints upon assassination. To my unspeakable astonishment and grief I found it empty! Every shelf, every chest, every coffer had been rifled. Of that unique and incomparable collection not a vestige remained! Yet I proved that until I had myself unlocked the massive metal door, not a bolt nor bar had been disturbed; the seals upon the lock had been intact.

I passed the night in alternate lamentation and research, equally fruitless; the mystery was impenetrable to conjecture, the pain invincible to balm. But never once throughout that dreadful night did my firm spirit relinquish its high design against

THE WIDOWER TURMORE

Elizabeth Mary, and daybreak found me more resolute than before to harvest the fruits of my marriage. My great loss seemed but to bring me into nearer spiritual relations with my dead ancestors, and to lay upon me a new and more inevitable obedience to the suasion that spoke in every globule of my blood.

My plan of action was soon formed, and procuring a stout cord I entered my wife's bedroom, finding her, as I expected, in a sound sleep. Before she was awake, I had her bound fast, hand and foot. She was greatly surprised and pained, but heedless of her remonstrances, delivered in a high key, I carried her into the now rifled strong-room, which I had never suffered her to enter, and of whose treasures I had not apprised her. Seating her, still bound, in an angle of the wall, I passed the next two days and nights in conveying bricks and mortar to the spot, and on the morning of the third day had her securely walled in, from floor to ceiling. All this time I gave no further heed to her pleas for mercy than (on her assurance of non-resistance, which I am bound to say she honorably observed) to grant her the freedom of her limbs. The space allowed her was about four feet by six. As I inserted the last bricks of the top course, in contact with the ceiling of the strong-room, she bade me farewell with what I deemed the composure of despair, and I rested from my work, feeling that I had faithfully observed the traditions of an ancient and illustrious family. My only bitter reflection, so far as my own conduct was concerned, came of the consciousness that in the performance of my design I had labored; but this no living soul would ever know.

After a night's rest I went to the Judge of the Court of Successions and Inheritances and made a true and sworn relation of all that I had done—except that I ascribed to a servant the manual labor of building the wall. His honor appointed a court commissioner, who made a careful examination of the work, and upon his report Elizabeth Mary Turmore was, at the end of a week, formally pronounced dead. By due process of law I was put into possession of her estate, and although this was not by hundreds of thousands of dollars as valuable as my lost treasures, it raised me from poverty to affluence and brought me the respect of the great and good.

Some six months after these events strange rumors reached me that the ghost of my deceased wife had been seen in several places about the country, but always at a considerable distance from Graymaulkin. These rumors, which I was unable to trace to any authentic source, differed widely in many particulars, but were alike in ascribing to the apparition a certain high degree of apparent worldly prosperity combined with an audacity most uncommon in ghosts. Not only was the spirit attired in most costly raiment, but it walked at noonday, and even drove! I was inexpressibly annoyed by these reports, and thinking there might be something more than superstition in the popular belief that only the spirits of the unburied dead still walk the earth, I took some workmen equipped with picks and crowbars into the now long unentered strong-room, and ordered them to demolish the brick wall that I had built about the partner of my joys. I was resolved to give the body of Elizabeth Mary such burial as I

THE WIDOWER TURMORE

thought her immortal part might be willing to accept as an equivalent to the privilege of ranging at will among the haunts of the living.

In a few minutes we had broken down the wall and, thrusting a lamp through the breach, I looked in. Nothing! Not a bone, not a lock of hair, not a shred of clothing—the narrow space which, upon my affidavit, had been legally declared to hold all that was mortal of the late Mrs. Turmore was absolutely empty! This amazing disclosure, coming upon a mind already overwrought with too much of mystery and excitement, was more than I could bear. I shrieked aloud and fell in a fit. For months afterward I lay between life and death, fevered and delirious; nor did I recover until my physician had had the providence to take a case of valuable jewels from my safe and leave the country.

The next summer I had occasion to visit my wine cellar, in one corner of which I had built the now long disused strong-room. In moving a cask of Madeira I struck it with considerable force against the partition wall, and was surprised to observe that it displaced two large square stones forming a part of the wall.

Applying my hands to these, I easily pushed them out entirely, and looking through saw that they had fallen into the niche in which I had immured my lamented wife; facing the opening which their fall left, and at a distance of four feet, was the brickwork which my own hands had made for that unfortunate gentlewoman's restraint. At this significant revelation I began a search of the wine cellar. Behind a row of casks I found four historically interesting but intrinsically valueless objects:

First, the mildewed remains of a ducal robe of state (Florentine) of the eleventh century; second, an illuminated vellum breviary with the name of Sir Aldebaran Turmore de Peters-Turmore inscribed in colors on the title page; third, a human skull fashioned into a drinking cup and deeply stained with wine; fourth, the iron cross of a Knight Commander of the Imperial Austrian Order of Assassins by Poison.

That was all—not an object having commercial value, no papers—nothing. But this was enough to clear up the mystery of the strong-room. My wife had early divined the existence and purpose of that apartment, and with the skill amounting to genius had effected an entrance by loosening the two stones in the wall.

Through that opening she had at several times abstracted the entire collection, which doubtless she had succeeded in converting into coin of the realm. When with an unconscious justice which deprives me of all satisfaction in the memory I decided to build her into the wall, by some malign fatality I selected that part of it in which were these movable stones, and doubtless before I had fairly finished my bricklaying she had removed them and, slipping through into the wine cellar, replaced them as they were originally laid. From the cellar she had easily escaped unobserved, to enjoy her infamous gains in distant parts. I have endeavored to procure a warrant, but the Lord High Baron of the Court of Indictment and Conviction[5] reminds me that she is legally dead, and says my only course is to go before the Master in Cadavery and move for a writ of disinterment and constructive revival. So it looks as if I must suffer without redress this great wrong at the hands of a woman devoid alike of principle and shame.

THE WIDOWER TURMORE

Wa 6, no. 36 (10 Jan. 1891): 13–14 (with subtitle: "A Chapter from the History of an Illustrious Family"); *CSTB* 221–29; *CW* **8.41–51**.

NOTES

AB was not only an admiring student of Poe when it was not fashionable to be such but he was also generations ahead of his time in his grasp of Poe's artistry—quite possibly the first significant American author to arrive at a just appreciation of it. It is evident in this story, which has a number of easily recognizable similarities to Poe's "The Cask of Amontillado" (1846), that AB, apart from deliberately using some of the plot of the earlier story, understood and was using Poe's technique of the unreliable narrator. "The Widower Turmore" establishes a clear bridge between Poe and AB's "Parenticide Club" tales, which series it also resembles and can now for the first time be seen as having been inspired by Poe. Until academics realized that Poe did not identify with his disturbed narrators but was instead satirizing their warped values, he was widely regarded as talented but perverse in his character. For the same reason, AB has suffered the same misunderstanding. Turmore in this story is patently an object of AB's satire.

1. The original name of the protagonist of "Oil of Dog" was Joram Turmore (see "Selected Textual Variants").
2. This title had been created in the original version of "Oil of Dog" (see "Selected Textual Variants"). Note also that the original title of "A Revolt of the Gods" was "The Ancient City of Grimaulquin."
3. "To labor is to err"—an ironic variation of the motto of the Benedictine order, *orare est laborare, laborare est orare* ("To pray is to labor, to labor is to pray").
4. I.e., Captain Doble of "A Cargo of Cat" (p. 427).
5. Cf. the Court of Commitment and Conviction in "Burbank's Crime" (p. 751).

HAÏTA THE SHEPHERD

In the heart of Haïta the illusions of youth had not been supplanted by those of age and experience. His thoughts were pure and pleasant, for his life was simple and his soul devoid of ambition. He rose with the sun and went forth to pray at the shrine of Hastur,[1] the god of shepherds, who heard and was pleased. After performance of this pious rite Haïta unbarred the gate of the fold and with a cheerful mind drove his flock afield, eating his morning meal of curds and oat cake as he went, occasionally pausing to add a few berries, cold with dew, or to drink of the waters that came away from the hills to join the stream in the middle of the valley and be borne along with it, he knew not whither.

During the long summer day, as his sheep cropped the good grass which the gods had made to grow for them, or lay with their forelegs doubled under their breasts and chewed the cud, Haïta, reclining in the shadow of a tree, or sitting upon a rock, played so sweet music upon his reed pipe that sometimes from the corner of his eye he got accidental glimpses of the minor sylvan deities, leaning forward out of the copse to hear; but if he looked at them directly they vanished. From this—for he must be thinking if he would not turn into one of his own sheep—he drew the solemn inference that happiness may come if not sought, but if looked for will never be seen; for next to the favor of Hastur, who never disclosed himself, Haïta most valued the friendly interest of his neighbors, the shy immortals of the wood and stream. At nightfall he drove his flock back to the fold, saw that the gate was secure and retired to his cave for refreshment and for dreams.

So passed his life, one day like another, save when the storms uttered the wrath of an offended god. Then Haïta cowered in his cave, his face hidden in his hands, and prayed that he alone might be punished for his sins and the world saved from destruction. Sometimes when there was a great rain, and the stream came out of its banks, compelling him to urge his terrified flock to the uplands, he interceded for the people in the cities which he had been told lay in the plain beyond the two blue hills forming the gateway of his valley.

"It is kind of thee, O Hastur," so he prayed, "to give me mountains so near to my dwelling and my fold that I and my sheep can escape the angry torrents; but the rest of the world thou must thyself deliver in some way that I know not of, or I will no longer worship thee."

And Hastur, knowing that Haïta was a youth who kept his word, spared the cities and turned the waters into the sea.

So he had lived since he could remember. He could not rightly conceive any other mode of existence. The holy hermit who dwelt at the head of the valley, a full hour's journey away, from whom he had heard the tale of the great cities where dwelt people—poor souls!—who had no sheep, gave him no knowledge of that early time, when, so he reasoned, he must have been small and helpless like a lamb.

It was through thinking on these mysteries and marvels, and on that horrible change to silence and decay which he felt sure must some time come to him, as he had seen it come to so many of his flock—as it came to all living things except the birds—that Haïta first became conscious how miserable and hopeless was his lot.

"It is necessary," he said, "that I know whence and how I came; for how can one perform his duties unless able to judge what they are by the way in which he was intrusted with them? And what contentment can I have when I know not how long it is going to last? Perhaps before another sun I may be changed, and then what will become of the sheep? What, indeed, will have become of me?"

Pondering these things Haïta became melancholy and morose. He no longer spoke cheerfully to his flock, nor ran with alacrity to the shrine of Hastur. In every breeze he heard whispers of malign deities whose existence he now first observed. Every cloud was a portent signifying disaster, and the darkness was full of terrors. His reed pipe when applied to his lips gave out no melody, but a dismal wail; the sylvan and riparian intelligences no longer thronged the thicket-side to listen, but fled from the sound, as he knew by the stirred leaves and bent flowers. He relaxed his vigilance and many of his sheep strayed away into the hills and were lost. Those that remained became lean and ill for lack of good pasturage, for he would not seek it for them, but conducted them day after day to the same spot, through mere abstraction, while puzzling about life and death—of immortality he knew not.

One day while indulging in the gloomiest reflections he suddenly sprang from the rock upon which he sat, and with a determined gesture of the right hand exclaimed: "I will no longer be a suppliant for knowledge which the gods withhold. Let them look to it that they do me no wrong. I will do my duty as best I can and if I err upon their own heads be it!"

Suddenly, as he spoke, a great brightness fell about him, causing him to look upward, thinking the sun had burst through a rift in the clouds; but there were no clouds. No more than an arm's length away stood a beautiful maiden. So beautiful she was that the flowers about her feet folded their petals in despair and bent their heads in token of submission; so sweet her look that the humming birds thronged her eyes, thrusting their thirsty bills almost into them, and the wild bees were about her lips. And such was her brightness that the shadows of all objects lay divergent from her feet, turning as she moved.

Haïta was entranced. Rising, he knelt before her in adoration, and she laid her hand upon his head.

"Come," she said in a voice that had the music of all the bells of his flock—"come, thou art not to worship me, who am no goddess, but if thou art truthful and dutiful I will abide with thee."

Haïta seized her hand, and stammering his joy and gratitude arose, and hand in hand they stood and smiled into each other's eyes. He gazed on her with reverence and rapture. He said: "I pray thee, lovely maid, tell me thy name and whence and why thou comest."

At this she laid a warning finger on her lip and began to withdraw. Her beauty underwent a visible alteration that made him shudder, he knew not why, for still she was beautiful. The landscape was darkened by a giant shadow sweeping across the valley with the speed of a vulture. In the obscurity the maiden's figure grew dim and indistinct and her voice seemed to come from a distance, as she said, in a tone of sorrowful reproach: "Presumptuous and ungrateful youth! must I then so soon leave thee? Would nothing do but thou must at once break the eternal compact?"

Inexpressibly grieved, Haïta fell upon his knees and implored her to remain—rose and sought her in the deepening darkness—ran in circles, calling to her aloud, but all in vain. She was no longer visible, but out of the gloom he heard her voice saying: "Nay, thou shalt not have me by seeking. Go to thy duty, faithless shepherd, or we shall never meet again."

Night had fallen; the wolves were howling in the hills and the terrified sheep crowding about Haïta's feet. In the demands of the hour he forgot his disappointment, drove his sheep to the fold and repairing to the place of worship poured out his heart in gratitude to Hastur for permitting him to save his flock, then retired to his cave and slept.

When Haïta awoke the sun was high and shone in at the cave, illuminating it with a great glory. And there, beside him, sat the maiden. She smiled upon him with a smile that seemed the visible music of his pipe of reeds. He dared not speak, fearing to offend her as before, for he knew not what he could venture to say.

"Because," she said, "thou didst thy duty by the flock, and didst not forget to thank Hastur for staying the wolves of the night, I am come to thee again. Wilt thou have me for a companion?"

"Who would not have thee forever?" replied Haïta. "Oh! never again leave me until—until I—change and become silent and motionless."

Haïta had no word for death.

HAÏTA THE SHEPHERD

"I wish, indeed," he continued, "that thou wert of my own sex, that we might wrestle and run races and so never tire of being together."

At these words the maiden arose and passed out of the cave, and Haïta, springing from his couch of fragrant boughs to overtake and detain her, observed to his astonishment that the rain was falling and the stream in the middle of the valley had come out of its banks. The sheep were bleating in terror, for the rising waters had invaded their fold. And there was danger for the unknown cities of the distant plain.

It was many days before Haïta saw the maiden again. One day he was returning from the head of the valley, where he had gone with ewe's milk and oat cake and berries for the holy hermit, who was too old and feeble to provide himself with food.

"Poor old man!" he said aloud, as he trudged along homeward. "I will return to-morrow and bear him on my back to my own dwelling, where I can care for him. Doubtless it is for this that Hastur has reared me all these many years, and gives me health and strength."

As he spoke, the maiden, clad in glittering garments, met him in the path with a smile that took away his breath.

"I am come again," she said, "to dwell with thee if thou wilt now have me, for none else will. Thou mayest have learned wisdom, and art willing to take me as I am, nor care to know."

Haïta threw himself at her feet. "Beautiful being," he cried, "if thou wilt but deign to accept all the devotion of my heart and soul—after Hastur be served—it is thine forever. But, alas! thou art capricious and wayward. Before to-morrow's sun I may lose thee again. Promise, I beseech thee, that however in my ignorance I may offend, thou wilt forgive and remain always with me."

Scarcely had he finished speaking when a troop of bears came out of the hills, racing toward him with crimson mouths and fiery eyes. The maiden again vanished, and he turned and fled for his life. Nor did he stop until he was in the cot of the holy hermit, whence he had set out. Hastily barring the door against the bears he cast himself upon the ground and wept.

"My son," said the hermit from his couch of straw, freshly gathered that morning by Haïta's hands, "it is not like thee to weep for bears—tell me what sorrow hath befallen thee, that age may minister to the hurts of youth with such balms as it hath of its wisdom."

Haïta told him all: how thrice he had met the radiant maid, and thrice she had left him forlorn. He related minutely all that had passed between them, omitting no word of what had been said.

When he had ended, the holy hermit was a moment silent, then said: "My son, I have attended to thy story, and I know the maiden. I have myself seen her, as have many. Know, then, that her name, which she would not even permit thee to inquire, is Happiness. Thou saidst the truth to her, that she is capricious for she imposeth conditions that man can not fulfill, and delinquency is punished by desertion. She cometh

HAÏTA THE SHEPHERD

only when unsought, and will not be questioned. One manifestation of curiosity, one sign of doubt, one expression of misgiving, and she is away! How long didst thou have her at any time before she fled?"

"Only a single instant," answered Haïta, blushing with shame at the confession. "Each time I drove her away in one moment."

"Unfortunate youth!" said the holy hermit, "but for thine indiscretion thou mightst have had her for two."

Wa 6, no. 38 (24 Jan. 1891): 11; *TSC* 277–87; *IML* 314–24; **CW** 3.297–307.

NOTES

No shortcoming of philosophy, especially that of the Stoicism to which he was otherwise attracted, was for AB more serious than its inability to promote happiness. "Haïta the Shepherd" reflects a mature AB who had come to the conclusion that happiness was one of life's greatest goods, so great, in fact, that even if it was based on illusion, it was more to be prized than wisdom.

1. Robert W. Chambers (1865–1933) borrowed Hastur in several stories in *The King in Yellow* (New York: F. Tennyson Neely, 1895), along with other terms from AB's fantasy tales; but in Chambers, Hastur is either a heavenly body ("Then from Carcosa, the Hyades, Hastur, and Aldebaran . . .": "The Repairer of Reputations") or a minor human character (see "The Demoiselle d'Ys"). H. P. Lovecraft (1890–1937) also mentions Hastur in a single story, "The Whisperer in Darkness" (1930), probably borrowing it from Chambers rather than from AB.

PARKER ADDERSON, PHILOSOPHER

"Prisoner, what is your name?"

"As I am to lose it at daylight to-morrow morning it is hardly worth while concealing it. Parker Adderson."

"Your rank?"

"A somewhat humble one; commissioned officers are too precious to be risked in the perilous business of a spy. I am a sergeant."

"Of what regiment?"

"You must excuse me; my answer might, for anything I know, give you an idea of whose forces are in your front. Such knowledge as that is what I came into your lines to obtain, not to impart."

"You are not without wit."

"If you have the patience to wait you will find me dull enough to-morrow."

"How do you know that you are to die to-morrow morning?"

"Among spies captured by night that is the custom. It is one of the nice observances of the profession."

The general so far laid aside the dignity appropriate to a Confederate officer of high rank and wide renown as to smile. But no one in his power and out of his favor would have drawn any happy augury from that outward and visible sign of approval. It was neither genial nor infectious; it did not communicate itself to the other persons exposed to it—the caught spy who had provoked it and the armed guard who had brought him into the tent and now stood a little apart, watching his prisoner in the yellow candle-light. It was no part of that warrior's duty to smile; he had been detailed for another purpose. The conversation was resumed; it was in character a trial for a capital offense.

"You admit, then, that you are a spy—that you came into my camp, disguised as you are in the uniform of a Confederate soldier, to obtain information secretly regarding the numbers and disposition of my troops."

"Regarding, particularly, their numbers. Their disposition I already knew. It is morose."

The general brightened again; the guard, with a severer sense of his responsibility, accentuated the austerity of his expression and stood a trifle more erect than before. Twirling his gray slouch hat round and round upon his forefinger, the spy took a leisurely survey of his surroundings. They were simple enough. The tent was a common "wall tent," about eight feet by ten in dimensions, lighted by a single tallow candle stuck into the haft of a bayonet, which was itself stuck into a pine table at which the general sat, now busily writing and apparently forgetful of his unwilling guest. An old rag carpet covered the earthen floor; an older leather trunk, a second chair and a roll of blankets were about all else that the tent contained; in General Clavering's command Confederate simplicity and penury of "pomp and circumstance" had attained their highest development. On a large nail driven into the tent pole at the entrance was suspended a sword-belt supporting a long saber, a pistol in its holster and, absurdly enough, a bowie-knife. Of that most unmilitary weapon it was the general's habit to explain that it was a souvenir of the peaceful days when he was a civilian.

It was a stormy night. The rain cascaded upon the canvas in torrents, with the dull, drum-like sound familiar to dwellers in tents. As the whooping blasts charged upon it the frail structure shook and swayed and strained at its confining stakes and ropes.

The general finished writing, folded the half-sheet of paper and spoke to the soldier guarding Adderson: "Here, Tassman, take that to the adjutant-general; then return."

"And the prisoner, General?" said the soldier, saluting, with an inquiring glance in the direction of that unfortunate.

"Do as I said," replied the officer, curtly.

The soldier took the note and ducked himself out of the tent. General Clavering turned his handsome face toward the Federal spy, looked him in the eyes, not unkindly, and said: "It is a bad night, my man."

"For me, yes."

"Do you guess what I have written?"

"Something worth reading, I dare say. And—perhaps it is my vanity—I venture to suppose that I am mentioned in it."

"Yes; it is a memorandum for an order to be read to the troops at *reveille* concerning your execution. Also some notes for the guidance of the provost-marshal in arranging the details of that event."

"I hope, General, the spectacle will be intelligently arranged, for I shall attend it myself."

"Have you any arrangements of your own that you wish to make? Do you wish to see a chaplain, for example?"

"I could hardly secure a longer rest for myself by depriving him of some of his."

"Good God, man! do you mean to go to your death with nothing but jokes upon your lips? Do you know that this is a serious matter?"

PARKER ADDERSON, PHILOSOPHER

"How can I know that? I have never been dead in all my life. I have heard that death is a serious matter, but never from any of those who have experienced it."

The general was silent for a moment; the man interested, perhaps amused him—a type not previously encountered.

"Death," he said, "is at least a loss—a loss of such happiness as we have, and of opportunities for more."

"A loss of which we shall never be conscious can be borne with composure and therefore expected without apprehension.[1] You must have observed, General, that of all the dead men with whom it is your soldierly pleasure to strew your path none shows signs of regret."

"If the being dead is not a regrettable condition, yet the becoming so—the act of dying—appears to be distinctly disagreeable to one who has not lost the power to feel."

"Pain is disagreeable, no doubt. I never suffer it without more or less discomfort. But he who lives longest is most exposed to it. What you call dying is simply the last pain—there is really no such thing as dying. Suppose, for illustration, that I attempt to escape. You lift the revolver that you are courteously concealing in your lap, and—"

The general blushed like a girl, then laughed softly, disclosing his brilliant teeth, made a slight inclination of his handsome head and said nothing. The spy continued: "You fire, and I have in my stomach what I did not swallow. I fall, but am not dead. After a half-hour of agony I am dead. But at any given instant of that half-hour I was either alive or dead. There is no transition period.[2]

"When I am hanged to-morrow morning it will be quite the same; while conscious I shall be living; when dead, unconscious. Nature appears to have ordered the matter quite in my interest—the way that I should have ordered it myself. It is so simple," he added with a smile, "that it seems hardly worth while to be hanged at all."

At the finish of his remarks there was a long silence. The general sat impassive, looking into the man's face, but apparently not attentive to what had been said. It was as if his eyes had mounted guard over the prisoner while his mind concerned itself with other matters. Presently he drew a long, deep breath, shuddered, as one awakened from a dreadful dream, and exclaimed almost inaudibly: "Death is horrible!"—this man of death.

"It was horrible to our savage ancestors," said the spy, gravely, "because they had not enough intelligence to dissociate the idea of consciousness from the idea of the physical forms in which it is manifested—as an even lower order of intelligence, that of the monkey, for example, may be unable to imagine a house without inhabitants, and seeing a ruined hut fancies a suffering occupant. To us it is horrible because we have inherited the tendency to think it so, accounting for the notion by wild and fanciful theories of another world—as names of places give rise to legends explaining them and reasonless conduct to philosophies in justification. You can hang me, General, but there your power of evil ends; you cannot condemn me to Heaven."

PARKER ADDERSON, PHILOSOPHER

The general appeared not to have heard; the spy's talk had merely turned his thoughts into an unfamiliar channel, but there they pursued their will independently to conclusions of their own. The storm had ceased, and something of the solemn spirit of the night had imparted itself to his reflections, giving them the sombre tinge of a supernatural dread. Perhaps there was an element of prescience in it. "I should not like to die," he said—"not to-night."

He was interrupted—if, indeed, he had intended to speak further—by the entrance of an officer of his staff, Captain Hasterlick, the provost-marshal. This recalled him to himself; the absent look passed away from his face.

"Captain," he said, acknowledging the officer's salute, "this man is a Yankee spy captured inside our lines with incriminating papers on him. He has confessed. How is the weather?"

"The storm is over, sir, and the moon shining."

"Good; take a file of men, conduct him at once to the parade ground and shoot him."

A sharp cry broke from the spy's lips. He threw himself forward, thrust out his neck, expanded his eyes, clenched his hands.

"Good God!" he cried hoarsely, almost inarticulately; "you do not mean that! You forget—I am not to die until morning."

"I have said nothing of morning," replied the general, coldly; "that was an assumption of your own. You die now."

"But, General, I beg—I implore you to remember; I am to hang! It will take some time to erect the gallows—two hours—an hour. Spies are hanged; I have rights under military law. For Heaven's sake, General, consider how short—"

"Captain, observe my directions."

The officer drew his sword and fixing his eyes upon the prisoner pointed silently to the opening of the tent. The prisoner hesitated; the officer grasped him by the collar and pushed him gently forward. As he approached the tent pole the frantic man sprang to it and with cat-like agility seized the handle of the bowie-knife, plucked the weapon from the scabbard and thrusting the captain aside leaped upon the general with the fury of a madman, hurling him to the ground and falling headlong upon him as he lay. The table was overturned, the candle extinguished and they fought blindly in the darkness. The provost-marshal sprang to the assistance of his superior officer and was himself prostrated upon the struggling forms. Curses and inarticulate cries of rage and pain came from the welter of limbs and bodies; the tent came down upon them and beneath its hampering and enveloping folds the struggle went on. Private Tassman, returning from his errand and dimly conjecturing the situation, threw down his rifle and laying hold of the flouncing canvas at random vainly tried to drag it off the men under it; and the sentinel who paced up and down in front, not daring to leave his beat though the skies should fall, discharged his rifle. The report alarmed

PARKER ADDERSON, PHILOSOPHER

the camp; the drums beat the long roll and bugles sounded the assembly, bringing swarms of half-clad men into the moonlight, dressing as they ran, and falling into line at the sharp commands of their officers. This was well; being in line the men were under control; they stood at arms while the general's staff and the men of his escort brought order out of confusion by lifting off the fallen tent and pulling apart the breathless and bleeding actors in that strange contention.

Breathless, indeed, was one: the captain was dead; the handle of the bowie-knife, protruding from his throat, was pressed back beneath his chin until the end had caught in the angle of the jaw and the hand that delivered the blow had been unable to remove the weapon. In the dead man's hand was his sword, clenched with a grip that defied the strength of the living. Its blade was streaked with red to the hilt.

Lifted to his feet, the general sank back to the earth with a moan and fainted. Besides his bruises he had two sword-thrusts—one through the thigh, the other through the shoulder.

The spy had suffered the least damage. Apart from a broken right arm, his wounds were such only as might have been incurred in an ordinary combat with Nature's weapons. But he was dazed and seemed hardly to know what had occurred. He shrank away from those attending him, cowered upon the ground and uttered unintelligible remonstrances. His face, swollen by blows and stained with gouts of blood, nevertheless showed white beneath his disheveled hair—as white as that of a corpse.

"The man is not insane," said the surgeon, preparing bandages and replying to a question; "he is suffering from fright. Who and what is he?"

Private Tassman began to explain. It was the opportunity of his life; he omitted nothing that could in any way accentuate the importance of his own relation to the night's events. When he had finished his story and was ready to begin it again nobody gave him any attention.

The general had now recovered consciousness. He raised himself upon his elbow, looked about him and, seeing the spy crouching by a camp-fire, guarded, said simply:

"Take that man to the parade ground and shoot him."

"The general's mind wanders," said an officer standing near.

"His mind does *not* wander," the adjutant-general said. "I have a memorandum from him about this business; he had given that same order to Hasterlick"—with a motion of the hand toward the dead provost-marshal—"and, by God! it shall be executed."

Ten minutes later Sergeant Parker Adderson, of the Federal army, philosopher and wit, kneeling in the moonlight and begging incoherently for his life, was shot to death by twenty men. As the volley rang out upon the keen air of the midnight, General Clavering, lying white and still in the red glow of the camp-fire, opened his big blue eyes, looked pleasantly upon those about him and said: "How silent it all is!"

The surgeon looked at the adjutant-general, gravely and significantly. The patient's eyes slowly closed, and thus he lay for a few moments; then, his face suffused with a smile of ineffable sweetness, he said, faintly: "I suppose this must be death," and so passed away.

E (22 Feb. 1891): 11–12 (as "James Adderson, Philosopher and Wit"); TSC 151–63; *CW* **2.133–45**.

NOTES

Another story implicitly skeptical of philosophy, this one challenges both the Epicurean ideas identified in the notes below and the Stoicism of Epictetus: "What disturbs men is not events but their judgments on events. For instance, death is nothing dreadful, or else Socrates would have thought it so. No, the only dreadful thing about it is man's judgment that it is dreadful" (*Manual* 5, trans. P. E. Matheson; Oates, *The Stoic and Epicurean Philosophers,* 469). Ironically, in the course of the story, Parker Adderson and General Clavering switch beliefs. For Adderson, death does become something dreadful. But at the end General Clavering is not only not troubled by the imminence of death, he is not troubled by the transition to it, either. The story, therefore, seems skeptically to suggest that empiricism does not favor one theory over the other. This skepticism may well have been inspired by the seventeenth-century author La Rochefoucauld, of whose *Maxims* AB was fond. Item no. 21, in particular, reads: "Condemned men sometimes affect a steadfastness and indifference to death which is really only fear of looking death in the face; thus it can be said that this steadfastness and indifference do for their spirit what the bandage does for their eyes."

1. The sentiment is Epicurean. Cf. Epicurus' *Letter to Herodotus:* "Death is nothing to us. For all good and evil consists in sensation, but death is deprivation of sensation." Cyril Bailey, *Epicurus: The Extant Fragments* (Oxford: Clarendon Press, 1926), 85. Cf. also Lucretius, *De Rerum Natura*, 3.898–901: "'Unhappy man,' they cry, 'unhappily cheated by one treacherous day [the day of death] out of all the uncounted blessings of life!' But they do not go on to say: 'And now no repining for these lost joys will oppress you any more'" (trans. Ronald Latham). The thought is found in "The Golampians," revised as "An Interview with Gnarmag-Zote."

2. This idea is also derived from Epicurus: "So death, the most terrifying of ills, is nothing to us, since so long as we exist, death is not with us; but when death comes, then we do not exist." *Letter to Menoeceus,* in Bailey, *Epicurus,* 85. Cf. "The Golampians" and "An Interview with Gnarmag-Zote."

A LADY FROM REDHORSE

I find myself more and more interested in him. It is not, I am sure, his—do you know any good noun corresponding to the adjective "handsome"? One does not like to say "beauty" when speaking of a man. He is beautiful enough, Heaven knows; I should not even care to trust you with him—faithfulest of all possible wives that you are—when he looks his best, as he always does. Nor do I think the fascination of his manner has much to do with it. You recollect that the charm of art inheres in that which is undefinable, and to you and me, my dear Irene, I fancy there is rather less of that in the branch of art under consideration than to girls in their first season. I fancy I know how my fine gentleman produces many of his effects and could perhaps give him a pointer on heightening them. Nevertheless, his manner is something truly delightful. I suppose what interests me chiefly is the man's brains. His conversation is the best I have ever heard and altogether unlike any one else's. He seems to know everything, as indeed he ought, for he has been everywhere, read everything, seen all there is to see—sometimes I think rather more than is good for him—and had acquaintance with the *queerest* people. And then his voice—Irene, when I hear it I actually feel as if I ought to have paid at the door, though of course it is my own door.

JULY 3.

I fear my remarks about Dr. Barritz must have been, being thoughtless, very silly, or you would not have written of him with such levity, not to say disrespect. Believe me, dearest, he has more dignity and seriousness (of the kind, I mean, which is not inconsistent with a manner sometimes playful and always charming) than any of the men that you and I ever met. And young Raynor—you knew Raynor at Monterey— tells me that the men all like him and that he is treated with something like deference everywhere. There is a mystery, too—something about his connection with the Blavatsky people in Northern India.[2] Raynor either would not or could not tell me the particulars. I infer that Dr. Barritz is thought—don't you dare to laugh!—a magician. Could anything be finer than that? An ordinary mystery is not, of course, so good as a scandal, but when it relates to dark and dreadful practices—to the exercise of unearthly powers—could anything be more piquant? It explains, too, the singular influence the man has upon me. It is the undefinable in his art—black art. Seriously, dear, I quite tremble when he looks me full in the eyes with those unfathomable orbs of his, which I have already vainly attempted to describe to you. How dreadful if he has the power to make one fall in love! Do you know if the Blavatsky crowd have that power—outside of Sepoy?[3]

JULY 16.

The strangest thing! Last evening while Auntie was attending one of the hotel hops (I hate them) Dr. Barritz called. It was scandalously late—I actually believe that he had talked with Auntie in the ballroom and learned from her that I was alone. I had been all the evening contriving how to worm out of him the truth about his connection with the Thugs[4] in Sepoy, and all of that black business, but the moment he fixed his eyes on me (for I admitted him, I'm ashamed to say) I was helpless. I trembled, I blushed, I—O Irene, Irene, I love the man beyond expression and you know how it is yourself.

Fancy! I, an ugly duckling from Redhorse—daughter (they say) of old Calamity Jim—certainly his heiress, with no living relation but an absurd old aunt who spoils me a thousand and fifty ways—absolutely destitute of everything but a million dollars and a hope in Paris,—I daring to love a god like him! My dear, if I had you here I could tear your hair out with mortification.

I am convinced that he is aware of my feeling, for he stayed but a few moments, said nothing but what another man might have said half as well, and pretending that he had an engagement went away. I learned to-day (a little bird told me—the bell-bird) that he went straight to bed. How does that strike you as evidence of exemplary habits?

JULY 17.

That little wretch, Raynor, called yesterday and his babble set me almost wild. He never runs down—that is to say, when he exterminates a score of reputations, more or less, he does not pause between one reputation and the next. (By the way, he inquired about you, and his manifestations of interest in you had, I confess, a good deal of *vraisemblance*.) Mr. Raynor observes no game laws; like Death (which he would inflict if slander were fatal) he has all seasons for his own.[5] But I like him, for we knew each other at Redhorse when we were young. He was known in those days as "Giggles," and I—O Irene, can you ever forgive me?—I was called "Gunny." God knows why;

A LADY FROM REDHORSE

perhaps in allusion to the material of my pinafores;[6] perhaps because the name is in allit-
eration with "Giggles," for Gig and I were inseparable playmates, and the miners may
have thought it a delicate civility to recognize some kind of a relationship between us.

Later, we took in a third—another of Adversity's brood, who, like Garrick[7] between Tragedy and Comedy, had a chronic inability to adjudicate the rival claims of
Frost and Famine. Between him and misery there was seldom anything more than a
single suspender and the hope of a meal which would at the same time support life and
make it insupportable. He literally picked up a precarious living for himself and an aged
mother by "chloriding the dumps," that is to say, the miners permitted him to search the
heaps of waste rock for such pieces of "pay ore" as had been overlooked; and these he
sacked up and sold at the Syndicate Mill. He became a member of our firm—"Gunny,
Giggles and Dumps" thenceforth—through my favor; for I could not then, nor can I
now, be indifferent to his courage and prowess in defending against Giggles the immemorial right of his sex to insult a strange and unprotected female—myself. After old Jim
struck it in the Calamity and I began to wear shoes and go to school, and in emulation
Giggles took to washing his face and became Jack Raynor, of Wells, Fargo & Co.,[8] and
old Mrs. Barts was herself chlorided to her fathers, Dumps drifted over to San Juan
Smith and turned stage driver, and was killed by road agents, and so forth.

Why do I tell you all this, dear? Because it is heavy on my heart. Because I walk the
Valley of Humility. Because I am subduing myself to permanent consciousness of my
unworthiness to unloose the latchet[9] of Dr. Barritz's shoe. Because, oh dear, oh dear,
there's a cousin of Dumps at this hotel! I haven't spoken to him. I never had much
acquaintance with him,—but do you suppose he has recognized me? Do, please give me
in your next your candid, sure-enough opinion about it, and say you don't think so. Do
you suppose He knows about me already, and that that is why He left me last evening
when He saw that I blushed and trembled like a fool under His eyes? You know I can't
bribe *all* the newspapers, and I can't go back on anybody who was civil to Gunny at
Redhorse—not if I'm pitched out of society into the sea. So the skeleton sometimes rat-
tles behind the door. I never cared much before, as you know, but now—*now* it is not
the same. Jack Raynor I am sure of—he will not tell Him. He seems, indeed, to hold
Him in such respect as hardly to dare speak to Him at all, and I'm a good deal that way
myself. Dear, dear! I wish I had something besides a million dollars! If Jack were three
inches taller I'd marry him alive and go back to Redhorse and wear sackcloth again to
the end of my miserable days.

JULY 25.

We had a perfectly splendid sunset last evening and I must tell you all about it. I
ran away from Auntie and everybody and was walking alone on the beach. I expect
you to believe, you infidel! that I had not looked out of my window on the seaward
side of the hotel and seen Him walking alone on the beach. If you are not lost to every
feeling of womanly delicacy you will accept my statement without question. I soon

established myself under my sunshade and had for some time been gazing out dreamily over the sea, when he approached, walking close to the edge of the water—it was ebb tide. I assure you the wet sand actually brightened about his feet! As he approached me he lifted his hat, saying, "Miss Dement, may I sit with you?—or will you walk with me?"

The possibility that neither might be agreeable seems not to have occurred to him. Did you ever know such assurance? Assurance? My dear, it was gall, downright *gall!* Well, I didn't find it wormwood, and replied, with my untutored Redhorse heart in my throat, "I—I shall be pleased to do *anything."* Could words have been more stupid? There are depths of fatuity in me, friend o' my soul, that are simply bottomless!

He extended his hand, smiling, and I delivered mine into it without a moment's hesitation, and when his fingers closed about it to assist me to my feet the consciousness that it trembled made me blush worse than the red west. I got up, however, and after a while, observing that he had not let go my hand I pulled on it a little, but unsuccessfully. He simply held on, saying nothing, but looking down into my face with some kind of smile—I didn't know—how could I?—whether it was affectionate, derisive or what, for I did not look at him. How beautiful he was!—with the red fires of the sunset burning in the depths of his eyes. Do you know, dear, if the Thugs and Experts of the Blavatsky region have any special kind of eyes? Ah, you should have seen his superb attitude, the godlike inclination of his head as he stood over me after I had got upon my feet! It was a noble picture, but I soon destroyed it, for I began at once to sink again to the earth. There was only one thing for him to do, and he did it; he supported me with an arm about my waist.

"Miss Dement, are you ill?" he said.

It was not an exclamation; there was neither alarm nor solicitude in it. If he had added: "I suppose that is about what I am expected to say," he would hardly have expressed his sense of the situation more clearly. His manner filled me with shame and indignation, for I was suffering acutely. I wrenched my hand out of his, grasped the arm supporting me and pushing myself free, fell plump into the sand and sat helpless. My hat had fallen off in the struggle and my hair tumbled about my face and shoulders in the most mortifying way.

"Go away from me," I cried, half choking. "O *please* go away, you—you Thug! How dare you think *that* when my leg is asleep?"

I actually said those identical words! And then I broke down and sobbed. Irene, I *blubbered!*

His manner altered in an instant—I could see that much through my fingers and hair. He dropped on one knee beside me, parted the tangle of hair and said in the tenderest way: "My dear girl, God knows I have not intended to pain you. How should I?—I who love you—I who have loved you for—for years and years!"

He had pulled my wet hands away from my face and was covering them with kisses. My cheeks were like two coals, my whole face was flaming and, I think,

A LADY FROM REDHORSE

steaming. What could I do? I hid it on his shoulder—there was no other place. And, O my dear friend, how my leg tingled and thrilled, and how I wanted to kick!

We sat so for a long time. He had released one of my hands to pass his arm about me again and I possessed myself of my handkerchief and was drying my eyes and my nose. I would not look up until that was done; he tried in vain to push me a little away and gaze into my face. Presently, when all was right, and it had grown a bit dark, I lifted my head, looked him straight in the eyes and smiled my best—my level best, dear.

"What do you mean," I said, "by 'years and years'?"

"Dearest," he replied, very gravely, very earnestly, "in the absence of the sunken cheeks, the hollow eyes, the lank hair, the slouching gait, the rags, dirt and youth, can you not—will you not understand? Gunny, I'm Dumps!"

In a moment I was upon my feet and he upon his. I seized him by the lapels of his coat and peered into his handsome face in the deepening darkness. I was breathless with excitement.

"And you are not dead?" I asked, hardly knowing what I said.

"Only dead in love, dear. I recovered from the road agent's bullet, but this, I fear, is fatal."

"But about Jack—Mr. Raynor? Don't you know——"

"I am ashamed to say, darling, that it was through that unworthy person's suggestion that I came here from Vienna."

Irene, they have roped in your affectionate friend,

MARY JANE DEMENT.

P. S.—The worst of it is that there is no mystery; that was the invention of Jack Raynor, to arouse my curiosity. James is not a Thug. He solemnly assures me that in all his wanderings he has never set foot in Sepoy.

E (15 Mar. 1891): 13 (as "An Heiress from Redhorse: Told in Letters from Coronado to San Francisco"); *TSC* 289–300; *CW* **2.373–84**. Reprinted in *Romance* 2, no. 1 (1891): 96–102 (as "An Heiress from Red Horse"); in Julian Hawthorne, ed., *Library of the World's Best Mystery and Detective Stories: American* (New York: Review of Reviews, 1907), 97–102 (as "An Heiress from Red Horse"); in Julian Hawthorne, ed., *The Lock and Key Library* (New York: Review of Reviews, 1909), 9:97–103 (as "An Heiress from Redhorse").

NOTES

This delightful story, the only romantic comedy AB wrote, belies by its good humor the portrait of him as a bitter misanthrope. His playful but adept characterization of a young woman falling in love is heightened by her last name, "Dement," which suggests that those in love are literally infatuated—that is, demented. The occasion of this story is almost certainly "A Strange Adventure," a charming anecdote *about* AB by W. C. Morrow, a friend of AB and also a short story author (whom AB praised in his *DD* entry for STORY). "A Strange Adventure" (see Appendix C) was dated 1 March 1891 and published in *Wa* on 7 March—the week before AB responded to it in *E* with "Redhorse." See Berkove, "'A Strange Adventure': The Story Behind a Bierce Tale."

A LADY FROM REDHORSE

1. Coronado Island, near San Diego, was—and still is—the site of a large resort hotel for the well-to-do, apparently the setting for the story.

2. The reference to Helena Petrovna Blavatsky (1831–91), a Russian mystic who founded the religion or philosophy known as theosophy in 1875, embodying its teachings in two large volumes, *Isis Unveiled* (1877) and *The Secret Doctrine* (1888). In 1878 she and a colleague, Henry S. Olcott, left for India, settling in Adyar, near Madras in southeastern (not northern) India; but accusations that she fabricated the miracles she claimed as validations of her teachings dogged her, and she left the country in 1885. The topic of theosophy received some attention in the feature sections of late-nineteenth-century periodicals, and a branch of the Theosophical Society existed in California. In "Prattle," *E* (11 Oct. 1891): 6, AB refers to Blavatsky as "the singed cat whose mental intestines supplied the fiddle-strings for Theosophy to make a pleasant noise upon." See also *CF*, no. 177.

3. AB refers both to the fact that Blavatsky attracted legions of fanatically devoted adherents and to the Sepoy Mutiny of 1857–58, a serious uprising of Indian soldiers (sepoys) serving in the British army. AB's character appears to be under the impression that there was a town in India named Sepoy.

4. The Thugs were members of an Indian criminal society in existence from as early as the twelfth century. They were heavily suppressed by the British in the 1830s; the last Thug was hanged in 1882.

5. Cf. Felicia Dorothea Hemans (1793–1835), "The Hour of Death" (1824), ll. 1–4:

> "Leaves have their time to fall,
> And flowers to wither at the north-wind's breath,
> And stars to set—but all,
> Thou hast all seasons for thine own, O Death!"

6. The suggestion is that Mary Jane's pinafores were made from gunnysacks; she alludes later on to her willingness to "wear sackcloth again."

7. David Garrick (1717–79), celebrated British actor and playwright.

8. Wells, Fargo & Co. was founded in 1852 by Henry Wells and George Fargo for the purpose of transacting express, banking, and freighting business in California.

9. "Latchet" is an archaic term for shoelace. Mary Jane is possibly alluding to the use of the term in John 1:27: "He it is, who coming after me is preferred before me, whose shoe's latchet I am not worthy to unloose."

THE BOARDED WINDOW

In 1830, only a few miles away from what is now the great city of Cincinnati, lay an immense and almost unbroken forest. The whole region was sparsely settled by people of the frontier—restless souls who no sooner had hewn fairly habitable homes out of the wilderness and attained to that degree of prosperity which to-day we should call indigence than impelled by some mysterious impulse of their nature they abandoned all and pushed farther westward, to encounter new perils and privations in the effort to regain the meager comforts which they had voluntarily renounced. Many of them had already forsaken that region for the remoter settlements, but among those remaining was one who had been of those first arriving. He lived alone in a house of logs surrounded on all sides by the great forest, of whose gloom and silence he seemed a part, for no one had ever known him to smile nor speak a needless word. His simple wants were supplied by the sale or barter of skins of wild animals in the river town, for not a thing did he grow upon the land which, if needful, he might have claimed by right of undisturbed possession. There were evidences of "improvement"—a few acres of ground immediately about the house had once been cleared of its trees, the decayed stumps of which were half concealed by the new growth that had been suffered to repair the ravage wrought by the ax. Apparently the man's zeal for agriculture had burned with a failing flame, expiring in penitential ashes.

The little log house, with its chimney of sticks, its roof of warping clapboards weighted with traversing poles and its "chinking" of clay,[1] had a single door and, directly opposite, a window. The latter, however, was boarded up—nobody could remember a time when it was not. And none knew why it was so closed; certainly not because of the occupant's dislike of light and air, for on those rare occasions when a hunter had passed that lonely spot the recluse had commonly been seen sunning himself on his doorstep if Heaven had provided sunshine for his need. I fancy there are few persons living to-day who ever knew the secret of that window, but I am one, as you shall see.

The man's name was said to be Murlock. He was apparently seventy years old, actually about fifty. Something besides years had had a hand in his aging. His hair and long, full beard were white, his gray, lusterless eyes sunken, his face singularly seamed with wrinkles which appeared to belong to two intersecting systems. In figure he was tall and spare, with a stoop of the shoulders—a burden bearer. I never saw him; these particulars I learned from my grandfather, from whom also I got the man's story when I was a lad. He had known him when living near by in that early day.

One day Murlock was found in his cabin, dead. It was not a time and place for coroners and newspapers, and I suppose it was agreed that he had died from natural causes or I should have been told, and should remember. I know only that with what was probably a sense of the fitness of things the body was buried near the cabin, alongside the grave of his wife, who had preceded him by so many years that local tradition had retained hardly a hint of her existence. That closes the final chapter of this true story—excepting, indeed, the circumstance that many years afterward, in company with an equally intrepid spirit, I penetrated to the place and ventured near enough to the ruined cabin to throw a stone against it, and ran away to avoid the ghost which every well-informed boy thereabout knew haunted the spot. But there is an earlier chapter—that supplied by my grandfather.

When Murlock built his cabin and began laying sturdily about with his ax to hew out a farm—the rifle, meanwhile, his means of support—he was young, strong and full of hope. In that eastern country whence he came he had married, as was the fashion, a young woman in all ways worthy of his honest devotion, who shared the dangers and privations of his lot with a willing spirit and light heart. There was no known record of her name; of her charms of mind and person tradition is silent and the doubter is at liberty to entertain his doubt; but God forbid that I should share it! Of their affection and happiness there is abundant assurance in every added day of the man's widowed life; for what but the magnetism of a blessed memory could have chained that venturesome spirit to a lot like that?

One day Murlock returned from gunning in a distant part of the forest to find his wife prostrate with fever, and delirious. There was no physician within miles, no neighbor; nor was she in a condition to be left, to summon help. So he set about the task of nursing her back to health, but at the end of the third day she fell into unconsciousness and so passed away, apparently, with never a gleam of returning reason.

From what we know of a nature like his we may venture to sketch in some of the details of the outline picture drawn by my grandfather. When convinced that she was dead, Murlock had sense enough to remember that the dead must be prepared for burial. In performance of this sacred duty he blundered now and again, did certain things incorrectly, and others which he did correctly were done over and over. His

THE BOARDED WINDOW

occasional failures to accomplish some simple and ordinary act filled him with aston-ishment, like that of a drunken man who wonders at the suspension of familiar nat-ural laws. He was surprised, too, that he did not weep—surprised and a little ashamed; surely it is unkind not to weep for the dead. "To-morrow," he said aloud, "I shall have to make the coffin and dig the grave; and then I shall miss her, when she is no longer in sight; but now—she is dead, of course, but it is all right—it *must* be all right, somehow. Things cannot be so bad as they seem."

He stood over the body in the fading light, adjusting the hair and putting the fin-ishing touches to the simple toilet, doing all mechanically, with soulless care. And still through his consciousness ran an undersense of conviction that all was right—that he should have her again as before, and everything explained. He had had no experience in grief; his capacity had not been enlarged by use. His heart could not contain it all, nor his imagination rightly conceive it. He did not know he was so hard struck; *that* knowledge would come later, and never go. Grief is an artist of powers as various as the instruments upon which he plays his dirges for the dead, evoking from some the sharpest, shrillest notes, from others the low, grave chords that throb recurrent like the slow beating of a distant drum. Some natures it startles; some it stupefies. To one it comes like the stroke of an arrow, stinging all the sensibilities to a keener life; to another as the blow of a bludgeon, which in crushing benumbs. We may conceive Murlock to have been that way affected, for (and here we are upon surer ground than that of conjecture) no sooner had he finished his pious work than, sinking into a chair by the side of the table upon which the body lay, and noting how white the profile showed in the deepening gloom, he laid his arms upon the table's edge, and dropped his face into them, tearless yet and unutterably weary. At that moment came in through the open window a long, wailing sound like the cry of a lost child in the far deeps of the darkening wood! But the man did not move. Again, and nearer than before, sounded that unearthly cry upon his failing sense. Perhaps it was a wild beast; perhaps it was a dream. For Murlock was asleep.

Some hours later, as it afterward appeared, this unfaithful watcher awoke and lifting his head from his arms intently listened—he knew not why. There in the black darkness by the side of the dead, recalling all without a shock, he strained his eyes to see—he knew not what. His senses were all alert, his breath was suspended, his blood had stilled its tides as if to assist the silence. Who—what had waked him, and where was it?

Suddenly the table shook beneath his arms, and at the same moment he heard, or fancied that he heard, a light, soft step—another—sounds as of bare feet upon the floor!

He was terrified beyond the power to cry out or move. Perforce he waited—waited there in the darkness through seeming centuries of such dread as one may know, yet live to tell. He tried vainly to speak the dead woman's name, vainly to stretch forth his hand across the table to learn if she were there. His throat was power-

THE BOARDED WINDOW

less, his arms and hands were like lead. Then occurred something most frightful. Some heavy body seemed hurled against the table with an impetus that pushed it against his breast so sharply as nearly to overthrow him, and at the same instant he heard and felt the fall of something upon the floor with so violent a thump that the whole house was shaken by the impact. A scuffling ensued, and a confusion of sounds impossible to describe. Murlock had risen to his feet. Fear had by excess forfeited control of his faculties. He flung his hands upon the table. Nothing was there!

There is a point at which terror may turn to madness; and madness incites to action. With no definite intent, from no motive but the wayward impulse of a madman, Murlock sprang to the wall, with a little groping seized his loaded rifle, and without aim discharged it. By the flash which lit up the room with a vivid illumination, he saw an enormous panther dragging the dead woman toward the window, its teeth fixed in her throat! Then there were darkness blacker than before, and silence; and when he returned to consciousness the sun was high and the wood vocal with songs of birds.

The body lay near the window, where the beast had left it when frightened away by the flash and report of the rifle. The clothing was deranged, the long hair in disorder, the limbs lay anyhow. From the throat, dreadfully lacerated, had issued a pool of blood not yet entirely coagulated. The ribbon with which he had bound the wrists was broken; the hands were tightly clenched. Between the teeth was a fragment of the animal's ear.

E (12 Apr. 1891): 11–12 (with subtitle: "An Incident in the Life of an Ohio Pioneer"); *TSC* 249–57; *IML* 273–82; **CW** 2.364–72.

NOTES

A ghost story, seeking to make readers believe in the incredible by its use of verisimilitude.

1. AB refers to the use of clay to fill up the chinks or gaps between the clapboards.

THE BOARDED WINDOW

THE SECRET OF
MACARGER'S GULCH

Northwestwardly from Indian Hill,[1] about nine miles as the crow flies, is Macarger's Gulch. It is not much of a gulch—a mere depression between two wooded ridges of inconsiderable height. From its mouth up to its head—for gulches, like rivers, have an anatomy of their own—the distance does not exceed two miles, and the width at bottom is at only one place more than a dozen yards; for most of the distance on either side of the little brook which drains it in winter, and goes dry in the early spring, there is no level ground at all; the steep slopes of the hills, covered with an almost impenetrable growth of manzanita and chemisal, are parted by nothing but the width of the water course. No one but an occasional enterprising hunter of the vicinity ever goes into Macarger's Gulch, and five miles away it is unknown, even by name. Within that distance in any direction are far more conspicuous topographical features without names, and one might try in vain to ascertain by local inquiry the origin of the name of this one.

About midway between the head and the mouth of Macarger's Gulch, the hill on the right as you ascend is cloven by another gulch, a short dry one, and at the junction of the two is a level space of two or three acres, and there a few years ago stood an old board house containing one small room. How the component parts of the house, few and simple as they were, had been assembled at that almost inaccessible point is a problem in the solution of which there would be greater satisfaction than advantage. Possibly the creek bed is a reformed road. It is certain that the gulch was at one time pretty thoroughly prospected by miners, who must have had some means of getting in with at least pack animals carrying tools and supplies; their profits, apparently, were not such as would have justified any considerable outlay to connect Macarger's Gulch with any center of civilization enjoying the distinction of a sawmill. The house, however, was there, most of it. It lacked a door and a window frame, and the chimney of mud and stones had fallen into an unlovely heap, overgrown with rank weeds. Such humble furniture as there may once have been, and much of the lower weather-boarding, had served as fuel in the camp fires of hunters; as had also, probably, the curbing of an old well, which at the time I write of existed in the form of a rather wide but not very deep depression near by.

One afternoon in the summer of 1874, I passed up Macarger's Gulch from the narrow valley into which it opens, by following the dry bed of the brook. I was quail-shooting and had made a bag of about a dozen birds by the time I had reached the house described, of whose existence I was until then unaware. After rather carelessly inspecting the ruin I resumed my sport, and having fairly good success prolonged it until near sunset, when it occurred to me that I was a long way from any human habi-tation—too far to reach one by nightfall. But in my game bag was food, and the old house would afford shelter, if shelter were needed on a warm and dewless night in the foothills of the Sierra Nevada, where one may sleep in comfort on the pine needles, without covering. I am fond of solitude and love the night, so my resolution to "camp out" was soon taken, and by the time that it was dark I had made my bed of boughs and grasses in a corner of the room and was roasting a quail at a fire that I had kin-dled on the hearth. The smoke escaped out of the ruined chimney, the light illumi-nated the room with a kindly glow, and as I ate my simple meal of plain bird and drank the remains of a bottle of red wine which had served me all the afternoon in place of the water, which the region did not supply, I experienced a sense of comfort which better fare and accommodations do not always give.

Nevertheless, there was something lacking. I had a sense of comfort, but not of security. I detected myself staring more frequently at the open doorway and blank window than I could find warrant for doing. Outside these apertures all was black, and I was unable to repress a certain feeling of apprehension as my fancy pictured the outer world and filled it with unfriendly entities, natural and supernatural—chief among which, in their respective classes, were the grizzly bear, which I knew was occasionally still seen in that region, and the ghost, which I had reason to think was not. Unfortunately, our feelings do not always respect the law of probabilities, and to me that evening, the possible and the impossible were equally disquieting.

Everyone who has had experience in the matter must have observed that one con-fronts the actual and imaginary perils of the night with far less apprehension in the open air than in a house with an open doorway. I felt this now as I lay on my leafy couch in a corner of the room next to the chimney and permitted my fire to die out. So strong became my sense of the presence of something malign and menacing in the place, that I found myself almost unable to withdraw my eyes from the opening, as in the deepening darkness it became more and more indistinct. And when the last little flame flickered and went out I grasped the shotgun which I had laid at my side and actually turned the muzzle in the direction of the now invisible entrance, my thumb on one of the hammers, ready to cock the piece, my breath suspended, my muscles rigid and tense. But later I laid down the weapon with a sense of shame and mortification. What did I fear, and why?—I, to whom the night had been

a more familiar face
Than that of man—[2]

I, in whom that element of hereditary superstition from which none of us is altogether free[3] had given to solitude and darkness and silence only a more alluring interest and charm! I was unable to comprehend my folly, and losing in the conjecture the thing conjectured of, I fell asleep. And then I dreamed.

I was in a great city in a foreign land—a city whose people were of my own race, with minor differences of speech and costume; yet precisely what these were I could not say; my sense of them was indistinct. The city was dominated by a great castle upon an overlooking height whose name I knew, but could not speak. I walked through many streets, some broad and straight with high, modern buildings, some narrow, gloomy and tortuous, between the gables of quaint old houses whose overhanging stories, elaborately ornamented with carvings in wood and stone, almost met above my head.

I sought someone whom I had never seen, yet knew that I should recognize when found. My quest was not aimless and fortuitous; it had a definite method. I turned from one street into another without hesitation and threaded a maze of intricate passages, devoid of the fear of losing my way.

Presently I stopped before a low door in a plain stone house which might have been the dwelling of an artisan of the better sort, and without announcing myself, entered. The room, rather sparely furnished, and lighted by a single window with small diamond-shaped panes, had but two occupants; a man and a woman. They took no notice of my intrusion, a circumstance which, in the manner of dreams, appeared entirely natural. They were not conversing; they sat apart, unoccupied and sullen.

The woman was young and rather stout, with fine large eyes and a certain grave beauty; my memory of her expression is exceedingly vivid, but in dreams one does not observe the details of faces. About her shoulders was a plaid shawl. The man was older, dark, with an evil face made more forbidding by a long scar extending from near the left temple diagonally downward into the black mustache; though in my dreams it seemed rather to haunt the face as a thing apart—I can express it no otherwise—than to belong to it. The moment that I found the man and woman I knew them to be husband and wife.

What followed, I remember indistinctly; all was confused and inconsistent—made so, I think, by gleams of consciousness. It was as if two pictures, the scene of my dream, and my actual surroundings, had been blended, one overlying the other, until the former, gradually fading, disappeared, and I was broad awake in the deserted cabin, entirely and tranquilly conscious of my situation.

THE SECRET OF MACARGER'S GULCH

My foolish fear was gone, and opening my eyes I saw that my fire, not altogether burned out, had revived by the falling of a stick and was again lighting the room. I had probably slept only a few minutes, but my commonplace dream had somehow so strongly impressed me that I was no longer drowsy; and after a little while I rose, pushed the embers of my fire together, and lighting my pipe proceeded in a rather ludicrously methodical way to meditate upon my vision.

It would have puzzled me then to say in what respect it was worth attention. In the first moment of serious thought that I gave to the matter I recognized the city of my dream as Edinburgh, where I had never been; so if the dream was a memory it was a memory of pictures and description. The recognition somehow deeply impressed me; it was as if something in my mind insisted rebelliously against will and reason on the importance of all this. And that faculty, whatever it was, asserted also a control of my speech. "Surely," I said aloud, quite involuntarily, "the MacGregors must have come here from Edinburgh."

At the moment, neither the substance of this remark nor the fact of my making it, surprised me in the least; it seemed entirely natural that I should know the name of my dreamfolk and something of their history. But the absurdity of it all soon dawned upon me: I laughed aloud, knocked the ashes from my pipe and again stretched myself upon my bed of boughs and grass, where I lay staring absently into my failing fire, with no further thought of either my dream or my surroundings. Suddenly the single remaining flame crouched for a moment, then, springing upward, lifted itself clear of its embers and expired in air. The darkness was absolute.

At that instant—almost, it seemed, before the gleam of the blaze had faded from my eyes—there was a dull, dead sound, as of some heavy body falling upon the floor, which shook beneath me as I lay. I sprang to a sitting posture and groped at my side for my gun; my notion was that some wild beast had leaped in through the open window. While the flimsy structure was still shaking from the impact I heard the sound of blows, the scuffling of feet upon the floor, and then—it seemed to come from almost within reach of my hand, the sharp shrieking of a woman in mortal agony. So horrible a cry I had never heard nor conceived; it utterly unnerved me; I was conscious for a moment of nothing but my own terror! Fortunately my hand now found the weapon of which it was in search, and the familiar touch somewhat restored me. I leaped to my feet, straining my eyes to pierce the darkness. The violent sounds had ceased, but more terrible than these, I heard, at what seemed long intervals, the faint intermittent gasping of some living, dying thing!

As my eyes grew accustomed to the dim light of the coals in the fireplace, I saw first the shapes of the door and window, looking blacker than the black of the walls. Next, the distinction between wall and floor became discernible, and at last I was sensible to the form and full expanse of the floor from end to end and side to side. Nothing was visible and the silence was unbroken.

With a hand that shook a little, the other still grasping my gun, I restored my fire and made a critical examination of the place. There was nowhere any sign that the cabin had been entered. My own tracks were visible in the dust covering the floor, but there were no others. I relit my pipe, provided fresh fuel by ripping a thin board or two from the inside of the house—I did not care to go into the darkness out of doors—and passed the rest of the night smoking and thinking, and feeding my fire; not for added years of life would I have permitted that little flame to expire again.

Some years afterward I met in Sacramento a man named Morgan, to whom I had a note of introduction from a friend in San Francisco. Dining with him one evening at his home I observed various "trophies" upon the wall, indicating that he was fond of shooting. It turned out that he was, and in relating some of his feats he mentioned having been in the region of my adventure.

"Mr. Morgan," I asked abruptly, "do you know a place up there called Macarger's Gulch?"

"I have good reason to," he replied; "it was I who gave to the newspapers, last year, the accounts of the finding of the skeleton there."

I had not heard of it; the accounts had been published, it appeared, while I was absent in the East.

"By the way," said Morgan, "the name of the gulch is a corruption; it should have been called 'MacGregor's.' My dear," he added, speaking to his wife, "Mr. Elderson has upset his wine."

That was hardly accurate—I had simply dropped it, glass and all.

"There was an old shanty once in the gulch," Morgan resumed when the ruin wrought by my awkwardness had been repaired, "but just previously to my visit it had been blown down, or rather blown away, for its débris was scattered all about, the very floor being parted, plank from plank. Between two of the sleepers still in position I and my companion observed the remnant of a plaid shawl, and examining it found that it was wrapped about the shoulders of the body of a woman, of which but little remained besides the bones, partly covered with fragments of clothing, and brown dry skin. But we will spare Mrs. Morgan," he added with a smile. The lady had indeed exhibited signs of disgust rather than sympathy.

"It is necessary to say, however," he went on, "that the skull was fractured in several places, as by blows of some blunt instrument; and that instrument itself—a pick-handle, still stained with blood—lay under the boards near by."

Mr. Morgan turned to his wife. "Pardon me, my dear," he said with affected solemnity, "for mentioning these disagreeable particulars, the natural though regrettable incidents of a conjugal quarrel—resulting, doubtless, from the luckless wife's insubordination."

"I ought to be able to overlook it," the lady replied with composure; "you have so many times asked me to in those very words."

THE SECRET OF MACARGER'S GULCH

I thought he seemed rather glad to go on with his story.

"From these and other circumstances," he said, "the coroner's jury found that the deceased, Janet MacGregor, came to her death from blows inflicted by some person to the jury unknown; but it was added that the evidence pointed strongly to her husband, Thomas MacGregor, as the guilty person. But Thomas MacGregor has never been found nor heard of. It was learned that the couple came from Edinburgh, but not—my dear, do you not observe that Mr. Elderson's boneplate has water in it?"

I had deposited a chicken bone in my finger bowl.

"In a little cupboard I found a photograph of MacGregor, but it did not lead to his capture."

"Will you let me see it?" I said.

The picture showed a dark man with an evil face made more forbidding by a long scar extending from near the temple diagonally downward into the black mustache.

"By the way, Mr. Elderson," said my affable host, "may I know why you asked about 'Macarger's Gulch'?"

"I lost a mule near there once," I replied, "and the mischance has—has quite—upset me."

"My dear," said Mr. Morgan, with the mechanical intonation of an interpreter translating, "the loss of Mr. Elderson's mule has peppered his coffee."

Wa 6, no. 51 (25 Apr. 1891): 13–14; *CSTB* 135–46; **CW 3.44–57.**

NOTES

Another ghost story, which also pokes fun at the narrator who vainly attempts to conceal his anxieties.

1. There were two mining towns in California named Indian Hill, one in El Dorado County between the South Fork of the American River and Weber Creek, north of Placerville, and another in Sierra County, five miles southwest of Goodyears Bar. Given AB's later mention of the foothills of the Sierra Nevada, the latter town appears to be the one he is referring to.

2. Byron, *Manfred* (1817), 3.4.4–5.

3. Cf. "A Watcher by the Dead": "'The superstitious awe with which the living regard the dead,' said Dr. Helberson, 'is hereditary and incurable'" (p. 699).

THE MOCKING-BIRD

The time, a pleasant Sunday afternoon in the early autumn of 1861. The place, a forest's heart in the mountain region of southwestern Virginia.[1] Private Grayrock of the Federal Army is discovered seated comfortably at the root of a great pine tree, against which he leans, his legs extended straight along the ground, his rifle lying across his thighs, his hands (clasped in order that they may not fall away to his sides) resting upon the barrel of the weapon. The contact of the back of his head with the tree has pushed his cap downward over his eyes, almost concealing them; one seeing him would say that he slept.

Private Grayrock did not sleep; to have done so would have imperiled the interests of the United States, for he was a long way outside the lines and subject to capture or death at the hands of the enemy. Moreover, he was in a frame of mind unfavorable to repose. The cause of his perturbation of spirit was this: during the previous night he had served on the picket-guard, and had been posted as a sentinel in this very forest. The night was clear, though moonless, but in the gloom of the wood the darkness was deep. Grayrock's post was at a considerable distance from those to right and left, for the pickets had been thrown out a needless distance from the camp, making the line too long for the force detailed to occupy it. The war was young, and military camps entertained the error that while sleeping they were better protected by thin lines a long way out toward the enemy than by thicker ones close in. And surely they needed as long notice as possible of an enemy's approach, for they were at that time addicted to the practice of undressing—than which nothing could be more unsoldierly. On the morning of the memorable 6th of April, at Shiloh, many of Grant's men when spitted on Confederate bayonets were as naked as civilians; but it should be allowed that this was not because of any defect in their picket line. Their error was of another sort: they had no pickets.[2] This is perhaps a vain digression. I should not care to undertake to interest the reader in the fate of an army; what we have here to consider is that of Private Grayrock.

For two hours after he had been left at his lonely post that Saturday night he stood stock-still, leaning against the trunk of a large tree, staring into the darkness in his front and trying to recognize known objects; for he had been posted at the same spot during the day. But all was now different; he saw nothing in detail, but only groups of things, whose shapes, not observed when there was something more of them to observe, were now unfamiliar. They seemed not to have been there before. A land-scape that is all trees and undergrowth, moreover, lacks definition, is confused and without accentuated points upon which attention can gain a foothold. Add the gloom of a moonless night, and something more than great natural intelligence and a city education is required to preserve one's knowledge of direction. And that is how it occurred that Private Grayrock, after vigilantly watching the spaces in his front and then imprudently executing a circumspection of his whole dimly visible environment (silently walking around his tree to accomplish it) lost his bearings and seriously impaired his usefulness as a sentinel. Lost at his post—unable to say in which direction to look for an enemy's approach, and in which lay the sleeping camp for whose secu-rity he was accountable with his life—conscious, too, of many another awkward fea-ture of the situation and of considerations affecting his own safety, Private Grayrock was profoundly disquieted. Nor was he given time to recover his tranquility, for almost at the moment that he realized his awkward predicament he heard a stir of leaves and a snap of fallen twigs, and turning with a stilled heart in the direction whence it came, saw in the gloom the indistinct outlines of a human figure.

"Halt!" shouted Private Grayrock, peremptorily as in duty bound, backing up the command with the sharp metallic snap of his cocking rifle—"who goes there?"

There was no answer; at least there was an instant's hesitation, and the answer, if it came, was lost in the report of the sentinel's rifle. In the silence of the night and the forest the sound was deafening, and hardly had it died away when it was repeated by the pieces of the pickets to right and left, a sympathetic fusillade. For two hours every unconverted civilian of them had been evolving enemies from his imagination, and peopling the woods in his front with them, and Grayrock's shot had started the whole encroaching host into visible existence. Having fired, all retreated, breathless, to the reserves—all but Grayrock, who did not know in what direction to retreat. When, no enemy appearing, the roused camp two miles away had undressed and got itself into bed again, and the picket line was cautiously re-established, he was discovered bravely holding his ground, and was complimented by the officer of the guard as the one sol-dier of that devoted band who could rightly be considered the moral equivalent of that uncommon unit of value, "a whoop in hell."

In the mean time, however, Grayrock had made a close but unavailing search for the mortal part of the intruder at whom he had fired, and whom he had a marksman's intuitive sense of having hit; for he was one of those born experts who shoot without aim by an instinctive sense of direction, and are nearly as dangerous by night as by day. During a full half of his twenty-four years he had been a terror to the targets of all the shooting-galleries in three cities. Unable now to produce his dead game he had the discretion to hold his tongue, and was glad to observe in his officer and comrades the natural assumption that not having run away he had seen nothing hostile. His "honorable mention" had been earned by not running away anyhow.

Nevertheless, Private Grayrock was far from satisfied with the night's adventure, and when the next day he made some fair enough pretext to apply for a pass to go outside the lines, and the general commanding promptly granted it in recognition of his bravery the night before, he passed out at the point where that had been displayed. Telling the sentinel then on duty there that he had lost something,—which was true enough—he renewed the search for the person whom he supposed himself to have shot, and whom if only wounded he hoped to trail by the blood. He was no more successful by daylight than he had been in the darkness, and after covering a wide area and boldly penetrating a long distance into "the Confederacy" he gave up the search, somewhat fatigued, seated himself at the root of the great pine tree, where we have seen him, and indulged his disappointment.

It is not to be inferred that Grayrock's was the chagrin of a cruel nature balked of its bloody deed. In the clear large eyes, finely wrought lips, and broad forehead of that young man one could read quite another story, and in point of fact his character was a singularly felicitous compound of boldness and sensibility, courage and conscience.

"I find myself disappointed," he said to himself, sitting there at the bottom of the golden haze submerging the forest like a subtler sea—"disappointed in failing to discover a fellow-man dead by my hand! Do I then really wish that I had taken life in the performance of a duty as well performed without? What more could I wish? If any danger threatened, my shot averted it; that is what I was there to do. No, I am glad indeed if no human life was needlessly extinguished by me. But I am in a false position. I have suffered myself to be complimented by my officers and envied by my comrades. The camp is ringing with praise of my courage. That is not just; I know myself courageous, but this praise is for specific acts which I did not perform, or performed—otherwise. It is believed that I remained at my post bravely, without firing, whereas it was I who began the fusillade, and I did not retreat in the general alarm because bewildered. What, then, shall I do? Explain that I saw an enemy and fired? They have all said that of themselves, yet none believes it. Shall I tell a truth which, discrediting my courage, will have the effect of a lie? Ugh! it is an ugly business altogether. I wish to God I could find my man!"

And so wishing, Private Grayrock, overcome at last by the languor of the afternoon and lulled by the stilly sounds of insects droning and prosing in certain fragrant shrubs, so far forgot the interests of the United States as to fall asleep and expose himself to capture. And sleeping he dreamed.

He thought himself a boy, living in a far, fair land by the border of a great river upon which the tall steamboats moved grandly up and down beneath their towering evolutions of black smoke, which announced them long before they had rounded the bends and marked their movements when miles out of sight. With him always, at his side as he watched them, was one to whom he gave his heart and soul in love—a twin brother. Together they strolled along the banks of the stream; together they explored the fields lying farther away from it, and gathered pungent mints and sticks of fragrant sassafras in the hills overlooking all—beyond which lay the Realm of Conjecture, and from which, looking southward across the great river, they caught glimpses of the Enchanted Land. Hand in hand and heart in heart they two, the only children of a widowed mother, walked in paths of light through valleys of peace, seeing new things under a new sun. And through all the golden days floated one unceasing sound—the rich, thrilling melody of a mocking-bird in a cage by the cottage door. It pervaded and possessed all the spiritual intervals of the dream, like a musical benediction. The joyous bird was always in song; its infinitely various notes seemed to flow from its throat, effortless, in bubbles and rills at each heart-beat, like the waters of a pulsing spring. That fresh, clear melody seemed, indeed, the spirit of the scene, the meaning and interpretation to sense of the mysteries of life and love.

But there came a time when the days of the dream grew dark with a sorrow in a rain of tears. The good mother was dead, the meadowside home by the great river was broken up, and the brothers were parted between two of their kinsmen. William (the dreamer) went to live in a populous city in the Realm of Conjecture, and John, crossing the river into the Enchanted Land, was taken to a distant region whose people in their lives and ways were said to be strange and wicked. To him, in the distribution of the dead mother's estate, had fallen all that they deemed of value—the mocking-bird. They could be divided, but it could not, so it was carried away into the strange country, and the world of William knew it no more forever. Yet still through the aftertime of his loneliness its song filled all the dream, and seemed always sounding in his ear and in his heart.

The kinsmen who had adopted the boys were enemies, holding no communication. For a time letters full of boyish bravado and boastful narratives of the new and larger experience—grotesque descriptions of their widening lives and the new worlds they had conquered—passed between them; but these gradually became less frequent, and with William's removal to another and greater city ceased altogether. But ever through it all ran the song of the mocking-bird, and when the dreamer opened his eyes and stared through the vistas of the pine forest the cessation of its music first apprised him that he was awake.

The sun was low and red in the west; the level rays projected from the trunk of each giant pine a wall of shadow traversing the golden haze to eastward until light and shade were blended in undistinguishable blue.

Private Grayrock rose to his feet, looked cautiously about him, shouldered his rifle and set off toward camp. He had gone perhaps a half-mile, and was passing a thicket of laurel, when a bird rose from the midst of it and perching on the branch of a tree above, poured from its joyous breast so inexhaustible floods of song as but one

THE MOCKING-BIRD

of all God's creatures can utter in His praise. There was little in that—it was only to open the bill and breathe; yet the man stopped as if struck—stopped and let fall his rifle, looked upward at the bird, covered his eyes with his hands and wept like a child! For the moment he was, indeed, a child, in spirit and in memory, dwelling again by the great river, over-against the Enchanted Land! Then with an effort of the will he pulled himself together, picked up his weapon and audibly damning himself for an idiot strode on. Passing an opening that reached into the heart of the little thicket he looked in, and there, supine upon the earth, its arms all abroad, its gray uniform stained with a single spot of blood upon the breast, its white face turned sharply upward and backward, lay the image of himself!—the body of John Grayrock, dead of a gunshot wound, and still warm! He had found his man.

As the unfortunate soldier knelt beside that masterwork of civil war the shrilling bird upon the bough overhead stilled her song and, flushed with sunset's crimson glory, glided silently away through the solemn spaces of the wood. At roll-call that evening in the Federal camp the name William Grayrock brought no response, nor ever again thereafter.

E (31 May 1891): 11–12 (with subtitle: "A Story of a Soldier Who Had a Dream"); *CSTB* 27–36; ***CW*** **2.218–29**. Reprinted in *E* (4 June 1893): special insert, n.p.

NOTES

As was done in related earlier stories, this tale exposes the true meaning of civil war in its examination of that kind of war on society's basic unit—the family. "A Horseman in the Sky" reveals the cost of the war to come down to parricide; "An Affair at Coulter's Notch" reveals it to be uxoricide and filicide; this story demonstrates fratricide. The beautiful settings of Nature, and their hints of more loveliness in the Realm of Conjecture and the Enchanted Land beyond do not prepare the story's innocents, the Grayrock brothers, for what the future will actually bring. All is wrapped up in the masterful final paragraph. Its bitter phrase "that masterwork of civil war" is placed among appreciations of the sublimities of Nature, but in the final analysis it is an indifferent Nature that unintentionally mocks with a bird song the stark tragedy on the forest floor. In its last sentence, this tale may anticipate Hemingway's *A Farewell to Arms*.

1. AB was stationed in western Virginia during this time, fighting in the battles of Cheat Mountain (3 Oct.) and Buffalo Mountain (December).

2. AB was sharply critical of Gen. Ulysses S. Grant for ineptitude at the battle of Shiloh. See "What I Saw of Shiloh" (*SS* 22–23).

THE MOCKING-BIRD

THE THING AT NOLAN

To the south of where the road between Leesville and Hardy, in the State of Missouri, crosses the east fork of May Creek stands an abandoned house.[1] Nobody has lived in it since the summer of 1879, and it is fast going to pieces. For some three years before the date mentioned above, it was occupied by the family of Charles May, from one of whose ancestors the creek near which it stands took its name. Mr. May's family consisted of a wife, and adult son and two young girls. The son's name was John—the names of the daughters are unknown to the writer of this sketch.

John May was of a morose and surly disposition, not easily moved to anger, but having an uncommon gift of sullen, implacable hate. His father was quite otherwise; of a sunny, jovial disposition, but with a quick temper like a sudden flame kindled in a wisp of straw, which consumes it in a flash and is no more. He cherished no resentments, and his anger gone, was quick to make overtures for reconciliation. He had a brother living near by who was unlike him in respect of all this, and it was a current witticism in the neighborhood that John had inherited his disposition from his uncle.

One day a misunderstanding arose between father and son, harsh words ensued, and the father struck the son full in the face with his fist. John quietly wiped away the blood that followed the blow, fixed his eyes upon the already penitent offender and said with cold composure, "You will die for that."

The words were overheard by two brothers named Jackson, who were approaching the men at the moment; but seeing them engaged in a quarrel they retired, apparently unobserved. Charles May afterward related the unfortunate occurrence to his wife and explained that he had apologized to the son for the hasty blow, but without avail; the young man not only rejected his overtures, but refused to withdraw his terrible threat. Nevertheless, there was no open rupture of relations: John continued living with the family, and things went on very much as before.

One Sunday morning in June, 1879, about two weeks after what has been related, May senior left the house immediately after breakfast, taking a spade. He said he was going to make an excavation at a certain spring in a wood about a mile away, so that the cattle could obtain water. John remained in the house for some hours, variously occupied in shaving himself, writing letters and reading a newspaper. His manner was very nearly what it usually was; perhaps he was a trifle more sullen and surly.

At two o'clock he left the house. At five, he returned. For some reason not connected with any interest in his movements, and which is not now recalled, the time of his departure and that of his return were noted by his mother and sisters, as was attested at his trial for murder. It was observed that his clothing was wet in spots, as if (so the prosecution afterward pointed out) he had been removing blood-stains from it. His manner was strange, his look wild. He complained of illness, and going to his room took to his bed.

May senior did not return. Later that evening the nearest neighbors were aroused, and during that night and the following day a search was prosecuted through the wood where the spring was. It resulted in little but the discovery of both men's footprints in the clay about the spring. John May in the meantime had grown rapidly worse with what the local physician called brain fever, and in his delirium raved of murder, but did not say whom he conceived to have been murdered, nor whom he imagined to have done the deed. But his threat was recalled by the brothers Jackson and he was arrested on suspicion and a deputy sheriff put in charge of him at his home. Public opinion ran strongly against him and but for his illness he would probably have been hanged by a mob. As it was, a meeting of the neighbors was held on Tuesday and a committee appointed to watch the case and take such action at any time as circumstances might seem to warrant.

On Wednesday all was changed. From the town of Nolan, eight miles away, came a story which put a quite different light on the matter. Nolan consisted of a school house, a blacksmith's shop, a "store" and a half-dozen dwellings. The store was kept by one Henry Odell, a cousin of the elder May. On the afternoon of the Sunday of May's disappearance Mr. Odell and four of his neighbors, men of credibility, were sitting in the store smoking and talking. It was a warm day; and both the front and the back door were open. At about three o'clock Charles May, who was well known to three of them, entered at the front door and passed out at the rear. He was without hat or coat. He did not look at them, nor return their greeting, a circumstance which did not surprise, for he was evidently seriously hurt. Above the left eyebrow was a wound—a deep gash from which the blood flowed, covering the whole left side of the face and neck and saturating his light-gray shirt. Oddly enough, the thought uppermost in the minds of all was that he had been fighting and was going to the brook directly at the back of the store, to wash himself.

Perhaps there was a feeling of delicacy—a backwoods etiquette which restrained them from following him to offer assistance; the court records, from which, mainly,

THE THING AT NOLAN

this narrative is drawn, are silent as to anything but the fact. They waited for him to return, but he did not return.

Bordering the brook behind the store is a forest extending for six miles back to the Medicine Lodge Hills. As soon as it became known in the neighborhood of the missing man's dwelling that he had been seen in Nolan there was a marked alteration in public sentiment and feeling. The vigilance committee went out of existence without the formality of a resolution. Search along the wooded bottom lands of May Creek was stopped and nearly the entire male population of the region took to beating the bush about Nolan and in the Medicine Lodge Hills. But of the missing man no trace was found.

One of the strangest circumstances of this strange case is the formal indictment and trial of a man for murder of one whose body no human being professed to have seen—one not known to be dead. We are all more or less familiar with the vagaries and eccentricities of frontier law, but this instance, it is thought, is unique. However that may be, it is of record that on recovering from his illness John May was indicted for the murder of his missing father. Counsel for the defense appears not to have demurred[2] and the case was tried on its merits. The prosecution was spiritless and perfunctory; the defense easily established—with regard to the deceased—an *alibi*. If during the time in which John May must have killed Charles May, if he killed him at all, Charles May was miles away from where John May must have been, it is plain that the deceased must have come to his death at the hands of some one else.

John May was acquitted, immediately left the country, and has never been heard of from that day. Shortly afterward his mother and sisters removed to St. Louis. The farm having passed into the possession of a man who owns the land adjoining, and has a dwelling of his own, the May house has ever since been vacant, and has the somber reputation of being haunted.

One day after the May family had left the country, some boys, playing in the woods along May Creek, found concealed under a mass of dead leaves, but partly exposed by the rooting of hogs, a spade, nearly new and bright, except for a spot on one edge, which was rusted and stained with blood. The implement had the initials C. M. cut into the handle.

This discovery renewed, in some degree, the public excitement of a few months before. The earth near the spot where the spade was found was carefully examined, and the result was the finding of the dead body of a man. It had been buried under two or three feet of soil and the spot covered with a layer of dead leaves and twigs. There was but little decomposition, a fact attributed to some preservative property in the mineral-bearing soil.

Above the left eyebrow was a wound—a deep gash from which blood had flowed, covering the whole left side of the face and neck and saturating the light-gray shirt. The skull had been cut through by the blow. The body was that of Charles May.

But what was it that passed through Mr. Odell's store at Nolan?

THE THING AT NOLAN

E (2 Aug. 1891): 11 (as "A Queer Story: Transcribed from the Notes of an Investigator"); *CSTB* 285–91; *CW* **3.405–12**.

NOTES

Another story in the supernatural mode, but which demonstrates AB's skill at verisimilitude.

1. The locations mentioned are fictitious.
2. In law, an objection by one party that the claim of the opposing party should not be allowed due to either a deficiency in law or to a defect in the claim.

THE THING AT NOLAN

A BABY TRAMP

If you had seen little Jo standing at the street corner in the rain, you would hardly have admired him. It was apparently an ordinary autumn rainstorm, but the water which fell upon Jo (who was hardly old enough to be either just or unjust,[1] and so perhaps did not come under the law of impartial distribution) appeared to have some property peculiar to itself: one would have said it was dark and adhesive—sticky. But that could hardly be so, even in Blackburg, where things certainly did occur that were a good deal out of the common.

For example, ten or twelve years before, a shower of small frogs had fallen, as is credibly attested by a contemporaneous chronicle, the record concluding with a somewhat obscure statement to the effect that the chronicler considered it good growing-weather for Frenchmen.[2]

Some years later Blackburg had a fall of crimson snow;[3] it is cold in Blackburg when winter is on, and the snows are frequent and deep. There can be no doubt of it—the snow in this instance was of the color of blood and melted into water of the same hue, if water it was, not blood. The phenomenon had attracted wide attention, and science had as many explanations as there were scientists who knew nothing about it. But the men of Blackburg—men who for many years had lived right there where the red snow fell, and might be supposed to know a good deal about the matter—shook their heads and said something would come of it.

And something did, for the next summer was made memorable by the prevalence of a mysterious disease—epidemic, endemic, or the Lord knows what, though the physicians didn't—which carried away a full half of the population. Most of the other half carried themselves away and were slow to return, but finally came back, and were now increasing and multiplying as before, but Blackburg had not since been altogether the same.

Of quite another kind, though equally "out of the common," was the incident of Hetty Parlow's ghost. Hetty Parlow's maiden name had been Brownon, and in Blackburg that meant more than one would think.

The Brownons had from time immemorial—from the very earliest of the old colonial days—been the leading family of the town. It was the richest and it was the best, and Blackburg would have shed the last drop of its plebeian blood in defense of the Brownon fair fame. As few of the family's members had ever been known to live permanently away from Blackburg, although most of them were educated elsewhere and nearly all had traveled, there was quite a number of them. The men held most of the public offices, and the women were foremost in all good works. Of these latter, Hetty was most beloved by reason of the sweetness of her disposition, the purity of her character and her singular personal beauty. She married in Boston a young scapegrace named Parlow, and like a good Brownon brought him to Blackburg forthwith and made a man and a town councilman of him. They had a child which they named Joseph and dearly loved, as was then the fashion among parents in all that region. Then they died of the mysterious disorder already mentioned, and at the age of one whole year Joseph set up as an orphan.

Unfortunately for Joseph the disease which had cut off his parents did not stop at that; it went on and extirpated nearly the whole Brownon contingent and its allies by marriage; and those who fled did not return. The tradition was broken, the Brownon estates passed into alien hands and the only Brownons remaining in that place were underground in Oak Hill Cemetery, where, indeed, was a colony of them powerful enough to resist the encroachment of surrounding tribes and hold the best part of the grounds. But about the ghost:

One night, about three years after the death of Hetty Parlow, a number of the young people of Blackburg were passing Oak Hill Cemetery in a wagon—if you have been there you will remember that the road to Greenton runs alongside it on the south. They had been attending a May Day festival at Greenton; and that serves to fix the date. Altogether there may have been a dozen, and a jolly party they were, considering the legacy of gloom left by the town's recent somber experiences. As they passed the cemetery the man driving suddenly reined in his team with an exclamation of surprise. It was sufficiently surprising, no doubt, for just ahead, and almost at the roadside, though inside the cemetery, stood the ghost of Hetty Parlow. There could be no doubt of it, for she had been personally known to every youth and maiden in the party. That established the thing's identity; its character as ghost was signified by all the customary signs—the shroud, the long, undone hair, the "far-away look"—everything. This disquieting apparition was stretching out its arms toward the west, as if in supplication for the evening star, which, certainly, was an alluring object, though obviously out of reach. As they all sat silent (so the story goes) every member of that party of merrymakers—they had merrymade on coffee and lemonade only—dis-

A BABY TRAMP

tinctly heard that ghost call the name "Joey, Joey!" A moment later nothing was there. Of course one does not have to believe all that.

Now, at that moment, as was afterward ascertained, Joey was wandering about in the sagebrush on the opposite side of the continent, near Winnemucca, in the State of Nevada.[4] He had been taken to that town by some good persons distantly related to his dead father, and by them adopted and tenderly cared for. But on that evening the poor child had strayed from home and was lost in the desert.

His after history is involved in obscurity and has gaps which conjecture alone can fill. It is known that he was found by a family of Piute Indians,[5] who kept the little wretch with them for a time and then sold him—actually sold him for money to a woman on one of the east-bound trains, at a station a long way from Winnemucca. The woman professed to have made all manner of inquiries, but all in vain: so, being childless and a widow, she adopted him herself. At this point of his career Jo seemed to be getting a long way from the condition of orphanage; the interposition of a multitude of parents between himself and that woeful state promised him a long immunity from its disadvantages.

Mrs. Darnell, his newest mother, lived in Cleveland, Ohio. But her adopted son did not long remain with her. He was seen one afternoon by a policeman, new to that beat, deliberately toddling away from her house, and being questioned answered that he was "a doin' home." He must have traveled by rail, somehow, for three days later he was in the town of Whiteville, which, as you know, is a long way from Blackburg. His clothing was in pretty fair condition, but he was sinfully dirty. Unable to give any account of himself he was arrested as a vagrant and sentenced to imprisonment in the Infants' Sheltering Home—where he was washed.

Jo ran away from the Infants' Sheltering Home at Whiteville—just took to the woods one day, and the Home knew him no more forever.[6]

We find him next, or rather get back to him, standing forlorn in the cold autumn rain at a suburban street corner in Blackburg; and it seems right to explain now that the raindrops falling upon him there were really not dark and gummy; they only failed to make his face and hands less so. Jo was indeed fearfully and wonderfully besmirched, as by the hand of an artist. And the forlorn little tramp had no shoes; his feet were bare, red and swollen, and when he walked he limped with both legs. As to clothing—ah, you would hardly have had the skill to name any single garment that he wore, or say by what magic he kept it upon him. That he was cold all over and all through did not admit of a doubt; he knew it himself. Any one would have been cold there that evening; but, for that reason, no one else was there. How Jo came to be there himself, he could not for the flickering little life of him have told, even if gifted with a vocabulary exceeding a hundred words. From the way he stared about him one could have seen that he had not the faintest notion of where (nor why) he was.

A BABY TRAMP

Yet he was not altogether a fool in his day and generation; being cold and hungry, and still able to walk a little by bending his knees very much indeed and putting his feet down toes first, he decided to enter one of the houses which flanked the street at long intervals and looked so bright and warm. But when he attempted to act upon that very sensible decision a burly dog came bowsing[7] out and disputed his right. Inexpressibly frightened and believing, no doubt (with some reason, too) that brutes without meant brutality within, he hobbled away from all the houses, and with gray, wet fields to right of him and gray, wet fields to left of him—with the rain half blinding him and the night coming in mist and darkness, held his way along the road that leads to Greenton. That is to say, the road leads those to Greenton who succeed in passing the Oak Hill Cemetery. A considerable number every year do not.

Jo did not.

They found him there the next morning, very wet, very cold, but no longer hungry. He had apparently entered the cemetery gate—hoping, perhaps, that it led to a house where there was no dog—and gone blundering about in the darkness, falling over many a grave, no doubt, until he had tired of it all and given up. The little body lay upon one side, with one soiled cheek upon one soiled hand, the other hand tucked away among the rags to make it warm, the other cheek washed clean and white at last, as for a kiss from one of God's great angels. It was observed—though nothing was thought of it at the time, the body being as yet unidentified—that the little fellow was lying upon the grave of Hetty Parlow. The grave, however, had not opened to receive him. That is a circumstance which, without actual irreverence, one may wish had been ordered otherwise.

Wa 7, no. 17 (29 Aug. 1891): 9; *CSTB* 263–70; ***CW* 3.185–93.**

NOTES

This tale, a curious mixture of the ironic and sentimental, was probably not a potboiler, for AB was regularly employed and well paid by Hearst's *E.* Its separate components evidence an ongoing scorn for supernatural and religious narratives but a long-established sympathy for young victims of circumstance.

1. Cf. Matt. 5:45: "That ye may be the children of your Father which is in heaven: for he maketh his sun to rise on the evil and on the good, and sendeth rain on the just and on the unjust."
2. French people, in coarse slang, are sometimes referred to disparagingly as "Frogs."
3. These are the kind of paranormal phenomena for which Charles Fort (1874–1932) became famous for recording in various books compiled in the first three decades of the twentieth century. Fort cites the *Scientific American* (12 July 1873) for "a shower of frogs which darkened the air and covered a long distance" in Kansas City, Missouri, and numerous instances of red or bloody rain—for example, from *Nature* (5 July 1877). AB could have heard of these or similar accounts in the newspapers of his day. See *The Book of the Damned* (1919), chaps. 3 and 7.

A BABY TRAMP

4. Winnemucca is the seat of Humboldt County in northwestern Nevada. It was founded in 1850 as a trading post.

5. The Piute, or Paiute, Indians are a Shoshonean tribe chiefly occupying portions of Utah and Nevada. See AB's early essay "The Pi-Ute Indians of Nevada," *Golden Era* 16, no. 32 (4 July 1868): [2–3].

6. See "A Providential Intimation," p. 292 note 2.

7. *To bowse* is slang for "to rush, come or go with a rush" *(DAE)*.

THE DEATH OF
HALPIN FRAYSER

For by death is wrought greater change than hath been shown. Whereas in general the spirit that removed cometh back upon occasion, and is sometimes seen of those in flesh (appearing in the form of the body it bore) yet it hath happened that the veritable body without the spirit hath walked. And it is attested of those encountering who have lived to speak thereon that a lich so raised up hath no natural affection, nor remembrance thereof, but only hate. Also, it is known that some spirits which in life were benign become by death evil altogether.—*Hali.*[1]

One dark night in midsummer a man waking from a dreamless sleep in a forest lifted his head from the earth, and staring a few moments into the blackness, said: "Catherine Larue." He said nothing more; no reason was known to him why he should have said so much.

The man was Halpin Frayser. He lived in St. Helena,[2] but where he lives now is uncertain, for he is dead. One who practices sleeping in the woods with nothing under him but the dry leaves and the damp earth, and nothing over him but the branches from which the leaves have fallen and the sky from which the earth has fallen, cannot hope for great longevity, and Frayser had already attained the age of thirty-two. There are persons in this world, millions of persons, and far and away the best persons, who regard that as a very advanced age. They are the children. To those who view the voyage of life from the port of departure the bark that has accomplished any considerable distance appears already in close approach to the farther shore. However, it is not certain that Halpin Frayser came to his death by exposure.

He had been all day in the hills west of the Napa Valley,[3] looking for doves and such small game as was in season. Late in the afternoon it had come on to be cloudy, and he had lost his bearings; and although he had only to go always downhill—everywhere the way to safety when one is lost—the absence of trails had so impeded him that he was overtaken by night while still in the forest. Unable in the darkness to penetrate the thickets of manzanita and other undergrowth, utterly bewildered and overcome with fatigue, he had lain down near the root of a large madroño and fallen into a dreamless sleep. It was hours later, in the very middle of the night, that one of God's mysterious messengers, gliding ahead of the incalculable host of his companions sweeping westward with the dawn line, pronounced the awakening word in the ear of the sleeper, who sat upright and spoke, he knew not why, a name, he knew not whose.

Halpin Frayser was not much of a philosopher, nor a scientist. The circumstance that, waking from a deep sleep at night in the midst of a forest, he had spoken aloud a name that he had not in memory and hardly had in mind did not arouse an enlightened curiosity to investigate the phenomenon. He thought it odd, and with a little perfunctory shiver, as if in deference to a seasonal presumption that the night was chill, he lay down again and went to sleep. But his sleep was no longer dreamless.[4]

He thought he was walking along a dusty road that showed white in the gathering darkness of a summer night. Whence and whither it led, and why he traveled it, he did not know, though all seemed simple and natural, as is the way in dreams; for in the Land Beyond the Bed[5] surprises cease from troubling and the judgment is at rest. Soon he came to a parting of the ways; leading from the highway was a road less traveled, having the appearance, indeed, of having been long abandoned, because, he thought, it led to something evil; yet he turned into it without hesitation, impelled by some imperious necessity.

As he pressed forward he became conscious that his way was haunted by invisible existences whom he could not definitely figure to his mind. From among the trees on either side he caught broken and incoherent whispers in a strange tongue which yet he partly understood. They seemed to him fragmentary utterances of a monstrous conspiracy against his body and soul.

It was now long after nightfall, yet the interminable forest through which he journeyed was lit with a wan glimmer having no point of diffusion, for in its mysterious lumination nothing cast a shadow. A shallow pool in the guttered depression of an old wheel rut, as from a recent rain, met his eye with a crimson gleam. He stooped and plunged his hand into it. It stained his fingers; it was blood! Blood, he then observed, was about him everywhere. The weeds growing rankly by the roadside showed it in blots and splashes on their big, broad leaves. Patches of dry dust between the wheelways were pitted and spattered as with a red rain. Defiling the trunks of the trees were broad maculations of crimson, and blood dripped like dew from their foliage.

All this he observed with a terror which seemed not incompatible with the fulfillment of a natural expectation. It seemed to him that it was all in expiation of some crime which, though conscious of his guilt, he could not rightly remember. To the menaces and mysteries of his surroundings the consciousness was an added horror.

THE DEATH OF HALPIN FRAYSER

Vainly he sought, by tracing life backward in memory, to reproduce the moment of his sin; scenes and incidents came crowding tumultuously into his mind, one picture effacing another, or commingling with it in confusion and obscurity, but nowhere could he catch a glimpse of what he sought. The failure augmented his terror; he felt as one who has murdered in the dark, not knowing whom nor why. So frightful was the situation—the mysterious light burned with so silent and awful a menace; the noxious plants, the trees that by common consent are invested with a melancholy or baleful character, so openly in his sight conspired against his peace; from overhead and all about came so audible and startling whispers and the sighs of creatures so obviously not of earth—that he could endure it no longer, and with a great effort to break some malign spell that bound his faculties to silence and inaction, he shouted with the full strength of his lungs! His voice, broken, it seemed, into an infinite multitude of unfamiliar sounds, went babbling and stammering away into the distant reaches of the forest, died into silence, and all was as before. But he had made a beginning at resistance and was encouraged. He said:

"I will not submit unheard. There may be powers that are not malignant traveling this accursed road. I shall leave them a record and an appeal. I shall relate my wrongs, the persecutions that I endure—I, a helpless mortal, a penitent, an unoffending poet!" Halpin Frayser was a poet only as he was a penitent: in his dream.

Taking from his clothing a small red-leather pocketbook, one-half of which was leaved for memoranda, he discovered that he was without a pencil. He broke a twig from a bush, dipped it into a pool of blood and wrote rapidly. He had hardly touched the paper with the point of his twig when a low, wild peal of laughter broke out at a measureless distance away, and growing ever louder, seemed approaching ever nearer; a soulless, heartless and unjoyous laugh, like that of the loon, solitary by the lakeside at midnight; a laugh which culminated in an unearthly shout close at hand, then died away by slow gradations, as if the accursed being that uttered it had withdrawn over the verge of the world whence it had come. But the man felt that this was not so—that it was near by and had not moved.

A strange sensation began slowly to take possession of his body and his mind. He could not have said which, if any, of his senses was affected; he felt it rather as a consciousness—a mysterious mental assurance of some overpowering presence—some supernatural malevolence different in kind from the invisible existences that swarmed about him, and superior to them in power. He knew that it had uttered that hideous laugh. And now it seemed to be approaching him; from what direction he did not know—dared not conjecture. All his former fears were forgotten or merged in the gigantic terror that now held him in thrall. Apart from that, he had but one thought: to complete his written appeal to the benign powers who, traversing the haunted wood, might some time rescue him if he should be denied the blessing of annihilation. He wrote with terrible rapidity, the twig in his fingers rilling blood without renewal; but in the middle of a sentence his hands denied their service to his will, his arms fell

THE DEATH OF HALPIN FRAYSER

to his sides, the book to the earth; and powerless to move or cry out, he found himself staring into the sharply drawn face and blank, dead eyes of his own mother, standing white and silent in the garments of the grave!

II

In his youth Halpin Frayser had lived with his parents in Nashville, Tennessee. The Fraysers were well-to-do, having a good position in such society as had survived the wreck wrought by civil war. Their children had the social and educational opportunities of their time and place, and had responded to good associations and instruction with agreeable manners and cultivated minds. Halpin being the youngest and not over robust was perhaps a trifle "spoiled." He had the double disadvantage of a mother's assiduity and a father's neglect. Frayser *père* was what no Southern man of means is not—a politician.[6] His country, or rather his section and State, made demands upon his time and attention so exacting that to those of his family he was compelled to turn an ear partly deafened by the thunder of the political captains and the shouting,[7] his own included.

Young Halpin was of a dreamy, indolent and rather romantic turn, somewhat more addicted to literature than law, the profession to which he was bred. Among those of his relations who professed the modern faith of heredity it was well understood that in him the character of the late Myron Bayne, a maternal great-grandfather, had revisited the glimpses of the moon—by which orb Bayne had in his lifetime been sufficiently affected to be a poet of no small Colonial distinction. If not specially observed, it was observable that while a Frayser who was not the proud possessor of a sumptuous copy of the ancestral "poetical works" (printed at the family expense, and long ago withdrawn from an inhospitable market) was a rare Frayser indeed, there was an illogical indisposition to honor the great deceased in the person of his spiritual successor. Halpin was pretty generally deprecated as an intellectual black sheep who was likely at any moment to disgrace the flock by bleating in meter. The Tennessee Fraysers were a practical folk—not practical in the popular sense of devotion to sordid pursuits, but having a robust contempt for any qualities unfitting a man for the wholesome vocation of politics.

In justice to young Halpin it should be said that while in him were pretty faithfully reproduced most of the mental and moral characteristics ascribed by history and family tradition to the famous Colonial bard, his succession to the gift and faculty divine[8] was purely inferential. Not only had he never been known to court the muse, but in truth he could not have written correctly a line of verse to save himself from the Killer of the Wise. Still, there was no knowing when the dormant faculty might wake and smite the lyre.

In the meantime the young man was rather a loose fish,[9] anyhow. Between him and his mother was the most perfect sympathy, for secretly the lady was herself a devout disciple of the late and great Myron Bayne, though with the tact so generally and justly admired in her sex (despite the hardy calumniators who insist that it is essentially the same thing as cunning) she had always taken care to conceal her weakness from all eyes but those of him who shared it. Their common guilt in respect of that was an added tie between them. If in Halpin's youth his mother had "spoiled" him, he had assuredly done his part toward being spoiled. As he grew to such manhood as is attainable by a Southerner who does not care which way elections go the attachment between him and his beautiful mother—whom from early childhood he had called Katy—became yearly stronger and more tender. In these two romantic natures was manifest in a signal way that neglected phenomenon, the dominance of the sexual element in all the relations of life, strengthening, softening, and beautifying even those of consanguinity.[10] The two were nearly inseparable, and by strangers observing their manners were not infrequently mistaken for lovers.

Entering his mother's boudoir one day Halpin Frayser kissed her upon the forehead, toyed for a moment with a lock of her dark hair which had escaped from its confining pins and said, with an obvious effort at calmness:

"Would you greatly mind, Katy, if I were called away to California for a few weeks?"

It was hardly needful for Katy to answer with her lips a question to which her telltale cheeks had made instant reply. Evidently she would greatly mind; and the tears, too, sprang into her large brown eyes as corroborative testimony.

"Ah, my son," she said, looking up into his face with infinite tenderness, "I should have known that this was coming. Did I not lie awake a half of the night weeping because, during the other half, Grandfather Bayne had come to me in a dream, and standing by his portrait—young, too, and handsome as that—pointed to yours on the same wall? And when I looked it seemed that I could not see the features; you had been painted with a face cloth, such as we put upon the dead. Your father has laughed at me, but you and I, dear, know that such things are not for nothing. And I saw below the edge of the cloth the marks of hands on your throat—forgive me, but we have not been used to keep such things from each other. Perhaps you have another interpretation. Perhaps it does not mean that you will go to California. Or maybe you will take me with you?"

It must be confessed that this ingenious interpretation of the dream in the light of newly discovered evidence did not wholly commend itself to the son's more logical mind; he had, for the moment at least, a conviction that it foreshadowed a more simple and immediate, if less tragic, disaster than a visit to the Pacific Coast. It was Halpin Frayser's impression that he was to be garroted on his native heath.

"Are there not medicinal springs in California?" Mrs. Frayser resumed before he had time to give her the true reading of the dream—"places where one recovers from rheumatism and neuralgia? Look—my fingers feel so stiff; and I am almost sure they have been giving me great pain while I slept."

THE DEATH OF HALPIN FRAYSER

She held out her hands for his inspection. What diagnosis of her case the young man may have thought it best to conceal with a smile the historian is unable to state, but for himself he feels bound to say that fingers looking less stiff, and showing fewer evidences of even insensible pain, have seldom been submitted for medical inspection by even the fairest patient desiring a prescription of unfamiliar scenes.

The outcome of it was that of these two odd persons having equally odd notions of duty, the one went to California, as the interest of his client required, and the other remained at home in compliance with a wish that her husband was scarcely conscious of entertaining.

While in San Francisco Halpin Frayser was walking one dark night along the water front of the city, when, with a suddenness that surprised and disconcerted him, he became a sailor. He was in fact "shanghaied" aboard a gallant, gallant ship[11] and sailed for a far countree.[12] Nor did his misfortunes end with the voyage; for the ship was cast ashore on an island of the South Pacific, and it was six years afterward when the survivors were taken off by a venturesome trading schooner and brought back to San Francisco.

Though poor in purse, Frayser was no less proud in spirit than he had been in the years that seemed ages and ages ago. He would accept no assistance from strangers, and it was while living with a fellow survivor near the town of St. Helena, awaiting news and remittances from home, that he had gone gunning and dreaming.

III

The apparition confronting the dreamer in the haunted wood—the thing so like, yet so unlike his mother—was horrible! It stirred no love nor longing in his heart; it came unattended with pleasant memories of a golden past—inspired no sentiment of any kind; all the finer emotions were swallowed up in fear. He tried to turn and run from before it, but his legs were as lead; he was unable to lift his feet from the ground. His arms hung helpless at his sides; of his eyes only he retained control, and these he dared not remove from the lusterless orbs of the apparition, which he knew was not a soul without a body, but that most dreadful of all existences infesting that haunted wood— a body without a soul! In its blank stare was neither love, nor pity, nor intelligence— nothing to which to address an appeal for mercy. "An appeal will not lie," he thought, with an absurd reversion to professional slang, making the situation more horrible, as the fire of a cigar might light up a tomb.

For a time, which seemed so long that the world grew gray with age and sin, and the haunted forest, having fulfilled its purpose in this monstrous culmination of its terrors, vanished out of his consciousness with all its sights and sounds, the apparition stood within a pace, regarding him with the mindless malevolence of a wild brute; then thrust its hands forward and sprang upon him with appalling ferocity! The act released his physical energies without unfettering his will; his mind was still spellbound, but his powerful body and agile limbs, endowed with a blind, insensate life of their own, resisted stoutly and well. For an instant he seemed to see this unnatural contest between a dead intelligence and a breathing mechanism only as a spectator—such fancies are in dreams; then he regained his identity almost as if by a leap forward into his body, and the straining automaton had a directing will as alert and fierce as that of its hideous antagonist.

But what mortal can cope with a creature of his dream? The imagination creating the enemy is already vanquished; the combat's result is the combat's cause. Despite his struggles—despite his strength and activity, which seemed wasted in a void, he felt the cold fingers close upon his throat. Borne backward to the earth, he saw above him the dead and drawn face within a hand's breadth of his own, and then all was black. A sound as of the beating of distant drums—a murmur of swarming voices, a sharp, far cry signing all to silence, and Halpin Frayser dreamed that he was dead.

IV

A warm, clear night had been followed by a morning of drenching fog. At about the middle of the afternoon of the preceding day a little whiff of light vapor—a mere thickening of the atmosphere, the ghost of a cloud—had been observed clinging to the western side of Mount St. Helena,[13] away up along the barren altitudes near the summit. It was so thin, so diaphanous, so like a fancy made visible, that one would have said: "Look quickly! in a moment it will be gone."

In a moment it was visibly larger and denser. While with one edge it clung to the mountain, with the other it reached farther and farther out into the air above the lower slopes. At the same time it extended itself to north and south, joining small patches of mist that appeared to come out of the mountain-side on exactly the same level, with an intelligent design to be absorbed. And so it grew and grew until the summit was shut out of view from the valley, and over the valley itself was an ever-extending canopy, opaque and gray. At Calistoga,[14] which lies near the head of the valley and the foot of the mountain, there were a starless night and a sunless morning. The fog, sinking into the valley, had reached southward, swallowing up ranch after ranch, until it had blotted out the town of St. Helena, nine miles away. The dust in the road was laid; trees were adrip with moisture; birds sat silent in their coverts; the morning light was wan and ghastly, with neither color nor fire.

Two men left the town of St. Helena at the first glimmer of dawn, and walked along the road northward up the valley toward Calistoga. They carried guns on their shoulders, yet no one having knowledge of such matters could have mistaken them for hunters of bird or beast. They were a deputy sheriff from Napa[15] and a detective from San Francisco—Holker and Jaralson, respectively. Their business was man-hunting.

"How far is it?" inquired Holker, as they strode along, their feet stirring white the dust beneath the damp surface of the road.

"The White Church? Only a half mile farther," the other answered. "By the way," he added, "it is neither white nor a church; it is an abandoned schoolhouse, gray with age and neglect. Religious services were once held in it—when it was white, and there is a graveyard that would delight a poet. Can you guess why I sent for you, and told you to come heeled?"[16]

"Oh, I never have bothered you about things of that kind. I've always found you communicative when the time came. But if I may hazard a guess, you want me to help you arrest one of the corpses in the graveyard."

"You remember Branscom?" said Jaralson, treating his companion's wit with the inattention that it deserved.

"The chap who cut his wife's throat? I ought; I wasted a week's work on him and had my expenses for my trouble. There is a reward of five hundred dollars, but none of us ever got a sight of him. You don't mean to say—"

"Yes, I do. He has been under the noses of you fellows all the time. He comes by night to the old graveyard at the White Church."

"The devil! That's where they buried his wife."

"Well, you fellows might have had sense enough to suspect that he would return to her grave some time."

"The very last place that any one would have expected him to return to."

"But you had exhausted all the other places. Learning your failure at them, I 'laid for him' there."

"And you found him?"

"Damn it! he found *me*. The rascal got the drop on me—regularly held me up and made me travel. It's God's mercy that he didn't go through me. Oh, he's a good one, and I fancy the half of that reward is enough for me if you're needy."

Holker laughed good-humoredly, and explained that his creditors were never more importunate.

"I wanted merely to show you the ground, and arrange a plan with you," the detective explained. "I thought it as well for us to be armed, even in daylight."

"The man must be insane," said the deputy sheriff. "The reward is for his capture and conviction. If he's mad he won't be convicted."[17]

Mr. Holker was so profoundly affected by that possible failure of justice that he involuntarily stopped in the middle of the road, then resumed his walk with abated zeal.

"Well, he looks it," assented Jaralson. "I'm bound to admit that a more unshaven, unshorn, unkempt, and uneverything wretch I never saw outside the ancient and honorable order of tramps.[18] But I've gone in for him, and can't make up my mind to let go. There's glory in it for us, anyhow. Not another soul knows that he is this side of the Mountains of the Moon."

"All right," Holker said; "we will go and view the ground," and he added, in the words of a once favorite inscription for tombstones: "'where you must shortly lie'—I

THE DEATH OF HALPIN FRAYSER

mean, if old Branscom ever gets tired of you and your impertinent intrusion. By the way, I heard the other day that 'Branscom' was not his real name."

"What is?"

"I can't recall it. I had lost all interest in the wretch, and it did not fix itself in my memory—something like Pardee. The woman whose throat he had the bad taste to cut was a widow when he met her. She had come to California to look up some relatives—there are persons who will do that sometimes. But you know all that."

"Naturally."

"But not knowing the right name, by what happy inspiration did you find the right grave? The man who told me what the name was said it had been cut on the headboard."

"I don't know the right grave." Jaralson was apparently a trifle reluctant to admit his ignorance of so important a point of his plan. "I have been watching about the place generally. A part of our work this morning will be to identify that grave. Here is the White Church."

For a long distance the road had been bordered by fields on both sides, but now on the left there was a forest of oaks, madroños and gigantic spruces whose lower parts only could be seen, dim and ghostly in the fog. The undergrowth was, in places, thick, but nowhere impenetrable. For some moments Holker saw nothing of the building, but as they turned into the woods it revealed itself in faint gray outline through the fog, looking huge and far away. A few steps more, and it was within an arm's length, distinct, dark with moisture and insignificant in size. It had the usual country-schoolhouse form—belonged to the packing-box order of architecture; had an underpinning of stones, a moss-grown roof and blank window spaces, whence both glass and sash had long departed. It was ruined, but not a ruin—a typical Californian substitute for what are known to guide-bookers abroad as "monuments of the past." With scarcely a glance at this uninteresting structure Jaralson moved on into the dripping undergrowth beyond.

"I will show you where he held me up," he said. "This is the graveyard."

Here and there among the bushes were small inclosures containing graves, sometimes no more than one. They were recognized as graves by the discolored stones or rotting boards at head and foot, leaning at all angles, some prostrate; by the ruined picket fences surrounding them; or, infrequently, by the mound itself showing its gravel through the fallen leaves. In many instances nothing marked the spot where lay the vestiges of some poor mortal—who, leaving "a large circle of sorrowing friends," had been left by them in turn—except a depression in the earth, more lasting than that in the spirits of the mourners. The paths, if any paths had been, were long obliterated; trees of a considerable size had been permitted to grow up from the graves and thrust aside with root or branch the inclosing fences. Over all was that air of abandonment and decay which seems nowhere so fit and significant as in a village of the forgotten dead.

THE DEATH OF HALPIN FRAYSER

As the two men, Jaralson leading, pushed their way through the growth of young trees, that enterprising man suddenly stopped and brought up his shotgun to the height of his breast, uttered a low note of warning and stood motionless, his eyes fixed upon something ahead. As well as he could, obstructed by brush, his companion, though seeing nothing, imitated the posture and so stood, prepared for what might ensue. A moment later Jaralson moved cautiously forward, the other following.

Under the branches of an enormous spruce lay the dead body of a man. Standing silent above it they noted such particulars as first strike the attention—the face, the attitude, the clothing; whatever most promptly and plainly answers the unspoken question of a sympathetic curiosity.

The body lay upon its back, the legs wide apart. One arm was thrust upward, the other outward; but the latter was bent acutely, and the hand was near the throat. Both hands were tightly clenched. The whole attitude was that of desperate but ineffectual resistance to—what?

Near by lay a shotgun and a game bag through the meshes of which was seen the plumage of shot birds. All about were evidences of a furious struggle; small sprouts of poison-oak were bent and denuded of leaf and bark; dead and rotting leaves had been pushed into heaps and ridges on both sides of the legs by the action of other feet than theirs; alongside the hips were unmistakable impressions of human knees.

The nature of the struggle was made clear by a glance at the dead man's throat and face. While breast and hands were white, those were purple—almost black. The shoulders lay upon a low mound, and the head was turned back at an angle otherwise impossible, the expanded eyes staring blankly backward in a direction opposite to that of the feet. From the froth filling the open mouth the tongue protruded, black and swollen. The throat showed horrible contusions; not mere finger-marks, but bruises and lacerations wrought by two strong hands that must have buried themselves in the yielding flesh, maintaining their terrible grasp until long after death. Breast, throat, face, were wet; the clothing was saturated; drops of water, condensed from the fog, studded the hair and mustache.

All this the two men observed without speaking—almost at a glance. Then Holker said:

"Poor devil! he had a rough deal."

Jaralson was making a vigilant circumspection of the forest, his shotgun held in both hands and at full cock, his finger upon the trigger.

"The work of a maniac," he said, without withdrawing his eyes from the inclosing wood. "It was done by Branscom—Pardee."

Something half hidden by the disturbed leaves on the earth caught Holker's attention. It was a red-leather pocketbook. He picked it up and opened it. It contained leaves of white paper for memoranda, and upon the first leaf was the name "Halpin Frayser." Written in red on several succeeding leaves—scrawled as if in haste and barely legible—were the following lines, which Holker read aloud, while his companion continued

THE DEATH OF HALPIN FRAYSER

scanning the dim gray confines of their narrow world and hearing matter of apprehension in the drip of water from every burdened branch:[19]

> "Enthralled by some mysterious spell, I stood
> In the lit gloom of an enchanted wood.
> The cypress there and myrtle twined their boughs,
> Significant, in baleful brotherhood.
>
> "The brooding willow whispered to the yew;
> Beneath, the deadly nightshade and the rue,
> With immortelles self-woven into strange
> Funereal shapes, and horrid nettles grew.
>
> "No song of bird nor any drone of bees,
> Nor light leaf lifted by the wholesome breeze:
> The air was stagnant all, and Silence was
> A living thing that breathed among the trees.
>
> "Conspiring spirits whispered in the gloom,
> Half-heard, the stilly secrets of the tomb.
> With blood the trees were all adrip; the leaves
> Shone in the witch-light with a ruddy bloom.
>
> "I cried aloud!—the spell, unbroken still,
> Rested upon my spirit and my will.
> Unsouled, unhearted, hopeless and forlorn,
> I strove with monstrous presages of ill!
>
> "At last the viewless—

Holker ceased reading; there was no more to read. The manuscript broke off in the middle of a line.

"That sounds like Bayne," said Jaralson, who was something of a scholar in his way. He had abated his vigilance and stood looking down at the body.

"Who's Bayne?" Holker asked rather incuriously.

"Myron Bayne, a chap who flourished in the early years of the nation—more than a century ago. Wrote mighty dismal stuff; I have his collected works. That poem is not among them, but it must have been omitted by mistake."

"It is cold," said Holker; "let us leave here; we must have up the coroner from Napa."

Jaralson said nothing, but made a movement in compliance. Passing the end of the slight elevation of earth upon which the dead man's head and shoulders lay, his foot struck some hard substance under the rotting forest leaves, and he took the trouble to kick it into view. It was a fallen headboard, and painted on it were the hardly decipherable words, "Catharine Larue."

THE DEATH OF HALPIN FRAYSER

"Larue, Larue!" exclaimed Holker, with sudden animation. "Why, that is the real name of Branscom—not Pardee. And—bless my soul! how it all comes to me—the murdered woman's name had been Frayser!"

"There is some rascally mystery here," said Detective Jaralson. "I hate anything of that kind."

There came to them out of the fog—seemingly from a great distance—the sound of a laugh, a low, deliberate, soulless laugh, which had no more of joy than that of a hyena night-prowling in the desert; a laugh that rose by slow gradation, louder and louder, clearer, more distinct and terrible, until it seemed barely outside the narrow circle of their vision; a laugh so unnatural, so unhuman, so devilish, that it filled those hardy man-hunters with a sense of dread unspeakable! They did not move their weapons nor think of them; the menace of that horrible sound was not of the kind to be met with arms. As it had grown out of silence, so now it died away; from a culminating shout which had seemed almost in their ears, it drew itself away into the distance, until its failing notes, joyless and mechanical to the last, sank to silence at a measureless remove.

Wa 7, no. 33 (19 Dec. 1891): 2–5; *CSTB* 1–26; ***CW* 3.13–43.**

NOTES

Although this story has long had much appeal for devotees of supernatural fiction, it is almost certainly a hoax, a trap for critics, with red herrings leading nowhere. Both M. E. Grenander (*Ambrose Bierce,* 1971) and William Bysshe Stein previously noted this apparently deliberate pattern of confusion in the tale, but Cathy N. Davidson's analysis of it in *The Experimental Fictions of Ambrose Bierce* makes a convincing case that beneath all its mysteries and intriguing hints it is but "a comic detective yarn" (103–14). As we have seen, AB learned the hoax technique from masters and used it for both serious and humorous purposes. Capitalizing on the popular appeals of the supernatural, the newly emerging detective story genre, and possibly even the early stirrings of Freudian criticism, "Halpin Frayser" is one of AB's most skillful hoaxes.

1. Hali is first mentioned in "An Inhabitant of Carcosa" (p. 457). The original attribution was to "Mannon's 'Thoughts on Immortality'" (see "Selected Textual Variants").

2. A town in Napa County, about fifty miles northeast of San Francisco. It has long been the center of California's wine country. When AB was forced in the early 1880s to leave San Francisco to relieve his asthma, he resided briefly in Saint Helena and, for several years, in the town of Angwin, about five miles northeast of Saint Helena.

3. A small wine-country valley situated within the Coastal Range, north of Pablo Bay in California.

4. The following dream-account was adapted from an actual dream of AB's, as recorded in his essay "Visions of the Night" (*SS* 308–9): "I was walking at dusk through a great forest of unfamiliar trees. Whence and whither I did not know. I had a sense of the vast extent of the wood, a consciousness that I was the only living thing in it. I was obsessed by some awful spell in expiation of a forgotten crime committed, as I vaguely surmised, against the sunrise. Mechanically and without hope, I moved under the arms of the giant trees along

a narrow trail penetrating the haunted solitudes of the forest. I came at length to a brook that flowed darkly and sluggishly across my path, and saw that it was blood. Turning to the right, I followed it up a considerable distance, and soon came to a small circular opening in the forest, filled with a dim, unreal light, by which I saw in the center of the opening a deep tank of white marble. It was filled with blood, and the stream that I had followed up was its outlet. All round the tank, between it and the enclosing forest—a space of perhaps ten feet in breadth, paved with immense slabs of marble—were dead bodies of men—a score; though I did not count them I knew that the number had some significant and portentous relation to my crime. Possibly they marked the time, in centuries, since I had committed it. I only recognized the fitness of the number, and knew it without counting. The bodies were naked and arranged symmetrically around the central tank, radiating from it like spokes of a wheel. The feet were outward, the heads hanging over the edge of the tank. Each lay upon its back, its throat cut, blood slowly dripping from the wound. I looked on all this unmoved. It was a natural and necessary result of my offense, and did not affect me; but there was something that filled me with apprehension and terror—a monstrous pulsation, beating with a slow, inevitable recurrence. I do not know which of the senses it addressed, or if it made its way to the consciousness through some avenue unknown to science and experience. The pitiless regularity of this vast rhythm was maddening. I was conscious that it pervaded the entire forest, and was a manifestation of some gigantic and implacable malevolence.

"Of this dream I have no further recollection. Probably, overcome by a terror which doubtless had its origin in the discomfort of an impeded circulation, I cried out and was awakened by the sound of my own voice."

5. Cf. the title of AB's "The Land Beyond the Blow." In a letter to S. O. Howes (2 May 1908), AB writes: "I find a fairly good 'essay' entitled 'The Land beyond the Bed'—all about dreams. Do you remember if it is in your book?" AB refers to Howes's compilation of AB's journalism into the "essays" he assembled for *The Shadow on the Dial* (1909). AB's own "Visions of the Night" had first appeared in *E* (24 July 1887). Possibly Howes had contemplated including this article—or another one containing other accounts of dreams by AB—in *The Shadow on the Dial*.

6. Cf. "An Occurrence at Owl Creek Bridge": "Peyton Farquhar was a well-to-do planter, of an old and highly respected Alabama family. Being a slave owner and like other slave owners a politician" (p. 727).

7. See "Chickamauga," p. 649 note 5.

8. William Wordsworth (1770–1850), *The Excursion* (1814) 1.79: "the vision and the faculty divine."

9. "Loose fish" is a colloquialism: "A person of irregular habits" *(C)*. In the sense that Herman Melville, in *Moby-Dick,* uses it, it can be someone not yet claimed by mastering convictions, obligations, or circumstances.

10. The comment is meant ironically, since AB himself was one of the most puritanical of men in regard to sexual matters. George Sterling recalled an incident with AB in 1893: "We had left the swimming-pool of the Bohemian Club and I was still attired in a bathing-suit which, though somewhat abbreviated, I thought sufficient to the demands of propriety. Before long we saw a canoe coming down the river, propelled by my wife and his niece. He ceased paddling and demanded: 'Do you intend to meet my niece in that costume?' 'Why not?' I innocently asked. 'All I have to say is,' he replied, 'that if you try it, I'll put a

bullet through your guts.'" George Sterling, "The Shadow Maker," *American Mercury* 6, No. 1 (Sept. 1925): 12.

11. Cf. William Vaughn Moody (1869–1901), "Gloucester Moors," ll. 35–36: "She swings and steadies to her keel / Like a gallant, gallant ship." The poem was published in Moody's *Gloucester Moors and Other Peoms* (1910), but it is unclear whether it appeared previously in a magazine or newspaper prior to the publication of AB's story.

12. Samuel Taylor Coleridge (1772–1834), *The Rime of the Ancient Mariner* (1797), ll. 517–18: "He loves to talk with marineres / That come from a far countree"; *Christabel* (1797), l. 225: "Like a lady of a far countrée."

13. A mountain (1,324 ft.) about twelve miles northwest of the town of Saint Helena. Robert Louis Stevenson spent his honeymoon in 1880 in a bunkhouse on the summit of the mountain, subsequently writing about the region in *The Silverado Squatters* (1883).

14. A town nine miles northwest of Saint Helena.

15. The seat of Napa County, about twenty miles southeast of Saint Helena.

16. "To heel" is Western slang for "to equip or arm" *(C)*.

17. AB, in his general support of capital punishment, was opposed to the plea of innocence on the grounds of insanity. "The only objection in the insanity plea in all these murder cases is a too narrow application: The benefit of it should be extended to the jury. That patient and tolerant body should be permitted to return a lawful verdict like this: "We find that the deed was committed, as charged, but that in committing it the prisoner was insane. Being that way ourselves, we find him guilty of murder in the first degree." "Prattle," *E* (4 Oct. 1896): 6.

18. AB expressed vigorous disapproval of the glamorization of the tramp life, especially by such writers as Jack London. "Damn the tramp and criminal in literature, say I. They stink." AB to George Sterling, 3 June 1907 (ms., NP). See also the essay "Ambrose Bierce Says: The Right to Labor Should Be Legally Defined," *NYJ* (15 June 1900): 8; *E* (19 June 1900): 6 (as "Concerning Legislation 'To Solve the Tramp Problem'").

19. The poem was first included in "Prattle," *E* (12 June 1887): 4; it has been considerably altered here (see "Selected Textual Variants"). The final stanza, omitted here, reads:

> At last, praise God! I broke the viewless chain,
> And, flying breathless to the sunny plain,
> Met Dr. Josselyn. He smiled. I sought
> The lesser horror of the wood again.

Dr. Charles Josselyn was the fire commissioner in San Francisco. He was evidently indicted on a charge of conspiracy to murder. See "Prattle," *E* (22 Aug. 1887): 4.

THE DEATH OF HALPIN FRAYSER

AN ADVENTURE AT BROWNVILLE*

I taught a little country school near Brownville, which, as every one knows who has had the good luck to live there, is the capital of a considerable expanse of the finest scenery in California. The town is somewhat frequented in summer by a class of persons whom it is the habit of the local journal to call "pleasure seekers," but who by a juster classification would be known as "the sick and those in adversity." Brownville itself might rightly enough be described, indeed, as a summer place of last resort. It is fairly well endowed with boarding-houses, at the least pernicious of which I performed twice a day (lunching at the schoolhouse) the humble rite of cementing the alliance between soul and body. From this "hostelry" (as the local journal preferred to call it when it did not call it a "caravanserai") to the schoolhouse the distance by the wagon road was about a mile and a half; but there was a trail, very little used, which led over an intervening range of low, heavily wooded hills, considerably shortening the distance. By this trail I was returning one evening later than usual. It was the last day of the term and I had been detained at the schoolhouse until almost dark, preparing an account of my stewardship for the trustees—two of whom, I proudly reflected, would be able to read it, and the third (an instance of the dominion of mind over matter) would be overruled in his customary antagonism to the schoolmaster of his own creation.

I had gone not more than a quarter of the way when, finding an interest in the antics of a family of lizards which dwelt thereabout and seemed full of reptilian joy for their immunity from the ills incident to life at the Brownville House, I sat upon a fallen tree to observe them. As I leaned wearily against a branch of the gnarled old trunk the twilight deepened in the somber woods and the faint new moon began casting visible shadows and gilding the leaves of the trees with a tender but ghostly light.

*This story was written in collaboration with Miss Ina Lillian Peterson, to whom is rightly due the credit for whatever merit it may have.

I heard the sound of voices—a woman's, angry, impetuous, rising against deep masculine tones, rich and musical. I strained my eyes, peering through the dusky shadows of the wood, hoping to get a view of the intruders on my solitude, but could see no one. For some yards in each direction I had an uninterrupted view of the trail, and knowing of no other within a half-mile thought the persons heard must be approaching from the wood at one side. There was no sound but that of the voices, which were now so distinct that I could catch the words. That of the man gave me an impression of anger, abundantly confirmed by the matter spoken.

"I will have no threats; you are powerless, as you very well know. Let things remain as they are or, by God! you shall both suffer for it."

"What do you mean?"—this was the voice of the woman, a cultivated voice, the voice of a lady. "You would not—murder us."

There was no reply, at least none that was audible to me. During the silence I peered into the wood in hope to get a glimpse of the speakers, for I felt sure that this was an affair of gravity in which ordinary scruples ought not to count. It seemed to me that the woman was in peril; at any rate the man had not disavowed a willingness to murder. When a man is enacting the rôle of potential assassin he has not the right to choose his audience.

After some little time I saw them, indistinct in the moonlight among the trees. The man, tall and slender, seemed clothed in black; the woman wore, as nearly as I could make out, a gown of gray stuff. Evidently they were still unaware of my presence in the shadow, though for some reason when they renewed their conversation they spoke in lower tones and I could no longer understand. As I looked the woman seemed to sink to the ground and raise her hands in supplication, as is frequently done on the stage and never, so far as I knew, anywhere else, and I am now not altogether sure that it was done in this instance. The man fixed his eyes upon her; they seemed to glitter bleakly in the moonlight with an expression that made me apprehensive that he would turn them upon me. I do not know by what impulse I was moved, but I sprang to my feet out of the shadow. At that instant the figures vanished. I peered in vain through the spaces among the trees and clumps of undergrowth. The night wind rustled the leaves; the lizards had retired early, reptiles of exemplary habits. The little moon was already slipping behind a black hill in the west.

I went home, somewhat disturbed in mind, half doubting that I had heard or seen any living thing excepting the lizards. It all seemed a trifle odd and uncanny. It was as if among the several phenomena, objective and subjective, that made the sum total of the incident there had been an uncertain element which had diffused its dubious character over all—had leavened the whole mass with unreality. I did not like it.

At the breakfast table the next morning there was a new face; opposite me sat a young woman at whom I merely glanced as I took my seat. In speaking to the high and mighty female personage who condescended to seem to wait upon us, this girl soon invited my attention by the sound of her voice, which was like, yet not altogether

AN ADVENTURE AT BROWNVILLE

like, the one still murmuring in my memory of the previous evening's adventure. A moment later another girl, a few years older, entered the room and sat at the left of the other, speaking to her a gentle "good morning." By *her* voice I was startled: it was without doubt the one of which the first girl's had reminded me. Here was the lady of the sylvan incident sitting bodily before me, "in her habit as she lived."[1]

Evidently enough the two were sisters. With a nebulous kind of apprehension that I might be recognized as the mute inglorious hero[2] of an adventure which had in my consciousness and conscience something of the character of eavesdropping, I allowed myself only a hasty cup of the lukewarm coffee thoughtfully provided by the prescient waitress for the emergency, and left the table. As I passed out of the house into the grounds I heard a rich, strong male voice singing an aria from "Rigoletto."[3] I am bound to say that it was exquisitely sung, too; but there was something in the performance that displeased me, I could say neither what nor why, and I walked rapidly away.

Returning later in the day I saw the elder of the two young women standing on the porch and near her a tall man in black clothing—the man whom I had expected to see. All day the desire to know something of these persons had been uppermost in my mind and I now resolved to learn what I could of them in any way that was neither dishonorable nor low.

The man was talking easily and affably to his companion, but at the sound of my footsteps on the gravel walk he ceased, and turning about looked me full in the face. He was apparently of middle age, dark and uncommonly handsome. His attire was faultless, his bearing easy and graceful, the look which he turned upon me open, free and devoid of any suggestion of rudeness. Nevertheless it affected me with a distinct emotion which on subsequent analysis in memory appeared to be compounded of hatred and dread—I am unwilling to call it fear. A second later the man and woman had disappeared. They seemed to have a trick of disappearing. On entering the house, however, I saw them through the open doorway of the parlor as I passed; they had merely stepped through a window which opened down to the floor.

Cautiously "approached" on the subject of her new guests my landlady proved not ungracious. Restated with, I hope, some small reverence for English grammar the facts were these: the two girls were Pauline and Eva Maynard of San Francisco; the elder was Pauline. The man was Richard Benning, their guardian, who had been the most intimate friend of their father, now deceased. Mr. Benning had brought them to Brownville in the hope that the mountain climate might benefit Eva, who was thought to be in danger of consumption.

Upon these short and simple annals[4] the landlady wrought an embroidery of eulogium which abundantly attested her faith in Mr. Benning's will and ability to pay for the best that her house afforded. That he had a good heart was evident to her from his devotion to his two beautiful wards and his really touching solicitude for their comfort. The evidence impressed me as insufficient and I silently found the Scotch verdict, "Not proven."[5]

AN ADVENTURE AT BROWNVILLE

Certainly, Mr. Benning was most attentive to his wards. In my strolls about the country I frequently encountered them—sometimes in company with other guests of the hotel—exploring the gulches, fishing, rifle shooting and otherwise wiling away the monotony of country life; and although I watched them as closely as good manners would permit I saw nothing that would in any way explain the strange words that I had overheard in the wood. I had grown tolerably well acquainted with the young ladies and could exchange looks and even greetings with their guardian without actual repugnance.

A month went by and I had almost ceased to interest myself in their affairs when one night our entire little community was thrown into excitement by an event which vividly recalled my experience in the forest.

This was the death of the elder girl, Pauline.

The sisters had occupied the same bedroom on the third floor of the house. Waking in the gray of the morning Eva had found Pauline dead beside her. Later, when the poor girl was weeping beside the body amid a throng of sympathetic if not very considerate persons, Mr. Benning entered the room and appeared to be about to take her hand. She drew away from the side of the dead and moved slowly toward the door.

"It is you," she said—"you who have done this. You—you—you!"

"She is raving," he said in a low voice. He followed her, step by step, as she retreated, his eyes fixed upon hers with a steady gaze in which there was nothing of tenderness nor of compassion. She stopped; the hand that she had raised in accusation fell to her side, her dilated eyes contracted visibly, the lids slowly dropped over them, veiling their strange wild beauty, and she stood motionless and almost as white as the dead girl lying near. The man took her hand and put his arm gently about her shoulders, as if to support her. Suddenly she burst into a passion of tears and clung to him as a child to its mother. He smiled with a smile that affected me most disagreeably— perhaps any kind of smile would have done so—and led her silently out of the room.

There was an inquest—and the customary verdict: the deceased, it appeared, came to her death through "heart disease." It was before the invention of heart *failure,* though the heart of poor Pauline had indubitably failed. The body was embalmed and taken to San Francisco by some one summoned thence for the purpose, neither Eva nor Benning accompanying it. Some of the hotel gossips ventured to think that very strange, and a few hardy spirits went so far as to think it very strange indeed; but the good landlady generously threw herself into the breach, saying it was owing to the precarious nature of the girl's health. It is not of record that either of the two persons most affected and apparently least concerned made any explanation.

One evening about a week after the death I went out upon the veranda of the hotel to get a book that I had left there. Under some vines shutting out the moonlight from a part of the space I saw Richard Benning, for whose apparition I was prepared by having previously heard the low, sweet voice of Eva Maynard, whom also I now discerned, standing before him with one hand raised to his shoulder and her eyes, as

AN ADVENTURE AT BROWNVILLE

nearly as I could judge, gazing upward into his. He held her disengaged hand and his head was bent with a singular dignity and grace. Their attitude was that of lovers, and as I stood in deep shadow to observe I felt even guiltier than on that memorable night in the wood. I was about to retire, when the girl spoke, and the contrast between her words and her attitude was so surprising that I remained, because I had merely forgotten to go away.

"You will take my life," she said, "as you did Pauline's. I know your intention as well as I know your power, and I ask nothing, only that you finish your work without needless delay and let me be at peace."

He made no reply—merely let go the hand that he was holding, removed the other from his shoulder, and turning away descended the steps leading to the garden and disappeared in the shrubbery. But a moment later I heard, seemingly from a great distance, his fine clear voice in a barbaric chant, which as I listened brought before some inner spiritual sense a consciousness of some far, strange land peopled with beings having forbidden powers. The song held me in a kind of spell, but when it had died away I recovered and instantly perceived what I thought an opportunity. I walked out of my shadow to where the girl stood. She turned and stared at me with something of the look, it seemed to me, of a hunted hare. Possibly my intrusion had frightened her.

"Miss Maynard," I said, "I beg you to tell me who that man is and the nature of his power over you. Perhaps this is rude in me, but it is not a matter for idle civilities. When a woman is in danger any man has a right to act."

She listened without visible emotion—almost I thought without interest, and when I had finished she closed her big blue eyes as if unspeakably weary.

"You can do nothing," she said.

I took hold of her arm, gently shaking her as one shakes a person falling into a dangerous sleep.

"You must rouse yourself," I said; "something must be done and you must give me leave to act. You have said that that man killed your sister, and I believe it—that he will kill you, and I believe that."

She merely raised her eyes to mine.

"Will you not tell me all?" I added.

"There is nothing to be done, I tell you—nothing. And if I could do anything I would not. It does not matter in the least. We shall be here only two days more; we go away then, oh, so far! If you have observed anything, I beg you to be silent."

"But this is madness, girl." I was trying by rough speech to break the deadly repose of her manner. "You have accused him of murder. Unless you explain these things to me I shall lay the matter before the authorities."

This roused her, but in a way that I did not like. She lifted her head proudly and said: "Do not meddle, sir, in what does not concern you. This is my affair, Mr. Moran, not yours."

AN ADVENTURE AT BROWNVILLE

"It concerns every person in the country—in the world," I answered, with equal coldness. "If you had no love for your sister I, at least, am concerned for you."

"Listen," she interrupted, leaning toward me. "I loved her, yes, God knows! But more than that—beyond all, beyond expression, I love *him*. You have overheard a secret, but you shall not make use of it to harm him. I shall deny all. Your word against mine—it will be that. Do you think your 'authorities' will believe you?"

She was now smiling like an angel and, God help me! I was heels over head in love with her! Did she, by some of the many methods of divination known to her sex, read my feelings? Her whole manner had altered.

"Come," she said, almost coaxingly, "promise that you will not be impolite again." She took my arm in the most friendly way. "Come, I will walk with you. He will not know—he will remain away all night."

Up and down the veranda we paced in the moonlight, she seemingly forgetting her recent bereavement, cooing and murmuring girlwise of every kind of nothing in all Brownville; I silent, consciously awkward and with something of the feeling of being concerned in an intrigue. It was a revelation—this most charming and apparently blameless creature coolly and confessedly deceiving the man for whom a moment before she had acknowledged and shown the supreme love which finds even death an acceptable endearment.

"Truly," I thought in my inexperience, "here is something new under the moon."[6] And the moon must have smiled.

Before we parted I had exacted a promise that she would walk with me the next afternoon—before going away forever—to the Old Mill, one of Brownville's revered antiquities, erected in 1860.

"If he is not about," she added gravely, as I let go the hand she had given me at parting, and of which, may the good saints forgive me, I strove vainly to repossess myself when she had said it—so charming, as the wise Frenchman has pointed out, do we find woman's infidelity when we are its objects, not its victims. In apportioning his benefactions that night the Angel of Sleep overlooked me.

The Brownville House dined early, and after dinner the next day Miss Maynard, who had not been at table, came to me on the veranda, attired in the demurest of walking costumes, saying not a word. "He" was evidently "not about." We went slowly up the road that led to the Old Mill. She was apparently not strong and at times took my arm, relinquishing it and taking it again rather capriciously, I thought. Her mood, or rather her succession of moods, was as mutable as skylight in a rippling sea. She jested as if she had never heard of such a thing as death, and laughed on the lightest incitement, and directly afterward would sing a few bars of some grave melody with such tenderness of expression that I had to turn away my eyes lest she should see the evidence of her success in art, if art it was, not artlessness, as then I was compelled to think it. And she said the oddest things in the most unconventional way, skirting sometimes unfathomable abysms of thought, where I had the courage to set foot. In

AN ADVENTURE AT BROWNVILLE

short, she was fascinating in a thousand and fifty different ways, and at every step I executed a new and profounder emotional folly, a hardier spiritual indiscretion, incurring fresh liability to arrest by the constabulary of conscience for infractions of my own peace.

Arriving at the mill, she made no pretense of stopping, but turned into a trail leading through a field of stubble toward a creek. Crossing by a rustic bridge we continued on the trail, which now led uphill to one of the most picturesque spots in the country. The Eagle's Nest, it was called—the summit of a cliff that rose sheer into the air to a height of hundreds of feet above the forest at its base. From this elevated point we had a noble view of another valley and of the opposite hills flushed with the last rays of the setting sun. As we watched the light escaping to higher and higher planes from the encroaching flood of shadow filling the valley we heard footsteps, and in another moment were joined by Richard Benning.

"I saw you from the road," he said carelessly; "so I came up."

Being a fool, I neglected to take him by the throat and pitch him into the treetops below, but muttered some polite lie instead. On the girl the effect of his coming was immediate and unmistakable. Her face was suffused with the glory of love's transfiguration: the red light of the sunset had not been more obvious in her eyes than was now the lovelight that replaced it.

"I am so glad you came!" she said, giving him both her hands; and, God help me! it was manifestly true.

Seating himself upon the ground he began a lively dissertation upon the wild flowers of the region, a number of which he had with him. In the middle of a facetious sentence he suddenly ceased speaking and fixed his eyes upon Eva, who leaned against the stump of a tree, absently plaiting grasses. She lifted her eyes in a startled way to his, as if she had *felt* his look. She then rose, cast away her grasses and moved slowly away from him. He also rose, continuing to look at her. He had still in his hand the bunch of flowers. The girl turned, as if to speak, but said nothing. I recall clearly now something of which I was but half-conscious then—the dreadful contrast between the smile upon her lips and the terrified expression in her eyes as she met his steady and imperative gaze. I know nothing of how it happened, nor how it was that I did not sooner understand; I only know that with the smile of an angel upon her lips and that look of terror in her beautiful eyes Eva Maynard sprang from the cliff and shot crashing into the tops of the pines below!

How and how long afterward I reached the place I cannot say, but Richard Benning was already there, kneeling beside the dreadful thing that had been a woman.

"She is dead—quite dead," he said coldly. "I will go to town for assistance. Please do me the favor to remain."

He rose to his feet and moved away, but in a moment had stopped and turned about.

AN ADVENTURE AT BROWNVILLE

"You have doubtless observed, my friend," he said, "that this was entirely her own act. I did not rise in time to prevent it, and you, not knowing her mental condition—you could not, of course, have suspected."

His manner maddened me.

"You are as much her assassin," I said, "as if your damnable hands had cut her throat."

He shrugged his shoulders without reply and, turning, walked away. A moment later I heard, through the deepening shadows of the wood into which he had disappeared, a rich, strong baritone voice singing *"La donna e mobile,"* from "Rigoletto."[7]

E (3 Apr. 1892): 18 (as by "Ina Lillian Peterson and Ambrose Bierce"; as "An Occurrence at Brownville"); *CSTB* 73–89; **CW 2.247–65**.

NOTES

Bordering at first on the uncanny, this story ends sensationally in its implication that both sisters were under the fatal mesmeric control of a cold-hearted villain. Apart from whatever Ina Peterson contributed to the story, AB had earlier given sensational treatment to the idea of sinister mesmerism in "The Realm of the Unreal" and touched on it briefly and humorously in "A Lady from Redhorse."

AB's purported collaborator, a niece of the poet Ina Coolbrith, was of the circle of admirers whom AB attracted and who looked to him for literary guidance. AB's footnote acknowledging her coauthorship, while courtly and generous, is also probably hyperbole. But for this collaboration it is doubtful she would be remembered.

1. Shakespeare, *Hamlet*, 3.4.36: "My father, in his habit as he lived!"
2. Thomas Gray, *Elegy Written in a Country Churchyard* (1751), l. 59: "Some mute inglorious Milton." AB also wrote verses that he eventually titled "A 'Mute Inglorious Milton'" (1883; *CW* 4.158–59).
3. The opera composed by Giuseppe Verdi, first performed 3 November 1851.
4. Another tag from Gray's *Elegy*: "The short and simple annals of the poor" (l. 32).
5. An alternative provided by Scotch law between "guilty" and "not guilty."
6. A twist on Eccles. 1:9: "The thing that hath been, it is that which shall be; and that which is done is that which shall be done: and there is no new thing under the sun." The use of the moon, however, gives the allusion an added force because the moon is a traditional symbol of mutability and change.
7. I.e., "the beautiful woman is fickle"—the aria is ironic in *Rigoletto*, as it seems to be here.

THE WIZARD OF BUMBASSA

Mr. George Westinghouse, the air-brake man,[1] did a cruel and needless thing in going out of his way to try to destroy humanity's hope of being shot along the ground at a speed of one hundred miles an hour. There is no trouble, it appears, in building locomotives able to snatch a small village of us through space at the required speed; the difficulty lies in making, with sufficient promptness, those unschedulary stops necessitated by open switches, missing bridges and various obstacles that industrial discontent is wont to grace the track withal. Even on a straight line—what the civil engineers find a pleasure in calling a tangent—the prosperous industrian at the throttle-valve cannot reasonably be expected to discern these hindrances at a greater distance than one thousand feet; and Mr. Westinghouse sadly confessed that in that distance his most effective appliance could not do more than reduce the rate from one hundred miles an hour to fifty—an obviously inadequate reduction. He held out no hope of being able to evolve from his inner consciousness either a brake of superior effectiveness or a pair of spectacles that would enable the engine driver to discover a more distant danger on a tangent, or to see round a curve.

All this begets an intelligent dejection. If we must renounce our golden dream of cannonading ourselves from place to place with a celerity suitable to our rank in the world's *fauna*—comprising the shark, the hummingbird, the hornet and the jackass-rabbit—civilization is indeed a failure.[2] But it is forbidden to the wicked pessimist to rejoice, for there is a greater than Mr. Westinghouse and he has demonstrated his ability to bring to a dead stop within its own length any railway train, however short and whatever its rate of speed. It were unwise, though, to indulge too high a hope in this matter, even if the gloomy vaticinations of the Westinghouse person are fallacious. Approaching an evidence of social unrest at a speed of one and two-thirds mile a minute on a down grade, even in a train equipped by a greater than Mr. Westinghouse, may not be an altogether pleasing performance.

This possibility can be best illustrated by recalling to the reader's memory the history of the Ghargaroo and Gallywest Railway in Bumbassa.[3] As is well known, the trains on that road attained a speed that had not theretofore been dreamed of except by the illustrious projector of the road.[4] But the King of Bumbassa was not content: with an indifference to the laws of dynamics which in the retrospect seems almost imperial, he insisted upon instantaneous stoppage. To the royal demand the clever and prudent gentleman who had devised and carried out the enterprise responded with an invention which he assured his Majesty would accomplish the desired end. A trial was made in the sovereign's presence, the coaches being loaded with his chief officers of state and other courtiers, and it was eminently successful. The train, going at a speed of ninety miles an hour, was brought to a dead stop within the length of the rhinoceros-catcher[5] and directly in front of the blue cotton umbrella beneath which his Majesty sat to observe the result of the test. The passengers, unfortunately, did not stop so promptly, and were afterward scraped off the woodwork at the forward ends of the cars and decently interred. The train-hands had all escaped by the ingenious plan of absenting themselves from the proceedings, with the exception of the engineer, who had thoughtfully been selected for the occasion from among the relatives of the projector's wife, and instructed how to shut off the steam and apply the brake. When hosed off the several parts of the engine he was found to have incurred a serious dispersal of the viscera.

The King's delight at the success of the experiment was somewhat mitigated by the reflection that if the train had been freighted with *bona fide* travelers instead of dignitaries whom he could replace by appointment the military resources of the state would have suffered a considerable loss; so he commanded the projector to invent a method of stopping the passengers and the trains simultaneously. This, after much experiment, was done by fixing the passengers to the seats by clamps extending across the abdomen and chest; but no provision being made for the head, a general decapitation ensued at each stop; and people who valued their heads preferred thereafter to travel afoot or ostrichback, as before. It was found, moreover, that, as arrested motion is converted into heat, the royal requirement frequently resulted in igniting and consuming the trains—which was expensive.

These various hard conditions of railroading in Bumbassa eventually subdued the spirits of the stockholders, drove the projector to drink and led at last to withdrawal of the concession—whereby one of the most promising projects for civilizing the Dark Continent was, in the words of the Ghargaroo *Palladium,* "knocked perfectly cold."

I have thought it well to recall this melancholy incident here for its general usefulness in pointing a moral, and for its particular application to the fascinating enterprise of a one-hundred-miles-an-hour electric road from New York to Chicago—a road whose trains, intending passengers are assured, will be under absolute control of the engineers and "can be stopped at a moment's notice." If I have said anything to discourage the enterprise I am sorry, but really it is not easy to understand why anybody should wish to go from New York to Chicago.

THE WIZARD OF BUMBASSA

E (28 Aug. 1892): 6 (as "Rabid Transit"; unsigned); *CW* **12.338–42**.

NOTES

The transition from expository to narrative satire occurs in the third paragraph. It is interesting to note that the nineteenth century not only conceived inventions that were not brought to practical development until generations later but also recognized some of the dangers and problems—including human ones—inherent in technological progress.

Title: AB also refers to Bumbassa in "An Ancient Hunter" (p. 1054).

1. George Westinghouse (1846–1914), American inventor of the air brake, which made high-speed rail travel possible, and founder in 1884 of the Westinghouse Electric Corporation.

2. Cf. AB's "Is Civilization a Failure" (*F,* 2 Oct. 1873), and the lines: "Is civilization a failure, / Or is the Caucasian played out?" Editorial, *W* no. 465 (20 June 1885): 4 (unsigned).

3. The name Ghargaroo was first coined by AB in a fable (*E,* 20 Mar. 1891), but this citation was removed when AB reprinted the fable in *CW* 6 (see *CF*, no. 252), probably because AB had used the name in "The Land Beyond the Blow" (*CW* 1), in the chapter "A Conflagration in Ghargaroo." AB refers to a "2330 Gallywest street, San Francisco," in "Our Medical Column," *W*, no. 497 (6 Feb. 1886): 3 (unsigned). "Galleywest," as in "knocked galley-west," means "into destruction or confusion." Bumbassa is probably intended as a parody of Mombasa, a major city in Kenya.

4. "Projector" has largely been replaced in our time by "promotor"—i.e., one who conceives and pushes enterprises. In the eighteenth century, however, "projector" took on a disparaging connotation for its association with impractical schemes. See, for example, Jonathan Swift's satire of projectors in chapters 4 and 5 of book 3 of *Gulliver's Travels* (1735).

5. "Rhinoceros-catcher" is a play on "cow-catcher," a slang term for "the inclined frame on the front of a locomotive for catching or thrusting aside cattle or other obstructions on the tracks of a railroad" (*DAE*).

THE APPLICANT

Pushing his adventurous shins through the deep snow that had fallen overnight, and encouraged by the glee of his little sister, following in the open way that he made, a sturdy small boy, the son of Grayville's most distinguished citizen, struck his foot against something of which there was no visible sign on the surface of the snow. It is the purpose of this narrative to show how it came to be there.

No one who has had the advantage of passing through Grayville by day can have failed to observe the large stone building crowning the low hill to the north of the railway station—that is to say, to the right in going toward Great Mowbray. It is a somewhat dull-looking edifice, of the Early Comatose order, and appears to have been designed by an architect who shrank from publicity, and although unable to conceal his work—even compelled, in this instance, to set it on an eminence in the sight of men—did what he honestly could to insure it against a second look. So far as concerns its outer and visible aspect, the Abersush Home for Old Men is unquestionably inhospitable to human attention. But it is a building of great magnitude, and cost its benevolent founder the profit of many a cargo of the teas and silks and spices that his ships brought up from the under-world when he was in trade in Boston; though the main expense was its endowment. Altogether, this reckless person had robbed his heirs-at-law of no less a sum than half a million dollars and flung it away in riotous giving. Possibly it was with a view to get out of sight of the silent big witness to his extravagance that he shortly afterward disposed of all his Grayville property that remained to him, turned his back upon the scene of his prodigality and went off across the sea in one of his own ships. But the gossips who got their inspiration most directly from Heaven declared that he went in search of a wife—a theory not easily reconciled with that of the village humorist, who solemnly averred that the bachelor philanthropist had departed this life (left Grayville, to wit) because the marriageable maidens had made it too hot to hold him.[1] However this may have been, he had not returned, and although at long intervals there had come to

Grayville, in a desultory way, vague rumors of his wanderings in strange lands, no one seemed certainly to know about him, and to the new generation he was no more than a name. But from above the portal of the Home for Old Men the name shouted in stone.

Despite its unpromising exterior, the Home is a fairly commodious place of retreat from the ills that its inmates have incurred by being poor and old and men. At the time embraced in this brief chronicle they were in number about a score, but in acerbity, querulousness and general ingratitude they could hardly be reckoned at fewer than a hundred; at least that was the estimate of the superintendent, Mr. Silas Tilbody. It was Mr. Tilbody's steadfast conviction that always, in admitting new old men to replace those who had gone to another and a better Home, the trustees had distinctly in will the infraction of his peace, and the trial of his patience. In truth, the longer the institution was connected with him, the stronger was his feeling that the founder's scheme of benevolence was sadly impaired by providing any inmates at all. He had not much imagination, but with what he had he was addicted to the reconstruction of the Home for Old Men into a kind of "castle in Spain," with himself as castellan, hospitably entertaining about a score of sleek and prosperous middle-aged gentlemen, consummately good-humored and civilly willing to pay for their board and lodging. In this revised project of philanthropy the trustees, to whom he was indebted for his office and responsible for his conduct, had not the happiness to appear. As to them, it was held by the village humorist aforementioned that in their management of the great charity Providence had thoughtfully supplied an incentive to thrift.[2] With the inference which he expected to be drawn from that view we have nothing to do; it had neither support nor denial from the inmates, who certainly were most concerned. They lived out their little remnant of life, crept into graves neatly numbered and were succeeded by other old men as like them as could be desired by the Adversary of Peace. If the Home was a place of punishment for the sin of unthrift the veteran offenders sought justice with a persistence that attested the sincerity of their penitence. It is to one of these that the reader's attention is now invited.

In the matter of attire this person was not altogether engaging. But for this season, which was midwinter, a careless observer might have looked upon him as a clever device of the husbandman indisposed to share the fruits of his toil with the crows that toil not, neither spin[3]—an error that might not have been dispelled without longer and closer observation than he seemed to court; for his progress up Abersush Street, toward the Home in the gloom of the winter evening, was not visibly faster than what might have been expected of a scarecrow blessed with youth, health and discontent. The man was indisputably ill-clad, yet not without a certain fitness and good taste, withal; for he was obviously an applicant for admittance to the Home, where poverty was a qualification. In the army of indigence the uniform is rags; they serve to distinguish the rank and file from the recruiting officers.

As the old man, entering the gate of the grounds, shuffled up the broad walk, already white with the fast-falling snow, which from time to time he feebly shook from

THE APPLICANT

its various coigns of vantage on his person, he came under inspection of the large globe lamp that burned always by night over the great door of the building. As if unwilling to incur its revealing beams, he turned to the left and, passing a considerable distance along the face of the building, rang at a smaller door emitting a dimmer ray that came from within, through the fanlight, and expended itself incuriously overhead. The door was opened by no less a personage than the great Mr. Tilbody himself. Observing his visitor, who at once uncovered, and somewhat shortened the radius of the permanent curvature of his back, the great man gave visible token of neither surprise nor displeasure. Mr. Tilbody was, indeed, in an uncommonly good humor, a phenomenon ascribable doubtless to the cheerful influence of the season; for this was Christmas Eve, and the morrow would be that blessed 365th part of the year that all Christian souls set apart for mighty feats of goodness and joy.[4] Mr. Tilbody was so full of the spirit of the season that his fat face and pale blue eyes, whose ineffectual fire served to distinguish it from an untimely summer squash, effused so genial a glow that it seemed a pity that he could not have lain down in it, basking in the consciousness of his own identity. He was hatted, booted, overcoated and umbrellaed, as became a person who was about to expose himself to the night and the storm on an errand of charity; for Mr. Tilbody had just parted from his wife and children to go "down town" and purchase the wherewithal to confirm the annual falsehood about the hunch-bellied saint who frequents the chimneys to reward little boys and girls who are good, and especially truthful. So he did not invite the old man in, but saluted him cheerily:

"Hello! just in time; a moment later and you would have missed me. Come, I have no time to waste; we'll walk a little way together."

"Thank you," said the old man, upon whose thin and white but not ignoble face the light from the open door showed an expression that was perhaps disappointment; "but if the trustees—if my application—"

"The trustees," Mr. Tilbody said, closing more doors than one, and cutting off two kinds of light, "have agreed that your application disagrees with them."

Certain sentiments are inappropriate to Christmastide, but Humor, like Death, has all seasons for his own.[5]

"Oh, my God!" cried the old man, in so thin and husky a tone that the invocation was anything but impressive, and to at least one of his two auditors sounded, indeed, somewhat ludicrous. To the Other—but that is a matter which laymen are devoid of the light to expound.

"Yes," continued Mr. Tilbody, accommodating his gait to that of his companion, who was mechanically, and not very successfully, retracing the track that he had made through the snow; "they have decided that, under the circumstances—under the very peculiar circumstances, you understand—it would be inexpedient to admit you. As superintendent and *ex officio* secretary of the honorable board"—as Mr. Tilbody "read his title clear"[6] the magnitude of the big building, seen through its veil of falling snow, appeared to suffer somewhat in comparison—"it is my duty to inform you that, in the

THE APPLICANT

words of Deacon Byram, the chairman, your presence in the Home would—under the circumstances—be peculiarly embarrassing. I felt it my duty to submit to the honorable board the statement that you made to me yesterday of your needs, your physical condition and the trials which it has pleased Providence to send upon you in your very proper effort to present your claims in person; but, after careful, and I may say prayerful, consideration of your case—with something too, I trust, of the large charitableness appropriate to the season—it was decided that we would not be justified in doing anything likely to impair the usefulness of the institution intrusted (under Providence) to our care."

They had now passed out of the grounds; the street lamp opposite the gate was dimly visible through the snow. Already the old man's former track was obliterated, and he seemed uncertain as to which way he should go. Mr. Tilbody had drawn a little away from him, but paused and turned half toward him, apparently reluctant to forego the continuing opportunity.

"Under the circumstances," he resumed, "the decision—"

But the old man was inaccessible to the suasion of his verbosity; he had crossed the street into a vacant lot and was going forward, rather deviously, toward nowhere in particular—which, he having nowhere in particular to go, was not so reasonless a proceeding as it looked.

And that is how it happened that the next morning, when the church bells of all Grayville were ringing with an added unction appropriate to the day, the sturdy little son of Deacon Byram, breaking a way through the snow to the place of worship, struck his foot against the body of Amasa Abersush, philanthropist.

Wa, Christmas 1892 (17 Dec. 1892): 16–17; *CSTB* 187–94; ***CW*** 2.281–89.

NOTES

The original publication of this story in the Christmas 1892 issue of *Wa* was a continuation of AB's lifelong campaign to arraign institutional Christianity for its unfaithfulness to the spirit of Christ. The tale's melodramatic ending is only slightly diffused by heavy-handed irony.

1. Cf. *DD*, s.v. "ABDICATION": "She [Queen Isabella] wisely left a throne too hot to hold her."
2. Another spoof of the argument from design; see "Oil of Dog," note 3.
3. Matt. 6:28: "And why take ye thought for raiment? Consider the lilies of the field, how they grow; they toil not, neither do they spin."
4. "How I hate Christmas! I'm one of the curmudgeons that the truly good Mr. Dickens found it profitable to hold up to the scorn of those who take such satisfaction in being decent and generous one day in 365." AB to C. W. Doyle (26 Dec. 1897); *MMM* 59.
5. See "The Lady from Redhorse," p. 779 note 5.
6. Isaac Watts, "When I Can Read My Title Clear," from *Hymns and Spiritual Songs* (1707).

THE APPLICANT

ONE KIND OF OFFICER

I
OF THE USES OF CIVILITY

"Captain Ransome, it is not permitted to you to know *anything*. It is sufficient that you obey my order—which permit me to repeat. If you perceive any movement of troops in your front you are to open fire, and if attacked hold this position as long as you can. Do I make myself understood, sir?"

"Nothing could be plainer. Lieutenant Price,"—this to an officer of his own battery, who had ridden up in time to hear the order—"the general's meaning is clear, is it not?"

"Perfectly."

The lieutenant passed on to his post. For a moment General Cameron and the commander of the battery sat in their saddles, looking at each other in silence. There was no more to say; apparently too much had already been said. Then the superior officer nodded coldly and turned his horse to ride away. The artillerist saluted slowly, gravely and with extreme formality. One acquainted with the niceties of military etiquette would have said that by his manner he attested a sense of the rebuke that he had incurred. It is one of the important uses of civility to signify resentment.

When the general had joined his staff and escort, awaiting him at a little distance, the whole cavalcade moved off toward the right of the guns and vanished in the fog. Captain Ransome was alone, silent, motionless as an equestrian statue. The gray fog, thickening every moment, closed in about him like a visible doom.

II
UNDER WHAT CIRCUMSTANCES MEN
DO NOT WISH TO BE SHOT

The fighting of the day before had been desultory and indecisive. At the points of collision the smoke of battle had hung in blue sheets among the branches of the trees till beaten into nothing by the falling rain. In the softened earth the wheels of cannon and ammunition wagons cut deep, ragged furrows, and movements of infantry seemed impeded by the mud that clung to the soldiers' feet as, with soaken garments and rifles imperfectly protected by capes of overcoats they went dragging in sinuous lines hither and thither through dripping forest and flooded field. Mounted officers, their heads protruding from rubber ponchos that glittered like black armor, picked their way, singly and in loose groups, among the men, coming and going with apparent aimlessness and commanding attention from nobody but one another. Here and there a dead man, his clothing defiled with earth, his face covered with a blanket or show-ing yellow and claylike in the rain, added his dispiriting influence to that of the other dismal features of the scene and augmented the general discomfort with a particular dejection. Very repulsive these wrecks looked—not at all heroic, and nobody was accessible to the infection of their patriotic example. Dead upon the field of honor, yes;[1] but the field of honor was so very wet! It makes a difference.

The general engagement that all expected did not occur, none of the small advan-tages accruing, now to this side and now to that, in isolated and accidental collisions being followed up. Half-hearted attacks provoked a sullen resistance which was sat-isfied with mere repulse. Orders were obeyed with mechanical fidelity; no one did any more than his duty.

"The army is cowardly to-day," said General Cameron, the commander of a Fed-eral brigade, to his adjutant-general.

"The army is cold," replied the officer addressed, "and—yes, it doesn't wish to be like that."

He pointed to one of the dead bodies, lying in a thin pool of yellow water, its face and clothing bespattered with mud from hoof to wheel.

The army's weapons seemed to share its military delinquency. The rattle of rifles sounded flat and contemptible. It had no meaning and scarcely roused to attention and expectancy the unengaged parts of the line-of-battle and the waiting reserves. Heard at a little distance, the reports of cannon were feeble in volume and *timbre:* they lacked sting and resonance. The guns seemed to be fired with light charges, unshot-ted. And so the futile day wore on to its dreary close, and then to a night of discom-fort succeeded a day of apprehension.[2]

An army has a personality. Beneath the individual thoughts and emotions of its component parts it thinks and feels as a unit. And in this large, inclusive sense of things lies a wiser wisdom than the mere sum of all that it knows. On that dismal morning this great brute force, groping at the bottom of a white ocean of fog among trees that seemed as sea weeds, had a dumb consciousness that all was not well; that a day's manœuvring had resulted in a faulty disposition of its parts, a blind diffusion of its strength. The men felt insecure and talked among themselves of such tactical errors as with their meager military vocabulary they were able to name. Field and line officers gathered in groups and spoke more learnedly of what they apprehended with

ONE KIND OF OFFICER

no greater clearness. Commanders of brigades and divisions looked anxiously to their connections on the right and on the left, sent staff officers on errands of inquiry and pushed skirmish lines silently and cautiously forward into the dubious region between the known and the unknown. At some points on the line the troops, apparently of their own volition, constructed such defenses as they could without the silent spade and the noisy ax.

One of these points was held by Captain Ransome's battery of six guns. Provided always with intrenching tools, his men had labored with diligence during the night, and now his guns thrust their black muzzles through the embrasures of a really formidable earthwork. It crowned a slight acclivity devoid of undergrowth and providing an unobstructed fire that would sweep the ground for an unknown distance in front. The position could hardly have been better chosen. It had this peculiarity, which Captain Ransome, who was greatly addicted to the use of the compass, had not failed to observe: it faced northward, whereas he knew that the general line of the army must face eastward. In fact, that part of the line was "refused"—that is to say, bent backward, away from the enemy. This implied that Captain Ransome's battery was somewhere near the left flank of the army; for an army in line of battle retires its flanks if the nature of the ground will permit, they being its vulnerable points. Actually, Captain Ransome appeared to hold the extreme left of the line, no troops being visible in that direction beyond his own. Immediately in rear of his guns occurred that conversation between him and his brigade commander, the concluding and more picturesque part of which is reported above.

III
HOW TO PLAY THE CANNON WITHOUT NOTES

Captain Ransome sat motionless and silent on horseback. A few yards away his men were standing at their guns. Somewhere—everywhere within a few miles—were a hundred thousand men, friends and enemies. Yet he was alone. The mist had isolated him as completely as if he had been in the heart of a desert. His world was a few square yards of wet and trampled earth about the feet of his horse. His comrades in that ghostly domain were invisible and inaudible. These were conditions favorable to thought, and he was thinking. Of the nature of his thoughts his clear-cut handsome features yielded no attesting sign. His face was as inscrutable as that of the sphinx. Why should it have made a record which there was none to observe? At the sound of a footstep he merely turned his eyes in the direction whence it came; one of his sergeants, looking a giant in stature in the false perspective of the fog, approached, and when clearly defined and reduced to his true dimensions by propinquity, saluted and stood at attention.

"Well, Morris," said the officer, returning his subordinate's salute.

"Lieutenant Price directed me to tell you, sir, that most of the infantry has been withdrawn. We have not sufficient support."

"Yes, I know."

"I am to say that some of our men have been out over the works a hundred yards and report that our front is not picketed."

"Yes."

"They were so far forward that they heard the enemy."

"Yes."

"They heard the rattle of the wheels of artillery and the commands of officers."

"Yes."

"The enemy is moving toward our works."

Captain Ransome, who had been facing to the rear of his line—toward the point where the brigade commander and his cavalcade had been swallowed up by the fog—reined his horse about and faced the other way. Then he sat motionless as before.

"Who are the men who made that statement?" he inquired, without looking at the sergeant; his eyes were directed straight into the fog over the head of his horse.

"Corporal Hassman and Gunner Manning."

Captain Ransome was a moment silent. A slight pallor came into his face, a slight compression affected the lines of his lips, but it would have required a closer observer than Sergeant Morris to note the change. There was none in the voice.

"Sergeant, present my compliments to Lieutenant Price and direct him to open fire with all the guns. Grape."

The sergeant saluted and vanished in the fog.

IV

TO INTRODUCE GENERAL MASTERSON

Searching for his division commander, General Cameron and his escort had followed the line-of-battle for nearly a mile to the right of Ransome's battery, and there learned that the division commander had gone in search of the corps commander. It seemed that everybody was looking for his immediate superior—an ominous circumstance. It meant that nobody was quite at ease. So General Cameron rode on for another half-mile, where by good luck he met General Masterson, the division commander, returning.

"Ah, Cameron," said the higher officer, reining up, and throwing his right leg across the pommel of his saddle in a most unmilitary way—"anything up? Found a good position for your battery, I hope—if one place is better than another in a fog."

"Yes, general," said the other, with the greater dignity appropriate to his less exalted rank, "my battery is very well placed. I wish I could say that it is as well commanded."

"Eh, what's that? Ransome? I think him a fine fellow. In the army we should be proud of him."

It was customary for officers of the regular army to speak of it as "the army." As the greatest cities are the most provincial, so the self-complacency of aristocracies is most frankly plebeian.

ONE KIND OF OFFICER

"He is too fond of his opinion. By the way, in order to occupy the hill that he holds I had to extend my line dangerously. The hill is on my left—that is to say the left flank of the army."

"Oh, no, Hart's brigade is beyond. It was ordered up from Drytown during the night and directed to hook on to you. Better go and—"

The sentence was unfinished: a lively cannonade had broken out on the left, and both officers, followed by their retinues of aides and orderlies making a great jingle and clank, rode rapidly toward the spot. But they were soon impeded, for they were compelled by the fog to keep within sight of the line-of-battle, behind which were swarms of men, all in motion across their way. Everywhere the line was assuming a sharper and harder definition, as the men sprang to arms and the officers, with drawn swords, "dressed" the ranks. Color-bearers unfurled the flags, buglers blew the "assembly," hospital attendants appeared with stretchers. Field officers mounted and sent their impedimenta to the rear in care of negro servants. Back in the ghostly spaces of the forest could be heard the rustle and murmur of the reserves, pulling themselves together.

Nor was all this preparation vain, for scarcely five minutes had passed since Captain Ransome's guns had broken the truce of doubt before the whole region was aroar: the enemy had attacked nearly everywhere.

V

HOW SOUNDS CAN FIGHT SHADOWS

Captain Ransome walked up and down behind his guns, which were firing rapidly but with steadiness. The gunners worked alertly, but without haste or apparent excitement. There was really no reason for excitement; it is not much to point a cannon into a fog and fire it. Anybody can do as much as that.

The men smiled at their noisy work, performing it with a lessening alacrity. They cast curious regards upon their captain, who had now mounted the banquette of the fortification and was looking across the parapet as if observing the effect of his fire. But the only visible effect was the substitution of wide, low-lying sheets of smoke for their bulk of fog. Suddenly out of the obscurity burst a great sound of cheering, which filled the intervals between the reports of the guns with startling distinctness! To the few with leisure and opportunity to observe, the sound was inexpressibly strange—so loud, so near, so menacing, yet nothing seen! The men who had smiled at their work smiled no more, but performed it with a serious and feverish activity.

From his station at the parapet Captain Ransome now saw a great multitude of dim gray figures taking shape in the mist below him and swarming up the slope. But the work of the guns was now fast and furious. They swept the populous declivity with gusts of grape and canister, the whirring of which could be heard through the thunder of the explosions. In this awful tempest of iron the assailants struggled forward foot by foot across their dead, firing into the embrasures, reloading, firing again, and at last falling in their turn, a little in advance of those who had fallen before. Soon the smoke was dense enough to cover all. It settled down upon the attack and, drifting back, involved the defense. The gunners could hardly see to serve their pieces, and when occasional figures of the enemy appeared upon the parapet—having had the good luck to get near enough to it, between two embrasures, to be protected from the guns—they looked so unsubstantial that it seemed hardly worth while for the few infantrymen to go to work upon them with the bayonet and tumble them back into the ditch.

As the commander of a battery in action can find something better to do than cracking individual skulls, Captain Ransome had retired from the parapet to his proper post in rear of his guns, where he stood with folded arms, his bugler beside him. Here, during the hottest of the fight, he was approached by Lieutenant Price, who had just sabered a daring assailant inside the work. A spirited colloquy ensued between the two officers—spirited, at least, on the part of the lieutenant, who gesticulated with energy and shouted again and again into his commander's ear in the attempt to make himself heard above the infernal din of the guns. His gestures, if coolly noted by an actor, would have been pronounced to be those of protestation: one would have said that he was opposed to the proceedings. Did he wish to surrender?

Captain Ransome listened without a change of countenance or attitude, and when the other man had finished his harangue, looked him coldly in the eyes and during a seasonable abatement of the uproar said:

"Lieutenant Price, it is not permitted to you to know *anything*. It is sufficient that you obey my orders."

The lieutenant went to his post, and the parapet being now apparently clear Captain Ransome returned to it to have a look over. As he mounted the banquette a man sprang upon the crest, waving a great brilliant flag. The captain drew a pistol from his belt and shot him dead. The body, pitching forward, hung over the inner edge of the embankment, the arms straight downward, both hands still grasping the flag. The man's few followers turned and fled down the slope. Looking over the parapet, the captain saw no living thing. He observed also that no bullets were coming into the work.

He made a sign to the bugler, who sounded the command to cease firing. At all other points the action had already ended with a repulse of the Confederate attack; with the cessation of this cannonade the silence was absolute.

VI
WHY, BEING AFFRONTED BY A, IT IS NOT BEST TO AFFRONT B

General Masterson rode into the redoubt. The men, gathered in groups, were talking loudly and gesticulating. They pointed at the dead, running from one body to another. They neglected their foul and heated guns and forgot to resume their outer clothing. They ran to the parapet and looked over, some of them leaping down into the ditch. A score were gathered about a flag rigidly held by a dead man.

"Well, my men," said the general cheerily, "you have had a pretty fight of it."

They stared; nobody replied; the presence of the great man seemed to embarrass and alarm.

Getting no response to his pleasant condescension, the easy-mannered officer whistled a bar or two of a popular air, and riding forward to the parapet, looked over at the dead. In an instant he had whirled his horse about and was spurring along in rear of the guns, his eyes everywhere at once. An officer sat on the trail of one of the guns, smoking a cigar. As the general dashed up he rose and tranquilly saluted.

"Captain Ransome!"—the words fell sharp and harsh, like the clash of steel blades—"you have been fighting our own men—our own men, sir; do you hear? Hart's brigade!"

"General, I know that."

"You know it—you know that, and you sit here smoking? Oh, damn it, Hamilton, I'm losing my temper,"—this to his provost-marshal. "Sir—Captain Ransome, be good enough to say—to say why you fought our own men."

"That I am unable to say. In my orders that information was withheld."

Apparently the general did not comprehend.

"Who was the aggressor in this affair, you or General Hart?" he asked.

"I was."

"And could you not have known—could you not see, sir, that you were attacking our own men?"

The reply was astounding!

"I knew that, general. It appeared to be none of my business."

Then, breaking the dead silence that followed his answer, he said:

"I must refer you to General Cameron."

"General Cameron is dead, sir—as dead as he can be—as dead as any man in this army. He lies back yonder under a tree. Do you mean to say that he had anything to do with this horrible business?"

Captain Ransome did not reply. Observing the altercation his men had gathered about to watch the outcome. They were greatly excited. The fog, which had been partly dissipated by the firing, had again closed in so darkly about them that they drew more closely together till the judge on horseback and the accused standing calmly before him had but a narrow space free from intrusion. It was the most informal of courts-martial, but all felt that the formal one to follow would but affirm its judgment. It had no jurisdiction, but it had the significance of prophecy.

"Captain Ransome," the general cried impetuously, but with something in his voice that was almost entreaty, "if you can say anything to put a better light upon your incomprehensible conduct I beg you will do so."

Having recovered his temper this generous soldier sought for something to justify his naturally sympathetic attitude toward a brave man in the imminence of a dishonorable death.

ONE KIND OF OFFICER

"Where is Lieutenant Price?" the captain said.

That officer stood forward, his dark saturnine face looking somewhat forbidding under a bloody handkerchief bound about his brow. He understood the summons and needed no invitation to speak. He did not look at the captain, but addressed the general:

"During the engagement I discovered the state of affairs, and apprised the commander of the battery. I ventured to urge that the firing cease. I was insulted and ordered to my post."

"Do you know anything of the orders under which I was acting?" asked the captain.

"Of any orders under which the commander of the battery was acting," the lieutenant continued, still addressing the general, "I know nothing."

Captain Ransome felt his world sink away from his feet. In those cruel words he heard the murmur of the centuries breaking upon the shore of eternity. He heard the voice of doom; it said, in cold, mechanical and measured tones: "Ready, aim, fire!" and he felt the bullets tear his heart to shreds. He heard the sound of the earth upon his coffin and (if the good God was so merciful) the song of a bird above his forgotten grave. Quietly detaching his saber from its supports, he handed it up to the provost-marshal.

E (1 Jan. 1893): 30; *CSTB* 167–86; ***CW* 2.178–96.**

NOTES

The clause "it is not permitted to you to know anything," with its tone of arrogant imperiousness, is the center of a complex of emotions and authorial attitudes in this fine story. The tragedy of an army unit firing on its own men or on innocents was one to which AB gave much consideration. "The Affair at Coulter's Notch" deals with a similar situation. AB was aware of at least two more such incidents, one involving Stonewall Jackson in the Mexican War, and another at Shiloh (see *PA* 198). All these tragedies have in common the military requirement that an order be obeyed regardless of whether or not a subordinate understands or agrees with it. This obedience goes to the heart of discipline, and discipline is essential to the military. At the same time, everyone would agree that some commands can be mistaken or, indeed, illegal; the absolutism of a command is therefore qualified by the realization that the giver of a command is not possessed of absolute knowledge or judgment. These are the horns of the dilemma in this story, and the subordinate cannot go between them but must choose one or the other.

In other words, a subordinate always must make a choice of whether to obey an order or to disobey it on the grounds of duty to a higher or sounder principle. The severe penalty that would surely follow upon being wrong is of course a great deterrent to subordinate disobedience but the penalty cuts both ways. In this case, Captain Ransome either risks his own life or knowingly kills fellow soldiers. In choosing to save himself by adopting the arbitrary hauteur of the bad officer General Cameron, he surrenders his conscience as well as his judgment and becomes essentially a robot, an unthinking cog in a machine. This is shown not only by his obedience to what he knew to be a bad order but by using the same language on the more conscientious Lieutenant Price that General Cameron used on him:

"it is not permitted to you to know anything." Ironically, therefore, Lieutenant Price pays Ransome back in his own coin by implicitly obeying his last command. "I know nothing," he replies to the crucial question put to him by General Masterson. AB's criticism of military discipline is therefore qualified by the title of the story. Officers even more than enlisted men have an absolute duty to the highest principles operant in a given situation and a mortal obligation to eschew ignorance or folly. Arrogant insistence upon an empty form of obedience is therefore not only foolish, it may be criminal. Ransome therefore gets what he deserves. See "The Crime at Pickett's Mill" (*SS* 37–44) for AB's more explicit opinion of pompous commanding officers.

1. See "Killed at Resaca," p. 512 note 3.
2. Possibly an adaptation of Sir Walter Scott, *The Lady of the Lake* (1810), canto 1, stanza 31: "Days of danger, nights of waking."

ONE KIND OF OFFICER

JOHN BARTINE'S WATCH

A Story by a Physician

"The exact time? Good God! my friend, why do you insist? One would think—but what does it matter; it is easily bedtime—isn't that near enough? But, here, if you must set your watch, take mine and see for yourself."

With that he detached his watch—a tremendously heavy, old-fashioned one—from the chain, and handed it to me; then turned away, and walking across the room to a shelf of books, began an examination of their backs. His agitation and evident distress surprised me; they appeared reasonless. Having set my watch by his, I stepped over to where he stood and said, "Thank you."

As he took his timepiece and reattached it to the guard I observed that his hands were unsteady. With a tact upon which I greatly prided myself, I sauntered carelessly to the sideboard and took some brandy and water; then, begging his pardon for my thoughtlessness, asked him to have some and went back to my seat by the fire, leaving him to help himself, as was our custom. He did so and presently joined me at the hearth, as tranquil as ever.

This odd little incident occurred in my apartment, where John Bartine was passing an evening. We had dined together at the club, had come home in a cab and—in short, everything had been done in the most prosaic way; and why John Bartine should break in upon the natural and established order of things to make himself spectacular with a display of emotion, apparently for his own entertainment, I could nowise understand. The more I thought of it, while his brilliant conversational gifts were commending themselves to my inattention, the more curious I grew, and of course had no difficulty in persuading myself that my curiosity was friendly solicitude. That is the disguise that curiosity usually assumes to evade resentment. So I ruined one of the finest sentences of his disregarded monologue by cutting it short without ceremony.

"John Bartine," I said, "you must try to forgive me if I am wrong, but with the light that I have at present I cannot concede your right to go all to pieces when asked the time o' night. I cannot admit that it is proper to experience a mysterious reluctance to look your own watch in the face and to cherish in my presence, without explanation, painful emotions which are denied to me, and which are none of my business."

To this ridiculous speech Bartine made no immediate reply, but sat looking gravely into the fire. Fearing that I had offended I was about to apologize and beg him to think no more about the matter, when looking me calmly in the eyes he said:

"My dear fellow, the levity of your manner does not at all disguise the hideous impudence of your demand; but happily I had already decided to tell you what you wish to know, and no manifestation of your unworthiness to hear it shall alter my decision. Be good enough to give me your attention and you shall hear all about the matter.

"This watch," he said, "had been in my family for three generations before it fell to me. Its original owner, for whom it was made, was my great-grandfather, Bramwell Olcott Bartine, a wealthy planter of Colonial Virginia, and as staunch a Tory as ever lay awake nights contriving new kinds of maledictions for the head of Mr. Washington, and new methods of aiding and abetting good King George. One day this worthy gentleman had the deep misfortune to perform for his cause a service of capital importance which was not recognized as legitimate by those who suffered its disadvantages. It does not matter what it was, but among its minor consequences was my excellent ancestor's arrest one night in his own house by a party of Mr. Washington's rebels. He was permitted to say farewell to his weeping family, and was then marched away into the darkness which swallowed him up forever. Not the slenderest clew to his fate was ever found. After the war the most diligent inquiry and the offer of large rewards failed to turn up any of his captors or any fact concerning his disappearance. He had disappeared, and that was all."

Something in Bartine's manner that was not in his words—I hardly knew what it was—prompted me to ask:

"What is your view of the matter—of the justice of it?"

"My view of it," he flamed out, bringing his clenched hand down upon the table as if he had been in a public house dicing with blackguards—"my view of it is that it was a characteristically dastardly assassination by that damned traitor, Washington, and his ragamuffin rebels!"

For some minutes nothing was said: Bartine was recovering his temper, and I waited. Then I said:

"Was that all?"

"No—there was something else. A few weeks after my great-grandfather's arrest his watch was found lying on the porch at the front door of his dwelling. It was wrapped in a sheet of letter paper bearing the name of Rupert Bartine, his only son, my grandfather. I am wearing that watch."

Bartine paused. His usually restless black eyes were staring fixedly into the grate, a point of red light in each, reflected from the glowing coals. He seemed to have

JOHN BARTINE'S WATCH

forgotten me. A sudden threshing of the branches of a tree outside one of the windows, and almost at the same instant a rattle of rain against the glass, recalled him to a sense of his surroundings. A storm had risen, heralded by a single gust of wind, and in a few moments the steady plash of the water on the pavement was distinctly heard. I hardly know why I relate this incident; it seemed somehow to have a certain significance and relevancy which I am unable now to discern. It at least added an element of seriousness, almost solemnity. Bartine resumed:

"I have a singular feeling toward this watch—a kind of affection for it; I like to have it about me, though partly from its weight, and partly for a reason I shall now explain, I seldom carry it. The reason is this: Every evening when I have it with me I feel an unaccountable desire to open and consult it, even if I can think of no reason for wishing to know the time. But if I yield to it, the moment my eyes rest upon the dial I am filled with a mysterious apprehension—a sense of imminent calamity. And this is the more insupportable the nearer it is to eleven o'clock—by this watch, no matter what the actual hour may be. After the hands have registered eleven the desire to look is gone; I am entirely indifferent. Then I can consult the thing as often as I like, with no more emotion than you feel in looking at your own. Naturally I have trained myself not to look at that watch in the evening before eleven; nothing could induce me. Your insistence this evening upset me a trifle. I felt very much as I suppose an opium-eater might feel if his yearning for his special and particular kind of hell were re-enforced by opportunity and advice.

"Now that is my story, and I have told it in the interest of your trumpery science; but if on any evening hereafter you observe me wearing this damnable watch, and you have the thoughtfulness to ask me the hour, I shall beg leave to put you to the inconvenience of being knocked down."

His humor did not amuse me. I could see that in relating his delusion he was again somewhat disturbed. His concluding smile was positively ghastly, and his eyes had resumed something more than their old restlessness; they shifted hither and thither about the room with apparent aimlessness and I fancied had taken on a wild expression, such as is sometimes observed in cases of dementia. Perhaps this was my own imagination, but at any rate I was now persuaded that my friend was afflicted with a most singular and interesting monomania. Without, I trust, any abatement of my affectionate solicitude for him as a friend, I began to regard him as a patient, rich in possibilities of profitable study. Why not? Had he not described his delusion in the interest of science? Ah, poor fellow, he was doing more for science than he knew: not only his story but himself was in evidence. I should cure him if I could, of course, but first I should make a little experiment in psychology—nay, the experiment itself might be a step in his restoration.

"That is very frank and friendly of you, Bartine," I said cordially, "and I'm rather proud of your confidence. It is all very odd, certainly. Do you mind showing me the watch?"

He detached it from his waistcoat, chain and all, and passed it to me without a word. The case was of gold, very thick and strong, and singularly engraved. After closely examining the dial and observing that it was nearly twelve o'clock, I opened it at the back and was interested to observe an inner case of ivory, upon which was painted a miniature portrait in that exquisite and delicate manner which was in vogue during the eighteenth century.

"Why, bless my soul!" I exclaimed, feeling a sharp artistic delight—"how under the sun did you get that done? I thought miniature painting on ivory was a lost art."

"That," he replied, gravely smiling, "is not I; it is my excellent great-grandfather, the late Bramwell Olcott Bartine, Esquire, of Virginia. He was younger then than later—about my age, in fact. It is said to resemble me; do you think so?"

"Resemble you? I should say so! Barring the costume, which I supposed you to have assumed out of compliment to the art—or for *vraisemblance,* so to say—and the no mustache, that portrait is you in every feature, line and expression."

No more was said at that time. Bartine took a book from the table and began reading. I heard outside the incessant plash of the rain in the street. There were occasional hurried footfalls on the sidewalks; and once a slower, heavier tread seemed to cease at my door—a policeman, I thought, seeking shelter in the doorway. The boughs of the trees tapped significantly on the window panes, as if asking for admittance. I remember it all through these years and years of a wiser, graver life.

Seeing myself unobserved, I took the old-fashioned key that dangled from the chain and quickly turned back the hands of the watch a full hour; then, closing the case, I handed Bartine his property and saw him replace it on his person.

"I think you said," I began, with assumed carelessness, "that after eleven the sight of the dial no longer affects you. As it is now nearly twelve"—looking at my own timepiece—"perhaps, if you don't resent my pursuit of proof, you will look at it now."

He smiled good-humoredly, pulled out the watch again, opened it and instantly sprang to his feet with a cry that Heaven has not had the mercy to permit me to forget! His eyes, their blackness strikingly intensified by the pallor of his face, were fixed upon the watch, which he clutched in both hands. For some time he remained in that attitude without uttering another sound; then, in a voice that I should not have recognized as his, he said:

"Damn you! it is two minutes to eleven!"

I was not unprepared for some such outbreak, and without rising replied, calmly enough:

"I beg your pardon; I must have misread your watch in setting my own by it."

He shut the case with a sharp snap and put the watch in his pocket. He looked at me and made an attempt to smile, but his lower lip quivered and he seemed unable to close his mouth. His hands, also, were shaking, and he thrust them, clenched, into the pockets of his sack-coat. The courageous spirit was manifestly endeavoring to subdue the coward body. The effort was too great; he began to sway from side to side, as from

JOHN BARTINE'S WATCH

vertigo, and before I could spring from my chair to support him his knees gave way and he pitched awkwardly forward and fell upon his face. I sprang to assist him to rise; but when John Bartine rises we shall all rise.

The *post-mortem* examination disclosed nothing; every organ was normal and sound. But when the body had been prepared for burial a faint dark circle was seen to have developed around the neck; at least I was so assured by several persons who said they saw it, but of my own knowledge I cannot say if that was true.

Nor can I set limitations to the law of heredity. I do not know that in the spiritual world a sentiment or emotion may not survive the heart that held it, and seek expression in a kindred life, ages removed. Surely, if I were to guess at the fate of Bramwell Olcott Bartine, I should guess that he was hanged at eleven o'clock in the evening, and that he had been allowed several hours in which to prepare for the change.

As to John Bartine, my friend, my patient for five minutes, and—Heaven forgive me!—my victim for eternity, there is no more to say. He is buried, and his watch with him—I saw to that. May God rest his soul in Paradise, and the soul of his Virginian ancestor, if, indeed, they are two souls.

E (22 Jan. 1893): 14 (with subtitle: "A Story Written from Notes of a Physician"); *CSTB* 239–48; *CW* 3.268–79.

NOTE

A story in the supernatural genre, depending for effect on the belief that the souls of the dead can usurp living bodies.

THE HYPNOTIST

By those of my friends who happen to know that I sometimes amuse myself with hypnotism, mind reading and kindred phenomena, I am frequently asked if I have a clear conception of the nature of whatever principle underlies them. To this question I always reply that I neither have nor desire to have. I am no investigator with an ear at the keyhole of Nature's workshop, trying with vulgar curiosity to steal the secrets of her trade. The interests of science are as little to me as mine seem to have been to science.

Doubtless the phenomena in question are simple enough, and in no way transcend our powers of comprehension if only we could find the clew; but for my part I prefer not to find it, for I am of a singularly romantic disposition, deriving more gratification from mystery than from knowledge. It was commonly remarked of me when I was a child that my big blue eyes appeared to have been made rather to look into than out of—such was their dreamful beauty, and in my frequent periods of abstraction, their indifference to what was going on. In those peculiarities they resembled, I venture to think, the soul which lies behind them, always more intent upon some lovely conception which it has created in its own image than concerned about the laws of nature and the material frame of things. All this, irrelevant and egotistic as it may seem, is related by way of accounting for the meagerness of the light that I am able to throw upon a subject that has engaged so much of my attention, and concerning which there is so keen and general a curiosity. With my powers and opportunities, another person might doubtless have an explanation for much of what I present simply as narrative.

My first knowledge that I possessed unusual powers came to me in my fourteenth year, when at school. Happening one day to have forgotten to bring my noon-day luncheon, I gazed longingly at that of a small girl who was preparing to eat hers. Looking up, her eyes met mine and she seemed unable to withdraw them. After a moment of hesitancy she came forward in an absent kind of way and without a word surrendered her little basket with its tempting contents and walked away. Inexpressibly pleased, I relieved my hunger and destroyed the basket. After that I had not the trouble to bring a luncheon for myself: that little girl was my daily purveyor; and not infrequently in satisfying my simple need from her frugal store I combined pleasure and profit by constraining her attendance at the feast and making misleading proffer of the viands, which eventually I consumed to the last fragment. The girl was always persuaded that she had eaten all herself; and later in the day her tearful complaints of hunger surprised the teacher, entertained the pupils, earned for her the sobriquet of Greedy-Gut and filled me with a peace past understanding.[1]

A disagreeable feature of this otherwise satisfactory condition of things was the necessary secrecy: the transfer of the luncheon, for example, had to be made at some distance from the madding crowd, in a wood; and I blush to think of the many other unworthy subterfuges entailed by the situation. As I was (and am) naturally of a frank and open disposition, these became more and more irksome, and but for the reluctance of my parents to renounce the obvious advantages of the new *régime* I would gladly have reverted to the old. The plan that I finally adopted to free myself from the consequences of my own powers excited a wide and keen interest at the time, and that part of it which consisted in the death of the girl was severely condemned, but it is hardly pertinent to the scope of this narrative.

For some years afterward I had little opportunity to practice hypnotism; such small essays as I made at it were commonly barren of other recognition than solitary confinement on a bread-and-water diet; sometimes, indeed, they elicited nothing better than the cat-o'-nine-tails. It was when I was about to leave the scene of these small disappointments that my one really important feat was performed.

I had been called into the warden's office and given a suit of civilian's clothing, a trifling sum of money and a great deal of advice, which I am bound to confess was of a much better quality than the clothing. As I was passing out of the gate into the light of freedom I suddenly turned and looking the warden gravely in the eye, soon had him in control.

"You are an ostrich," I said.

At the *post-mortem* examination the stomach was found to contain a great quantity of indigestible articles mostly of wood or metal. Stuck fast in the œsophagus and constituting, according to the Coroner's jury, the immediate cause of death, one door-knob.

I was by nature a good and affectionate son, but as I took my way into the great world from which I had been so long secluded I could not help remembering that all my misfortunes had flowed like a stream from the niggard economy of my parents in the matter of school luncheons; and I knew of no reason to think they had reformed.

On the road between Succotash Hill and South Asphyxia is a little open field which once contained a shanty known as Pete Gilstrap's Place, where that gentleman used to murder travelers for a living. The death of Mr. Gilstrap and the diversion of nearly all the travel to another road occurred so nearly at the same time that no one has ever been able to say which was cause and which effect. Anyhow, the field was now a desolation and the Place had long been burned. It was while going afoot to South Asphyxia, the home of my childhood, that I found both my parents on their way to the Hill. They had hitched their team and were eating luncheon under an oak tree in the center of the field. The sight of the luncheon called up painful memories of my school days and roused the sleeping lion in my breast. Approaching the guilty couple, who at once recognized me, I ventured to suggest that I share their hospitality.

"Of this cheer, my son," said the author of my being, with characteristic pomposity, which age had not withered, "there is sufficient for but two. I am not, I hope, insensible to the hunger-light in your eyes, but—"

My father has never completed that sentence; what he mistook for hunger-light was simply the earnest gaze of the hypnotist. In a few seconds he was at my service. A few more sufficed for the lady, and the dictates of a just resentment could be carried into effect. "My former father," I said, "I presume that it is known to you that you and this lady are no longer what you were?"

"I have observed a certain subtle change," was the rather dubious reply of the old gentleman; "it is perhaps attributable to age."

"It is more than that," I explained; "it goes to character—to species. You and the lady here are, in truth, two *broncos*—wild stallions both, and unfriendly."

"Why, John," exclaimed my dear mother, "you don't mean to say that I am—"

"Madam," I replied, solemnly, fixing my eyes again upon hers, "you are."

Scarcely had the words fallen from my lips when she dropped upon her hands and knees, and backing up to the old man squealed like a demon and delivered a vicious kick upon his shin! An instant later he was himself down on all-fours, headed away from her and flinging his feet at her simultaneously and successively. With equal earnestness but inferior agility, because of her hampering body-gear, she plied her own. Their flying legs crossed and mingled in the most bewildering way; their feet sometimes meeting squarely in midair, their bodies thrust forward, falling flat upon the ground and for a moment helpless. On recovering themselves they would resume the combat, uttering their frenzy in the nameless sounds of the furious brutes which they believed themselves to be—the whole region rang with their clamor! Round and round they wheeled, the blows of their feet falling "like lightnings from the mountain cloud."[2] They plunged and reared backward upon their knees, struck savagely at each other with awkward descending blows of both fists at once, and dropped again upon their hands as if unable to maintain the upright position of the body. Grass and pebbles were torn from the soil by hands and feet; clothing, hair, faces inexpressibly defiled with dust and blood. Wild, inarticulate screams of rage attested the delivery of the blows; groans, grunts and gasps their receipt. Nothing more truly military was ever seen at Gettysburg or Waterloo: the valor of my dear parents in the hour of danger can never cease to be to me a source of pride and gratification. At the end of it all two battered, tattered, bloody and fragmentary vestiges of mortality attested the solemn fact that the author of the strife was an orphan.

Arrested for provoking a breach of the peace, I was, and have ever since been, tried in the Court of Technicalities and Continuances[3] whence, after fifteen years of proceedings, my attorney is moving Heaven and earth to get the case taken to the Court of Remandment for New Trials.

Such are a few of my principal experiments in the mysterious force or agency known as hypnotic suggestion. Whether or not it could be employed by a bad man for an unworthy purpose I am unable to say.

E (10 Sept. 1893): 11 (as "John Bolger, Hypnotist"); ***CW* 8.177–84**. Reprinted in *Figaro* (London), no. 187 (28 Sept. 1893): 58–59 (as "John Bolger—Hypnotist").

NOTES

The fourth in the set of four tales that AB designated "The Parenticide Club." Like "The Widower Turmore," this tale also reveals some influence of Poe in its use of a well-spoken, intelligent, and initially impressive narrator who gradually exposes himself as a psychopath. AB, like Poe, most definitely did not identify with such characters but, rather, drew them so that their faults and flaws of reasoning might be recognized. AB's tendency to both overrate the power of hypnotism and to represent it negatively appears to stem as much from his assumption that it could circumvent the defensive powers of reason and understanding as from his fears that it was a secret and mysterious ability. See AB's discussion of a speech by William Jennings Bryan: "To be quite honest, I do not entirely believe that Orator Bryan's words and gestures had anything to do with it. I have long been convinced that personal persuasion is a matter of animal magnetism—what in its more obvious manifestation we now call hypnotism. At the back of the words and the postures, and independent of them, is that secret, mysterious power, addressing, not the ear, not the eye, nor, through them, the understanding, but through its matching quality in the auditor, captivating the will and enslaving it. That is how persuasion is effected; the spoken words merely supply a pretext for surrender." "Prattle," *E* (19 July 1896): 6. On mind reading and hypnotism, see the unsigned editorial "'Mind-Reading,'" *E* (7 Jan. 1892): 6.

1. Phil. 4:7: "And the peace of God, which passeth all understanding, shall keep your hearts and minds through Christ Jesus."
2. Fitz-Greene Halleck (1790–1867), "Marco Bozzaris" (1825), l. 30 ("As" for "like" in Halleck).
3. An adaptation of the Court of Technicalities and Exceptions in "Burbank's Crime" (p. 751).

A JUG OF SIRUP

This narrative begins with the death of its hero. Silas Deemer died on the 16th day of July, 1863, and two days later his remains were buried. As he had been personally known to every man, woman and well-grown child in the village, the funeral, as the local newspaper phrased it, "was largely attended." In accordance with a custom of the time and place, the coffin was opened at the graveside and the entire assembly of friends and neighbors filed past, taking a last look at the face of the dead. And then, before the eyes of all, Silas Deemer was put into the ground. Some of the eyes were a trifle dim, but in a general way it may be said that at that interment there was lack of neither observance nor observation; Silas was indubitably dead, and none could have pointed out any ritual delinquency that would have justified him in coming back from the grave. Yet if human testimony is good for anything (and certainly it once put an end to witchcraft in and about Salem) he came back.

I forgot to state that the death and burial of Silas Deemer occurred in the little village of Hillbrook, where he had lived for thirty-one years. He had been what is known in some parts of the Union (which is admittedly a free country) as a "merchant"; that is to say, he kept a retail shop for the sale of such things as are commonly sold in shops of that character. His honesty had never been questioned, so far as is known, and he was held in high esteem by all. The only thing that could be urged against him by the most censorious was a too close attention to business. It was not urged against him, though many another, who manifested it in no greater degree, was less leniently judged. The business to which Silas was devoted was mostly his own— that, possibly, may have made a difference.

At the time of Deemer's death nobody could recollect a single day, Sundays excepted, that he had not passed in his "store," since he had opened it more than a quarter-century before. His health having been perfect during all that time, he had been unable to discern any validity in whatever may or might have been urged to lure him astray from his counter; and it is related that once when he was summoned to the county seat as a witness in an important law case and did not attend, the lawyer who had the hardihood to move that he be "admonished" was solemnly informed that the Court regarded the proposal with "surprise." Judicial surprise being an emotion that attorneys are not commonly ambitious to arouse, the motion was hastily withdrawn and an agreement with the other side effected as to what Mr. Deemer would have said if he had been there—the other side pushing its advantage to the extreme and making the supposititious testimony distinctly damaging to the interests of its proponents. In brief, it was the general feeling in all that region that Silas Deemer was the one immobile verity of Hillbrook, and that his translation in space would precipitate some dismal public ill or strenuous calamity.

Mrs. Deemer and two grown daughters occupied the upper rooms of the building, but Silas had never been known to sleep elsewhere than on a cot behind the counter of the store. And there, quite by accident, he was found one night, dying, and passed away just before the time for taking down the shutters. Though speechless, he appeared conscious, and it was thought by those who knew him best that if the end had unfortunately been delayed beyond the usual hour for opening the store the effect upon him would have been deplorable.

Such had been Silas Deemer—such the fixity and invariety of his life and habit, that the village humorist (who had once attended college) was moved to bestow upon him the sobriquet of "Old Ibidem," and, in the first issue of the local newspaper after the death, to explain without offense that Silas had taken "a day off." It was more than a day, but from the record it appears that well within a month Mr. Deemer made it plain that he had not the leisure to be dead.

One of Hillbrook's most respected citizens was Alvan Creede, a banker. He lived in the finest house in town, kept a carriage and was a most estimable man variously. He knew something of the advantages of travel, too, having been frequently in Boston, and once, it was thought, in New York, though he modestly disclaimed that glittering distinction. The matter is mentioned here merely as a contribution to an understanding of Mr. Creede's worth, for either way it is creditable to him—to his intelligence if he had put himself, even temporarily, into contact with metropolitan culture; to his candor if he had not.

One pleasant summer evening at about the hour of ten Mr. Creede, entering at his garden gate, passed up the gravel walk, which looked very white in the moonlight, mounted the stone steps of his fine house and pausing a moment inserted his latchkey in the door. As he pushed this open he met his wife, who was crossing the passage from the parlor to the library. She greeted him pleasantly and pulling the door further back held it for him to enter. Instead he turned and, looking about his feet in front of the threshold, uttered an exclamation of surprise.

"Why!—what the devil," he said, "has become of that jug?"

A JUG OF SIRUP

"What jug, Alvan?" his wife inquired, not very sympathetically.

"A jug of maple sirup—I brought it along from the store and set it down here to open the door. What the—"

"There, there, Alvan, please don't swear again," said the lady, interrupting. Hillbrook, by the way, is not the only place in Christendom where a vestigial polytheism forbids the taking in vain of the Evil One's name.[1]

The jug of maple sirup which the easy ways of village life had permitted Hillbrook's foremost citizen to carry home from the store was not there.

"Are you quite sure, Alvan?"

"My dear, do you suppose a man does not know when he is carrying a jug? I bought that sirup at Deemer's as I was passing. Deemer himself drew it and lent me the jug, and I—"

The sentence remains to this day unfinished. Mr. Creede staggered into the house, entered the parlor and dropped into an arm-chair, trembling in every limb. He had suddenly remembered that Silas Deemer was three weeks dead.

Mrs. Creede stood by her husband, regarding him with surprise and anxiety.

"For Heaven's sake," she said, "what ails you?"

Mr. Creede's ailment having no obvious relation to the interests of the better land he did not apparently deem it necessary to expound it on that demand; he said nothing—merely stared. There were long moments of silence broken by nothing but the measured ticking of the clock, which seemed somewhat slower than usual, as if it were civilly granting them an extension of time in which to recover their wits.

"Jane, I have gone mad—that is it." He spoke thickly and hurriedly. "You should have told me; you must have observed my symptoms before they became so pronounced that I have observed them myself. I thought I was passing Deemer's store; it was open and lit up—that is what I thought; of course it is never open now. Silas Deemer stood at his desk behind the counter. My God, Jane, I saw him as distinctly as I see you. Remembering that you had said you wanted some maple sirup, I went in and bought some—that is all—I bought two quarts of maple sirup from Silas Deemer, who is dead and underground, but nevertheless drew that sirup from a cask and handed it to me in a jug. He talked with me, too, rather gravely, I remember, even more so than was his way, but not a word of what he said can I now recall. But I saw him—good Lord, I saw and talked with him—and he is dead! So I thought, but I'm mad, Jane, I'm as crazy as a beetle; and you have kept it from me."

This monologue gave the woman time to collect what faculties she had.

"Alvan," she said, "you have given no evidence of insanity, believe me. This was undoubtedly an illusion—how should it be anything else? That would be too terrible! But there is no insanity; you are working too hard at the bank. You should not have attended the meeting of directors this evening; any one could see that you were ill; I knew something would occur."

It may have seemed to him that the prophecy had lagged a bit, awaiting the event, but he said nothing of that, being concerned with his own condition. He was calm now, and could think coherently.

"Doubtless the phenomenon was subjective," he said, with a somewhat ludicrous transition to the slang of science. "Granting the possibility of spiritual apparition and even materialization, yet the apparition and materialization of a half-gallon brown clay jug—a piece of coarse, heavy pottery evolved from nothing—that is hardly thinkable."

As he finished speaking, a child ran into the room—his little daughter. She was clad in a bedgown. Hastening to her father she threw her arms about his neck, saying: "You naughty papa, you forgot to come in and kiss me. We heard you open the gate and got up and looked out. And, papa dear, Eddy says mayn't he have the little jug when it is empty?"

As the full import of that revelation imparted itself to Alvan Creede's understanding he visibly shuddered. For the child could not have heard a word of the conversation.

The estate of Silas Deemer being in the hands of an administrator who had thought it best to dispose of the "business," the store had been closed ever since the owner's death, the goods having been removed by another "merchant" who had purchased them *en bloc*. The rooms above were vacant as well, for the widow and daughters had gone to another town.

On the evening immediately after Alvan Creede's adventure (which had somehow "got out") a crowd of men, women and children thronged the sidewalk opposite the store. That the place was haunted by the spirit of the late Silas Deemer was now well known to every resident of Hillbrook, though many affected disbelief. Of these the hardiest, and in a general way the youngest, threw stones against the front of the building, the only part accessible, but carefully missed the unshuttered windows. Incredulity had not grown to malice. A few venturesome souls crossed the street and rattled the door in its frame; struck matches and held them near the window; attempted to view the black interior. Some of the spectators invited attention to their wit by shouting and groaning and challenging the ghost to a footrace.

After a considerable time had elapsed without any manifestation, and many of the crowd had gone away, all those remaining began to observe that the interior of the store was suffused with a dim, yellow light. At this all demonstrations ceased; the intrepid souls about the door and windows fell back to the opposite side of the street and were merged in the crowd; the small boys ceased throwing stones. Nobody spoke above his breath; all whispered excitedly and pointed to the now steadily growing light. How long a time had passed since the first faint glow had been observed none could have guessed, but eventually the illumination was bright enough to reveal the whole interior of the store; and there, standing at his desk behind the counter, Silas Deemer was distinctly visible!

The effect upon the crowd was marvelous. It began rapidly to melt away at both flanks, as the timid left the place. Many ran as fast as their legs would let them; others moved off with greater dignity, turning occasionally to look backward over the shoulder. At last a score or more, mostly men, remained where they were, speechless, staring, excited. The apparition inside gave them no attention; it was apparently occupied with a book of accounts.

Presently three men left the crowd on the sidewalk as if by a common impulse and crossed the street. One of them, a heavy man, was about to set his shoulder against the door when it opened, apparently without human agency, and the courageous investigators passed in. No sooner had they crossed the threshold than they were seen by the awed observers outside to be acting in the most unaccountable way. They thrust out their hands before them, pursued devious courses, came into violent collision with the counter, with boxes and barrels on the floor and with one another. They turned awkwardly hither and thither and seemed trying to escape, but unable to retrace their steps. Their voices were heard in exclamations and curses. But in no way did the apparition of Silas Deemer manifest an interest in what was going on.

By what impulse the crowd was moved none ever recollected, but the entire mass—men, women, children, dogs—made a simultaneous and tumultuous rush for the entrance. They congested the doorway, pushing for precedence—resolving themselves at length into a line and moving up step by step. By some subtle spiritual or physical alchemy observation had been transmuted into action—the sightseers had become participants in the spectacle—the audience had usurped the stage.

To the only spectator remaining on the other side of the street—Alvan Creede, the banker—the interior of the store with its inpouring crowd continued in full illumination; all the strange things going on there were clearly visible. To those inside all was black darkness. It was as if each person as he was thrust in at the door had been stricken blind, and was maddened by the mischance. They groped with aimless imprecision, tried to force their way out against the current, pushed and elbowed, struck at random, fell and were trampled, rose and trampled in their turn. They seized one another by the garments, the hair, the beard—fought like animals, cursed, shouted, called one another opprobrious and obscene names. When, finally, Alvan Creede had seen the last person of the line pass into that awful tumult the light that had illuminated it was suddenly quenched and all was as black to him as to those within. He turned away and left the place.

In the early morning a curious crowd had gathered about "Deemer's." It was composed partly of those who had run away the night before, but now had the courage of sunshine, partly of honest folk going to their daily toil. The door of the store stood open; the place was vacant, but on the walls, the floor, the furniture, were shreds of clothing and tangles of hair. Hillbrook militant had managed somehow to pull itself out and had gone home to medicine its hurts and swear that it had been all night in bed. On the dusty desk, behind the counter, was the sales-book. The entries in it, in Deemer's handwriting, had ceased on the 16th day of July, the last of his life. There was no record of a later sale to Alvan Creede.

A JUG OF SIRUP

That is the entire story—except that men's passions having subsided and reason having resumed its immemorial sway, it was confessed in Hillbrook that, considering the harmless and honorable character of his first commercial transaction under the new conditions, Silas Deemer, deceased, might properly have been suffered to resume business at the old stand without mobbing. In that judgment the local historian from whose unpublished work these facts are compiled had the thoughtfulness to signify his concurrence.

E (17 Dec. 1893): 19–20 (with subtitle: "Some Fantastic Passages from the Chronicles of a Village"; *CW* **3.155–68**.

NOTES

This seemingly conventional tale of the supernatural proves to be more complex than is evident on first reading. As recorded in the "Selected Textual Variants," AB had initially written that the sale of the jug to Alvan Creede *was* recorded in Deemer's sales book, making the story emphatically supernatural. The elimination of this detail makes the story much more ambiguous, leaving open the possibility of a collective hallucination on the part of the townspeople who saw the ghost of Deemer in his store, or some other nonsupernatural explanation.

1. Cf. AB's celebrated comment when Doubleday, Page retitled his *Devil's Dictionary* as *The Cynic's Word Book*: "Here in the East the Devil is a sacred personage (the Fourth Person of the Trinity, as an Irishman might say) and his name must not be taken in vain." AB to George Sterling (6 May 1906); *MMM* 151.

THE DAMNED THING

ONE DOES NOT ALWAYS EAT
WHAT IS ON THE TABLE

By the light of a tallow candle which had been placed on one end of a rough table a man was reading something written in a book. It was an old account book, greatly worn; and the writing was not, apparently, very legible, for the man sometimes held the page close to the flame of the candle to get a stronger light on it. The shadow of the book would then throw into obscurity a half of the room, darkening a number of faces and figures; for besides the reader, eight other men were present. Seven of them sat against the rough log walls, silent, motionless, and the room being small, not very far from the table. By extending an arm any one of them could have touched the eighth man, who lay on the table, face upward, partly covered by a sheet, his arms at his sides. He was dead.

The man with the book was not reading aloud, and no one spoke; all seemed to be waiting for something to occur; the dead man only was without expectation. From the blank darkness outside came in, through the aperture that served for a window, all the ever unfamiliar noises of night in the wilderness—the long nameless note of a distant coyote; the stilly pulsing thrill of tireless insects in trees; strange cries of night birds, so different from those of the birds of day; the drone of great blundering bee-tles, and all that mysterious chorus of small sounds that seem always to have been but half heard when they have suddenly ceased, as if conscious of an indiscretion. But nothing of all this was noted in that company; its members were not overmuch addicted to idle interest in matters of no practical importance; that was obvious in every line of their rugged faces—obvious even in the dim light of the single candle. They were evidently men of the vicinity—farmers and woodsmen.

858

The person reading was a trifle different; one would have said of him that he was of the world, worldly,[1] albeit there was that in his attire which attested a certain fellowship with the organisms of his environment. His coat would hardly have passed muster in San Francisco; his foot-gear was not of urban origin, and the hat that lay by him on the floor (he was the only one uncovered) was such that if one had considered it as an article of mere personal adornment he would have missed its meaning. In countenance the man was rather prepossessing, with just a hint of sternness; though that he may have assumed or cultivated, as appropriate to one in authority. For he was a coroner. It was by virtue of his office that he had possession of the book in which he was reading; it had been found among the dead man's effects—in his cabin, where the inquest was now taking place.

When the coroner had finished reading he put the book into his breast pocket. At that moment the door was pushed open and a young man entered. He, clearly, was not of mountain birth and breeding: he was clad as those who dwell in cities. His clothing was dusty, however, as from travel. He had, in fact, been riding hard to attend the inquest.

The coroner nodded; no one else greeted him.

"We have waited for you," said the coroner. "It is necessary to have done with this business to-night."

The young man smiled. "I am sorry to have kept you," he said. "I went away, not to evade your summons, but to post to my newspaper an account of what I suppose I am called back to relate."

The coroner smiled.

"The account that you posted to your newspaper," he said, "differs, probably, from that which you will give here under oath."

"That," replied the other, rather hotly and with a visible flush, "is as you please. I used manifold paper[2] and have a copy of what I sent. It was not written as news, for it is incredible, but as fiction. It may go as a part of my testimony under oath."

"But you say it is incredible."

"That is nothing to you, sir, if I also swear that it is true."

The coroner was silent for a time, his eyes upon the floor. The men about the sides of the cabin talked in whispers, but seldom withdrew their gaze from the face of the corpse. Presently the coroner lifted his eyes and said: "We will resume the inquest."

The men removed their hats. The witness was sworn.

"What is your name?" the coroner asked.

"William Harker."

"Age?"

"Twenty-seven."

"You knew the deceased, Hugh Morgan?"

"Yes."

THE DAMNED THING

"You were with him when he died?"

"Near him."

"How did that happen—your presence, I mean?"

"I was visiting him at this place to shoot and fish. A part of my purpose, however, was to study him and his odd, solitary way of life. He seemed a good model for a character in fiction. I sometimes write stories."

"I sometimes read them."

"Thank you."

"Stories in general—not yours."

Some of the jurors laughed. Against a somber background humor shows high lights. Soldiers in the intervals of battle laugh easily, and a jest in the death chamber conquers by surprise.

"Relate the circumstances of this man's death," said the coroner. "You may use any notes or memoranda that you please."

The witness understood. Pulling a manuscript from his breast pocket he held it near the candle and turning the leaves until he found the passage that he wanted began to read.

II
WHAT MAY HAPPEN IN A FIELD OF WILD OATS

". . . The sun had hardly risen when we left the house. We were looking for quail, each with a shotgun, but we had only one dog. Morgan said that our best ground was beyond a certain ridge that he pointed out, and we crossed it by a trail through the *chaparral.* On the other side was comparatively level ground, thickly covered with wild oats. As we emerged from the *chaparral* Morgan was but a few yards in advance. Suddenly we heard, at a little distance to our right and partly in front, a noise as of some animal thrashing about in the bushes, which we could see were violently agitated.

"'We've started a deer,' I said. 'I wish we had brought a rifle.'

"Morgan, who had stopped and was intently watching the agitated *chaparral,* said nothing, but had cocked both barrels of his gun and was holding it in readiness to aim. I thought him a trifle excited, which surprised me, for he had a reputation for exceptional coolness, even in moments of sudden and imminent peril.

"'O, come,' I said. 'You are not going to fill up a deer with quail-shot, are you?'

"Still he did not reply; but catching a sight of his face as he turned it slightly toward me I was struck by the intensity of his look. Then I understood that we had serious business in hand and my first conjecture was that we had 'jumped' a grizzly. I advanced to Morgan's side, cocking my piece as I moved.

"The bushes were now quiet and the sounds had ceased, but Morgan was as attentive to the place as before.

THE DAMNED THING

"'What is it? What the devil is it?' I asked.

"'That Damned Thing!' he replied, without turning his head. His voice was husky and unnatural. He trembled visibly.

"I was about to speak further, when I observed the wild oats near the place of the disturbance moving in the most inexplicable way. I can hardly describe it. It seemed as if stirred by a streak of wind, which not only bent it, but pressed it down—crushed it so that it did not rise; and this movement was slowly prolonging itself directly toward us.

"Nothing that I had ever seen had affected me so strangely as this unfamiliar and unaccountable phenomenon, yet I am unable to recall any sense of fear. I remember—and tell it here because, singularly enough, I recollected it then—that once in looking carelessly out of an open window I momentarily mistook a small tree close at hand for one of a group of larger trees at a little distance away. It looked the same size as the others, but being more distinctly and sharply defined in mass and detail seemed out of harmony with them. It was a mere falsification of the law of aërial perspective, but it startled, almost terrified me. We so rely upon the orderly operation of familiar natural laws that any seeming suspension of them is noted as a menace to our safety, a warning of unthinkable calamity. So now the apparently causeless movement of the herbage and the slow, undeviating approach of the line of disturbance were distinctly disquieting. My companion appeared actually frightened, and I could hardly credit my senses when I saw him suddenly throw his gun to his shoulder and fire both barrels at the agitated grain! Before the smoke of the discharge had cleared away I heard a loud savage cry—a scream like that of a wild animal—and flinging his gun upon the ground Morgan sprang away and ran swiftly from the spot. At the same instant I was thrown violently to the ground by the impact of something unseen in the smoke—some soft, heavy substance that seemed thrown against me with great force.

"Before I could get upon my feet and recover my gun, which seemed to have been struck from my hands, I heard Morgan crying out as if in mortal agony, and mingling with his cries were such hoarse, savage sounds as one hears from fighting dogs. Inexpressibly terrified, I struggled to my feet and looked in the direction of Morgan's retreat; and may Heaven in mercy spare me from another sight like that! At a distance of less than thirty yards was my friend, down upon one knee, his head thrown back at a frightful angle, hatless, his long hair in disorder and his whole body in violent movement from side to side, backward and forward. His right arm was lifted and seemed to lack the hand—at least, I could see none. The other arm was invisible. At times, as my memory now reports this extraordinary scene, I could discern but a part of his body; it was as if he had been partly blotted out—I cannot otherwise express it—then a shifting of his position would bring it all into view again.

"All this must have occurred within a few seconds, yet in that time Morgan assumed all the postures of a determined wrestler vanquished by superior weight and strength. I saw nothing but him, and him not always distinctly. During the entire incident his shouts and curses were heard, as if through an enveloping uproar of such sounds of rage and fury as I had never heard from the throat of man or brute!

"For a moment only I stood irresolute, then throwing down my gun I ran forward to my friend's assistance. I had a vague belief that he was suffering from a fit, or some form of convulsion. Before I could reach his side he was down and quiet. All sounds had ceased, but with a feeling of such terror as even these awful events had not inspired I now saw again the mysterious movement of the wild oats, prolonging itself from the trampled area about the prostrate man toward the edge of a wood. It was only when it had reached the wood that I was able to withdraw my eyes and look at my companion. He was dead."

III
A MAN THOUGH NAKED MAY BE IN RAGS

The coroner rose from his seat and stood beside the dead man. Lifting an edge of the sheet he pulled it away, exposing the entire body, altogether naked and showing in the candle-light a claylike yellow. It had, however, broad maculations of bluish black, obviously caused by extravasated blood from contusions. The chest and sides looked as if they had been beaten with a bludgeon. There were dreadful lacerations; the skin was torn in strips and shreds.

The coroner moved round to the end of the table and undid a silk handkerchief which had been passed under the chin and knotted on the top of the head. When the handkerchief was drawn away it exposed what had been the throat. Some of the jurors who had risen to get a better view repented their curiosity and turned away their faces. Witness Harker went to the open window and leaned out across the sill, faint and sick. Dropping the handkerchief upon the dead man's neck the coroner stepped to an angle of the room and from a pile of clothing produced one garment after another, each of which he held up a moment for inspection. All were torn, and stiff with blood. The jurors did not make a closer inspection. They seemed rather uninterested. They had, in truth, seen all this before; the only thing that was new to them being Harker's testimony.

"Gentlemen," the coroner said, "we have no more evidence, I think. Your duty has been already explained to you; if there is nothing you wish to ask you may go outside and consider your verdict."

The foreman rose—a tall, bearded man of sixty, coarsely clad.

"I should like to ask one question, Mr. Coroner," he said. "What asylum did this yer last witness escape from?"

"Mr. Harker," said the coroner, gravely and tranquilly, "from what asylum did you last escape?"

Harker flushed crimson again, but said nothing, and the seven jurors rose and solemnly filed out of the cabin.

"If you have done insulting me, sir," said Harker, as soon as he and the officer were left alone with the dead man, "I suppose I am at liberty to go?"

"Yes."

Harker started to leave, but paused, with his hand on the door latch. The habit of his profession was strong in him—stronger than his sense of personal dignity. He turned about and said:

"The book that you have there—I recognize it as Morgan's diary. You seemed greatly interested in it; you read in it while I was testifying. May I see it? The public would like—"

"The book will cut no figure in this matter," replied the official, slipping it into his coat pocket; "all the entries in it were made before the writer's death."

As Harker passed out of the house the jury reëntered and stood about the table, on which the now covered corpse showed under the sheet with sharp definition. The foreman seated himself near the candle, produced from his breast pocket a pencil and scrap of paper and wrote rather laboriously the following verdict, which with various degrees of effort all signed:

"We, the jury, do find that the remains come to their death at the hands of a mountain lion, but some of us thinks, all the same, they had fits."

IV
AN EXPLANATION FROM THE TOMB

In the diary of the late Hugh Morgan are certain interesting entries having, possibly, a scientific value as suggestions. At the inquest upon his body the book was not put in evidence; possibly the coroner thought it not worth while to confuse the jury. The date of the first of the entries mentioned cannot be ascertained; the upper part of the leaf is torn away; the part of the entry remaining follows:

". . . would run in a half-circle, keeping his head turned always toward the center, and again he would stand still, barking furiously. At last he ran away into the brush as fast as he could go. I thought at first that he had gone mad, but on returning to the house found no other alteration in his manner than what was obviously due to fear of punishment.

"Can a dog see with his nose? Do odors impress some cerebral center with images of the thing that emitted them? . . .

"Sept. 2.—Looking at the stars last night as they rose above the crest of the ridge east of the house, I observed them successively disappear—from left to right. Each was eclipsed but an instant, and only a few at the same time, but along the entire length of the ridge all that were within a degree or two of the crest were blotted out. It was as if something had passed along between me and them; but I could not see it, and the stars were not thick enough to define its outline. Ugh! I don't like this." . . .

Several weeks' entries are missing, three leaves being torn from the book.

THE DAMNED THING

"Sept. 27.—It has been about here again—I find evidences of its presence every day. I watched again all last night in the same cover, gun in hand, double-charged with buckshot. In the morning the fresh footprints were there, as before. Yet I would have sworn that I did not sleep—indeed, I hardly sleep at all. It is terrible, insupportable! If these amazing experiences are real I shall go mad; if they are fanciful I am mad already.

"Oct. 3.—I shall not go—it shall not drive me away. No, this is *my* house, *my* land. God hates a coward. . . .

"Oct. 5.—I can stand it no longer; I have invited Harker to pass a few weeks with me—he has a level head. I can judge from his manner if he thinks me mad.

"Oct. 7.—I have the solution of the mystery; it came to me last night—suddenly, as by revelation. How simple—how terribly simple!

"There are sounds that we cannot hear. At either end of the scale are notes that stir no chord of that imperfect instrument, the human ear. They are too high or too grave. I have observed a flock of blackbirds occupying an entire tree-top—the tops of several trees—and all in full song. Suddenly—in a moment—at absolutely the same instant—all spring into the air and fly away. How? They could not all see one another—whole tree-tops intervened. At no point could a leader have been visible to all. There must have been a signal of warning or command, high and shrill above the din, but by me unheard. I have observed, too, the same simultaneous flight when all were silent, among not only blackbirds, but other birds—quail, for example, widely separated by bushes—even on opposite sides of a hill.

"It is known to seamen that a school of whales basking or sporting on the surface of the ocean, miles apart, with the convexity of the earth between, will sometimes dive at the same instant—all gone out of sight in a moment. The signal has been sounded—too grave for the ear of the sailor at the masthead and his comrades on the deck—who nevertheless feel its vibrations in the ship as the stones of a cathedral are stirred by the bass of the organ.

"As with sounds, so with colors. At each end of the solar spectrum the chemist can detect the presence of what are known as 'actinic' rays.[3] They represent colors—integral colors in the composition of light—which we are unable to discern. The human eye is an imperfect instrument; its range is but a few octaves of the real 'chromatic scale.' I am not mad; there are colors that we cannot see.

"And, God help me! the Damned Thing is of such a color!"

TT 30, no. 23 (7 Dec. 1893): 23–24; *E* (13 Sept. 1896): 25; *IML* 325–42; ***CW*** **3.280–96.** Reprinted in *Tales from "Town Topics"* (New York: Town Topics, 1896), 238-53; *Anti-Philistine*, no. 3 (15 Aug. 1897): 139–50; in William Patten, ed., *Short Story Classics (American)* (New York: P. F. Collier & Son, 1905), 1301–15.

THE DAMNED THING

NOTES

In "Prattle" (*E*, 31 Mar. 1894; see appendix), AB addressed the charge that "The Damned Thing" was a plagiarism of Fitz-James O'Brien's story "What Was It?" (*Harper's*, Mar. 1859). AB recognized that that story had been published earlier and that a denial of having read it would be a weak defense, so he argued his own originality as follows: "In O'Brien's story a man is attacked by, and overcomes, a supernatural and impossible being, invisible because transparent; in mine a man is attacked and killed by a wild animal that cannot be seen because, although opaque, like other animals, it is of an invisible color." AB further argued the greater plausibility of his story by noting that there are colors in nature invisible to the human eye, but they are colors nevertheless and may be visible to some creatures. He claimed that his story was inspired by a personal experience on a hunting trip during which his dog was terrified by something it apprehended but AB could not.

1. See "The Middle Toe of the Right Foot," p. 750 note 4.

2. Manifold paper was an early type of carbon paper devised in the early nineteenth century for making multiple copies of either handwritten or (later) typewritten documents. AB's later mention of a "manuscript" suggests that this document was handwritten.

3. The term "actinic rays" was a feature of a now-outdated assumption that there were three distinct kinds of radiation—thermal, luminous, and actinic, the last referring chiefly to infrared and ultraviolet rays that produced the greatest chemical effects (e.g., on photographic plates). It is now understood that the three types of rays are merely different effects of the same kind of radiation.

SELECTED TEXTUAL VARIANTS

ABBREVIATIONS

C	*Can Such Things Be?* (1893)
CW	*Collected Works* (1909–12; 12 vols.)
E	*San Francisco Examiner*
H	Manuscript copy of *CW*, Huntington Library (San Marino, CA)
I	*In the Midst of Life* (1898)
O	*Oakland Tribune*
T	*Tales of Soldiers and Civilians* (1891)
TT	*Town Topics*
Wa	*Wave*

KILLED AT RESACA

507.7	part] portion, *E, T*
507.13	so] similarly *E, T, I*
507.19	Stone's] Stone *E*
508.9	cover;] the trees. *E*
508.17	of personal dignity.] in which considerations of personal dignity cut a figure. *E*
508.20	exposed.] ~. ¶ *E*
508.22	prone] *om. E*
508.29	perilous] horrible *E, T, I*
508.36	would. ¶] ~.^ *E, T*
509.13	seldom] never *E, T, I*
509.19	the enemy's fortified line being] *om. E*
509.29	damned] —— *E*
509.31	and his horse] *om. E*; and horse *T*
509.35	erect] straight and soldierly *E*
510.9	drawn] averted *E, T, I*
510.13	saw . . . him.] divined the cause of his inaction. *E, T, I*
510.17	now were] stood *E*; were *T*

510.19–20	and leapt into it.] *om. E, T*
510.29–30	A generous . . . brave.] A tattered battle flag upon the parapet was lowered to half-mast. *E*
510.33	me.] ~ and was put away without examination. *E*
510.35	Out . . . letter] A letter fell out—a letter *E*
510.40	Marian Mendenhall.] which I must be pardoned for not disclosing; the lady is living. *E*
511.9	a hundred] one thousand *E*
511.10	Miss . . . letter] the writer of that letter to return it *E*
511.11	a handsome] an elegantly furnished *E*
511.24	to rescue . . . me,] *om. E*
511.27	its page.] the letter. *E*
511.28	as this detestable creature.] *om. E*

THE MAN OUT OF THE NOSE

513.12	is] ~ indescribably *E*
514.7	more and more] further and further *E*
514.15	day. ¶] ~.^ *E, C*
514.17	destroy] drive away *E*
514.20	distinctly] greatly *E, C*
514.21	neatly,] well, *E*
514.26	permit.] ~. ¶ This man's name does not concern us—nor do the names of any persons whom I may mention in the course of this narrative. I have too sincere a respect for the lady already mentioned—the washerwoman at North Beach—to turn the bull's-eye lantern of the press full upon the shadow of her saintly life. We will call her husband John Hardshaw. *E*
514.38	On these occasions] At these latter times, *E, C*
515.35	later] subsequent *E, C*
516.7	arrest.] crime. *E, C*
516.23	physician.] medico. *E*
516.24	suggestion] direction *E*
517.17	the region] the lowland region *E*
517.23	her body] her beautiful body *E, C*
517.32	sound] crash *E*
517.36	bleeding body] the bleeding, the *burst* Thing *E*; the bleeding form *C*
518.6	Dolores,] *om. E, C*
518.12	man's] old gentleman's *E, C*

A BOTTOMLESS GRAVE

520.5	surprise] astonish *E*
520.7	surprising] astonishing *E*
520.17	remove] kill *E*
520.19	disposition,] ~ to bloodshed, *E*
520.21	removed] shot *E*

521.21	had disappeared . . . unknown.] was found dead in a ditch, with his throat cut from ear to ear. *E*
521.40	music,] astronomy, *E*
521.40–522.1	bugler . . . mutes;] comet-seeker in a neighboring asylum for the blind; *E*
522.10	goods] ~, crackers *E*
522.33	faint] *om. E*
322.35	tainted] loaded *E*
522.37–38	disturbed earth] grave *E*
522.38	the edges . . . grave] its edges *E*
523.14	care] *E*; dare *CW [not corrected in H]*
523.30–31	our eyes . . . grave.] he was still in his hole and our eyes had deceived us. *E*
523.31	an enormous] a valuable *E*
523.36	one. ¶] ~.^ *E*
523.39	that fateful cellar. ¶] the cellar of the house.^ *E*
524.11	him— . . . crime.] him. Let the lesson of his error sink deeply into the human heart. *E*

ONE OF THE MISSING

525.1	Jerome] Early in the morning of July 3, 1864, Jerome *E*
525.2	Kennesaw] Kenesaw *E, T, I*
525.8	division] brigade *E*
525.12	young,] ~—it is surprising how young we all were in those days!—*E, T, I*
525.13	division] brigade *E*
525.18	corps] division *E*
526.6	fellows] Johnnies *E*
526.19	rifle-pits.] picket-pits. *E*
526.40	finger. ¶] ~.^ *E, T, I*
527.2	Kennesaw] Kenesaw *E, T, I*
527.4	enemy, . . . sunlight.] enemy. *E*
527.7	Confederates] infantry *E, T, I*
527.11	habit] pleasure *E, T, I*
527.15	discernible,] ~ to our consciousness, *E*
527.17	pattern.] ~. ¶ *T, I*
527.23–25	officer . . . officer] sergeant . . . sergeant *E*
527.34	Confederate] *om. E, T*
527.34–35	while . . . off,] *om. E*
528.1–2	a certain kind of] *om. E*
528.7	dust!] ~! ¶ Lieutenant Adrian Searing, in command of the picket guard on that part of the line through which his brother Jerome had passed on his mission, sat with attentive ears in his breastwork behind the line. Not the faintest sound escaped him: the cry of a bird, the barking of a squirrel, the noise of the wind among the pines—all were anxiously noted by his overstrained sense. Suddenly, directly in front of his line, he heard a faint, confused rumble, like the clatter of a falling building

translated by distance. At the same moment an aide-de-camp approached him on foot from the rear and saluted. ¶ "Lieutenant," said the aide, "the General directs that you move forward your line and feel the enemy if you find him. If not, continue the advance until directed to halt. The Forty-second will support you. There is reason to think that the enemy has retired." ¶ The Lieutenant nodded and said nothing; the aide retired. In a moment the men, apprised of their duty by the non-commissioned officers in low tones, had deployed from their rifle-pits and were moving forward in skirmishing order, with set teeth and beating hearts. The Lieutenant mechanically looked at his watch. Six o'clock and eighteen minutes. *E, T, I*

528.19	lines;] ~; in the center a bright ring of metal—*E, T, I*
528.26	trap." ¶] ~."^ *E*
528.38	free.] ~, but he could not get it from under the heavy timber athwart his chest, nor move it outward more than six inches at the elbow. *E*
528.38–40	But . . . elbow.] *om. E*
529.16	legs. ¶] ~.^ *E*
529.29	forehead. ¶] ~.^ *E*
530.20	were,] seemed, *E, T*
530.32	irrelevantly,] irreverently, *E*
531.29	incessant.] constant. *E, T*
532.15	wince.] scream. *E, T, I*
532.34–533.10	Lieutenant . . . This line] A little later a line *E*; A line *T, I*
533.10	skirmishers] Federal ~ *T, I*
	sweeps] swept *E, T, I*
533.11	pass] passed *E, T, I*
533.12	their commander comes.] came their commander, Lieutenant Adrian Searing. *E, T, I*
533.13–14	is Confederate gray.] looks gray—a Confederate soldier. *E*
533.19	on and absently] on, mechanically *E*; on mechanically *T*; on and mechanically *I*

FOR THE AHKOOND

535.1	4591] 3940 *E*
	Citrusia] California *E*
535.5	distinction] notoriety *E*
535.6	Darkest] *om. E*
535.13	isochronophone] telephonagraphine *E*
535.23	Kikago,] Kicago, *E*
536.8	vines. ¶] ~.^ *E*
536.20	Forgotten Continent." ¶] Dark Continent."^ *E*
536.23	those of oxen] a horse *E*
536.27	the ancient] our greatest living *E*
536.32	urging] paddling *E*
536.34	on examination] my experienced eye at once *E*
537.2	1945!] 1920! *E*

537.8	isochronophone] telephonagraphine *E*
537.13	times: in 1920.] times—as late as the year 1895. *E*
537.18	vast sea of mud] shoreless sea of slickens *E*
537.30	you!" ¶] ~!"^ *E*
537.31	dessert, and served badly.] dessert. *E*
538.3	lessening] disappearance *E*
	from evaporation] *om. E*
538.4	recovered. ¶] ~.^ *E*
538.6–7	primitive and monstrous] monstrous and primitive *E*
539.14	*coprets*] surindas *E*
539.21	origin. ¶] ~.^ *E*
539.24	winter,] Blizzard, *E*
	eternal. ¶] ~*E*
539.25	archæthermograph,] archæthermometer, *E*
539.26	winters] Blizzards *E*
539.31	insupportable.] intolerable. *E*
539.34	winter] Blizzard *E*
539.36	Californians,] Citrusians, *E*
540.2	1943,] 1915, *E*
540.12	Coons. ¶] ~. *E*
540.17	*smig*] rod *E*
540.19	successors. ¶] ~. *E*
540.26	frequent] annual *E*
540.27	point] acre *E*
540.28	half century] half-dozen years *E*
	no footnote in E
540.33	Californians] Citrusians *E*
541.2	1946] 1945 *E*
541.4	isochronophone] telephonographine [*sic*] *E*

HADES IN TROUBLE

544.35	these] this *E*
545.38	remembrance,] rememberance, *E*
551.32	Nick?] ~. *E*

THE FALL OF THE REPUBLIC

556.18–19	"Decline . . . Republics,"] *Decline . . . Republics, E*
556.19	"History . . . Government,"] *History . . . Government, E*
556.19–20	"Monarchical Renascence"] *Monarchical Renascence E*
556.20–21	"Rise, . . . States,"] *Rise, . . . States, E*
563.36	"Memoirs"] *Memoirs E*

THE KINGDOM OF TORTIRRA

567.2	*Jabez Jones,*] Jabez Jones, *E*
567.5	*Ecuador,*] Ecuador, *E*
567.13	*Ecuador,*] Ecuador, *E*

567.14   *Arethusa,*] Arethusa, *E*
568.1   *Jabez Jones,*] Jabez Jones, *E*
568.2   *Ecuador,*] Ecuador, *E*
571.31   nation] nations *E*

A SON OF THE GODS

Subtitle: Present] Historical ~ *E, T, I*
599.16   were] had been *E*
599.22   beyond. ¶] ~.^ *E*
599.23   had seemed!] seemed! *E, T, I*
599.25   had related] retained; *E*; related *T, I*
600.7   them. ¶] ~.^ *E*
600.38   hill!] ~. He is deathly pale. *E, T, I*
600.39   six] three *E*
601.2   How] Ah! How beautiful he is!—how *E*
601.8–9   him . . . laughed!] him; we are but "dead men all." We no longer even
              know that we laughed. *E*; him; we are but "dead men all." But we re-
              member that we laughed! *T, I*
601.19   thunder] shock *E*
601.32   has not retreated] occupies that hill, *E*
602.13   Our] One *E*
602.15   parallel] *om. E*
602.25   directly] *om. E*
603.1   musketry is] musketry, faintly and fitfully heard as the wind serves, is
              nevertheless *E*
603.1–2   target] billet *E*
603.14   toward us.] to the enemy. *E, T*
603.15   to us,] to the enemy, to us, *E, T*
603.33   sound] shock *E*
603.38   one] *one E*
603.39   pitiless perfection] consistency *E*

MY FAVORITE MURDER

612.2   charging the jury,] summing up, *E, C*
612.4   away. ¶] ~.^ *E*
612.6   agreeable] pleasant *E*
612.8   (if . . . called)] *om. E, C*
612.9   victim.] deceased. *E*
612.13   hard] impossible *E, C*
613.2   year] week *E*
613.9   1856] 1836 *E*
613.10   later] declining *E*
613.11   Head,] Tent, *E [et seq.]*
613.14–15   event . . . trial] night when I had the misfortune to murder my mother
              as she lay by his side *E*
614.28   proof] guaranty *E*; guarantee *C*

614.29	wounded] shot *E*
614.32	win. ¶] ~.^ *E*
614.37	rifle.] Winchester. *E*
614.40	*tendo*] *tendon E, C*
615.3	generous.] liberal about this thing. *E, C*
615.10	knees] thighs *E*
615.16	wind. ¶] ~:^ *E*; ~.^ *C*
615.20	large, fine] huge *E, C*
615.33	method] *E, C*; methods *CW*
616.4	Instantly] In a moment *E*
616.13	forward,] upward *E*; ~ *C*
617.11–13	Evidently . . . indeed.] *om. E*
617.24	unspeakable] inexpressible *E*
617.27	heron. ¶] ~.^ *E, C*
617.28	height] hight *E*
	fond . . . view,] nearly as I could judge, *E, C*
617.31	me] my head *E*
617.36–37	a . . . seismic,] *om. E, C*
617.38	southwest.] south. *E, C*
617.39	artistic] *om. E, C*

A TOUGH TUSSLE

619.2	was] was then, and still is, *E, T, I*
619.16	writing] speaking *E, T, I*
619.24–25	author . . . dispositions] young Lieutenant *E*; young lieutenant *T*
620.20	incur.] encounter. *E, T*
620.32	grotesque. ¶] ~.^ *E*
621.1	footfall] footstep *E, T*
621.30	body.] man. *E, T*
622.2	slowly on,] westward *E, T, I*
622.13	extended,] all abroad, *E*
623.4	run] flown *E*
623.30	grumble] beat *E*
623.39	plunging] screaming *E*
624.12–13	It . . . own.] *om. E*

ONE OF TWINS

631.3	the natural . . . acquaintance.] such natural laws as we have acquaintance with. *E, C*
631.11	tattooing] branding *E*
631.12	the operator . . . reckoning;] "they mixed the babies up"; *E*
631.19	"Jehnry."] "Jenry." *E, C*
632.30	queer,"] funny," *E, C*
633.1	which] ~, feeling that I was myself unobserved, *E, C*
633.4–5	a fashionably] an elegantly *E*
633.5	woman] lady *E*

633.15	shame.] consciousness of any moral obliquity. *E*
633.20	beauty] marvelous ~ *E*
633.21–22	the marvelous . . . face] it *E*
633.23	surroundings.] environment. *E*
633.24–25	enduring . . . experience,] enduring *E, C*
633.27	gravity: ¶] ~:^ *E*
633.36	pale,] deathly ~, *E*
	entirely] perfectly *E, C*
633.40	It] There was good stuff in this little sinner. It *E*
633.41	needless. ¶] ~.^ *E*
634.5	continued, with agitation:] continued: *E*
634.15	manner. ¶] ~.^ *E*
634.26	endeavored] ~ vainly *E, C*
634.38	frightened] thoroughly ~ *E*
634.39	move.] ~. A chill crept up my back and passed over my scalp—the sensation which is called the rising of the hair. *E*
634.40	myself] ~, "clothed and in my right mind," *E*
635.7	chest, inflicted] chest unskillfully inflicted *E*
635.24–28	But . . . hospital. ¶] *om. E*
635.36	should be] is *E*

THE CITY OF THE GONE AWAY

643.2	coin.] dollar. *E*
643.9	salute] welcome *E*
643.10	welcoming] rewarding *E*
643.13	its benediction] the blessings of their influence *E*
643.15	taste. ¶] ~.^ *E*
644.1	priest,] preacher, *E*
644.2	penny.] dollar. *E*
644.23	made] *om. E*
644.31	incalculable multitudes.] such incalculable multitudes that a writer in one of the public prints, alluding to their escorting friends and my uncommon fees, said: "The blockade of impatients in front of Dr. Gringhast's expensary is the only case of congestion that he will not treat." *E*
644.34	parliament.] Legislature. *E*
645.13	signify] express *E*
645.16	had] been known to have *E*
646.7	severity] austerity *E*
646.15	work. ¶] ~.^ *E*
646.19	kink] curl *E*
646.36	greater part of the] whole *E*
647.2–5	*cadavres . . . cadavres*] *cadavers . . . cadavers E*
647.4	diplomas, degrees] diplomas *E*
647.10	Badelina Fatti] *om. E*

CHICKAMAUGA

648.4	thousands] many thousands *E, T, I*
648.5	victories] victorious *E*
648.6	cities] great cities *E*
648.16	space] interspaces *E*; spaces *T*
649.7–8	sat, bolt . . . a] bolt . . . sat a *E, T*
649.9	with inarticulate cries for] upon *E*
649.12	erring] aimless *E*
649.13	in a narrow space] *om. E*
649.20	hedges] hedgerows *E, T*
649.40	moving] moving forward *E, T, I*
650.10	motionless.] as dead. *E*
650.13	elder] older *E, T, I*
650.15	unfamiliarly] some of them were singularly *E*; some of them were unfamiliarly *T*
650.24	"making believe" they were] fancying them *E*
650.25	The man] He *E*
650.33	clumsy] uncanny *E, T*
651.12	rifle] musket *E, T*
651.19	battalions,] battalions' lines, *E*
652.4	illumination,] illumination of its interspaces, *E*
652.18	stumbling] aimless *E*
652.20	out] all abroad *E*
652.23	bubbles—the] bubbles. The *E*
652.24	The child] He *E*

ONE OFFICER, ONE MAN

654.1	Captain] "I shall break down! I shall break down!" ¶ These words kept repeating themselves in the mind of Captain *E*
	Graffenreid] Traylor [*et seq.*] as he *E*
654.3–4	The left . . . miles.] Both flanks were veiled by woods. *E*
654.9	motionless,] as ~ as statues, *E, C*
655.21	waived] foregone *E*
	devotion to duty] position *E, C*
655.24	hope. ¶] ~.^ *E*
655.26	Anderton Graffenreid.] he. *E*
655.36	dark] ~ blue *E, C*
655.41	deep, jarring] sharp shock of an *E*
656.3	attention to note] the ear to discern *E*
656.13	officer] General *E*; general *C*
656.36	rifle;] musket; *E, C*
656.39	erect;] standing; *E*
656.40	low . . . rear.] hills. *E*
657.1	the dead man,] his dead, *E*
657.5	company. ¶] ~.^ *E*

657.8	black] ~ and brazen *E*
657.12	side. ¶] ~.^ *E, C*
657.15	disappointing.] ~. He expressed it to himself in four words: "I shall break down." *E*
657.20	moment] ~ for the Federal center *E*
657.25–26	chorus of voices,] confusion of stray voices, *E*
657.38	reminded by vertigo.] apprised by vertigo. These symptoms of excitement he interpreted as cowardice, and was filled with apprehensions of disgrace. "I shall break down! I shall break down!" Over and over the words repeated themselves with mechanical iteration. He thought he spoke them audibly—believed that he screamed them so that all could hear. *E*
657.39–658.11	Glancing . . . died.] He had glanced downward at his naked sword and—God knows how—it had reminded him of an ancient Roman antidote to military dishonor. He grasped the hilt in both hands, set the point against his breast and bent his arms with all their strength, thrusting the keen blade through his body till it came out at the back; then falling heavily forward upon the dead man, he died. *E*

A HORSEMAN IN THE SKY

[No sections divisions in E, T, I]	
660.10	to that point] for two miles *E*
	west,] ~ at that point, *E*
660.11	one hundred] fifty *E*
660.13	northward,] from the ridge to the ~, *E, T*
660.16	angle . . . lay] soldier's station *E*
661.19	Virginia.] ~ a quarter-century ago. *E*
661.23	"Well, go, sir,] "Go, Carter, *E, T*
661.24	Virginia, to . . . traitor,] Virginia *E*
662.11	confronting] *om. E*
662.17	eminence] commanding ~ *E, T, I*
662.30	pale;] deathly ~; *E, T*
662.34–35	of emotion.] and excitement. *E*
663.5	through] below. Through *E*; below, through *T*
663.6	sea. He] sea, he *E*
663.9	dozen] hundred *E, T, I*
663.11–14	But . . . duty." *om. E*
663.17	conquered;] silenced conscience; *E*
663.19	An] At this moment an *E*; At that moment an *T*
663.20	with aimless feet] climbing the slope *E*
663.25	It] At some distance away to his right it *E, T, I*
663.32	hands were] right hand was *E, T*
664.3	distant] a half-mile *E, T*
664.13	The . . . smiled.] *om. E*
664.23	It . . . cliff."] I am a great marksman; you know I once shot a match with the Devil in hell and beat him." *E*

664.24	The] The Sergeant was shocked and startled. He looked searchingly at Druse. The *E*
664.24–25	white, . . . understand.] white; his eyes were restless and glittered with a strange uncanny light. The Sergeant, still on hands and knees, involuntarily backed a little away from him. *E*
664.27	anybody . . . horse?"] anybody—anybody at all—except the horse?" *E*
664.29	"Well?"] "Who?" *E, T*
664.30	away . . . said.] rapidly down the road and toward the valley. *E*

THE COUP DE GRÂCE

666.4–5	the forest,] *T, I*; the interspaces of the forest, *E*; the forests, *CW*
666.7	neglect] exposure *E, T*
666.10	it.] ~. Those of the vanquished party forego it altogether; their patience is without reward. *E*
666.17	afterward] *om. E, T*
667.3	presumably] *om. E, T, I*
667.15	small] young *E*
667.15–16	narrowly.] ~, the crimson light suffusing it and fringing its confused outlines with fire. *E*
667.17	Downing Madwell,] Lewis Marriner [*et seq.*] *E*
667.18	man. ¶] ~.^ *E*
667.19	Halcrow— . . . Halcrow.] Searle—John and Francis. [*et seq.*] *E*
667.28	gulf] social ~ *E, T*
667.34	services. ¶] ~.^ *E*
667.38	said:] ~: ¶ *E*
668.8	1862.] 1863. *E*
668.20	loop of] lacerated end of the *E, T*
668.37	what? ¶] ~?^ *E*
668.39	formulate . . . death.] beg for death. *E*
669.4	that silent] its piteous *E*; its silent *T*; his silent *I*
	plea. ¶] ~.^ *E*
669.7	*grâce.* ¶] ~.^ *E*
669.8	friend.] ~: "Frank, Frank, do you not know me?" *E*
669.27	Presently] Suddenly *E, T, I*
669.30	horse. ¶] ~.^ *E, T*
670.6–7	stretcher. ¶ The] stretcher; the *E*

THE SUITABLE SURROUNDINGS

677.3–4	lost himself while] been *E, T, I*
677.4	near midnight was] at nightfall found himself *E, T, I*
677.5	unfamiliar.] but partly familiar. *E, T, I*
677.16	the other end] a destination *E*
677.17	there?"] ~? I don't like it." *E, T, I*
677.26	thing. ¶] ~.^ *E*
678.18	stopped] paused in his flight *E, T, I*

678.19	all.] ~. He endeavored to still the beating of his heart by holding his breath until half suffocated. *E, T, I*
	blood forsaking] deadly whiteness of *E, T*
678.36	me?"] *me?" E, T*
678.37	breakfast] dinner *E, T*
679.2	enjoyment?] admiration? *E, T, I*
680.16	ghostly] ghastliest *E, T, I*
680.33	spirits;] ~ apparently; *E, T, I*
680.38	unlocked] bolted on the inside, *E, T, I*
680.39	ceremony.] further ceremony than breaking it down. *E, T, I*
681.1–2	They . . . man.] These two doors also were fastened, and were broken in. They entered at random the one on the left first. It was vacant. In the room on the right—the one which had the blank front windows— was the dead body of a man! [man. *T,* I] *E, T, I*
681.12	glooming] gloaming *E*
681.14	the man read:] *om. E, T, I*
681.19	tragic] gloomy *E, T, I*
681.24	twelve] ten *E*
681.30–31	Here . . . aloud.] *om. E, T, I*
681.37–38	manuscript,] ~, sealed, *E*
682.4	*twelve*] *10 E*
682.7–8	the candle . . . lighted.] one of the others had picked up the candle and lighted it. *E*
682.10–12	The man . . . contained.] *sentences reversed in E*
682.21–22	Most . . . large."] It is thought that his malady is due to grief and excite- ment caused by the recent mysterious death of his friend Willard Marsh. *E*

THE AFFAIR AT COULTER'S NOTCH

684.5–6	in a . . . extolled.] Captain Coulter's courage had been too highly extolled in a recent conversation between them. *E, T, I*
684.13–14	Federal] a line of *E*
684.17	two batteries] an entire battery *E*
684.19	on an open lawn] *om. E, T;* in an open lawn *I*
684.21–22	exposure— . . . fire.] exposure: the rifles of that day would not carry a mile without such an elevation as made the fire, in a military sense, harmless: it might kill here and there but could not dislodge. *E*
685.10	twelve."] six." [*et seq.*] *E*
685.15	deprecation. ¶] ~.^ *E, T, I*
686.8	statuesque.] motionless as an equestrian statue. *E, T, I*
686.8–9	road . . . headlong] *om. CW*
686.9	behind a wood.] around a corner. *E*
686.16	slope,] declivity, *E*
	deafening report] sharp shock which turned up the white of the forest leaves like a storm *E*

686.31	house.] ~, with which it was accurately in line. *E*, *T*
687.4–16	A young . . . guns.] *om. E*
688.16–17	disabled— . . . another.] disabled. *E*
688.28–31	The colonel . . . there] There *E*
689.10	to anybody,] facetiously, *E*, *T*
689.23	supper] ~ that evening *E*, *T*
689.37	side.] feet. *E*, *T*, *I*
690.1–3	away, . . . foot.] away lay an infant's foot. It was near an irregular depression in the beaten earth which formed the cellar's floor—a fresh excavation with a convex bit of iron, having jagged edges, visible in one of the sides. *E*, *T*
690.17	And these?"] Who then are—were these?" *E*
690.18	I] Colonel, I *E*

A WATCHER BY THE DEAD

697.3	man, . . . sheet.] man in a coffin. *E*
697.8	the man.] a man covered from head to foot with a sheet. *E*
	as also the corpse,] including the body, *E*
697.18	an indolence] a deliberation *E*
697.21	body.] coffin. *E*
698.11	by those having it] *om. E*
698.28	regard.] ~. It was a picture to delight a Rembrandt. *E*
697.37	gravest] eldest *E*, *T*, *I*
	Dr. Helberson,] whom we may call ~, *E*
699.17	it."] ~ under ordinary circumstances." *E*
699.25	Cæsarian section."] the Cæsarian operation." *E*
699.30	here;] in California; *E*, *T*, *I*
699.31	loads] dead ~ *E*, *T*, *I*
700.4	*no section division in E*
700.25	Then,] Suddenly, *E*, *T*, *I*
701.12	insupportable] horrible *E*, *T*
701.14	know] *know E*
702.7	accordance] virtual but not literal ~ *E*
702.15	closed] colored *E*
702.19	Harper] ~, who was now deathly pale, *E*, *T*, *I*
702.24	men.] people. *E*, *T*, *I*
703.15	six] two *E*, *T*, *I*
703.20	shifting his lantern] *om. E*; he shifted the lantern and *T*
704.9	replied: ¶] ~:^ *E*
704.11	suddenly, rose and went white.] suddenly and grew deathly pale. *E*, *T*, *I*
704.19	Harper . . . his] both men . . . their *E*, *T*, *I*
704.29–30	to come . . . him] *om. E*
704.38	Hell-born] Helborn *E*; Hellborn *T*, *I*
705.5	High Supreme] Chief *E*

THE MAJOR'S TALE

E prefaces text with the following paragraph: The Major's Impressions Regarding Men's Ages—How to Tell a Story: "Straight Away to the End Without Digression"—The Lady-Killer's Hard Lot—Decadence of Womanly Worth—The Narrative Strolls on Through Paths of Flowery Ease to the Denouement—The Practical Joke.

706.1	Civil War] civil war *E*
706.3	evermore] *om. E, C*
706.11	really is;] *is; E, C*
706.17	more than forty,] above forty-five, *E, C*
707.26	remark, as is my way.] remark. *E*
707.26	comrades.] companions. *E, C*
707.29	eager] anxious *E, C*
707.38	he has had] you have had *E*
708.7	digression. ¶] ~.^ *E*
708.16	about him.] in illustration. *E*
708.18	admiration] ~ and favor *E*
709.2	insurgent] rebellious *E*
709.15	done. ¶] ~.^ *E*
709.34	little dance] bottle and his rigadoon *E*
710.8–9	an *édition* . . . Deportment."] a blue-and-gold edition of *Masher on Deportment. E*
710.18	in appearance] *om. E*
710.21	words without sense] manuscript without meaning *E*
710.31	possessing . . . hands] putting his arms about her waist *E*
710.34	erect. ¶] ~.^ *E*

THE STORY OF A CONSCIENCE

713.7	He] This man *E*
713.8	civilian—a] civilian. He was a *E*
713.14	neglected] ill cared-for *E, C*
713.24	coat.] "butternut" ~. *E*
714.1	"You-all"] "You 'uns *E, C*
714.14–15	a company . . . artillery,] two companies of infantry and a battery of artillery, *E*
714.17–18	It . . . "discovered."] *om. E*
715.15	saying: ¶] ~:^ *E*
715.25	Brune,] ~, a deserter from the Federal army, *E*
715.38	enigmatical] extraordinary *E, C*
716.20	who . . . you.] was placed on guard over you who had just returned from a long, fatiguing march. *E, C*
717.7	silence. ¶] ~.^ *E, C*
717.15	shame] fear and ~ *E*
717.17	heard about you."] heard." *E, C*
717.19	colors.] ~—'the bonnie blue flag.' *E*
717.20–21	I . . . punishment."] *om. E*

718.3	solemn] *om. E*
719.23	that . . . gratitude] which I meanly accepted, *E*; which I accepted without gratitude *C*

THE MAN AND THE SNAKE

720.23	higher] ~ types *E, T*
720.32	splendor. ¶] ~.^ *E*
721.10	affected] *om. E*
721.23	mind . . . decision.] consciousness before he made the least movement in precaution. He had not even withdrawn his eyes from those of the serpent. How, however, he had "made up his mind" what to do: he flattered himself that thought had ripened to action. Passively submitting himself to the stress of a thousand sets of opposing influences, and recognizing the instant predominance of one set over the others, he gave the process the customary names—consideration and decision. *E*
721.31	backward] ~ without obstruction and find the door *E, T*
722.9	needles. ¶] ~.^ *E*
722.30	knew] realized *E, T*
722.39	assured . . . triumph,] knowing its triumph assured, *E, T*
723.31	daubed] defiled *E*

AN OCCURRENCE AT OWL CREEK BRIDGE

725.2	A man] One morning in the summer of 1862 a man *E*
725.9	was] stood *E*
725.17	curving,] ~ to the right, *E*
725.19	topped] crowned *E, T, I*
726.8	habit,] dress, *E, T*
726.15	persons,] people, *E, T*
	excluded.] ~ if patriotic and daring. *E*
727.6	their lines;] them: *E*
727.28	fetching] gone to fetch *E, T, I*
	horseman] cavalryman *E*
727.32	north] other *E, T*
728.17	periodicity.] ~ of abatement and augmentation. *E*
728.30	darkness] blackness *E, T*
728.31	fainter and fainter] dimmer and dimmer *E*
728.32	glimmer.] point. *E*
729.3	neck. They] neck, *E*
729.28	soldiers upon] soldiers. Upon *E*
729.30	him. The captain] him; the Captain *E*; him; the captain *T, I*
729.32	he . . . report and] *om. E*
729.33	He . . . report, and] A sharp report followed, and he *E*
730.19	again,] *om. E*
730.20	swimming] ~, consciously and *E*
730.37	forest,] *E, T, I,* H; forests, *CW*

731.5	diamonds,] gold, like ~, *E, T*
732.7	neck,] ~ and suspended by as stout a rope as ever rewarded the zeal of a civilian patriot in war-time, *A*

THE REALM OF THE UNREAL

734.2	Newcastle] ~, in Placer county, *E*
734.6	off] over the bank *E*
734.9	ravine,] gulch, *E*
734.10	saw] ~ the figure of *E, C*
734.14	vehicle;] buggy, *E, C*
735.31	reporter.] liar. *E*
736.29	Bewildered] Inexpressibly bewildered *E, C*
736.30	retired] fled *E*
736.32	came near crying] cried *E*
736.39	sidewalk,] ~ was absolutely *E, C*
737.2	Dupont] Stockton *E*
737.8	Oakland. ¶] ~.^ *E*
737.18	lived,] stayed^ *E*
737.20	ladies. ¶] ~.^ *E, C*
737.30–31	was . . . was . . . was] is . . . is . . . is *E*
737.32–36	were . . . were . . . grew . . . had . . . were . . . overran . . . was . . . wandered . . . was] are . . . are . . . grow . . . have . . . are . . . overrun . . . is . . . wander . . . is *E*
737.36	God. ¶] ~.^ *E, C*
738.1	ghostly] ghastly *E, C*
738.8	I] My friends, you must excuse me—I *E*
738.14–15	*Paragraphs reversed in* E
739.3	disquieting."] alarming. *E*

THE MIDDLE TOE OF THE RIGHT FOOT

744.10	material] fundamental *E, T*
744.19	dwellings] *E, T, I,* H; dwelling *CW*
	It] The house *E, T, I*
745.11	to me] *om. E*
745.28	structure. ¶] architecture.^ *E, T;* ~. *I*
745.29	candle.] ~; they might have been a *tableau vivant* after a painting by Rembrandt. *E*
745.32	features,] face, *E*
746.30	startling.] appalling! *E, T*
746.34	door;] ~ and its locking; *E*
746.35	building.] ~. Instantly—audible without and within—a strange wild shriek resounded through the vacant upper chambers, and a startled owl, dashing clumsily out of one of the blank windows, flew away through the night to the nearest wood. *E*
747.2	(. . .)] *om. E, T, I*
747.9–10	Southern] Missouri *E*

747.29	parted] cut *E, T*
747.34	"That chap"] That person *E, T*; That chap *I*
748.20	disregard] unconsciousness *E, T, I*
748.31	beneficent] *om. E*
	State] ~ of Missouri *E*
748.40	obedience . . . command.] obedience. He had intended going away— but in other company. *E, T*
749.1	which . . . locked,] *om. E*
749.2	amazed] surprised *E*
7449.11	threshold.] ~—halt and hold their breath. *E*
749.16	dead.] ~—dead of terror! *E, T*
749.18	In the thick] *E, T, I,* H; In thick *CW*
749.32	was!" ¶] ~!"^ *E*
749.38	comprehend. ¶] ~.^ *E*
750.1	affected . . . terror.] struck him with an invincible terror. *E, T, I*
750.7	attention, horribly pale.] attention. *E*
750.11	Brewer.] ~. Another moment, and that gentleman, staggering and clutching at nothing, sank awkwardly to the floor in a dead faint. Under strong emotions men will sometimes do that. *E*

OIL OF DOG

754.1	Boffer Bings.] Joram Turmore. [*et seq.*] *O*
754.2	manufacturer of] retail dealer in *O*
754.14	persons] people *O*
754.18	days,] ~ of prosperity and happiness^ *O*
755.19	was] he had *O*
755.28	but] for *O*
756.18	dagger. ¶] ~.^ *O*
756.19	profit] pleasure and ~ *O*
756.21	indescribable] inconceivable *O*
756.26	apart. ¶] ~.^ *O*
756.27	and . . . contact.] was covered with blood, and blood was dripping from the dagger which my mother still retained. *O*
756.30	resistance,] the repeated blows of the dagger, *O*
756.35	Otumwee,] Graymaulkin, *O*
756.35–37	where . . . disaster.] in whose ancient University I have long held the Regius Professorship of Cats.

THE WIDOWER TURMORE

758.7	I] As related elsewhere (*Lives of the Gods*—Bancroft, San Jurasco) I *Wa, C*
758.18	the Noble Science,] Felinology, *Wa, C*
758.21	even . . . salary.] my meagre salary. *Wa*
759.18	conspirators,] and best, *Wa, C*
	computation. There were] the dreams of avarice—*Wa*; computation—*C*
759.20	king's] mother's *Wa*
759.26	imagination,] ~ and the powers of expression, *Wa, C*

759.35–36	Yet I proved] Yet, I satisfied myself *Wa, C*
760.1	more resolute than before] as resolute as ever *Wa, C*
760.3–4	obedience] obligation to prove myself obedient *Wa, C*
760.29	good.] ~. I remain a widower to this day, having never again married. *Wa*
761.2	living. ¶] ~.^ *Wa, C*
761.23	colors] Latin *Wa*
	skull] ~, apparently that of a female, *Wa*
761.29	wall. ¶] ~.^ *Wa, C*
761.38	Indictment] Arrest *Wa, C*
761.40	constructive] *om. Wa, C*

HAÏTA THE SHEPHERD

763.1–2	youth . . . age and experience.] learning and experience . . . youth. *Wa*
763.9	whither. ¶] ~.^ *Wa*
763.12	chewed] indolently ~ *Wa, T, I*
763.14	accidental] *om. Wa*
765.5	brightness] radiance *Wa*
765.7	before her] at her feet *Wa*
765.13	into each other's] in one another's *Wa, T*; in each other's *I*
765.21	youth!] man! *Wa, T*
765.31	Hastur . . . flock,] Hastur, *Wa*
766.21	thine] yours *Wa, T, I*
766.25	bears came] wolves sprang *Wa, T*
766.26	crimson mouths and fiery eyes.] fiery eyes and dreadful howls. *Wa*
766.27	cot] humble dwelling *Wa*
766.28	bears] wolves, *Wa, T*
766.31	bears] wolves *Wa, T*

PARKER ADDERSON, PHILOSOPHER

768.3	Parker] James [*et seq.*] *E*
768.3	my answer] if I answered that it *E, T*
769.2	morose."] most unamiable." *E*
769.3	brightened] smiled *E*
769.10	leather] hair *E, T, I*
769.15	that . . . weapon] the last *E*
769.16	souvenir] cherished ~ *E, T, I*
	peaceful] blameless *E*
769.25	note] ~, saluted again and *E*
769.26	handsome] ~, clean-cut *E, T, I*
769.41	know] not ~ *E, T*
770.2	it."] ~. I suspect, too, that they know as little about it as we." *E*
770.16	lap,] ~ below the edge of the table^ *E*
770.18	continued:] ~: ¶ *E*
770.19	fire,] ~, but in the haste and confusion of the moment your aim has been taken badly *E*

770.21–22	There . . . same;] The pain was possibly equal to that produced by an attack of gout, which we regard with apprehension but not with horror. We are unreasonable: the fact that a certain case of pain has death as its outcome makes it neither more nor less severe. To-morrow morning you will cause me to be hanged. It is not known if hanging is painful, but this I know: *E*
771.8	Captain Hasterlick,] *om. E*
771.27	grasped] seized *E*
772.11	hilt. ¶] ~.^ *E*
772.26	attention. ¶] ~.^ *E*
772.38	Clavering, . . . camp-fire,] Clavering *E*
772.41– 773.1	then, . . . sweetness,] then smiling again, *E*

A LADY FROM REDHORSE

774.1	CORONADO,] *om. E*
774.4	beautiful] handsome *E, T, I*
774.10–11	give . . . heighten] instruct him how to heighten *E*
775.24	him!] Him! *E*
775.32	exterminates] does run down *E*
775.35	*vraisemblance.*] genuine ~. *E*
775.37	young.] ~ and truehearted and barefooted. *E, T*
	days] far fair ~ *E, T*
776.3	civility] compliment *E, T, I*
776.6	misery] the grave *E, T, I*
778.21	roped in your] played it upon / Your *E*; played it upon your *T, I*

THE BOARDED WINDOW

780.1	1830,] 1845, *E*
780.3	habitable] comfortable *E, T*
780.7	the meager] *om. E, T*
780.17	ax.] axe [ax *T, I*] at some distant day. *E, T, I*
781.1	as] ~ in due time *E, T*
781.8	grandfather,] father, [*et seq.*] *E*
781.19	spot.] ~. As this record grows naturally out of my personal relation to what it records, that circumstances [circumstance *T*], as a part of the relation, has a certain relevancy. *E, T*
781.23–24	fashion,] ~ *in juvento mundi*, *E*
781.28	abundant assurance] assurance abundant *E*
781.34–35	fell into unconsciousness] passed into a comatose state *E, T*
783.6	feet. Fear] feet and terror *E*; feet, and terror *T*

THE SECRET OF MACARGER'S GULCH

784.1	Indian Hill,] Mammon Hill, *Wa*
784.10	five . . . name.] it is known even by name, five miles away. *Wa*
784.12	try] ~ a long time *Wa, C*

785.21	supply,] afford, *Wa, C*
785.22	give. ¶] ~.^ *Wa, C*
785.25	black,] bleak, *Wa*
785.27	unfriendly] uncanny *Wa*
785.31	disquieting. ¶] ~.^ *Wa, C*
785.34	now] keenly *Wa*
786.2	But] A moment *Wa, C*
786.9	And then I dreamed. ¶] And sleeping, I dreamed.^ *Wa*; And, sleeping, I dreamed. ¶ *C*
786.16	head. ¶] ~.^ *Wa, C*
786.21	Presently] At last *Wa*
786.34	husband and wife. ¶] man and wife.^ *Wa*; husband and wife.^ *C*
786.39	situation. ¶] ~.^ *Wa*
787.6	vision. ¶] ~.^ *Wa, C*
787.10	pictures and description.] pictures. *Wa*
787.18	aloud,] audibly, *Wa, C*
787.35	living, dying thing!] living thing at the point of death! *Wa*; living thing! *C*
788.22	all.] ~, from my lips. *Wa*
788.28	the body of a woman,] a female body, *Wa*
789.1	story. ¶] ~.^ *Wa*
789.7	water in it?"] water, is wet?" *Wa*

THE MOCKING-BIRD

790.2	southwestern] Western *E, C*
790.25	vain] *om. E, C*
790.26	that of] *om. E*
791.1	two hours] some minutes *E*
791.10	knowledge] sense *E, C*
791.20	a stilled heart] his heart in his mouth *E*
791.26	when it was repeated by] when, bang! bang! went *E*
791.34	complimented] highly ~ *E, C*
792.32	of themselves] *om. E, C*
792.40	moved] sped *E, C*
793.4	away from it,] back, *E*
793.5	overlooking] back of *E*
793.11	intervals] interspaces *E*
793.18	kinsmen.] wealthy ~. *E*
793.27	kinsmen] wealthy ~ *E*
793.34	awake. ¶] ~.^ *E, C*
794.11	man. ¶] ~.^ *E*

THE THING AT NOLAN

795.1	To] Just to *E*
	Hardy,] Hurdy, *E*
795.5	took its name.] was named. *E*

795.6	young girls.] girls "in their teens." *E*
795.10	quick] ~, hot *E, C*
795.10–11	kindled . . . which] which is kindled in a wisp of straw, *E*; which, kindled in a wisp of straw, *C*
796.2	spade.] ~ with him. *E*
796.7	five,] 4.25^ *E*; five^ *C*
796.27	light on] aspect upon *E, C*
797.2	return. ¶] ~.^ *E, C*
797.20	the deceased] "the deceased" *E*
797.25	haunted.] ~. An extraordinary fact in its later history is that within its walls death has overtaken no fewer than three of the five men who testified to the presence of Charles May in Mr. Odell's store at Nolan. Two of them, Abner Gray and Parker Robinson, took shelter in it from a storm, quarreled—about what no one knows—and fatally shot one another. The other, Amasa T. Filder, entered it one dark night in a spirit of bravado and was found next day in the principal room, stone dead of what the Coroner's jury was pleased to name "a visitation of God." But that is later history. *E*
797.26	day] ~ in September, 1879, directly *E, C*
797.40	what was it] who was that man *E*

A BABY TRAMP

799.7	common.¶] ~.^ *Wa*
799.9	credibly] veritably *Wa, C*
799.16	science . . . scientists] scientific men . . . scientific men *Wa*
800.3	think. ¶] ~.^ *Wa, C*
800.9	traveled,] ~ "abroad," *Wa, C*
800.25	three] five *Wa, C*
800.38	an alluring] a splendid *Wa*
801.4	on the . . . continent.] *om. Wa*
801.8	obscurity] the greatest ~ *Wa, C*
801.16	disadvantages. ¶] ~.^ *Wa, C*
801.21	Whiteville,] Dryville, *Wa*
801.25	Whiteville] Dryville *Wa*
801.30–31	wonderfully] ~, almost indelibly—*Wa*
801.31	forlorn] *om. Wa*
801.39	not the faintest] no *Wa, C*
802.11	A considerable] Quite a *Wa, C*
802.20	unidentified] "unidentified" *Wa, C*
802.21	Parlow. The grave,] Parlow—which, *Wa*

THE DEATH OF HALPIN FRAYSER

E = "Prattle," *E* (12 June 1887): 4.

804.3	that removed] that hath removed *Wa*
804.8	*Hali.*] *Mannon's "Thoughts on Immortality." Wa*
804.9	forest] ~ in the Napa Valley *Wa, C*

804.13	St. Helena,] San Francisco, *Wa*
804.17	thirty-two.] twenty-seven. *Wa*
804.18–19	persons . . . persons, . . . persons,] people . . . people, . . . people, *Wa*, *C*
804.20	port] haven *Wa*
804.22	it is . . . exposure.] Halpin Frayser did not come to his death by exposure, as we shall see. *Wa*
805.7	sweeping] who swept *Wa*, *C*
805.8	who sat] who, as we have noted, sat *Wa*, *C*
805.11	spoken] mentioned *Wa*, *C*
805.23	imperious] malign *Wa*
805.24–25	invisible existences whom] malevolent existences, invisible, and whom *Wa*, *C*
805.25	trees] black bodies of the ~ A
805.28	soul. ¶] his ~.^ *Wa*, *C*
805.30	mysterious] uncanny *Wa*
805.37	foliage. ¶] ~.^ *Wa*, *C*
805.38	terror which] terror, which, however, *Wa*, *C*
	not incompatible with] but *Wa*
806.5	whom nor why.] why nor whom. *Wa*, *C*
806.12–13	unfamiliar] various *Wa*
806.23	peal of laughter] laugh *Wa*, *C*
806.29	moved. ¶] ~.^ *Wa*, *C*
807.6	well-to-do,] ~ people, *Wa*, *C*
807.20	Bayne] he *Wa*
807.30	politics. ¶] ~.^ *Wa*, *C*
807.35	truth] point of fact *Wa*, *C*
807.37–38	lyre. ¶ In . . . anyhow.] lyre.^ In . . . anyhow. ¶ *Wa*, *C*
808.3	those of him] his *Wa*, *C*
808.3–4	guilt in . . . If in] guilt was a tie that bound them very closely together; and if in *Wa*
808.4	his mother] she *Wa*
808.9	signal] conspicuous *Wa*
808.21	son,"] boy," *Wa*
808.38	had] had had *Wa*
809.20	had gone] went *Wa*, *C*
	dreaming.] ~, as we have seen. *Wa*
809.28	apparition,] ghost, *Wa*
809.32	reversion . . . slang,] attrusion of professional memories^ *Wa*, *C*
810.6	antagonist. ¶] ~.^ *Wa*, *C*
810.12	beating] grumble *Wa*
810.29	The] And the *Wa*, *C*
811.20	them,] *them, Wa*
811.20–21	'laid for him' there."] laid for him *there." Wa*; laid for him there." *C*
811.23	Damn] D—n *C*
811.28–29	you," . . . explained. "I] you. I *Wa*

811.31	conviction.] *conviction. Wa*
811.35	wretch] galoot *Wa*
811.39	go] ~, anyhow, *Wa*
812.5	memory . . . Pardee.] memory. Yes, I remember—it is Pardee. *Wa, C*
812.10	what the name was] that the name was Pardee *Wa*
812.17	spruces] firs *Wa*
812.25	long departed.] been long removed by Time and his ally, the small boy. *Wa, C*
812.31	discolored stones or] *om. Wa, C*
812.40	significant] right *Wa*
812.41	forgotten] *om. Wa, C*
813.2	trees,] madroños, *Wa*
813.6	moved cautiously] strode *Wa, C*
813.7	spruce] madroño *Wa*
813.11	legs wide] legs spread wide *Wa*
813.19	theirs;] ~, and *Wa, C*
	hips] waist *Wa, C*
	knees. ¶] ~.^ *Wa, C*
814.1–2	apprehension] suspicion *Wa, C*
814.3	"Enthralled . . . spell,] If 'twas a dream I know not, but *E*
814.4	In . . . enchanted] Within the gloom of an infernal *E*
814.7	"The . . . yew;] The myrtle whispered to the brooding yew. *E*
814.11	any drone of] murmuring of *E*; droning of the *Wa*
814.13	Silence was] silence seemed *E*
814.15–18	"Conspiring . . . bloom.] *om. E*
814.30–31	works. That . . . them, but] works, and if that . . . them it *Wa*
814.31	mistake."] ~. It is—" *Wa*
814.32–815.5	"It is cold . . . kind." *placed after* There came . . . remove. *in Wa*
814.32	"It] The men looked at one another, consciously pale and visibly shuddering. "It *Wa*
	said . . . we] they explained, both at once; and, "let us leave here," added Holker; "we A
814.37–38	hardly decipherable] *om. A*

AN ADVENTURE IN BROWNVILLE

Footnote omitted in E.

818.6	summer] *om. E*
818.17	creation. ¶] ~.^ *E, C*
819.7	That . . . gave] One was that of a man, evidently, the tone, though deep and low, giving *E, C*
819.20	seemed] appeared to be *E*; appeared *C*
	woman wore,] woman, wearing *E*
819.21	gray stuff.] clinging gray stuff, was short, *E*; clinging gray stuff. *C*
819.29	vanished.] ~. ¶ *E, C*
819.32	west. ¶] ~.^ *E, C*

819.39	merely glanced] glanced carelessly *E, C*
820.5	lived." ¶] ~"!^ *E*; ~!"^ *C*
820.40	found the] "recorded" the mental *E*
821.4–5	manners] breeding *E, C*
821.14	her.] her~ in the bed. *E, C*
821.18	"you who] "you, monster, who *E*
821.28	inquest] ~—perhaps an autopsy *E, C*
822.2	singular] peculiar *E, C*
822.7	"as] "~ you did Mary's two years ago—as *E* Pauline's.] ~'s last week. *E, C*
822.21	rude] impertinence *E, C*
822.23	visible] apparent *E, C*
822.25	said. ¶] ~.^ *E, C*
822.37	murder.] ~—of double murder. *E*
823.2	for you."] for—" *E, C*
823.13–14	seemingly . . . bereavement,] *om. E*; apparently forgetting her recent bereavement, *C*
823.20	moon."] sun." *E*
823.36	as if . . . death,] *om. E*
824.3	constabulary] invisible ~ *E, C*
824.9	hundreds of] a hundred *E*

THE WIZARD OF BUMBASSA

826.1	George] *om. E* did] has done *E*
826.3	hour.] ~. There is nothing in the railroad situation as it is to justify it, he thinks, and to this dismal view we may all have to come. *E*
826.10	confessed] confesses *E*
826.20–21	has . . . ability] confidently affirms his power *E*
826.21–22	short . . . speed.] long and however fast it may be going. This ingenious gentleman, upon whom it is hardly too much to say the hopes of civilization rest, lives in Missouri, and his name is Jowers. He has not as yet seen fit to describe his invention to anybody but an unknown clerk in the Patent Office, but he seems to have found certain well-to-do persons who are willing to "stake" him in its manufacture and introduction. If it is all his fancy paints it, and the one-hundred-miles-an-hour locomotive may now confidently evolve itself, the future is so full of promise that one may with-out offense be almost reluctant to die. Compared with the possibility of going in comparative safety from San Francisco to Chicago in twenty hours and getting away again in half the time, the prospect of death is a minor joy. ¶ *E*
826.22	were unwise,] is not wise, *E*
826.22–23	in this matter,] *om. E*
826.23	if] ~ that of Mr. Jowers is fulfilled and *E*
826.24	social unrest] industrial discontent *E*

826.25–26   on a . . . performance. ¶] in a train equipped with even the Jowers
             brake may not be the picnic that one might think it, or that Mr. Jowers,
             thinking through his hat, as it were, might represent it.^ *E*
827.1   This possibility] But this point *E*
827.3–4   of . . . road.] of, and the secret of which perished with the illustrious
             projector. *E*
827.10   ninety] seventy *E*
827.19   incurred] sustained *E*
827.25   the passengers] them *E*
827.28   afoot . . . before.] afoot. *E*
827.30   trains— . . . expensive.] trains, and sometimes the stations and adjacent
             buildings. *E*
827.34   was, . . . cold." ¶] was knocked perfectly cold.^ *E*
827.35   I] We *E*
             well] worth while *E*
             this . . . incident] its . . . history *E*
827.38   assured,] ~ (probably with Mr. Jowers in mind) *E*
827.39–40   I . . . I am] we . . . we are *E*

THE APPLICANT

829.10   architect] artist *Wa*
829.14   founder] erector *Wa*
830.10   better] bitter *Wa*
830.34   Home . . . not] Home, was not, in the gloom of the winter evening, *Wa, C*
831.10   season] ~ (to say nothing of bird) *Wa*
831.20   good, and especially truthful.] good and truthful. *Wa*; good and espe-
             cially truthful. *C*
832.17   deviously,] *Wa, C*; ~ *CW*
832.18   reasonless] aimless *Wa*

ONE KIND OF OFFICER

833.2   OF] ONE OF *E, C*
833.5   fire, . . . can.] fire on them. *E*
833.16   important] chief *E*
833.23   SHOT] KILLED *E*
835.6   ax. ¶] ~.^ *E, C*
835.40   not sufficient] no *E, C*
837.13   mounted] dismounted *E, C*
837.14   impedimenta] horses *E, C*
837.19   nearly] with inconceivable fury *E, C*
837.34   activity. ¶] ~.^ *E, C*
838.6   for the few infantrymen] *om. E, C*
838.7   bayonet] saber and revolver *E, C*
838.17   Did . . . surrender?] *om. E, C*
838.31   ended] ~ for the time being *E, C*

838.40	flag] Federal ~ *E*
839.38	incomprehensible] extraordinary *E, C*
840.12	cruel] *om. E, C*

JOHN BARTINE'S WATCH

842.8	reasonless.] altogether ~. *E, C*
842.10	timepiece] watch *E, C*
842.11	unsteady.] ~. A slight pallor had come into his face. *E, C*
842.17	cab] hack *E, C*
842.25	disregarded] *om. E, C*
843.12	give me your attention] persuade me to have a fresh cigar *E, C*
843.19	as . . . disadvantages.] by those who suffered its disadvantages as legitimate. *E, C*
843.26–35	Something . . . all?"] *om. E*
843.36	my great-grandfather's] his *E*
843.38	Rupert] *Elizabeth E, C*
843.38–39	son, my grandfather.] daughter, my grandmother. *E, C*
844.1	me.] my existence. *E, C*
844.4	heard.] audible. *E, C*
844.17	looking at your own.] consulting your own timepiece. *E*
844.22	your trumpery] *om. E*
844.26	delusion] hallucination *E, C*
845.7	feeling a sharp] experiencing the keenest *E, C*
845.21	key] watchkey *E, C*
846.2–3	face . . . rise. ¶] face—dead! ^ *E*; face—dead! ¶ *C*
846.5	circle] ~, as if made by contusion, *E, C*
846.7–15	true. ¶ Nor . . . that.] true. *E*
846.8	set . . . law] affirm my knowledge of the limitations of the principle *C*
846.9–10	world . . . removed.] as in the temporal world, natural laws have no *post-facto* validity. *C*

THE HYPNOTIST

847.16	material] *om. E*
848.2	destroyed] returned her *E*
848.15	my] ~ dear *E*
848.24	one] second *E*
848.31–32	a great . . . metal.] the following articles: One pound of shingle-nails; one hammer-head for driving them; three fragments of beer bottles; one piece of iron chain; one short section of gaspipe; one part of a felt hat; one paper of carpet-tacks; one boot-heel; one gold watch (not belonging to the deceased); one pocket handkerchief; two brass keys; one feather boa; one spinning-top, and two daily newspapers. *E*
848.33	door-knob.] hen. *E*
848.37	reformed.] ~, although they had made a great deal of money from my young sister's ingenious invention for smothering babes. *E*

849.3	was] ~ then that, *E*
849.4	that I found] I met *E*
849.15	former father,"] father," *E*
849.23	when] before *E*
849.26	successively.] turn about. *E*
849.40	valor] heroism *E*

A JUG OF SIRUP

Silas Deemer named John Deemer in E.

851.1–2	This . . . 1863,] On the 16th day of July, in the year 1863, John Deemer died, *E*
851.14	Hillbrook,] ~, in the State of Missouri, *E*
851.19	not] *not E*
851.22	that, possibly,] that *E*
852.20	that] had led *E*
	was moved] *om. E*
852.32	candor] truthfulness *E*
853.7	village] Southwestern ~ *E*
853.9	quite sure, Alvan?"] *quite* sure, Alv—" *E*
853.13	unfinished. Mr. Creede] unfinished: Mr. Creede's face suddenly became as pale as faces of the dead. He *E*
853.28	said you wanted] expressed a wish for *E*
853.29	bought . . . bought] purchased . . . purchased *E*
854.2	condition.] thoughts. *E*
854.14	For . . . conversation.] *om. E*
854.15	administrator] executor *E*
854.20	town. ¶] ~.^ *E*
855.2	score or more,] hundred, *E*
855.3	excited.] pale. *E*
855.23	clearly visible.] visibly conspicuous. ¶ *E*
855.24	black darkness] black—a darkness unthinkable! *E*
	door] ~ by the pressure of those behind him *E*
855.25	blind, . . . mischance.] stone blind. *E*
855.26	imprecision,] ~ of movement, *E*
	force] turn and ~ *E*
	current, pushed] current. They pushed *E*
855.27	in their turn.] others with vengeful emphasis. *E*
855.28	another] ~ blindly *E*
	cursed,] ~, shrieked, *E*
855.30	awful] horrible *E*
855.32	place.] spot. *E*
855.35	courage] boldness *E*
855.36–37	on . . . hair.] there were blood-spots here and there on the walls and furniture, stray tangles of hair on the floor and fragments of clothing. *E*
855.37	somehow] *om. E*
855.38	out] together somehow *E*

855.40	16th] 15th *E*
855.41	July, . . . life.] July—the day before his death. *E*
	There . . . Creede.] No; there was another, freshly written. It recorded the sale, on the 7th day of August, to Alvan Creede, of one half gallon of maple sirup. *E*
856.2	its immemorial] her *E*
	confessed] thought *E*
856.3	commercial] *om. E*
856.4	deceased,] *defunctus, E*
	resume] continue in *E*
856.5	at the old stand] *om. E*
	local historian] Distinguished Authority *E*
856.6	work] monograph *E*
856.6–7	had . . . concurrence.] heartily concurs. *E*

THE DAMNED THING

858.21	of] of—of *TT*
858.26	please.] choose. *TT, I*
858.31	The coroner . . . time,] The coroner was apparently not greatly affected by the young man's manifest resentment. He was silent for some moments, *TT, I*
859.10	Some] The witness was not visibly affected in any way, but some *TT*
859.24	but] *om. TT*
859.35	intensity . . . look.] pallor of it. *TT, I*
860.21	grain!] grass! *TT, I*
861.7	again] *om. TT*
861.12	THOUGH] IF *TT*
862.26	". . . would] ". . . up his bristles, growling and uncovering his teeth, making sudden dashes, then backing away, as if in fear. Sometimes he would *TT*
862.31	cerebral] olfactory *TT, I*
863.11	mystery;] problem; *TT, I*
863.14	chord] cord *TT, I*
863.24	between,] ~ them, *TT, I*
863.25	moment.] second. *TT*
863.34	such a] that *TT*